Women's Movements Facing the Reconfigured State

Women's Movements Facing the Reconfigured State examines the relationship between women's movements and states in West Europe and North America, as states have relocated their formal powers and policy-making responsibilities. Since the 1980s, North American and West European states have reduced the scope and volume of their national responsibilities, increasingly employing neoliberal free market rhetoric, and developed transnational economic and political authorities. Simultaneously, second-wave women's movements have been transformed. Movements that were revolutionary in rhetoric, autonomous from states, and largely informally organized in the 1970s are, by the 1990s, employing moderate neoliberal rhetoric, entering state institutions as active participants, and creating more formal organizations. Utilizing a common theoretical framework, the contributors examine how movements have influenced the reconfiguration of nation-states and how these changes have influenced the goals, mobilization, tactics, success, and rhetoric of women's movements in various West European and North American countries. This volume contributes new theoretical insights and empirical evidence to the growing literature on states and movements.

Lee Ann Banaszak is associate professor of political science and women's studies at The Pennsylvania State University. Her research focuses on women's movements in the United States and Europe and the comparative study of public opinion on abortion, gender roles, and feminism. She is the author of *Why Movements Succeed or Fail* (1996).

Karen Beckwith is professor of political science at the College of Wooster. Former president of the Women and Politics Research Section of the American Political Science Association, she is the author of *American Women and Political Participation* (1986) and numerous articles on women and politics. Her research interests include mass political participation, comparative women's movements, and women and political representation.

Dieter Rucht is professor of sociology at the Social Science Research Center Berlin and honorary professor at the Free University of Berlin. His research interests include modernization processes in comparative perspective, political participation, social movements, and political protest. One of his recent books is *Zwischen Palaver und Diskurs* (1998).

Women's Movements Facing the Reconfigured State

Edited by

LEE ANN BANASZAK
The Pennsylvania State University

KAREN BECKWITH
The College of Wooster

DIETER RUCHT
Wissenschaftszentrum Berlin für Sozialforschung

CAMBRIDGE
UNIVERSITY PRESS

PUBLISHED BY THE PRESS SYNDICATE OF THE UNIVERSITY OF CAMBRIDGE
The Pitt Building, Trumpington Street, Cambridge, United Kingdom

CAMBRIDGE UNIVERSITY PRESS
The Edinburgh Building, Cambridge CB2 2RU, UK
40 West 20th Street, New York, NY 10011-4211, USA
477 Williamstown Road, Port Melbourne, VIC 3207, Australia
Ruiz de Alarcón 13, 28014 Madrid, Spain
Dock House, The Waterfront, Cape Town 8001, South Africa

http://www.cambridge.org

First published 2003

Printed in the United States of America

Typeface Sabon 10/12 pt.   *System* LATEX 2$_\varepsilon$ [TB]

A catalog record for this book is available from the British Library.

Library of Congress Cataloging in Publication Data
Women's movements facing the reconfigured state / edited by Lee Ann Banaszak,
Karen Beckwith, Dieter Rucht.
    p.   cm.
Includes bibliographical references and index.
ISBN 0-521-81278-X – ISBN 0-521-01219-8 (pbk.)
 1. Feminism – Europe, Western.   2. Feminism – North America.   3. Women in
politics – Europe, Western.   4. Women in politics – North America.   5. Europe,
Western – Politics and government – 1989–   6. North America – Politics and government.
 I. Banaszak, Lee Ann, 1960–   II. Beckwith, Karen, 1950–   III. Rucht, Dieter.
HQ1587 .W68 2003
305.42'094–dc21   2002067620

ISBN 0 521 81278 x hardback
ISBN 0 521 01219 8 paperback

Contents

Tables and Figures

FIGURES

Acronyms

ACGF	[French] Action catholique générale féminine
ACN	Action Canada Network
AFDC	Aid to Families with Dependent Children
AFFDU	[French] Association française des femmes diplômées des universités
BQ	[Canadian] Bloc Québécois
CA	Canadian Alliance
CACSW	Canadian Advisory Council on the Status of Women
CADAC	[French] Coordination pour le Droit à l'avortement et à la contraception
CCOO	[Spanish] Comisiones Obreras
CELEM	[Spanish] Coordinadora Española para el Lobby Europeo de Mujeres
CETA	Comprehensive Employment and Training Act
CGT	[French] Confédération Générale du Travail
CLC	Canadian Labour Congress
CLEF	[French] Coordination française pour le lobby européen des femmes
CLUW	Coalition of Labor Union Women
CSEP	[French] Conseil superieur de l'égalité professionnel
DAIP	Domestic Abuse Intervention Project
DGB	[German] Deutscher Gewerkschaftsbund
DKP	[German] Deutsche Kommunistische Partei
ECJ	European Court of Justice
EOC	[British] Equal Opportunity Commission
EP	European Parliament
ERA	Equal Rights Amendment
EU	European Union
FEW	Federally Employed Women
FTA	[Canada/U.S.] Free Trade Agreement

GATT	General Agreement on Tariffs and Trade
GLC	Greater London Council
HUD	Housing and Urban Development
IGC	Intergovernmental Conference
IM	[Spanish] Instituto de la Mujer
IMF	International Monetary Fund
IPU	Inter-Parliamentary Union
IU	[Spanish] Izquierda Unida
JAWS	Journalism and Women Symposium
JOBS	Job Opportunities and Basic Skills Training
KPD	[German] Kommunistische Partei Deutschlands
LAMAR	[Spanish] Lucha Antiautoritaria de Mujeres Antipatriarcales Revolucionarias
LCER	[British] Labour Campaign for Electoral Reform
LWN	[British] Labour Women's Network
MDF	[French] Mouvement démocratique et féminin
MDHC	[British] Mersey Docks and Harbour Company
MDM	[Spanish] Movimiento Democrático de Mujeres
MEP	Member of European Parliament
MIFAS	[French] Mouvement pour l'intégration des femmes à l'action sociale
MLF	[French] Mouvement de libération des femmes
MP	Member of Parliament
NAC	[Canadian] National Action Committee on the Status of Women
NAFTA	North American Free Trade Agreement
NATO	North Atlantic Treaty Organization
NCADV	National Coalition Against Domestic Violence
NDP	[Canadian] New Democratic Party
NI	[Spanish] Nueva Izquierda
NIWC	Northern Ireland Women's Coalition
NOW	National Organization for Women
NWAC	Native Association of Women of Canada
NWAPC	[British] National Women Against Pit Closures
OECD	Organisation for Economic Co-operation and Development
ORT	[Spanish] Organización Revolucionaria de Trabajadores
PC	[Canadian] Progressive Conservative Party
PCE	[Spanish] Partido Comunista de España
PCF	[French] Parti Communiste Français
PCI	[Italian] Partito Comunista Italiano
PDS	[German] Party of Democratic Socialism
POS	Political Opportunity Structure
PP	[Spanish] Partido Popular
PR	Proportional Representation

PRA	Personal Responsibility and Work Opportunity Reconciliation Act
PS	[French] Parti socialiste
PSOE	[Spanish] Partido Socialista Obrero Españo
PTE	[Spanish] Partido del Trabajo en España
ROKS	National Organization for Battered Women's Shelters in Sweden (Riksorganisationen för Kvinnojourer i Sverige)
RPR	[French] Rassemblement pour la République
SLP	Scottish Labour Party
SMO	Social Movement Organization
SMP	Scottish Member of Parliament
SMP	Single-Member Plurality
SNCC	Student Nonviolent Coordinating Committee
SNP	Scottish National Party
SPD	[German] Sozialdemokratische Partei Deutschlands
STUC	Scottish Trade Union Congress
SWCF	Scottish Women's Consultative Forum
TANF	Temporary Assistance to Needy Families
TGWU	[British] Transport and General Workers Union
TUC	[British] Trades Union Congress
UDF	[French] Union pour la Démocratie Française
UDI	[Italian] Unione Donne Italiane
UFCS	[French] Union féminine civique et sociale
UGT	[Spanish] Unión General de Trabajadores
UK	United Kingdom
UNESCO	United Nations Educational, Scientific, and Cultural Organization
UPF	[French] Union professionnelle féminine
WCG	[Scottish] Women's Coordination Group
WEAL	Women's Equity Action League
WISP	Women in Scholarly Publishing
WIZO	[French] Organisation internationale des femmes sionistes
WMA	Military Women Aviators
WNC	[British] Women's National Commission
WOPA	Women's Officers Professional Association
WOW	[British] Women of the Waterfront
WTO	World Trade Organization

Contributors

Lee Ann Banaszak, associate professor of political science at The Pennsylvania State University, has written on comparative women's movements and the determinants of feminist attitudes among the mass public in the United States and Europe. She is the author of *Why Movements Succeed or Fail: Opportunity, Culture and the Struggle for Woman Suffrage* (Princeton 1996) and has published articles in the *American Political Science Review, Political Research Quarterly,* and *Public Opinion Quarterly.* Her current research examines movement activists within the state and their effect on the U.S. women's movement.

Karen Beckwith is professor of political science at the College of Wooster. Former president of the Women and Politics Research Section of the American Political Science Association, she is the author of *American Women and Political Participation* (Greenwood Press 1986) and numerous articles on women and politics. Her research interests include mass political participation, comparative women's movements, and women and political representation.

Donatella della Porta is professor of sociology at the European University Institute (Fiesole, Italy). Author of *Social Movements, Political Violence, and the State* (Cambridge University Press 1995), her research focuses on political violence, political corruption, and social movements.

Alexandra Dobrowolsky is associate professor of political science at Saint Mary's University (Canada). She teaches in the areas of Canadian, comparative, and women and politics. She has published the book, *The Politics of Pragmatism: Women, Representation and Constitutionalism* in Canada. She is currently coediting *Women, Politics and Constitutional Change,* a collection that compares women's constitutional interventions in the United Kingdom with women's experiences abroad. She has written articles concerned with theories and practices of political mobilization, representation, and democracy. Her most recent research traces shifts in social policy that reflect changing state and citizenship regimes in Canada and Great Britain.

R. Amy Elman is associate professor of political science at Kalamazoo College, where she is also codirector of the Center for West European Studies and director of the Women's Studies Program. She is the editor of *Sexual Politics and the European Union* (Berghahn Books 1996) and author of *Sexual Subordination and State Intervention: Comparing Sweden and the United States* (Berghahn Books 1996). Her forthcoming work offers an account of European Union "progress" toward sexual equality in matters of migration, matrimony, and male violence.

Jane Jenson is professor of political science at the University of Montreal. Her scholarly work includes extensive publication on women and politics in France, labor and employment policies in North America, and the changing nature of welfare states and the political economy. Her most recent book, with Mariette Sineau, is *Who Cares? Women's Work, Childcare and Welfare State Redesign* (University of Toronto Press 2001).

Mary Fainsod Katzenstein is a professor of government and women's studies at Cornell University. She writes on social movement activism, cross-nationally focusing on the United States, India, and Europe. She is the co-editor with Carol Mueller of the *Women's Movements of the United States and Western Europe* (Temple University Press 1987). More recently, she is the author of *Faithful and Fearless: Moving Feminist Protest inside the Church and Military* (Princeton University Press 1998) and is the editor with Judith Reppy of *Beyond Zero Tolerance: Discrimination and Military Culture in the U.S.* (Rowman and Littlefield 1999). She is currently writing on prison reform activism after holding a Russell Sage Fellowship in 2001–2002 and is coediting a book on social movement politics and poverty with Raka Ray.

John D. McCarthy is professor of sociology at The Pennsylvania State University. His recent research focusing on media bias in the reporting of protest events, the policing of protest, and the role of social movement organizations in mobilizing citizen action has appeared in the *American Sociological Review* and *Social Forces*. He also coedited *Comparative Perspectives on Social Movements* (Cambridge University Press 1996).

David S. Meyer is associate professor of sociology and political science at the University of California, Irvine. He is the author or editor of four books and numerous articles on social movements, and he is interested in the connections among institutional politics, public policy, and social movements.

Carol McClurg Mueller is professor of sociology at Arizona State University. She has written extensively on social movements, women's movements in Europe and the United States, and the gender gap. Her recent work focuses on social movements in transitional democracies and has appeared in the *American Sociological Review, American Journal of Sociology,* and *Social Problems.*

Dieter Rucht is professor of sociology at the Social Science Research Center Berlin and honorary professor at the Free University of Berlin. His research interests include modernization processes in comparative perspective, political participation, social movements, and political protest. Among his recent books are *Acts of Dissent* (Rowman and Littlefield 1999 with Ruud Koopmans and Friedhelm Neidhardt, eds.) and *Social Movements in a Globalizing World* (Macmillan 1999 with Donatella della Porta and Hanspeter Kriesi, eds.).

Celia Valiente, lecturer in sociology at the Universidad Carlos III de Madrid, has published extensively on women and politics in Spain. Her research interests include comparative women and politics, European Union policies on women's employment and sexual harassment, and the women's movements of southern Europe. She is also a member of the Research Network on Gender, Politics, and the State.

Foreword

On June 12, 1997, eight scholars from Canada, West Europe, and the United States met at the Wissenschaftszentrum Berlin für Sozialforschung to discuss women's movements in comparative perspective and to consider how a specific study of women's movements in West Europe and North America might contribute to the development of social movement theory. As the three coprincipal investigators, and with initial funding from the Council for European Studies, we convened a research planning group around the theme of "Women's Movements in Comparative Perspective: Building Theory from Case Studies." Over three days, Donatella della Porta (University of Florence), Drude Dahlerup (University of Aarhus), Amy Elman (Kalamazoo College), Jane Jenson (University of Montreal), Mary Fainsod Katzenstein (Cornell University), Lee Ann Banaszak (Pennsylvania State University), Karen Beckwith (College of Wooster), and Dieter Rucht (Wissenschaftszentrum Berlin) discussed social movement theories and frameworks, shared examples from the multiple-country cases on which our prior research had been based, and argued across national specificities to identify the changes in women's movements, and in states, across the past three decades. We raised questions about commonalities across movements, debated the differences between feminist movements and women's movements, found some components of existing social movement theory helpful and others inadequate or irrelevant, and began to map changes in women's movements with developments in the location of state powers. On the last day, we were joined by Myra Marx Ferree (University of Wisconsin), who offered us the helpful and dispassionate critical comments that come more easily to someone outside a project than to those enlivened by days of discussion and debate. By the end of this first meeting, we had shaped the basic contours of a collaborative project entitled "Women's Movements Facing the Reconfigured State."

In the course of the next two years, research presentation meetings were organized during which these ideas were further honed and developed.

Convening at The Pennsylvania State University in May 1998, we were joined by three social movement colleagues whose contributions to our work were synthetic and conclusive. David Meyer's task was to write a critical summary assessment, comparing cases, that considered similarities and differences across national women's movements. John McCarthy and Carol Mueller agreed to coauthor a chapter that, in a broader perspective, would highlight the persistence of ideological and cultural features within the women's movements and would also contribute to the general critical discussion shaping both our joint theoretical framework and individual chapters.

Three graduate students – Erin Cross and Heather Gollmar-Casey from Penn State and Heidi Swarts from Cornell – joined us for this second meeting. In addition, Alexandra Dobrowolsky (St. Mary's University) and Celia Valiente (Universidad Carlos III de Madrid) joined the project at this meeting and contributed greatly to the further development and elaboration of the substantive analysis. Our active collaborative work concluded at the College of Wooster in May 1999, when we met for the final discussion of the theoretical framework on women's movements and reconfigured states and to reflect on the intersections of the individual chapters, whose country examples range from Canada and the United States to Britain, France, Germany, the Republic of Ireland, Italy, the Netherlands, Northern Ireland, Scotland, Spain, and Sweden. As is the case for this volume, most individual chapters were comparative not only across time but across nations.

THE PROJECT: WHAT IT IS

This project focuses on state reconfiguration and the changing relationship between women's movements and states in West Europe and North America. By state reconfiguration, we mean the rearrangement of formal state powers and conventional policy responsibilities that states have been undertaking in the past three decades. In the first chapter of this book, we argue that nations have been reconfiguring state powers, relocating state authority and functions, and relinquishing many of the policy commitments of the social welfare state. We define this concept, elaborating its various dimensions, and then argue that women's movements and states have both influenced and been affected by each other in the process of state reconfiguration. The individual chapters of this volume are all inspired by a shared theoretical framework, one that we developed collectively across three joint meetings and that is provided in full in the first chapter.

The various chapters in this volume provide systematic investigations of specific women's movements and the states within which they are located. Although we employ the term *women's movements* throughout this volume, in most (but not all) cases our chapters examine feminist movements and their relationship with states (for a clarification of these terms, see Chapter 1). All chapters are written from a comparative perspective, including those with a single-nation focus. Beyond the cross-national comparative strengths of the chapters, both individually and as a collective whole, the chapters share a theoretically informed longitudinal methodology of examining changes in women's movement-state relationships from the 1970s to the 1990s. In combination with the shared theoretical framework and comparative perspective, the result is a volume that is thoroughly collaborative (and, we happily acknowledge, collegial). As is the case with comparative political research of this scope, collective endeavor was essential for addressing the range of nations, the range of women's movements, and the panoply of changes across three decades. No individual scholar could encompass the range of nations and women's movements, across time, undertaken in this volume.

THE PROJECT: WHAT IT ISN'T

Given our cross-national, longitudinal framework for investigating movement-state interactions in the context of state reconfiguration, we are limited in the number of issues that could be addressed in this volume, despite a range of crucial related concerns. Our awareness and recognition of these issues, however, have not permitted more space to be devoted to them in an already rich and lengthy volume.

Readers will readily note, for example, that public opinion, changes in government, party system shifts, and the role of potential alliance actors, including labor unions, are only modestly discussed, if at all, in Chapter 1. This is not the result of a lack of appreciation of the import of these factors, but rather because we realize that an emphasis on state reconfiguration and state-movement interactions will necessarily require a detailed discussion across individual nations and cross-national comparisons. To varying extents, individual chapters give attention to these factors as they contribute to our critical understanding of states and women's movements in the context of state reconfiguration. We also acknowledge that *Women's Movements Facing the Reconfigured State* does not provide detailed, descriptive accounts of individual women's movements located in a range of nations. Several excellent edited collections, including Katzenstein and Mueller, ed., *The Women's Movements of the United States and Western Europe*; Threlfall, ed., *Mapping the Women's Movement*; Basu, ed., *The Challenge of Local Feminisms*; and Nelson and Chowdhury, eds., *Women and Politics Worldwide*, already provide such high-quality accounts, and we felt we could not equal the already high standard of work in this area.

In the following chapters, we distinguish our work on state reconfiguration from several other existing literatures on changes in the state. Despite the fact that relinquishing state authority to international authorities is one dimension of the concept of state reconfiguration, we are not merely arguing that states are engaging in federal state building, particularly in the case of the European Union. State reconfiguration is both more extensive – including international organizations besides the European Union – and more limited – occurring within single nations – than is encompassed in the emerging literature on the European Union as a suprastate.

We also distinguish our project from work on globalization. Again, while clearly related to our project, globalization is both more extensive and less specific to the changes in states where powers have been relocated. State reconfiguration is, in large part, influenced by those more encompassing international or even global transformations. At the same time, a number of other case-specific factors also contribute to the national changes that encompass the concept of state reconfiguration. These include, with considerable variation across nations, a shift away from Keynesian to neoliberal policies, austerity programs, cuts in the welfare state, privatization, and the increase of public-private partnerships. These issues have been the focus of considerable conversation and debate among us, particularly among the editors. A general analysis of postwar economic and political changes, however, is not the focus of this project.

Finally, we make no claim that our arguments are generalizable beyond West Europe and North America. The editors and contributors to this volume have regional scholarly expertise in West Europe and North America and recognize both the similarities that justify a focus on these two regions of the world and the political, economic, cultural, and developmental differences between these regions and others. Our arguments in this volume, therefore, are bounded in regional and temporal terms. Although our conclusions are case-specific and suggestive, we nonetheless believe that our framework and our findings can serve to identify hypotheses that can be tested in other regions.

ACKNOWLEDGMENTS

Women's Movements Facing the Reconfigured State would not have been possible without generous funding and support from the Council for European Studies at Columbia University, then directed by Ioannis Sinanoglou, and from the College of Wooster and the Pennsylvania State University. The Council provided the grant through money made available by the German Marshall Fund of the United States under the Council's Research Planning Group program. The College of Wooster provided us with a grant from the Luce Fund for Distinguished Scholarship, which supported our final project meeting in May 1999 and an editors' meeting in Berlin in June 2000, as well as other expenses associated with this project. Particular thanks are due to former Acting Vice President Hayden Schilling and former Dean of Faculty Susan Figge, whose interest in and support of this project helped make it possible. The Pennsylvania State University's Continuing and Distance Education Program Innovation Fund provided complete funding for the second meeting, which was held at Penn State. Finally, the Wissenschaftszentrum

Berlin für Sozialforschung hosted us and provided logistical support in our first meeting. We thank each of these institutions for their generosity and hope that this volume vindicates their confidence in our project across the six years their help sustained it.

We also thank, with the most profound appreciation, our colleagues who worked with us over the years to construct, critique, and complete this volume. Their names and contributions are listed in the first section of this Foreword: Donatella della Porta, Alexandra Dobrowolski, R. Amy Elman, Celia Valiente, Jane Jenson, and Mary Fainsod Katzenstein. The last two colleagues were especially helpful with distinctive contributions during our early sessions as we began to develop the concept of the reconfigured state. Moreover, we wish to thank John McCarthy, David S. Meyer, and Carol Mueller, who took on challenging synthesis tasks. We also benefited from the contributions, in two early meetings, of Myra Marx Ferree and Drude Dahlerup and the three graduate students mentioned previously: Erin Cross, Heather Gollmar-Casey, and Heidi Swarts. Although they were not participants in the ongoing project, they nonetheless emerged as participant–observers with thoughtful contributions to the discussion and, ultimately, this volume, for which we thank them.

Multiple anonymous reviewers reviewed this manuscript at various stages of development. We closely read their comments and critiques and, for the most part, responded to them in subsequent revisions (and asked our contributors to do so as well). Theda Skocpol generously served as the final reviewer on selected chapters of this volume, discussing them as they were presented on the panel "When Power Relocates" at the 2001 American Political Science Association meeting in San Francisco. Final revisions to these chapters incorporated many of her comments and observations, and we thank her for her participation during what must have been her busiest APSA meeting.

As coeditors who each have children and close family members, we are also grateful to those who suffered from our engagement and, in one form or another, helped to sustain each of us, respectively. Lee Ann Banaszak thanks Eric Plutzer for uncomplainingly taking the lion's share of the household work during the many conferences and meetings and Clara and Isaac, who joined the family in the course of this project and have had to patiently share their mother's attention. Fitz Beckwith-Collings and Piper Beckwith-Collings were patient with Karen Beckwith's attention to work, understanding of her frequent absences from home, and unflaggingly cheerful and encouraging, for which she is exceedingly grateful. Dieter Rucht thanks Evelin Riefer-Rucht, Sarah, and Daniel for their patience and understanding. Two meetings in Berlin – one collectively and one as editors only – were transformed by the welcome extended to us all by Evelin. She provided us with the most generous reception, for which we express our gratitude.

Finally, we are very grateful to those who have helped us modify this manuscript from a collection of manuscripts into a book. Eliot Walker was instrumental in turning a bunch of computer files into the coherent manuscript. Lew Bateman and Jennifer Carey have been wonderfully helpful in marshalling the manuscript through the various stages of production. Catherine Fox provided invaluable help with the indexing of the book.

In launching and steering the collective project through all its stages, we three coeditors look back in gratitude (and relief!). We were able to communicate and collaborate on an egalitarian and noncompetitive basis, relieving each other in cases when one of us was committed to other duties, dividing our work according to our particular strengths, but also working in such an integrated way that it would be impossible to reconstruct our individual contributions. Hence it was a singular pleasure for each of us to have engaged in this joint coeditorship. We list ourselves in alphabetical order since no one of us can be said to have contributed more than another.

Lee Ann Banaszak
The Pennsylvania State University

Karen Beckwith
The College of Wooster

Dieter Rucht
Social Science Center Berlin

When Power Relocates: Interactive Changes in Women's Movements and States

Lee Ann Banaszak, Karen Beckwith, and Dieter Rucht

INTRODUCTION: WHERE IS THE WOMEN'S MOVEMENT?

Feminist activity for childcare in the United States took two forms during the 1970s. First, local feminist groups were active in building community day-care centers. Groups like the Women's Action Alliance (1974) and Resources for Community Change (1974) encouraged women to form cooperative day-care centers, allowing parents and local community members to direct child-care implementation and institute a curriculum that minimized sex role differences and encouraged social change. Second, the National Organization for Women and feminist legislators fought hard to pass the Comprehensive Child Development Act of 1971, which would have provided federally regulated and funded child-care centers open to parents of all incomes on a sliding fee basis. Although the bill passed Congress with bipartisan support, Nixon vetoed the bill in December 1971.[1] Both local community organizers and those who pushed for federally funded day care protested nascent corporate interest in profit-making, privatized day-care centers ("Kentucky Fried Children," as Featherstone [1970] called them). Radical and diverse, both autonomous and state-involved, the U.S. women's movement argued for a national child-care policy that was woman centered, independent of financial circumstances of parents, state funded, and community controlled.

By the 1990s, the U.S. feminist movement's concern with childcare had diminished,[2] and the site for discussion had shifted location. Childcare, even among feminists, was discussed primarily in the context of women's employment, and as child centered and concerned with child safety and development, rather than as an issue essential to the full human actualization of women with children. Moreover, child-care policy had acquired a two-class resolution: no child-care provision by the state for poor mothers, private child-care provision arranged by individuals for middle- and upper-class mothers. Female, and even many feminist, members of Congress, by voting for the Personal Responsibility

---

[1] Attempts at similar legislation in 1974 and 1975 were unsuccessful.
[2] See, however, the efforts of the National Organization for Women, in Mink 1998: 7, 162–163n85.

and Work Opportunity Act (PRA) of 1996, disempowered poor single mothers and advanced a welfare child-care policy considerably less feminist than its precursor (the Child Development Act of 1971) twenty-five years earlier. The PRA ended child-care entitlements for welfare recipients, eliminated "welfare-related child-care programs" and did not provide enough funding to supply affordable childcare to poor mothers compelled by the PRA to work (Mink 1998: 114). Thus, by the late 1990s, feminists had abandoned their previous concern about poor women's access to childcare as well as the larger concerns about the ideological content and locus of control of child-care solutions.

These changes in the policy concerns of women's movements in the United States are not unique. They neither occurred only in the United States nor were they restricted to the particular issue of daycare. As with the United States, women's movements[3] in West Europe and Canada with radical and even revolutionary antecedents transformed their feminist policy concerns and their relationship with the state. They have moved from an early radicalism, autonomy, and challenge to the state in the 1970s, to a more moderate, state-involved, and accommodationist stance by the 1990s. Some parts of the movement even employ a neoliberal rhetoric that would have been unthinkable within the movement's ranks in the 1970s. This pattern of change, although not perfectly replicated in every West European and North American women's movement, is nonetheless evidenced in each of them.

Can our claim about the dramatic change of the women's movements in North America and Western Europe be substantiated? And if so, why have these movements, situated in widely differing contexts, followed a similar trajectory? These are the two key questions that this volume seeks to answer. In doing so, we maintain that a crucial factor in explaining this trajectory is that women's movements today no longer confront the state they faced in the 1970s. We argue instead that the state has reshaped, relocated, and rearticulated its formal powers and policy responsibilities throughout the 1980s and 1990s. Women's movements in North America and West Europe have been interactively engaged with this "reconfiguring" state, and this relational interaction has transformed feminist movements. As a result, changes

---

[3] We conceive of *women's movements* as those movements whose definition, content, leadership, development, or issues are specific to women and their gender identity (Beckwith 2000). Such a definition includes feminist movements, liberal women's groups, and [even] some conservative women's organizations, and provides us with the analytical flexibility to compare women's movements within and across West European and North American nations. From the European perspective, the term *women's movement* is often equated with feminism, particularly those aspects that are associated with the radical branch of the movement. This branch is distinctive in its critique of state institutions and society as patriarchal, compared to, for example, a liberal strand of the women's movement, which accepts institutional arrangements and struggles for women's equal access to them. Our definition of women's movements permits us to incorporate a wider array of groups than a more restrictive definition would allow.

in feminist movements cannot be seen simply as interior to the movement; for example, as the result of the movement's natural lifecycle (Tarrow 1998), of personnel changes (see della Porta, this volume for refutation of this position), or the natural waning of activists' enthusiasm and energy (Hirschman 1982). Rather, women's movements face a reconfigured state that offers them opportunities for advancing feminist agendas and that also threatens feminist successes.

Moreover, by interacting with governments that are reconfiguring state power, women's movements have also contributed to state reconfiguration and facilitated and resisted the changes that accompany it. In this regard, we do not see women as "the objects of state policy" or the state as "something 'out there' and external to women's lives... over which they have little control" (Waylen 1998: 4). Rather, we see both states and feminist movements as "sites of struggle" (Waylen 1998: 15) in dynamic interaction. Neither is homogeneous or monolithic; instead they are engaged in complex, flexible, nonteleological interaction with each other. This book, then, investigates the pattern of change in women's movements in West Europe and North America as they interact with states that are reconfiguring state powers. Given this central theme, our task in the rest of this introductory chapter is twofold. First, we clarify the concept of state reconfiguration and outline its extent and evidence in three exemplary nations. Second, we demonstrate how state reconfiguration influences concrete interactions between states and women's movements and discuss the effects of these interactions on both states and women's movements.

THE RECONFIGURATION OF STATES IN WEST EUROPE
AND NORTH AMERICA

The fundamental character of the nation-state is undergoing change. Underlying this claim is the assumption that the postwar period represents a stage of state development which, in spite of national variances, was structurally similar across most Western nations insofar as they were all modeled according to the capitalist welfare state. In the European context, this state was often characterized as "Keynesian" or "Fordist." Economic and social changes have contributed to the gradual abandonment of this state model. At the same time, fundamental changes in the nature of the state have emerged, reconfiguring formal and informal state powers, potentially shaping a new state model, and thereby changing the relationship between states and civil societies. Several authors have attributed state changes to more global economic transformations by labeling a new state model as neo-Fordist or post-Fordist[4] (Hirsch 1985; Hirsch and Roth 1986; Jessop 1990; Nielsen 1991).

---

[4] The term post-Fordist or neo-Fordist describes a state that has moved beyond relying on economic mass production and industry, Keynesian economics, and extensive welfare provisions to a state encouraging flexible production and globalization of the economy.

We prefer a more neutral term – *the reconfiguration of the state* – which reflects both the developing, incomplete, and flexible nature of changes in West European and North American states and which is less emphatic in stressing the economic aspects of this transformation. As was the case with the formation of nation states (Anderson 1974a, 1974b; Bright and Harding 1984) and the creation and development of welfare states (Castles and Mitchell 1993; Esping-Andersen 1990; Rieger and Leibfried 1995), the process of reconfiguration is highly differentiated, starting at different time points, taking different guises, and evoking different levels of support and resistance depending on the specific context in which it takes place. Nevertheless, for the sake of analytical clarity, we describe reconfiguration as an *ideal-type* process, and illustrate the various dimensions and aspects of the process with empirical references to particular states and policies.

Reconfiguration is evidenced, first, by structural changes within the state and, second, by the changing relationship between the state and civil society. These changes are accompanied, and partly reflected, by a changing discourse about the role of the state – an aspect that we will discuss further below.

Structural Changes within the State

These structural changes imply a relocation of formal state authority and/or a transfer of state policy responsibilities from one governmental level or branch to another. This relocation can first occur in a vertical direction by shifting power, which was mainly concentrated at the level of the nation-state, upward or downward. Much state authority has been *uploaded* to supranational organizations such as the European Union (EU), various UN bodies, the International Monetary Fund (IMF), and the World Trade Organization (WTO). Member nations of the EU, for example, having relinquished independent formal state powers to the EU, are subject to "supreme legal powers residing in the European Court of Justice, . . . and the autonomous capacity for action of the European Commission. . . . [T]he Treaties and Directives of the EU have a direct effect on every citizen of the EU" (Walby 1999: 120). Whereas Walby argues that the EU is best understood as a new federal suprastate, we conceive the transfer of formal decision-making competencies by individual nations to the EU as a vertical reconfiguration of power. Other examples of uploading include the transfer of economic decision-making powers by the United States and Canada to the North American Free Trade Agreements and to the WTO. In these arrangements, nations have relinquished autonomy of decision making in policy-specific areas, and hence, have ceded some state authority to supranational organizations.

Vertical reconfiguration of formal state decision-making powers is also evidenced by *downloading*, that is, by the relocation of national state authority or responsibility for specific tasks to substate, provincial, or regional governments. For example, the devolution of formal decision making from the British Parliament to the new Scottish Parliament constitutes a transfer of state power and authority and the formal empowerment of a national region. Two Scottish referenda and elections to a new Scottish Parliament in May 1999 indicate that formal state powers, formerly the purview of the House of Commons, have been relinquished to Scotland and would be difficult to recover (Bogdanor 1999, 1997). The content and implementation of policy decisions by the new Scottish Parliament will likewise be irrefutable by the House of Commons. In addition to downloading formal authority, national governments have been reducing their responsibility for tasks by downloading these to subnational territorial units, without transferring the authority over policy arenas. For example, the Personal Responsibility Act mentioned previously increases the discretion of individual states, but "also imposed additional procedural, administrative, and financial burdens on states" (Mink 1998: 61–62; see also Schram and Weissert 1997).

Parallel to these vertical changes in state authority and responsibility, shifts of power occurred across the traditional representative spheres of the state, particularly the legislative and executive arenas. As a rule, there has been a weakening of the power of elected state spheres and a growing reliance on other and partly nonelected state bodies to make policy. We refer to these changes in state responsibility as *lateral loading*.[5] The national state maintains its decision-making powers, yet policy decisions increasingly occur in the courts, quasi-nongovernmental organizations (quangos), and executive agencies of government. Jessop (1991b: 150) notes that there has been a "decentralization of new supply-side powers…through the creation of single-function non-elected government agencies."[6] For example, in Great Britain, the Housing Act of 1988 led to the replacement of elected officials from the local authority housing departments by appointed officials on housing trusts (Lewis 1991).

The movement of policy decisions to nonelected state bodies is important because each policy venue influences the specific characteristics of policy decisions (Baumgartner and Jones 1993; Kirp 1982). In particular, as Baumgartner and Jones note (1993: 32–33), electoral politics allow activists greater influence over the framing of issues. When issues move from the Parliament to the administration, they tend to become more invisible and depoliticized. Similarly, issues may become depoliticized when they move to the judiciary. For example, the German Constitutional Court's decision on the 1992 abortion law changed the character of the German abortion

---

[5] We thank Michael Lewis-Beck for suggesting this term.

[6] Baumgartner and Jones (1993: 38–39) argue that as individual groups and issues gain recognition within the system, they may effect long-term structural changes in how policies are decided. This may be one cause of the increased power in nonelected state bodies. For example, as gender issues have gained more recognition, new and more independent bureaucracies concerned with gender were created.

debate. It effectively removed the issue from the arena of public debate, and constrained Parliament in their ability to determine abortion policy.[7] As governments have increasingly engaged in lateral loading, women's movements have been presented with an increasingly depoliticized and remote set of state policy-making agencies at the national level. Thus, the relocation of responsibility to nonelected state bodies eventually reduces social movement influence.

Structural Changes in the Relationship between State and Civil Society

States have not only shifted their power within their own realm but also have reduced their own power and authority vis-à-vis civil society. Perhaps the most visible part of such a shift in power and authority involves states' decisions to offload their traditional responsibilities onto nonstate venues such as the community, the family, the market, or intermediary organizations. In the United States, Germany, and Great Britain, for example, the state has shifted away from being the sole provider of welfare and the primary authority for equalizing economic inequalities. Instead, some of these responsibilities are now part of the economic market or, in the case of alleviating poverty, have become the charge of the community or of civil society (Birkinshaw, Harden, and Lewis 1990). In policy areas such as education, health, and housing, there has been a move toward "private interest government" (Jessop 1991a; Streeck 1995; Streeck and Schmitter 1983). In this case, individual social groups may become regulating agencies of the state. This differs from existing corporatist institutions in that the emphasis lies not in "interorganizational concertation" but in creating institutions and parameters for groups to act independently or at best in "informal cooperation" (Jessop 1990: 140). One result of offloading has been that families (particularly women) increasingly bear the burdens of caring for the aged and disabled (Bashevkin 1998).

Related to the rise in power of nonelected state bodies has been the proliferation of civil society representation within the state itself. Quangos, regulatory agencies, and corporatist institutions usually include representatives of civil groups. For example, beginning in the 1980s, educational policy in the United States was increasingly decided by quasi-governmental organizations (Fuhrman 1994). Members of these organizations are appointed by national or state political leaders, who usually seek representatives of business, teachers, and policymakers. Thus, as the number of such bodies has increased in the last ten years, so has the presence of certain parts of civil society within official state organizations (Levine and Trachtman 1988).

---

[7] Some social movement scholars have argued that access to the judiciary is a powerful political opportunity for social movements, by providing access to policy change (Kitschelt 1986; Kriesi 1995). We do not disagree. Rather here we are arguing that when the locus of policy making is removed from elected systems, social movements lose.

TABLE 1.1. *Reconfiguration Processes*

	Changes within the State	Changes in State/Society Relations
Vertical shifts	Downloading of power and responsibility to lower state levels	
	Uploading of power and reponsibility to higher state levels	Offloading of state power to nonstate actors
Horizontal shifts	Lateral loading by the delegation of competencies to nonelected state bodies	

These changes in the institutions of the state reflect a new power relationship between the state and other actors. On the one hand, there is a decline of the traditional neocorporatist arrangements of the past (Schmitter 1989). To the extent that states have lost macroeconomic control and businesses have moved toward more flexible forms of production, neocorporatist institutions, which engage in price and wage controls, have become less useful and less powerful (Jessop 1991a). Two groups appear to have lost more as a result of this shift. First, some industries, previously key to corporatist institutions (such as steel, coal, and large industrial manufacturing firms), are less relevant to the new economy and therefore no longer have the same power vis-à-vis the state that they once did (Jessop 1991a). Second, the new power constellations have also excluded traditional trade unions or only included more privileged groups of workers (Hirsch 1991, 1985; Jessop 1991a). For example, Jessop (1991b: 148) notes that under Thatcher the British system of tripartite corporatism was altered, often by eliminating or downgrading those institutions where trade unions were strong. On the other hand, the structural changes described previously, particularly the offloading of state responsibilities, mean that an increase in public-private partnerships provides new power to particular private interests. Certain policy areas are increasingly seen as specifically geared to serving business interests (for example, education, health, security, prisons) and, as a result, private corporations have increased power over certain types of state policy.

To summarize, reconfiguration is a multifaceted process that can be conceptualized as a syndrome of four specific transformations: Within the state we witness processes of horizontal and vertical shifts of power and policy responsibility, namely *uploading, downloading,* and *lateral loading.* At the same time, the relationship between the state and civil society has undergone fundamental changes insofar as states have *offloaded* responsibilities by simply withdrawing from particular functions and/or by delegating tasks to actors in civil society. These four processes are located in Table 1.1.

As the overall political and social power structure, including the organization and competencies of the state, is reconfigured, it affects a broad range of policy domains and social actors. To the extent that state reconfiguration is the result of large scale transformations in the global economic structure and international world order, states will experience widespread and long-lasting structural alterations, to which nonstate actors such as women's movements will have to adapt and of which they can take advantage. We argue that these reconfiguration processes are crucial for women's movements insofar as they provide negative as well as positive opportunities that differ fundamentally from the state context that women's movements faced in the 1960s and early 1970s.

Structural changes in the state are accompanied by a rhetoric and discourse of the state that has provided the rationale for state reconfiguration. That West European and North American states have developed, especially throughout the 1980s, a neoliberal discourse is not surprising, given the right-wing governments of Thatcher in Britain, Mulroney in Canada, Kohl in Germany, and Reagan in the United States. This discourse helped to shift and justify citizens' perceptions from a vision of states as activist centers of policy initiatives to one of states as limited, morally and economically, in their responsibilities and to an image of citizens as customers. Relying on frames developed in multinational industry and banking (Hirsch 1991, 1985; Jessop 1991b; Nielsen 1991), states articulated a neoliberal politics of individualism, meritocracy, self-reliance, and minimalist state responsibility. For example, Elman (this volume) argues that in the United States during the 1990s both the women's movement and the government emphasized the economic benefits to corporations of policies attacking violence against women. In addition, states altered their discourse about citizen participation from a vision of individuals as citizens with basic rights and of political participation, particularly voting, as the basis for citizen equality in the 1970s to a neoliberal discourse in the 1980s where citizens are seen as clients or consumers whose primary legitimate demand upon the state is for the satisfaction of specific needs (Brown 1995: 194).[8] For example, the Citizens' Charter in Great Britain, despite its name, lists rights that clients of the National Health Service or riders of British Rail have as consumers of these services.

Examples of Reconfiguration in Three Nations

Although we argue that all nations in West Europe and North America have experienced state reconfiguration, we also recognize that not all nations reconfigured in the same ways, at the same pace, and to the same extent. We discuss the cases of Britain, France and Germany, which serve as examples of different experiences with state reconfiguration from the 1970s to the 1990s, as follows.

[8] Indeed, a vision akin to the "civic man" of Berelson, Lazarsfeld, and McPhee (1954).

Britain

Britain's major reconfiguration of state powers is evidenced in its 1) program of radical privatization of state-owned enterprises, 2) shift of many former social welfare commitments and responsibilities away from the national state, by defunding and abolishing some programs, and by transferring implementation responsibilities to local venues, 3) transfer of responsibilities to nonelected venues within the state, and 4) devolution of some powers to Scotland.

Although British nationalization policy in the mid-1970s involved "a bipartisan element in the approach to public enterprise (i.e., the Conservatives had tolerated it and Labour had been enthusiastically in favour of it)" (Swann 1988: 7), by the mid-1990s, formerly nationalized industries and utilities had been sold to private owners.[9] The extensive privatization program, initiated under the Thatcher government and pursued by the Major government, included privatization of the coal industry (1992–3) and the gradual sell off of the railway system (1987 through the mid-1990s). The Blair government has not reversed these policies, in contrast to the French experience (see the following).

During this same period, state responsibility for traditional social welfare policies was reconfigured through a combination of defunding, reorganizing, and relocating policy implementation to local or nonstate venues. For example, under the Thatcher governments of the 1980s, state responsibility for public housing was partially relinquished by offloading public housing stock to the private sector (Studlar 1996: 172). As the British state downloaded and offloaded policy responsibilities, however, it not only maintained its authority over local councils and agencies, but also increased its formal authority in the 1980s by abolishing several local councils, such as the Greater London Council (see Birch 1998: 193–195).

The establishment of quasi-nongovernmental organizations (quangos), which removed various social policy decision making from democratic accountability, also dispersed policy responsibilities without relinquishing ultimate formal authority (Wolfe 2001). By 1990–1, British "quangos were spending three times as much as they had in 1978–79" (Krieger 1996: 69), despite a reorganization by Margaret Thatcher; by 1994, quangos were "responsible for one-fifth of all public spending and more than three-quarters of local government spending" (Krieger 1996: 69). Hutton claims that by 1996, the Conservative government had established 7,700 new quangos (Hutton 1995: 4–5).

Recently, state powers have also been devolved to Scotland and, to a lesser extent, Wales. In Scotland, two referenda (approving a Scottish Parliament and additional powers of taxation) and parliamentary elections in May 1999 formalized the devolution of state powers over such areas as school policy

[9] For a list of privatized industries in Britain, see Table 2 in the Appendix of Swann (1988).

and some environmental policies, previously the purview of the Scottish minister. Although devolution involves less transfer of power than would a federal reconfiguration of British powers (Bogdanor 1997), state authority recently ceded to Scotland will be exceedingly difficult for Britain to recover (Bogdanor 1999).

On the other hand, Britain has not been as active as France and Germany in uploading formal state powers to supranational organizations, specifically the European Union. Britain's membership in the EU has been marked by a series of fits and starts; since joining the EU, Britain has conditioned its membership by reserving for itself specific policy exceptions. For example, Britain signed the Maastricht Treaty but negotiated a series of "opt-outs" from workers' rights provisions in the Social Charter of the Treaty,[10] and from its unitary monetary and currency provisions. Britain's resistance to ceding these sovereign powers to the EU is shared by both the Conservative and Labour Parties (see, for example, Butler and Westlake 1995).

France

The French state varies considerably in all reconfiguration dimensions from Great Britain. France's state reconfiguration has been limited; the French state has continued central state authority within national boundaries, and maintained its commitment to state social welfare provisions. Nonetheless, France has moved toward reconfiguration, decentralizing policy implementation to local governments and relinquishing some authority to the European Union.

On its face, a major reconfiguration of state power would appear to be the decentralization policy of the Mitterrand government. In the 1980s, the Socialists introduced the *loi Defferre*, restructuring and increasing municipal, *département*, and regional powers and responsibilities. For example, *départements* assumed authority over "general medical facilities, maternity care, family welfare and special forms of social assistance for the elderly and physically disabled" (Mazey 1994: 160). Formal regional authorities were established and charged with economic development responsibilities, including vocational training and employment responsibilities. Despite the Socialists' initiatives at the local level, France has not ceded state authority by transferring formal authority (such as the power to tax) to local or regional authorities.[11] As Mazey claims, "the decentralised structures remain, for the time being at least, dominated by traditional political and administrative elites who have once again demonstrated their capacity to adapt to changing circumstances" (1994: 167, see also Mény 1998).

[10] The Social Charter, as it is referred to by other EU member states, is formally the "Community Charter of the Fundamental Social Rights of Workers."

[11] Transfer of implementation responsibilities was strongly resisted by the various Ministries (see Ashford 1990: 52). Ashford also argues that "most local spending is more or less obligatory and provides little room for discretion" (59).

The French experience with privatization in the late 1980s similarly involves modest state changes rather than radical ones. The French engaged in a series of nationalizations and privatizations throughout the 1970s and 1980s as governments changed. However, nationalization, privatization, and renationalization have not evinced fundamental changes in state authority; "parties of [both] the Right and the Left have for the most part nurtured and expanded the size and scope of the French public sector" (Zahariadis 1995: 118). In marked contrast to Britain's program of privatization, the first Mitterrand government (1981–2) introduced a program of bank nationalizations. In response, in 1986 the Chirac government privatized "65 industries – 9 industrial groups, 38 banks, 13 insurance companies, 4 finance companies" (Zahariadas 1995: 117) and communications groups (but not rail or coal), involving 900,000 jobs.[12] It did not, however, attack the principle of state ownership of economic enterprises; nor was it antistatist in its intentions or rhetoric; indeed most privatizations are more rightly characterized as reprivatizations, since most of these industries had only recently been nationalized by Mitterrand. French privatizations also lacked the ideological underpinnings of free market neoliberalism typical of Britain during the same period (Maclean 1995; Zahariadas 1995: 122–123). These privatizations continued (albeit at a much slower pace) when the Socialist Party resumed power in 1991 and increased again with the return of the center right in 1993 (Maclean 1995: 273).

Similarly, in France there has been little evidence of the types of horizontal shifts in policy responsibility we have labeled lateral loading. No specific policy agencies representing women have developed a lasting place within the French state. Rather, the French state has shifted policy responsibility for women's rights back and forth often depending on the party in power (see Mazur 1995: 78). For example, in 1974 President Giscard D'Estaing created a deputy ministry office for women (the Secrétariat d'Etat à la Condition Féminine) that disappeared in a governmental reorganization two years later. Moreover, France has evidenced little transfer of responsibilities to nonelected state bodies, in part because the executive branch in the Fifth Republic already controls more state authority and responsibility than its counterpart in the United Kingdom.

France's greatest step toward reconfiguration is its membership in the European Union, with commitments to monetary union and to the social and economic components of the Maastricht Treaty. As a founding member of the Common Market (1957), France has had longstanding political commitments to Europe as a unified entity as evidenced in its transfer of state power through the Single European Act (1987) and the Treaty of Maastricht (1993). In contrast to Britain, France has not reserved specific state powers

---

[12] For a list of French privatizations, see Table 5.1 in Zahariadas (1995: 118).

for itself as a condition of EU monetary union or, obviously, as a condition of EU membership.

Germany

Germany's degree of reconfiguration lies somewhere in between those of France and the United Kingdom; Germany has participated in the construction of a stronger European Union, has engaged in privatization, has downloaded some previous responsibilities to the states, and has offloaded others to the private sector. However, much of this reconfiguration has occurred within the context of continual support for a strong and active state. Thus, it has not gone as far as Great Britain in reducing the scope of state responsibility and authority. On the other hand, there have been more attempts to reduce state responsibility than in France.

Germany, like France, has been one of the strongest supporters of the European Union. Under Helmut Kohl, Germany signed the Maastricht Treaty and forged ahead with the Economic and Monetary Union. Under Gerhard Schröder, Germany has pushed for a stronger EU presence in social policy, particularly in the area of alleviating unemployment. Thus, both left and center-right governments have been responsible for shifting state authority from the national level to the European Union.

As a federal state, Germany has always had a more decentralized system than either Britain or France, with individual *Länder* having independent autonomy in some issue areas (for example, education) and responsibility for the implementation of many national policies. However, the responsibility of the *Länder* has increased in the 1980s. In areas such as industrial policy and social policy, the national government delegated to the *Länder* tasks that were previously under joint control by withdrawing funding from policy areas (particularly social welfare) that previously had been jointly funded (Benz 1989: 212–214; Jeffery 1996: 80). As a result, *Länder* governments find that they have increased decision-making power although this has occurred at a time of decreased revenues.

Despite the fact that the 1990 unification with East Germany created added pressure for state expenditures and control, the German state has also moved to privatize industries – particularly transportation and communications firms – and tried to reduce – though with little effect – the size of the state. These changes, however, have largely consisted of a series of small steps, such as the 1996 program to reduce the state's share of the GDP back to 1989 levels (Flockton 1996: 221). In the area of privatization, the German state has cut its participation in Lufthansa over the course of several years (Flockton 1996). Other firms, like Deutsche Telecom, have become joint-stock companies with the government maintaining some interest. Attempts to reduce state spending began in the late 1970s, under Helmut Schmidt's second term as chancellor, and were expanded by Helmut Kohl (Lawson 1996). The Social Democratic-Green coalition under

Gerhard Schröder has continued many of these efforts. Much of the retrenchment of the welfare state has been in the form of reductions in benefits or tightening eligibility requirements (Mangen 1996). Despite these moves to retrench the state, the neoliberal rhetoric is checked by a consensus (expressed in Basic Law and reiterated by every government) in a socially active state.[13]

Germany also has a long tradition of civil society participating in public policy, both in the decision-making process and in policy implementation (Katzenstein, P. 1987). For example, German churches have long played a role in providing welfare benefits with state funding (Katzenstein, P. 1987). As the German state reduced its funding of some benefits during the 1980s and 1990s, it increased the responsibility of nonprofit groups. However, compared to Great Britain, offloading has been fairly limited in scope.

The horizontal transfer of state responsibility has also been fairly limited in Germany. As far as women's issues are concerned, there was a gradual concentration of competencies that were previously scattered across various departments of the Ministry for Family and Youth. In 1986, the Ministry explicitly added women to its title and eventually became known, in shorthand, as the Ministry for Women. Similarly, although Germany has had extensive "parapublic institutions" and a strong bureaucracy in the postwar period (Katzenstein, P. 1987), there have been only limited increases in the number and size of these institutions. In contrast to Great Britain, there has not been a wholesale transfer of power from elected to appointed bodies.

COMPARING THE THREE COUNTRIES

As the preceding discussion indicates, Britain, France, and Germany have reconfigured their powers differently along the different dimensions of configuration, and even within each nation, changes are not uniform or unidirectional (see Table 1.2). Given this caveat, a pattern of state change from the 1970s to the 1990s emerges. First, each of the three nations has transferred some of its state sovereignty, in regard to economic policy, to supranational authoritative bodies. Second, social policies have been transferred from national responsibility to lower-level governmental arenas; national governments in the early 1990s have less responsibility for implementing and funding social welfare programs than they did in the mid-1970s. Third, states in the 1980s and 1990s have abandoned a range of social welfare supports that they instituted in the 1970s or earlier, leaving social problems to be addressed (or absorbed) by corporations, charitable and voluntary organizations, and/or the family and private individuals. On these dimensions

---

[13] For example, abortion, though illegal in principle, continues to be state-funded for poor women.

TABLE 1.2. *State Reconfiguration in Britain, France, and Germany (1970s–1990s)*

| Nation | Uploading | Downloading | | Offloading | Lateral Loading |
		Formal Power	Policy		
Britain	limited	none/reversed (centralization since 1983, e.g., GLC; exception is 1999 devolution)	extensive	extensive	extensive (e.g., establishment and increased funding of quangos)
Germany	extensive	none (federal state)	extensive	limited	limited
France	extensive	limited	extensive with reversals (e.g., 1981 bank nationalizations)	mixed	limited

of state reconfiguration differences between nations are matters of degree. France and Germany have ceded more formal powers to the European Union than has Britain. On the other hand, from the mid-1970s to the early 1990s, France (and to a lesser extent Germany) has retained more policy responsibilities than Britain, which has transferred these to other venues or relinquished them altogether.

Only with regard to devolving formal state powers and the horizontal shifts in state responsibility is there distinctive variation across the three nations. Britain recouped some formal power by abolishing county councils and directly governing major cities, such as London, but then devolved power in the late 1990s. France experimented with limited decentralization of policy implementation under the Socialists between 1981 and 1986. Germany, already decentralized, downloaded more responsibilities (but not authority) to the *Länder* by withdrawing from areas previously under joint responsibility. Great Britain engaged in extensive lateral loading of state responsibility onto nonelected state bodies with the establishment and increased funding of quangos. While neither Germany nor France has engaged in such extensive lateral loading to nonelected state bodies, in Germany we also see how the increased importance of gender in politics has led to the concentration of responsibilities on policies related to women into a single ministry.

These three examples illustrate that individual nations vary in the extent and forms that these changes in the state assume. We argue that all nation-states in West Europe and North America are experiencing state reconfiguration to some degree. Women's movements, which have interacted with nation-states in the context of these developments, have been both empowered and constrained by state reconfiguration. Moreover, second-wave women's movements have arisen to have powerful impacts on the discourse, policy, and even institutions of these nations. Women's movements are part of the historical context that shapes the specific relocation of power that has occurred in these countries.

CHANGING INTERACTIONS BETWEEN WOMEN'S MOVEMENTS AND STATES IN WEST EUROPE AND NORTH AMERICA

State reconfiguration, as a process of political restructuring and relocation of power, affects nonstate groups to the extent that these groups depend upon and interact with the state. How, in the context of state reconfiguration, have women's movements and states interacted? In the following pages, we first conceptualize state-movement interaction. Second, we present a generalized picture of the changing interactions between women's movements and states beginning in the 1970s, and, finally, we describe interactions between states and women's movements, with particular emphasis on their effects on both actors.

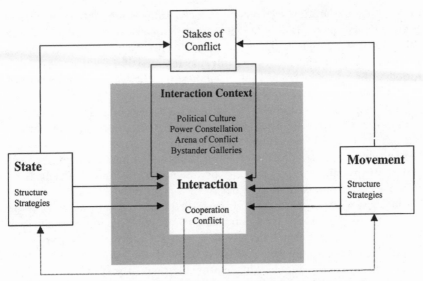

FIGURE 1.1. A Model of Interaction between States and Social Movements

Conceptualizing Movement-State Interactions

Theoretical literatures on the relationship between states and social movements falls into two general categories. First, structural approaches view states as stable entities challenged by social movements (for example, Birnbaum 1988; Kitschelt 1986; Tilly 1978). States are seen as largely coherent entities with a fixed range of political institutions that respond consistently to a range of social movements and their demands (if not always positively or explicitly). A second literature emphasizes that states are not necessarily stable and homogenous structures but are rather composed of, or represented by, various sets of actors who engage in diverse and dynamic relationships with social movements (della Porta and Rucht 1995; Flam 1994; Tarrow 1998). From this perspective, states, or their various components, can be engaged by social movements in ways that alter state behavior, elicit distinctive policy responses, or mobilize some, rather than other, state actors or agencies. We adopt this perspective in our treatment of movement-state interaction, as do all contributors to this volume.

By definition, a social interaction is the interplay of at least two actors. The general properties of these actors – their structure, their overall strategies[14] – as well as the nature of the specific issue at stake and the context in which the interaction takes place, all have an impact on the concrete character of the interaction (for a graphic illustration of this model see Figure 1.1). As

[14] "...Strategy refers to a conscious, long range, planned and integrated general conception of an actor's conflict behavior based on the overall context (including third parties and potential allies), and with special emphasis on the inherent strengths and weaknesses of the major opponents" (Rucht 1990: 161).

we have already discussed the changing structures of states, we now address the remaining factors affecting state-movement interactions in the following pages.

The *strategies* of states and women's movements can be arrayed along a scale from assimilative to confrontational (see Kitschelt 1986). Women's movements may choose to use strictly persuasive and legal means to become confrontational and even potentially to employ physical violence. The choice of strategies may affect (although it does not determine) the reactions by the state. More disruptive strategies may provoke strong state reactions.

The issues at stake for women's movements and states may be classified as 1) those that do not fundamentally affect the existing distribution of power and 2) those that constitute direct and serious challenge to existing power arrangements. Examples of the former include criticizing an ineffective public agency and campaigning for tax deductions for child-care expenses. These demands may engender strong resistance but they do not challenge systemic power arrangements. In contrast, issues that directly question the social and political order increase the stakes of the conflict for both the movement and the state; in these cases, movements risk harsh resistance by state authorities and other groups. A notable example was Greenham Common, where activist women protested the placement of U.S. cruise missiles on British soil as part of the dominant violent [male] political order. The response of the British police and the U.S. military included violent removals and the destruction of make-shift camps at individual base gates (see Roseneil 1995).

Finally, the interaction between women's movements and the state is also shaped by its context (Edmondson 1997; Hyvarinen 1997). The context of interaction can be conceived as a set of layers ranging from very general, deeply rooted, and relatively stable conditions to more variable, particular, and temporary settings which influence the form and outcome of interaction (Kriesi 1995; McAdam 1996; Tarrow 1998). Major components of the interaction context,[15] applicable to both movements and states, include political culture, the configuration of power, the policy agenda, and arenas and audiences.

The first and most general context variable is the *overall political culture* of a given society (Almond and Verba 1965; Johnston and Klandermans 1995; Laitin 1997; Steinmetz 1999). The political culture includes basic and widely accepted values to which women's movements and the state can appeal (Banaszak 1996). Moreover, the political culture sets evaluative standards about which kinds and forms of conflicts are legitimate and defines the roles and rights of certain kinds of actors in a given society. Although the character of the political culture does not determine the concrete strategies and reactions of women's movements and states, it makes some

---

[15] Our concept of interaction context differs from the concept of political opportunity structure only in its applicability to the state as well as movements.

strategies and reactions more likely than others. For example, authorities in the Netherlands tend to be more relaxed about breaches of legal rules (for example, squatting) than those in Germany or France.

A second contextual element that influences the interactions between women's movements and states is the *configuration of power* (Kriesi 1995: 179–192), that is, the cleavage structure as represented by major interest groups, the balance of power among political parties, and the composition of government. Conflicts between women's movements and states are shaped by the lines of established cleavages, the involvement of other actors as parties to the conflict, and governments' stances in opposing or supporting the movement.

The power configuration of the specific policy field within which the movement's issues are articulated is an important contextual variable. Some policy fields are long established, rest on stable constellations, have established agendas, and are fairly regulated. In these cases, particularly for corporatist structures with a few but powerful key actors, women's movement issues are likely to be incorporated into established policy agendas without concessions to the movement. This, for example, explains why equal pay policies in many nations have been resolved with more influence by labor unions than by the women's movement (see Banaszak this volume). Other policy fields, particularly those not yet firmly established such as domestic violence, are more open and more pluralistic. In such contexts, women's movements have more opportunity to shape the policy agenda.

The third contextual element likely to shape the forms of interaction is the *forum*[16] where the interaction occurs. It consists of two components: 1) an arena where the interaction takes place and 2) a gallery or audience where bystanders observe and react to the interaction (Ferree, Gamson, Gerhards, and Rucht 2002; see also Schattschneider 1960). In interactions between women's movements and states, some major arenas are the mass media, parliaments, and courts. The choice of the arena has implications for the kinds of interactions that are possible, insofar as some arenas (for example, parliaments, courts) are regulated and controlled by the state, whereas others (for example, the streets) are open to a wider range of interactions. We can expect that states prefer to confine conflict to strongly regulated arenas.

The activities and outcomes in different arenas are often interconnected. For instance, if the women's movement loses on an issue in parliament, it may shift its struggle to the courts or raise the issue in European Union institutions. Similarly, a campaign to win the support of the media may precede a parliamentary campaign.

Women's movements and states act not only in relation to each other but also with regard to the gallery (Schattschneider 1960). The gallery may be

---

[16] A forum is a visible place defined by certain roles and rules (Gerhards, Neidhardt, and Rucht 1998).

defined as everything from the small number of those who are physically present during an interaction to the mass public observing events and processes via the media. In democratic societies the reactions of the gallery play a decisive role in many political struggles since the majority of the voters ultimately affect which groups get into positions of formal decision making. Because of this (and the potential mobilizing power of public opinion), movements and states calculate the effect of their actions on the gallery.

As Figure 1.1 suggests, we recognize the importance of feedback loops in understanding state-movement interactions. Earlier interactions structure subsequent ones. Movement and state experiences within the previous interaction and particularly their evaluations of its outcome are incorporated into the next round of interaction. For example, women's movements may change their strategies, reorganize, or redefine the stakes of the conflict based on past experiences. In this perspective, interactions between women's movements and states are episodes in an ongoing process that, at each stage, can only be fully understood in the light of the past.

The Dynamics of State-Movement Interaction

How has the interaction of states and women's movements in North America and West Europe changed over time? As our model suggests, the interaction between states and women's movements is structured by previous interactions as well as the characteristics of both actors and the political context. In this section, we present a rough overview of the shifting nature of this interaction since the 1970s, with the caveat that the generalizations presented here occurred in varying degrees in specific countries.

In the 1970s, women's movements' interactions with states were characterized in part by radical if not revolutionary rhetoric made by largely informally organized and locally based wings of the movements. The section of the second wave of the women's movement that grew out of New Left groups adhered to socialist and Marxist ideas and advocated revolutionary change in everyday life (see, for example, Echols 1989; Firestone 1970; Freeman 1975; Morgan 1970; Randall 1992; Salper 1972; Tanner 1971; see also della Porta, and Jenson and Valiente this volume). It was this section of the women's movement in particular that sought to eliminate patriarchal and capitalist institutions, demanding the creation of a new political system and economic order.

Other wings of the women's movement, such as those composed of trade union women or liberal movement organizations, were concerned with specific policy reforms of the state. Yet, even their demands (for example, regarding violence against women, reproductive rights, and sexuality) challenged established political arrangements and were not easily contained or captured by existing politics. While the exact character of these sections of the women's movement varied from state to state, in the 1970s they were relatively limited in size and scope. Despite a need for political allies, the women's movement had few inroads to established politics through political parties, trade unions, or governmental institutions. Moreover, during this period, the new women's movements tended to keep their distance from established parties, even those of the left, insisting on the movement's "autonomy" (Beckwith 1987; Ferree 1987; Hellman 1987; Jenson 1987). At these early stages, the concerns and demands of the women's movement were novel and unfamiliar to the larger public, attracting little public support. As a result, women's movements often focused not just on influencing states but also on changing social norms and practices.

Thus, in the beginning stages of the second wave, both the constellation of power and most bystanders were unreceptive to women's movements' demands. While different sections of the women's movement utilized different arenas, the early women's movement was characterized by greater reliance on venues outside of the state. Moreover, the issues at stake largely challenged the existing distribution of power. Particularly challenging were those demands that called for complete restructuring of the patriarchal system.

The novelty of the women's movement's demands and the lack of political allies or widespread public support allowed states to ignore most movement claims. Nonetheless, states did make some concessions to initial demands, although these varied depending on the specific historical and political context. Most West European and North American states acceded in very minimal ways to demands for equal opportunity, equal pay, and increased political inclusion, demands which were the least challenging to existing state structures and harmonized with the political norms of a liberal democratic state. In addition, many states also altered their policies in the issue areas of contraception and abortion, where women's movements' use of extrastate protest was greatest, and where larger changes in societal gender roles underlay movement positions. Outside the state, women's movements' activities over the decade led to increasingly sympathetic public opinion toward some of the less revolutionary demands of the women's movement.

In the 1980s and 1990s, as states began to reconfigure, the political context of state–women's movement interaction was different. Women's issues had permeated many social and political groups as well as a broad range of more formal organizations and institutions. For example, the issue of sexual harassment spread from the women's movement into even more conservative state institutions such as the military (Katzenstein 1998a; Stiehm 1989). This does not necessarily imply that women's movements made outstanding substantial gains but rather that women's issues are raised and debated in many more and wider circles than ever before. Moreover, initial demands for inclusion in political institutions increased the links between women's movements and political parties. In some cases, movements established strongholds in left-libertarian parties, such as the Greens, which were likely to advance the movements' cause. Other left and left-center parties (and some center-right parties) offered organized women access to political office (see Darcy and Beckwith 1991; Studlar and Matland 1996).[17] Demands for access to political institutions also contributed to the rise of feminists in public administration, even in traditionally "male" areas such as the military.

Increased public acceptance and links to other political allies made women's movements in many countries large, diverse, and multilayered. Women's movements now included loosely coupled networks that extended into many nonmovement areas, permitting the formation of broad alliances and the aggregation of heterogeneous resources (see Keck and Sikkink 1998; Banaszak this volume). However, in some cases, this meant that women's movements became so highly fragmented that they no longer exhibited an identifiable ideological and social core and hence jeopardized their ability to act strategically.

Finally, although in most countries a more radical component of the women's movement persists and retains independence from the state and mainstream political actors, the discourse and identity of this segment are no longer tied to revolutionary rhetoric. For example, Ryan (1992) finds that the original radical feminist groups in the United States gave way to a different form of group activism, exemplified by local service projects (for example, women's shelters; see also Schmidt and Martin 1999 on self-help groups; Taylor 1999) that were justified by their focus on women's culture rather than on antipatriarchal and revolutionary rhetoric. In other cases, a neoliberal discourse of individual opportunity, capacity, and merit has underlain the movement's emphasis on parity issues (see Jenson 1996; Jenson and Valiente this volume). In the United States and Britain, for example, class-based feminist discourse has virtually disappeared, again superseded by neoliberal claims (see Katzenstein, Beckwith this volume).

These considerably altered women's movements faced a reconfigured state that had relinquished its authority in some areas, had actively empowered political decision making by other political actors through offloading and lateral loading, and had adopted an ideology that precluded some forms of action. On the other hand, the state was also more sympathetic to some women's movements' concerns and had adopted at least some forms of gender discourse. The resulting interactions for upper- and middle-class feminists were decidedly less conflictual although limited to issues that corresponded with state discourse and ideology. However, as Beckwith (this volume) shows, parts of the women's movement and their issues continued

---

[17] In other cases, however, changes in party competition and in party systems jeopardized women's movements' relationship with and reliance upon established parties to achieve movement goals (see Randall 1995). As left-wing parties lost elections, newly governing parties were unreceptive to organized feminists and their issues, and feminist movements found themselves without influence in government (for example, Britain, Canada).

to be excluded from this institutionalized interaction. Those segments of the women's movements that do not engage in institutionalized interactions with the state continue to engage in confrontational tactics. They are hampered in large part by a lack of resources and political allies. While public opinion and other bystanders are sensitized to some movement discourse and to more institutionalized interactions, the existence of these interactions has marginalized the other wings of the movement, giving them little opportunity to gain support of bystander publics or other political allies.

Given the evolving nature of state-movement interactions since the 1970s, we turn now to an examination of the different ways that the reconfiguration of the state has effected changes in women's movements and has also been, in part, affected by women's movement activism.

The Effect of State-Movement Interactions on Women's Movements

As states have reconfigured their structures, relocated their policy responsibilities by delegating or abrogating them, and rearticulated their policy discourse, how have feminist movements responded? We argue that the effects of state-movement interactions on women's movements' development, tactics, discourse, and policy outcomes are both numerous and discernible. Some of the effects on women's movement organization have already been investigated; for example, the effect of shifting power to supranational levels in the specific case of the European Union (EU) has been examined by several authors (Elman 1996a; Hoskyns 1996). In a limited number of policy areas, the increasing power of the EU has required women to organize collectively at that level (Hoskyns 1996: 16; see also Elman this volume) and to use that venue to wrest policy results from individual nations (see Carter 1988). We expect to see similar responses as feminist movements alter their organizing efforts to be consistent with other dimensions of state reconfiguration. For example, as states decentralize their power, feminist organizing, as well as feminist office seeking, is likely to increase at the local level. The offloading of state responsibility to private organizations may also lead women's movements to mobilize in ways that would allow them to acquire resources through offloading (see Katzenstein this volume). Such mobilization may encourage the transformation of local feminist groups into service organizations and self-help groups. Ironically, women's movements have solidified relationships with the national state and feminists have moved into state institutions and elected bodies at the same time as the traditional responsibilities afforded these institutions are dissipating through state reconfiguration.

We expect that these changes will affect women's movements' strategies, as well as their ability to articulate and to pursue their own agenda. For example, one interesting question is whether state-movement interactions played a role in the decline of radical feminist ideology and identity, and how differences in radical and autonomist stances of women's movements across nations might vary accordingly. We hypothesize that a revolutionary ideology and discourse was first abandoned in countries that traditionally lacked a strong left (most notably the United States and Canada), since these countries had no bystanders or political allies who might be swayed by such a discourse. Revolutionary ideology and discourse is also likely to disappear where states were relatively accessible and responsive to women's movements' demands. As women's movements had some initial policy successes in the 1970s (for example, divorce reform, liberalization of abortion), some strands within the movements learned to employ a neoliberal state discourse in achieving their ends. This is apparent in the successes of women's movements' emphasis on equality of opportunity and on equal access to employment, housing, social services, and legislative representation, even where equality may be posited on a male model. Finally, in nations where women's movements employed a state involvement rather than an autonomous political strategy, women's movements were unlikely to adopt revolutionary discourse.

We are also interested in how established party links and feminist presence within the state affect state-movement interactions. We hypothesize that strong links between women's movements and other social actors, including other movements, interest groups, and political parties are likely to facilitate women's movements' access to the state and their influence on state policy making. Banaszak (this volume) suggests that such links might facilitate policy successes during offloading and horizontal shifts to nonelected bodies because women's movements still receive less state recognition as a private interest than political parties and trade unions.

On the other hand, as women's movements establish such links and broaden their scope, they may also moderate their tactics, their demands, and their rhetoric. Movement action dependent upon alliances with other social groups and political parties may be constrained by the nature of the institutions themselves and by the (un)willingness of allies to engage in particular tactics. Such links also multiply the number of networks and organizations involved in the women's movement, making coordination among movement actors more difficult. In the creation and expansion of political alliances, the more radical components of the movement may find themselves marginalized.

Similarly, the changes in discourse wrought by state-movement interaction and by the process of state reconfiguration may alter the frames and issues of women's movements. While a moderate feminist discourse has gained a legitimate place within the political debate, the neoliberal, anticollectivist rhetoric of the reconfigured state also limits women's movements to issues that will resonate with a wider public. Moreover, the policy discourse of the state is itself limited to certain views of women (for example, as mothers or workers), which may again constrain the range of potential movement action.

Thus, the interaction of states and women's movements, while providing legitimacy to some types of women's issues, restricts the acceptability of others and eliminates still others from the political agenda.

Effects of State-Movement Interactions on the State

Given the central role of the modern interventionist state, women's movements must engage the state to bring about political and societal changes. As Brown argues for the North American cases, "the state figures prominently in a number of issues currently occupying and often dividing... feminists... [In addition], an unprecedented and growing number of women... are today directly dependent upon the state for survival" (Brown 1995: 168). Although hostility toward the state and a distaste for male-dominated national politics have been characteristic of some sectors of second-wave feminism (see Jenson and Sineau 1994; Lovenduski and Randall 1993; Randall 1998), feminist movements in the 1980s and 1990s have directed their efforts toward states, by becoming state authorities or agents (for example, elected or appointed officials, bureaucrats), by mobilizing for policy change, and by involving themselves in state reform projects.

Because the state is targeted by multiple and often conflicting groups, ranging from competing social movements to conventional pressure groups to political parties, the impact of women's movements on the general structures of the state remains limited. It is unlikely that any single social movement would be able to change the fundamental structure of the state, and thus we cannot easily attribute major changes in state reconfiguration (for example, decentralization) to the women's movement. Women's movements, in conjunction with other social forces, nonetheless contributed to structural changes; for example, new power constellations between state and nonstate actors developed as the result of the weakening, or even abolition, of corporatist arrangements in some countries. In other nations, the decentralization of state structures and downloading of state responsibilities may have been encouraged and supported by autonomous women's groups positioned to undertake control of these functions at the local level. In still other cases, women's movements may have helped to shape new state structures in the making, for example, in the case of constructing new federalist arrangements in Canada (Dobrowolsky this volume) or in shaping the structure of devolution in Scotland (Brown 1995).

In which countries and in which respects have women's movements been most successful in effecting state changes and how can this been explained? Have feminist movements been able to cast these transformations in West European and North American states in forms and modes potentially more receptive to these movements, their issues, and their constituencies? We suggest that women's movements have been more likely to effect changes in state structures, institutional practices, policy priorities, state personnel and authorities, and state rhetoric – that is, to facilitate state reconfiguration – under the following conditions.

First, when women's movements are positioned to form an alliance with other movements, or when a sympathetic carrying agent (for example, a left, left-libertarian, or radical political party) seeks similar ends and can advance these issues within the state, women's movements are more likely to be able to influence state changes above and beyond specific policy achievements (see della Porta this volume). Conversely, where such allies were not available or did not share or pursue structural or policy changes, women's movements are not likely to contribute to state reconfiguration (see Beckwith, Katzenstein this volume).

Second, when policy arenas related to women's issues (for example, equal employment opportunity) or of specific concern to women (for example, schooling) have high saliency for the state, women's movements will be better positioned not only to shape the debate, but also to influence the locations of policy implementation and to direct the construction of new state agencies or quasi-nongovernmental organizations (see Banaszak this volume). In those policy domains that directly relate to most women's issues, women's movements are likely to have an impact by supporting an increase in women's representation within the state apparatus and by interjecting new women's issues, such as sexual violence, into the policy-making process. In several countries, this trend has even resulted in the establishment of women's state secretariats, women's bureaus, and other agencies that are geared to advancing the cause of women (Stetson and Mazur 1995); in Germany, for example, all medium-sized and large cities employ *Gleichstellungsbeauftragte* (commissioners for the advancement of gender equality). As states abandon women's policy issues, or as such issues become less salient for states, women's movements are less likely to be able to influence or to resist state structural or implementation changes.[18]

Third, are there state structural settings that are more-or-less conducive to influence by women's movements? We suggest that where policy issues involve feminist struggles against implementation rather than active support for new policy initiatives, women's movements are more likely to be advantaged in their efforts by multiple centers of power. In this regard, we ask whether women's movements' support of local politics and critiques of the state actually facilitate state reconfiguration. Conversely, where state power is centralized and unitary, women's movements may be advantaged in attempts to advance policy initiatives which, confirmed by a central state structure, are then uniformly applicable nationwide (see Katzenstein and

---

[18] Note that we recognize that potentially all policy issues and state formations are gendered insofar as male power and masculine attributes are actively, although not perfectly, enacted through state mechanisms, practices, and discourses (see Brown 1995: ch. 7; Dodson forthcoming).

Banaszak this volume; see also Mink 1998). In addition, decentralization of state powers (implicated in but not coterminous with multiple locations of state power) may also open political opportunities for organized women; we therefore consider whether decentralization creates state structures that tend to be more responsive to women's movement demands than centralization of power.

Finally, state and feminist discourses have intersected in ways that also serve to feminize state discourse; that is, a shared discourse developed from the interaction between women's movements and states, as women targeted the state as a venue for issue resolution. States increasingly interact discursively with women's movements by employing a gendered discourse, that is, a discourse about women that is not necessarily feminist or change oriented. This has been evidenced in two ways. First, states have recognized gender as a legitimate and crucial venue for state rhetoric and discourse. Many controversies about rights and responsibilities now include discussions of gender, at least in the area of reproduction, work, and political representation. Moreover, reference to equality of the sexes is increasingly included in discussions around constitutional issues and basic rights. For example, gender questions have been highlighted by the French, British, Italian, German, and Norwegian states (Bystydzienski 1995; Chamberlayne 1993), and lack of women's representation within the British Conservative Party was used to criticize the party in Scotland. In some cases, a feminized state discourse is purely symbolic and deflects state responsibility for policy change (for example, in the United States the gender inclusive language of the 1984 Republican Party platform).

Second, states have employed a gendered discourse that relies upon neutral or inclusive language. In many cases gender has been recognized only in a few areas of state discourse and has been constrained by preexisting state and societal conceptions of gender. For example, in Britain, child-care policies continue to articulate concern with "heads of households," apparently neutral language that nonetheless functions as a male trope (Lewis 1998). Such feminized state discourse can serve to mask real differences in circumstance and power between women and men, despite face efforts to address women's issues. In these cases, while the state's focus on gender appears to be both a success of the women's movement and an opportunity for further activity, it also reflects the limits of and political constraints on women's movements.

THE APPROACH OF THIS STUDY

As the preceding section has argued, our focus is on interaction processes and how these impact upon both the state and the women's movement. Two additional characteristics of our joint approach are worth emphasizing. First, because of our interest in state reconfiguration, the work focuses on over-time

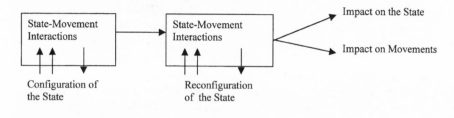

Period 1: Early 1970s   Period 2: 1990s

FIGURE I.2. Model of Research Design

comparisons. We contrast two periods indicative of different levels of state reconfiguration whose juxtaposition demonstrates the significant changes in women's movements, their relevant societal and political context, and their effects on states. Our starting point is the early 1970s, the period when the second generation of women's movements gained momentum. We contrast the interactions between states and movements in this period with those in the late 1980s and 1990s. In this most recent period, as we have already suggested, the movements have changed their ideology, structure, and strategy, mainly because, as we hypothesize, they confront a restructured state that forces movements in turn to adapt in order to remain, or to become, influential players. Although the analytical focus of our studies is the comparison of interactions in these two periods, our ultimate concern is to assess and to understand the impact of the contemporary interactions on both the women's movement and a reconfigured state, as illustrated in the model of our research design (see Figure I.2).

Secondly, we employ a comparative cross-national and cross-policy perspective. Most of the individual chapters take a comparative view instead of treating individual countries. Because of the competencies and preferences of the contributors to this volume, however, we also chose not to limit our discussion to a small number of issues to be covered in the same set of countries. We have opted instead for a less stringent and more flexible pattern of comparison in examining our principal questions. Nonetheless, we believe that a cross-national comparative analysis written to a common theoretical framework will provide valuable insights into our understanding of the interaction between states and women's movements and their effects.

Plan of the Book

The structure of this volume reflects our ambition to create an integrated collaborative product using the authors' multinational expertise in women's movements and social movements more generally. The book is divided into two major parts. We first present eight substantive chapters, each of which considers one particular aspect of the interaction between women's movements and the state. Celia Valiente's chapter on Spain and Donatella della

Porta's chapter on Italy provide two in-depth examinations of changing state-movement interactions over time; together they present a comparative assessment of women's movements in South European states, which made democratic transitions in the post–World War II period and where state reconfiguration has a distinctive and limited pattern.

These two single-nation assessments are followed by explicitly cross-national explorations of women's movements and state reconfiguration. Jane Jenson and Celia Valiente's chapter on parity movements in France and Spain traces the development of an electorally focused strategy in the 1990s and the conditions that shaped this turn. R. Amy Elman's discussion of women's shelter movements in Sweden, the United Kingdom, and the United States shows how state involvement in feminist programs can function to professionalize service delivery as it renders feminist activists more conservative. Alexandra Dobrowolsky's chapter assesses the explicit attempts of women's movements to shape constitutional construction in the United Kingdom and Canada. Women's movements' ability to effect change depended in part on the existing opportunities in these nations and on the particular constellation of identity politics within those movements.

Three additional chapters in this section analyze the effects of state–women's movement interaction on state policy and state governance. Lee Ann Banaszak's chapter examines how policy outcomes are influenced by the level of state reconfiguration and by an issue's centrality to issues of reconfiguration. Banaszak investigates the impact of state reconfiguration on policy using comparative case studies of abortion in Germany and Ireland and equal pay in Britain and France. Karen Beckwith similarly considers state reconfiguration in Britain, France, and the United States, and assesses changes in women's movements in the three nations, both in terms of the movements' shift to emphasizing women's access to elective office and of women's actual electoral success in different venues of state power. Mary Fainsod Katzenstein's chapter concludes this set of chapters by analyzing the conditions under which the U.S. women's movement (and implicitly many of the other movements dealt with in the volume) turned away from its radical socialist commitments to poor women in the 1970s as poor women in the 1990s became negative policy targets in the reconfiguration of the U.S. state.

The second section of the volume contains three analytical chapters designed to broaden the specific perspectives of the substantive chapters in various ways. The chapter by John McCarthy and Carol Mueller focuses on political cultural issues and underscores that structural changes unfold within the cultural specificities in individual nations. Relying on the examples of feminist movements detailed in various chapters, McCarthy and Mueller seek to classify feminist movement types in the context of reconfiguring states. A second chapter by Dieter Rucht links our findings to work on interactions between the states and movements other than women's movements. This allows us to answer the question of whether or not we can identify more general trends and patterns of interaction. One finding is that women's movements and environmental movements exhibit striking similarities in their changing interactions with states over time, while the same cannot be said for various other movements. A final chapter by David S. Meyer draws together findings from the substantive chapters in order to assess both divergences and convergences across time, issues, and space. Despite national differences in political opportunities and political culture, Meyer finds that the substantive chapters all evidence an institutionalizing of women's movements that provides greater opportunities for some types of movement activity and success, while precluding others. These chapters link the theory and empirical cases to broader questions about women's movements and social movements in general, state structures and public policies, and the interaction between civil society and states.

2

The Feminist Movement and the Reconfigured State in Spain (1970s–2000)*

Celia Valiente

The so-called "political process" approach to the study of social movements (Eisinger 1973; Jenkins and Perrow 1977; Kitschelt 1986; Kriesi 1995; 1996; McAdam 1982; Tarrow 1996; Tilly 1978, among others) proposes that in contemporary polities the structural and conjunctural characteristics of the state influence social movements over time causing their organizational features, goals, strategies, and even outcomes to develop in particular ways. This chapter studies the influence of the state on the feminist movement in Spain since the 1970s.[1] The first section of this chapter argues that the Spanish second-wave feminist movement has been affected by state-centered variables related to the democratization process of the country. From the mid-1930s to 1975, Spain was governed by a right-wing authoritarian regime that actively opposed the advancement of women's rights and status. The first feminist groups were set up in the late 1960s and early 1970s in a period of liberalization of the authoritarian political regime. Many of the first feminists were active in the opposition to the dictatorship, where they encountered illegal left-wing political parties and trade unions. These have been the (uneasy) allies of the feminist movement ever since. Numerous feminists mobilized in favor of equal rights for women, but also pursued broader political reforms, such as the establishment of a democratic regime using mainly (but not exclusively) conventional repertoires of political action. Feminists

* Some of the material in this chapter is drawn from della Porta et al. 1997. I would like to thank Kerman Calvo, Manuel Jiménez, and Gracia Trujillo for their invaluable comments on an earlier draft.
[1] This chapter does not describe the evolution of the Spanish feminist movement in and of itself but rather focuses only on the changes over time in terms of state/movement interactions. Readers interested in more general accounts of the Spanish feminist movement may consult (among other secondary sources): Borreguero, Catena, de la Gándosa, and Salas 1986; della Porta, Valiente, and Kousis 1997; Di Febo 1979; Durán and Gallego 1986; Escario et al. 1996; Folguera 1988b; Kaplan 1992; Pineda 1995; Puleo 1996; Salas 1996; Scanlon 1976, 1990; Sundman 1999; Threlfall 1985, 1996.

have been unable to build strong, encompassing, and long-lasting umbrella organizations, partly because of the differences among feminists across party lines.[2]

At least three important reconfigurations of the state have taken place in the last three decades in Spain as well as in other Western countries: *downloading* of central state authority to lower territorial levels (chiefly to regions and not so much to localities); *uploading* authority to higher levels (the European Union, EU); and horizontal redistribution of responsibility within the state among governmental departments (called *lateral loading* in this book) with the creation of bureaucracies concerned with gender. State-society relations have also been transformed by states' decisions to *offload* their traditional responsibilities onto nonstate venues such as the community, the family, or the market (see the introductory chapter this volume).

The second section of this chapter shows that the aforementioned dimensions of the reconfiguration of the state and state-society relations have had an impact on the Spanish feminist movement. Because national power has been translated to alternative territorial levels, feminists have reoriented their actions to the regions and the EU. The regionalization of Spanish politics has made the establishment of nationally based umbrella organizations very difficult, while the European dimension of Spanish politics might have intensified joint action undertaken by different feminist groups. The establishment of institutions to promote gender equality has meant for the Spanish feminist movement the availability of state subsidies for groups, a very limited point of access to the state, and a redirection of media attention from the movement to the state. In Spain, some services for citizens are increasingly provided by partnerships of state and nonstate actors. This trend has provided women's groups that deliver services with state monies.

Generally speaking, the "political process" literature on social movements makes (usually passing) reference to the influence of social movements on the state. The best known example here is the formation of Green parties and their incorporation into the party system over time (Müller-Rommel 1989). There are several reasons why the influence of movements on the state is less studied than that of the state on movements, among others the theoretical arduousness associated with the definition of "success" and "failure" of movements (Gamson 1990 [1975]; Giugni 1998; Kitschelt 1986); "the methodological difficulties involved in separating social movement organization impact from the effects of other forces" (Burstein, Einwohner, and Hollander 1995: 293); or the rare success of social movements in changing particular public policies (Rochon and Mazmanian 1993). Nevertheless, since it is increasingly recognized that states and movements influence each

---

[2] As the chapter by Elman for this book states, writing an account of the feminist movement implies making generalizations about a collective actor. However, it is important to remember that social movements are composed of many diverse groups and individuals.

other in dynamic ways and continually interact with each other (McAdam, Tarrow, and Tilly 2001: ch. 1), it is mandatory to study both processes of influence, rather than analyzing mainly or exclusively the impact that the state exercises on movements.

The third section of this chapter defends the claim that in the interaction of the movement with the state, the former managed to change the later at least in two regards. On the one hand, the feminist movement has intervened in the policy area of gender equality mobilizing public opinion in favor of the need to improve women's status and putting pressure on state officials to be more active in tackling the problem of women's subordination. Feminists have also managed to feminize the state to some degree. It has been principally thanks to feminists' pressures within left-wing political parties (among other causes) that an increasing number of women occupy political decision-making positions.[3]

THE DEMOCRATIZATION PROCESS AND THE FEMINIST MOVEMENT

As shown next, state-centered factors relative to the democratization process have had an impact on the feminist movement in Spain regarding its political allies, its aims, its organizational structures, and its repertoires of action.

The Political Allies of the Feminist Movement

Some of the first feminists were active in the opposition to the authoritarian regime where they encountered mainly left-wing illegal political parties and trade unions (López-Accotto 1999: 114–115). Second-wave feminists have allied themselves with left-wing parties and unions ever since (see also the chapter on Italy in this volume for a similar alliance between feminists and the left).

The first feminist groups appeared at a time of liberalization of the authoritarian regime when there was some (restricted) space for the development of civil society. This was the case (among others) of the Democratic Women's Movement (*Movimiento Democrático de Mujeres*, MDM), which was linked to the clandestine communist party (*Partido Comunista de España*, PCE),[4] although some MDM members were not members of any political party

---

[3] The research for this chapter consists of analysis of published secondary sources. Only the feminist part of the women's movement in Spain is analyzed here. The reason for not including the nonfeminist branch of the movement (housewives' organizations, widows' associations, mothers' movements, and religious associations, among others) in this study is the acute scarcity of secondary research on the issue.

[4] The PCE was the main party in the illegal opposition to the Francoist regime. Since 1986, the PCE has been included in the electoral coalition called United Left (*Izquierda Unida*, IU). Since the 1977 general election, the PCE/IU has obtained a third position among nationally based political parties, except in the 1982 and 1986 general elections, when it obtained a fourth position.

(Escario, Alberdi, and López-Accotto 1996: 363; Kaplan 1999; Pardo 1988: 134; Seminario de Estudios sobre la Mujer 1986a: 333; Threlfall 1996: 115–116).[5] After 1975, feminist groups mushroomed. Many of them were also very close to left-wing political parties, such as the Women's Democratic Association (*Asociación Democrática de la Mujer*) which related to the Spanish Workers' Party (*Partido del Trabajo en España*, PTE) and the Union for Women's Liberation (*Unión para la Liberación de la Mujer*) which is connected to the Workers' Revolutionary Organization (*Organización Revolucionaria de Trabajadores*, ORT) (Pardo 1988: 137).[6]

During the transition to democracy, other women organized themselves as feminists within left-wing parties and unions. Therefore, since the origins of the Spanish second wave of feminist activism, the frontier between the movement and conventional political actors has been blurred. Feminists have been active within the Spanish Socialist Workers' Party (*Partido Socialista Obrero Español*, PSOE) since the beginning of the transition to democracy, trying to win organizational status within the party.[7] In 1976, a women's caucus, "Woman and Socialism" (*Mujer y Socialismo*) was formed. It was no more than a study group. In 1981, one of its members was elected to the PSOE Executive Committee and others followed her in successive years. In December 1984, the women's caucus was raised by the party to the status of a Women's Secretariat at the Federal Executive level (Threlfall 1985). The Communist Party set up a highly ranked Women's Committee in 1977 when the party was legalized (Durán and Gallego 1986: 213). In 1977, feminists within the trade union the Workers' Commissions (*Comisiones Obreras*, CCOO) managed to create a Women's Secretariat at the highest organizational level. Feminists within the trade union General Workers' Union (*Unión General de Trabajadores*, UGT) established a woman's department at an organizational level lower than that of CCOO.

Only a minority of feminists remained independent of left-wing political parties and trade unions. These include the Antiauthoritarian Struggle of Antipatriarchal and Revolutionary Women (*Lucha Antiautoritaria de Mujeres Antipatriarcales Revolucionarias*, LAMAR); and small autonomous groups called "feminist collectives," for instance, the Feminist Collective Seminar of Madrid (*Seminario Colectivo Feminista de Madrid*) (Durán and Gallego 1986: 211).

---

[5] Since the 1970s, many feminist organizations appeared, and some of them also disappeared very quickly in Spain (Seminario de Estudios sobre la Mujer 1986a: 33). To give the names of all feminist groups since the 1970s is an almost impossible task. Therefore, only a few names are mentioned in this chapter as an illustration. An annotated list of organizations and platforms can be consulted in, among other places, Escario et al. (1996: 342–373).

[6] The PTE, the ORT, and other small left-wing political forces comprised the so-called extra-parliamentarian left, since they did not win representation in parliament.

[7] The PSOE was the main party in opposition between the general elections of 1977 and 1982 and again since 1996. In 1982, the PSOE took office, where it remained up to 1996.

In Spain, the association between feminism and the Left has been as troublesome as in other Western democracies, because left-wing parties have always been much more concerned with class inequalities than with gender differences. Feminist goals have always been viewed by the majority of party members and leaders either as bourgeois (and therefore illegitimate), or merely as distractions to the central goal of reaching a more egalitarian society (in terms of social classes) (Escario et al. 1996: 66; López-Accotto 1999: 116; Threlfall 1996: 121). Feminists have made herculean (and successful) efforts to add some clauses to left-wing political party congress resolutions, electoral programs, and other documents, making these parties more sensitive to gender inequalities.

The Aims of the Feminist Movement

In Spain, democracy was not a political regime taken for granted but one to be built. Many Spanish feminists took part in collective action in order to achieve not only the advancement of women's status but also the political transformation of the country (Scanlon 1990: 96). The majority (but not the totality) of second-wave Spanish feminists maintained a preference (not exempt of suspicion in some cases) for democracy, which implied at least the recognition of basic civil and political rights and equality of women and men before the law. Important strands of the second-wave feminist movement in Spain have maintained an interest in political reforms up until now. As explained by Jenson and Valiente in their chapter for this book, one of the main aims of some Spanish feminist groups since the 1990s has been a higher number of women in political decision-making positions (Puleo 1996: 57).

The focus of many Spanish feminists on political change has possibly meant that Spanish feminists have fought for the development of a common identity, countercultural change, and alternative lifestyles to a lesser extent than feminists in other western countries that were already consolidated democracies in the 1970s. However, in Spain as well, since the 1970s, a minority of feminist groups argued that reform in the political arena was not the main aim that feminists had to pursue. These activists thought that what women had to do was to develop their womanly characteristics (different groups had different opinions about which characteristics these were). The best way to develop this womanly side was to participate in nonhierarchical all-women groups. Some of these feminists abandoned grand utopias, proposing instead to experiment with new models of society and new lifestyles departing from daily realities.

The Organizational Structures of the Feminist Movement

As noted above, in the 1970s, many feminists combined membership in a feminist group and in another type of organization, such as a left-wing political party or trade union, in order to participate in the democratization of the country and include feminist concerns in mainstream political life. This position was called the double membership position (*doble militancia*) (Escario et al. 1996: 166–175; Scanlon 1990: 96–97). In contrast, champions of the single membership position in feminist associations (*militancia única*) thought that the improvement of women's status could not be pursued in feminist terms within traditional "malestream" organizations such as parties and unions because these contributed to the perpetuation of the unequal relationship between women and men. Women had to discover themselves (their capacities and wishes repressed in a male-dominated society) and create bonds of solidarity with other women while participating in nonhierarchical only-female groups. The dilemma between single versus double membership split the feminist movement in the late 1970s and was one of the main (if not the most important) points of discussion and disagreement in many feminist gatherings at that time (Durán and Gallego 1986: 208–209; Threlfall 1996: 116–117).

Political divisions of feminists across party lines (but also the multiplicity of theoretical positions; Pineda 1995: 102–103) have impeded the establishment of umbrella structures that represent a high number of groups, are often active for concerted actions, and persist across time. Although some umbrella organizations exist (or have existed), for instance, the Federation of Feminist Organizations of the State (*Coordinadora de Organizaciones Feministas del Estado Español*), comparatively speaking Spanish coordinating platforms are fewer, less representative, less active, and less long lasting than in other western countries. Political divergences across party lines also made very difficult the establishment of feminist organizations formed by women who belonged to different parties (Bella 1999: 160–167).

The Repertoire of Actions of the Feminist Movement

Social movements have an ample repertoire of actions to use, which include "conventional" actions such as lobbying or signing petitions and nonconventional actions, for instance, violent rioting. As political scientist Mary Katzenstein (1998b: 196) rightly points out, "constrained by traditional gender role stereotypes and by political choice, feminist activists' arsenal of political activism has drawn only fleetingly on demonstrative protest activities and even more rarely on violent activism." This pattern has probably been especially accentuated in Spain. The interest in political reform gave incentives to feminists to use conventional forms of collective action. The Spanish transition to democracy was of a consensual and peaceful type. Although some violent actions by political and social actors were undertaken, these actions were by no means the norm.

THE INFLUENCE OF THE RECONFIGURED STATE ON THE FEMINIST MOVEMENT

I next argue that four dimensions of the reconfiguration of the Spanish state and state-society relations have had a marked influence on the feminist movement: downloading central state power to the regions; uploading authority to the EU; lateral loading of power to gender equality institutions; and off-loading state responsibilities to alternative venues (voluntary associations in civil society, the family, or the market).

Downloading Central State Powers to the Regions

The shift of competences from the central state to the regions has had consequences for the organizational structure of the feminist movement. Unful-filled aspirations to self-government existed or appeared in several regions of Spain at the beginning of the transition to democracy. These regionalist demands made the establishment of nationally based coordinating platforms difficult because these could be seen as centralist efforts of Madrid feminists to impose umbrella structures upon activists in the regions (Threlfall 1996: 123). In contrast, feminists have succeeded in organizing national meetings in which hundreds or thousands of women participated. For instance, the four-day conference titled "Feminism Is...and Will Be" (*Feminismo es... y será*), organized by the Federation of Feminist Organizations of the Spanish State held in Cordoba in December 2000, was attended by more than three thousand women from very different feminist groups (*El País* 7 December 2000: 34). Reflecting the regionalization of Spanish politics, regional feminist meetings have also been organized in the last three decades (Escario et al. 1996: 228; Pineda 1995: 115).

Uploading Authority to the European Union

The transfer of authority to the EU has provided Spanish feminist groups with important incentives for concerted actions. On September 22, 1990, the European Women's Lobby was established. It includes Europe-wide women's groups and women's umbrella organizations from each EU member-state. The purpose of this lobby is to promote women's interests at the level of the EU (Hoskyns 1996: 185–186). The Spanish Association to Support the European Women's Lobby was founded in March 1993. It is an umbrella association of nationally based Spanish feminist groups funded mainly with European money and has close ties to the Spanish Socialist Party. Feminists active in left-wing parties with parliamentary representation have increasingly mobilized through this association in the battle for higher numbers of women in political decision-making positions (see Jenson and Valiente this book).

Lateral Loading State Authority within Departmental Units: State Feminism

Institutions whose purpose is the advancement of women's rights and status have been established in all western countries since the 1970s. These institutions are called women's policy machineries (or bureaucracies) or state feminist institutions. People who work in them are usually called "state feminists" or "femocrats" (Stetson and Mazur 1995). Regarding the Spanish central state, the main state feminist institution, the Women's Institute (*Instituto de la Mujer*, IM), was created in 1983, six years after the first democratic elections were held in Spain and one year after the Socialist Party (PSOE) first came to power.[8] In general, members of feminist groups did not issue a strong unified call for the creation of women's equality institutions in the 1970s and early 1980s (Escario et al. 1996: 288–289; Threlfall 1996: 124). The IM was established thanks to the efforts of feminists within the PSOE, many of whom were (or had been) members of feminist groups in civil society as well.[9]

The IM is an administrative unit that was first attached to the Ministry of Culture and then moved to the Ministry of Social Affairs created in 1988.[10] In spite of its late establishment in comparison with feminist machineries in other western countries, the IM is now comparable to those organizations in terms of personnel, budget, and the extent of its functions (Threlfall 1996: 124, 1998). The IM has its own director, staff (around 250 members), facilities, and independent budget. The staff and resources of the IM have constantly increased. In 2000, the IM had an annual budget of about 3.4 billion Spanish pesetas (*El País* 28 September 1999: 70). The major IM objective is to promote policy initiatives for women. The IM has neither the power nor the budget to formulate and implement most gender equality policies. Instead, it has to convince more powerful state offices, which usually have more resources, to elaborate women's equality policies.[11]

[8] The predecessor of the Women's Institute was the Women's Sub-Directorate (*Subdirección General de la Mujer*, SGM), which was created in 1978 and was dependent on the General Directorate of Youth and Socio-Cultural Development (*Dirección General de Juventud y Promoción Sociocultural*). Histories of the Spanish feminist movement make only passing references to the SGM (Kaplan 1992: 202; López-Accotto 1999: 128–129; Seminario de Estudios sobre la Mujer 1986a: 29–30, 1986b: 14–15). Since so little is known about the SGM, it is not covered in this chapter.

[9] A history of the establishment of the IM, the role played by the IM in the policy-making process, and the relationships between state feminists and activists in the feminist movement can be found in Threlfall (1996, 1998) and Valiente (1995b; 1997b).

[10] In 1996, the Ministry of Social Affairs and the Ministry of Labor and Social Security were merged into the Ministry of Labor and Social Affairs, upon which the IM depends.

[11] According to the IM act of foundation and its regulations (Act Number 6 of 24 October 1983 and Royal Decree Number 1,456 of 1 August 1984) the IM is also in charge of studying all aspects of women's situation in Spain, overseeing the implementation of women's policies, receiving and handling women's discrimination complaints, and increasing women's knowledge of their rights.

The main impact of the establishment of the IM on the feminist movement has been the availability of state subsidies for service provision activities
(rather than within-group activities oriented to develop and maintain a collective identity). Since its establishment, the IM has dedicated between 10
and 15% of its budget to subsidize women's organizations (not all of them
feminist). Generally speaking, and with some exceptions, the IM does not
give subsidies to feminists to maintain their associations or organize activities
directed to their own members. For example, the IM does not offer money to
feminist organizations to rent premises where feminists can meet, or organize
conferences and workshops where activists can elaborate theory and develop
political strategies. The IM confers subsidies upon feminists for the management of projects that usually consist of service delivery. Moreover, since the
late 1980s, the IM subsidizes only projects of service delivery strictly defined
in accordance with the IM's priorities. The pattern of subsidizing service
delivery started under socialist governments and is present nowadays under
the government of the Conservative Party (see the following).

The foundation of the IM has also meant a (very limited) point of access to
the state for (very few) feminist groups. Feminists' access to decision making
in the IM is restricted to the participation of some feminists in the meetings of
the IM advisory council (*Consejo Rector*).[12] For instance, in the early 1990s,
the government invited three representatives of feminist organizations (the
Association of Separated and Divorced Women, and Young Women) and
representatives of the women's departments of the two major Spanish unions
(UGT and CCOO) to serve on the *Consejo Rector*.

Another consequence of the establishment of the IM for the feminist movement (also less important than state subsidies) has been the increased attention paid by the mass media to state feminism rather than to the feminist
movement. The movement has always had the problem of not receiving high
media coverage for many reasons including the movement's lack of capacity
to convoke mass demonstrations. Nevertheless, according to Puleo (1996),
the fact that feminist demands and actions are not news in Spain may be
good news. Many feminist demands have been assimilated by broad sectors
of the population and are no longer seen as exotic requests advanced by a
minority of extremist militants.

The regionalization of Spanish politics has implied that gender equality
machineries have also been set up at the regional level since the late 1980s
(therefore, later than the establishment of the IM) (Bustelo 1999; Elizondo
and Martínez 1995; Granados 1999). Local women's policy machineries
were founded mainly in the 1990s (Sampedro 1992; Valiente 1998–1999).
We know very little about these regional and local machineries and whether
they advance the status of women. These regional and local institutions

---

[12] The *Consejo Rector* is an organ that advises the IM director. The *Consejo Rector* is mainly
composed of representatives of the ministries.

have also subsidized the women's movement. In fact, many regional and local women's organizations in civil society have appeared because of the existence of state subsidies and femocrats' efforts to organize female citizens in voluntary associations. Hence, regional and local institutions have created or helped establish part of the women's movement. As in the case of the IM, the existence of regional and local women's machineries at times has meant for representatives of women's groups points of (limited) access to the state. Some regional and local feminist institutions have fostered the establishment of platforms of women's organizations (whether feminist or otherwise) to advise equality institutions. These platforms have been given different names, the most common being that of "Women's Councils" (*Consejos de la Mujer*). The function of these regional and local women's councils varies widely. Some women's councils have provided feminists with a real opportunity to lobby state feminists, while other women's councils hardly met and their resolutions were not considered by feminist authorities. Finally, in regard to media coverage, the mass media has often paid more attention to the activities of regional and local machineries than to the feminist movement, as has happened at the central state level.

Offloading: Partnerships between State and Nonstate Actors Delivering Services

Western states have decided to offload some of their traditional responsibilities onto nonstate venues such as the community, the market, or the family. In Spain, this offloading process has been distinctive since some of these responsibilities of western states had not traditionally been exercised by the state. In some cases, the Spanish state started to provide some services for its citizens in partnership with nonstate actors, such as associations of civil society. Feminist organizations have been increasingly busy delivering services for women (this is not a particularity of Spain, since it is a pattern noticeable in the feminist movements of other countries such as Italy or in the shelter movement – see della Porta and Elman this book).

The provision of services for women has been an activity of Spanish feminists since the 1970s. Services were seen by feminists as a bridge between them and broader sectors of the female population. The first lawyers' office run exclusively by feminists was set up in Madrid in 1975. These feminist lawyers provided legal advice to women in cases of marital separation. They usually charged fees, but did not do so to women without an ability to pay (Escario et al. 1996: 86). Some pilot services were also organized in the area of violence. During the transition, there was hardly any service delivered by authorities in this policy area. Feminists gave refuge to some battered women in their own apartments, and organized self-defense groups to fight back against violent men (López-Accotto 1999: 124). An area in which feminists were particularly active was that of reproductive rights. The information, diffusion, and selling of contraceptives was a crime until 1978. Abortion was a crime in all circumstances until 1985. Thus, to provide services in this area was an act of civil disobedience. Since the late 1960s, some women from left-wing parties disseminated information and means regarding contraception (López-Accotto 1999: 123). Later, birth control centers (called "family planning centers") were created mainly by feminists. In them, information about sexuality, contraception, and (later) abortion was spread. The first center was established in 1976 in Madrid. Centers were organized in other cities and feminists managed to set up a coordinating platform (*Coordinadora Estatal de Grupos de Planning Familiar*) which organized a national meeting in 1977 (Escario et al. 1996: 137–150, 359). Family planning centers were located mainly in working-class neighborhoods, the assumption being that working-class women had less access to contraception (especially when it was forbidden) than did upper-class women (López-Accotto 1999: 122–124; Threlfall 1996: 119). These centers also organized trips for women to have abortions abroad, chiefly in England, France, or the Netherlands; abortions were later performed in Spain.

Some of these services provided by feminists during the transition were later supplied by the state. For instance, family planning became one of the provisions offered by the public health system. Nevertheless, the increased state intervention in the area of services for women did not mean that feminists stopped being active in this regard. Quite the contrary, since the 1980s state units (gender equality bureaucracies but also many other institutions) have given subsidies to nongovernmental organizations that provide services. Through these subsidies, the state has pushed numerous feminist organizations along the line of service provision (such as organizing job training courses, or providing psychological support to victims of violence). This has even happened to the feminist associations that in the 1970s did not provide any service and at that time "specialized" in the denunciation of gender inequalities and authorities' passivity regarding this problem through engaging in street demonstrations and other forms of protest (Pineda 1995: 109–111). A project-oriented culture has developed in the Spanish feminist movement in which writing proposals for funds and managing the subsidized projects have become one of the most important activities (if not the only activity) of many feminist groups.

The most important (sometimes the only) income source of feminist organizations is state money.[13] Members of feminist groups pay very small fees or do not pay fees at all. Feminist organizations rarely receive private donations and sponsorship. Therefore, the state has a lot of room to influence feminists' activities because state money is crucial for the economic survival of many feminist groups. Given the high rates of unemployment in Spain (since 1982,

---

[13] This pattern of dependence on the state for economic resources can also be found in many Spanish social movements, such as the environmental movement (Jiménez 1999).

the unemployment rate has always been higher than 15%),[14] some feminist activists have found temporary employment working in the projects administered by feminist organizations. State subsidies are also crucial for these feminists to survive as waged workers in the crowded Spanish labor market.

State subsidies have provided numerous feminist groups with more money than they have ever had to run projects that contribute to the improvement of the position of women as a group in Spanish society. With the help of these state monies, feminists have been able to deliver services to women beyond simply members of feminist groups, therefore expanding their roots into society. On the other hand, some feminists have complained that the bureaucratization of the application process has increased over time and feminists have to spend a lot of time writing submissions and reporting to authorities the accounts and results of their projects. The state may be attacking feminists' autonomy by imposing its own criteria about the types of activities feminist groups have to undertake in order to receive subsidies. Some feminists fear that state subsidies have tamed the movement. It is risky for activists to participate in visible protest activities against authorities (especially against those that subsidize part of the movement) because these actions may jeopardize future subsidies. In fact, the feminist movement is now less protest oriented than in the 1970s (as is also the case in other countries, for instance Italy – see della Porta this volume). This trend might have been reinforced by the state policy of subsidies but other factors also influenced this tendency, such as the absence of unifying and mobilizing causes (with the main exception of violence against women).

INFLUENCES OF THE FEMINIST MOVEMENT ON THE STATE

In what follows, I state that the Spanish feminist movement has been able to exert a nonnegligible influence on the state in the last three decades. Policymakers have reacted to feminist demands by elaborating gender equality policies. Thanks to feminist activism, the proportion of women in elected and appointed political positions has significantly increased.

Gender Equality Policies

Since the 1970s, feminists have pressured policymakers to elaborate gender equality policies. When the dictatorship ended in 1975, women and men were not equal before the law. Therefore, many reforms that had already taken place in other western countries had to be implemented in Spain. After 1975, policymakers began to dismantle the discriminatory legislation

---

[14] The unemployment rate is the proportion of unemployed individuals out of the active population (workers and unemployed people).

inherited from Franco's time and to promote women's rights and status. Many women's policies in the democratic period are the opposite of those implemented during Franco's time. For instance, whereas the Franco regime actively promoted sex-segregated schooling, the post-Franco government encouraged girls and boys to go to school together. This is currently the norm (with very few exceptions). The 1978 constitution explicitly states that women and men are equal before the law and sex discrimination is prohibited. It was during the rule of the center-right coalition of parties, the Union of Democratic Center (*Unión de Centro Democrático*) that some very important legal reforms took place, for instance: the abolition of the harder punishment for committing adultery for women than men (1978); the decriminalization of advertising and selling of contraceptives (1978); or the law that permitted divorce (1981). However, other reforms had to wait longer. It was only in 1985 (under a Socialist government) that abortion was permitted in three circumstances: when pregnancy is the result of rape; when pregnancy seriously endangers the physical or mental health of the mother; and when the fetus has malformations.[15] Although many gender equality policies were installed under the Socialist Party government (1982–1996), for the most part, all have been sustained since 1996 when the Conservative Party, the *Partido Popular*, took power.[16]

There is not yet a study that systematically assesses the impact of the feminist movement on the policy area of gender equality regarding the central state. It has become commonplace in analyses of the elaboration of specific gender equality policies to affirm that most central state gender equality policies have been promoted in Spain in the last three decades mainly by state feminists and/or feminists within parties and unions (Threlfall 1996; Valiente 1995a, 1996, 1997a, 1998). Feminist Members of Parliament (MPs) have also been crucial actors. For instance, "publicity and sale of contraceptives were legalized after an opposition motion eloquently defended by the feminist deputy Carlota Bustelo" (Threlfall 1996: 120). Public policy studies argue that the feminist movement has not been one of the central actors in the policy area of gender equality in Spain in the last three decades.

In contrast, Trujillo (1999) seems to suggest that some public policy analysts tend to be social-movement blind since they often focus their attention

---

[15] While in Spain feminists have pressured policymakers to change legislation, in other countries, for instance the United States, feminists have also sought reform through other means such as litigation (see Elman this book).

[16] A description and assessment of the major gender equality policies undertaken by the central state in the last three decades are beyond the scope of this chapter. For a description across policy areas see: Martínez 1997; Sensat and Varella 1998; Threlfall 1996; Valiente 2001. Research on specific policy areas includes abortion (Barreiro 1998); child care (Valiente 1995a); violence against women (Valiente 1996); equal opportunities in the labor market (Valiente 1997a); sexual harassment in the workplace (Valiente 1998); and job training (Valiente 2000).

on the visible and final parts of the negotiations that precede political decision making. Subsequently, analysts have hastily concluded that the Spanish feminist movement is not a major policy actor because it is not present at the negotiating tables where political decisions are made. Histories of the feminist movement document that since the 1970s feminists mobilized endlessly in order to raise awareness of the unequal legal situation of women and/or press authorities to pass legal reforms (Durán and Gallego 1986; Escario et al. 1996; Folguera 1988a: 122–123; Scanlon 1990; Threlfall 1985; among others). This literature seems to suggest (implicitly) that the movement played a nonnegligible role in the elaboration of central-state measures aimed at improving the status of women.

Let me use the case of abortion liberalization to illustrate the two opposite conclusions reached by scholars while analyzing the impact of the feminist movement in gender equality policy making at the central-state level. Barreiro (1998) argues that the feminist movement did not have a direct influence in the 1985 decriminalization of abortion. She also contends that state feminism had a moderate impact in abortion regulation, since the Women's Institute (IM) successfully negotiated with policymakers for the elaboration of the implementation proceedings facilitating access to induced abortion. In contrast, Trujillo (1999) proposes that in the 1970s and 1980s the Spanish feminist movement was the only actor that systematically and endlessly mobilized for and demanded abortion liberalization. The feminist movement contributed to the creation of a climate of opinion in civil society favorable to the acceptance of abortion reform. Conducive climates of this type permit politicians to make decisions around very conflictual issues such as abortion. I also state elsewhere (Valiente 2000) that part of the feminist movement's impact on the central state abortion liberalization was achieved through the movement's pressure on the IM. In the 1970s and 1980s a sector of the feminist movement (concretely part of the so-called radical branch) was clearly against the creation of gender equality institutions and constantly accused the IM of being very moderate regarding many topics. This radical sector chose the issue of abortion to fight against the IM in order to show that women's policy machineries meant the deradicalization of the movement. According to these radical feminists the IM would always promote measures that were far behind what many activists in the feminist movement asked: abortion on demand performed free of charge in the public health system. This radical sector of the movement constantly insisted that the IM demand a broad decriminalization of abortion. This radical sector was composed of very few women, but some of them were "historical feminists," that is, companions in battle in the 1970s and early 1980s of some feminists who later became part of the IM directive team. Some of these radical feminists were active in Madrid, where the headquarters of the IM are located. These radical feminists attempted to boycott some public activities organized by the IM, protesting against the IM's position on abortion, which was considered too moderate in their view.[17]

The transference of power from the central state to the regions meant that the regions, and not only the central state, became the main political reference for many feminists. Some feminists pressured their own regional government (and not so much the central government) in favor of gender equality policies (Fernández and Aierdi 1997:193). As for local women's policy machineries, these focus on the provision of services for women more than central and regional feminist institutions. Then, local machineries are in a structural position that pushes them toward paying more attention to women's demands, since they do not want to be in the unenviable position of offering services and activities that nobody is interested in, that nobody uses, and where nobody participates. Some local policy machineries have then been sensitive to the demands of the women's movement while elaborating measures to improve women's status (Valiente 1998–1999). Little more is known about the impact of the feminist movement on gender equality policies at the regional and local level. This is an area where future research will have to be conducted.

Increasing Numbers of Women in Political Decision-Making Positions

The second impact of the feminist movement on the state has been the increasing feminization of the political elite. As explained by Jenson and Valiente in their chapter for this book, the low number of women in political decision-making positions has been a concern for many Spanish feminists interested in political reforms since the transition to democracy in Spain. These feminists lobbied within their left-wing political parties for the establishment of mechanisms to increase the proportion of women in political posts. For instance, PSOE feminists managed to include the 25% quota for women in the statutes of their party in 1988. This quota was raised to 40% in 1997. The United Left (IU), which is an electoral coalition of parties to the left of the PSOE and which includes the Spanish Communist Party, established a quota since its foundation in 1986. Although the conservative party (the PP, *Partido Popular*) does not have a quota, and strongly opposes it, in practice it has also included an increasing number of women in its lists.

As a result of feminists' mobilization (among other factors), the presence of women in political decision-making positions has increased (although not always continually) throughout the democratic period. No woman has ever occupied the position of prime minister in contemporary Spain. Three women are ministers in the cabinet. Regarding the presence of women in

---

[17] This description of radical feminism in Spain and its position and tactics regarding abortion and the IM is in part deduced from a personal interview that I conducted with Justa Montero (Pro-Abortion Commission) on 25 May 1994 for another work (Valiente 1995b).

the central state parliament, Spain occupies a middle position in the EU, since 28% of seats of the lower chamber of the Spanish parliament and 23% of those in the upper house are occupied by women. The proportion of seats of the lower house occupied by female representatives in Spain (28%) is the seventh highest in the EU. In this regard, Spain is behind: Sweden (43%); Denmark (37%); Finland (36%); Norway (36%); the Netherlands (36%); and Germany (31%). Spain is ahead of: Austria (27%); Belgium (23%); Portugal (19%); the United Kingdom (18%); Luxembourg (17%); Ireland (12%); Italy (11%); and France (11%) (Women in National Parliaments 2000). The presence of women in the lower chamber is the highest in the social democratic PSOE (37%) followed by the conservative PP and the leftist coalition IU (25%) (Instituto de la Mujer 2000). In the European Parliament, one third (34%) of Spanish europarliamentarians are women, which is a proportion higher than the EU average (30%). In this regard, Spain also occupies a middle position among EU member states after Finland (44%), Sweden (41%), France (40%), Austria (38%), Denmark (37%), Germany (36%), and the Netherlands (35%) (Instituto de la Mujer 2000).

With respect to the regional level, in 1999 no woman was the president of any region. Two regions had no women in the executive, one region had fewer than 10% of women, nine regions had between 10 and 20% of women (both included), four regions had between 21 and 30%, and one region had 43% (*El País* 29 April 2000: 26; Instituto de la Mujer 2000). The regional data on functional specialization confirm a tendency that can be observed in all levels of government: When women reach the leadership, they are usually in charge of "soft" issues such as education, culture, or health. Women are hardly ever in charge of those departments considered more important, for instance, the economy. In 1999, women amounted to 29% of all regional MPs, although significant differences existed among regions (Instituto de la Mujer 2000).

At the local level, the presence of women in the leadership and the assembly is lower than at the central state, regional, and European levels: in 1999, only 10% of mayors and 16% of city councilors were women (Instituto de la Mujer 2000). The difference between the local and the other levels merits attention, since it is often argued that women have more chances of entering the political elite at the local level.

CONCLUSION

State-centered factors related to the democratization of the country and some dimensions of the reconfiguration of the state and state-society relations have profoundly affected the Spanish feminist movement since the 1970s. The first feminist groups appeared in the milieu of the opposition to the authoritarian regime, where other political and social forces were also active, such as left-wing political parties and trade unions (among others). These have been the allies of many feminists ever since. The mobilization of women as feminists in groups in civil society and/or within left-wing parties and trade unions blurred the frontier between the movement and conventional political actors from the very foundation of the second wave of feminist activism.

The relationship with political parties and the state was the main issue that split the feminist movement in the late 1970s. The main dividing dilemma within the movement was whether to collaborate with political parties and labor unions or not, rather than with which party or union to cooperate more fruitfully. The political opportunity structure (POS) favored the existing majoritarian position that supports working together with parties and unions. By the late 1970s, it was clear that an electoral victory of the Socialist Party would be possible in the near future. The governing of the country by a left-wing party was seen by many feminists interested in political reform as a major opportunity to work through the state in order to improve women's status. Had a conservative party governed Spain between the early 1980s and mid-1990s, more feminist groups would probably have turned their energies toward the achievement of cultural change and the development of robust common identities. Therefore, the Spanish case between the 1970s and 1990s shows us the inappropriateness of considering a POS positive or negative for the feminist movement as a whole. Given the fact that the Spanish feminist movement is composed of a majoritarian branch interested chiefly in instrumental goals and a minority strand pursuing mainly identity development, a given political context may be conducive for one of the branches but one of the worst scenarios for the other one, as was the case in Spain in the past decades.

The trend of *downloading* central state power to regions made it difficult for the movement to establish nationally based umbrella organizations. Some feminists have increasingly put their efforts into lobbying regional powers rather than central state authorities to tackle the problem of women's subordination. The pattern of *uploading* authority to the EU has facilitated concerted actions among different feminists, since joint activities by different groups are encouraged and subsidized by Europe. The drift of *lateral loading* authority to new agencies such as state feminist institutions and *offloading* the performance of traditional state functions to partnerships of state and nonstate actors have provided feminist groups with strong incentives (state subsidies) to focus increasingly on the delivery of services for women. Feminist groups have been busier managing their subsidized projects and less active in protesting against authorities.

Our knowledge of the impact of the feminist movement on the state is weaker, scarcer, and more superficial than that of the influence of the state on the movement. In this regard, Spain is no different than other western countries, where social scientists have dedicated more attention to the analysis of the influence of the political opportunity structure on social movements than the impact of movements on the state. Thanks in part to feminist mobilization, central state, regional, and local authorities have been implementing public policies with the aim of improving the status of women as a group. Gender equality policies have affected a higher number of women than those in direct contact with feminist activists. However, the feminist movement may have also lost some degree of autonomy vis-à-vis the state, since it is increasingly defining the priorities of gender equality policy. For example, the current conservative government at the central-state level has chosen two priority areas for its gender equality policy: violence against women and the combination of professional and family responsibilities. While most feminists would think that both issues are principal concerns of many women, other topics may also be conceptualized as societal problems deserving state intervention, such as reproductive rights. Partly thanks to feminist activism within left-wing parties, an increasing proportion of women belong to the political elite. Some of these women are feminists. As their numbers increase and as the feminist movement continues to organize for improvements in women's status and public policies, Spanish women may finally have their voices heard, even in the traditional male arena of parliamentary politics.

3

The Women's Movement, the Left, and the State

Continuities and Changes in the Italian Case

Donatella della Porta

INTRODUCTION

The Italian women's movement has traditionally shown strong similarities to "sister movements" in other western democracies. After a first wave of mobilization on women's rights developed at the turn of the twentieth century, the so-called second wave of the women's movement rose in the early 1970s. Autonomous feminist groups grew out of the New Left, denouncing the authoritarianism of sexual discrimination present even within the protest movement itself (Mormino and Guarnieri 1988: 31). They interacted with existing organizations concerned with the women's question, especially the Unione Donne Italiane (UDI) with its ties to the Communist Party (PCI). The years between 1975 and 1977 marked the period of greatest visibility of the women's movement. Mass mobilizations took place in response to the referendum demanded by Catholic organizations for the repeal of the divorce law and also in favor of the liberalization of abortion. Among other things, the latter campaign brought with it collaboration between the feminist organizations and groups of women in the PCI and the trade unions. In the second half of the 1970s forms of protest became more radical, but at the same time a massive wave of terrorism dramatically reduced the space for collective protest action. Mobilization declined in 1977, after a young feminist, Giorgiana Masi, was killed during a violent police charge while returning from a demonstration to mark the anniversary of the divorce referendum victory. The violence associated with social movements probably furthered this political distancing.

What happened after mobilization declined? Did the women's movement die, as many feminists feared at that time, or did it adapt to the environmental conditions, alternating phases of latency with phases of visibility? And if the women's movement is still vibrant, what are the continuities and discontinuities, comparing the women's movement of the 1990s with that of the 1970s? A first aim of this chapter is to describe, on the basis of a secondary analysis of social science research and some field research (in particular on a case study of the city of Florence[1]), the main characteristics of the Italian women's movement at the turn of the millennium. Although the focus on one city makes generalization to all countries difficult, it allows for an in-depth analysis of the women's movement in its privileged geographical level of intervention: the local one. As Florence belongs to the so-called "red subculture" – with a tradition of strength of the left-wing party both in local government and in society – the case study will allow the development of hypotheses on a characteristic of the Italian women's movement, and more generally, the southern European women's movements: the strong alliance of the movement with the Old Left.[2] I will suggest that the mobilization of the 1970s set the basis for what can be called the long wave of the women's movement that continued well into the 1990s.

Once similarities and differences, continuities and discontinuities are assessed, the next step is to explain the evolution of the women's movement. In doing this, I shall in particular focus on the characteristics of the state's response, and its own evolution. First of all, the state is a counterpart for the movement. Possessing the monopoly of the legitimate use of force and as the guarantor of public order, the state uses the police to control protest, limiting the resources available for collective action. Protest policing is a particularly relevant issue for understanding the relationship between social movements and the state (della Porta 1995; della Porta and Reiter 1998). This was also the case with the women's movement – notwithstanding a relatively low degree of actual confrontation with the repressive state apparatuses. In Italy, the interaction of radical protest and hard policing contributed to the alliance

---

[1] I will refer in particular to two research projects conducted by Sara Valenza (1999) and Paola Carlucci (1999) on the groups active on women's issues in Florence. Sara Valenza analyzed archive materials on the women's groups active in Florence from the 1960s to the 1990s; moreover, she interviewed representatives of twenty-six groups active in the 1990s: thirteen of them were classified (according to previous membership of the founding members, organizational history of the group, networking with other groups, and self-perception) as belonging to the women's movement, while the other thirteen were defined as concerned with women's issues but not part of the women's movement. Carlucci interviewed representatives of the thirty-five groups active on women's issues, fourteen of which she defined (on similar indicators as the ones used by Valenza) as part of the women's movement. Both studies used a list of women's groups developed by two women's organizations with the sponsorship of the local government integrated with information from additional written and oral sources. Both researchers used semistructured questionnaires with questions referring to the organizational activities, group structure, its relationship with the public administration, and networking with other groups in society. In this presentation, I shall focus on the groups that showed continuities with the women's movement of the 1970s, but I will often compare them with those that emerged outside it.

[2] The alliance with the left and the experience of exclusive strategy by the state characterized all southern European women's movements. For a systematic comparison, see della Porta, Valiente, and Kousis forthcoming.

of the new social movements – the women's movement among them – with the Old Left.

The state, however, is far from being just the "enemy," or the "repressor" of the challengers, as old "Marxist" approaches would have suggested many years ago.[3] It is "simultaneously target, sponsor, and antagonist for social movements as well as the organizer of the political system and the arbiter of victory" (Jenkins and Klandermans 1995: 3). A basic assumption of the literature on political opportunity structure is indeed that states provide not only repression but also facilitation for social movements. Far from being the "personification" of the interest of the capitalist states or the "patriarchy," public bureaucrats can become committed to social movements' causes. In particular, social movement organizations may exploit, for their own purposes, the tendency of the state bureaucracy to expand their power by expanding social expenditures (among others, Poggi 1990: chs. 7, 8). The development of specific institutions for dealing with women's issues – state feminism, as it has been defined – produced some niches with easier access for women's organizations, as well as vested interest in the development of specific policy networks.

This does not mean that the state is a neutral arena. As the social science literature on neocorporativism emphasizes, public decision making "favors organized as against not-organized interests; organizations which can as against organizations which cannot advance the cause of the administrative units with which they deal; organizations led by people who share the social background, the language, the cognitive assumptions, the moral and political preferences of administrative elites, as against those led by other kinds of people" (Poggi 1990: 134). In the case of the women's movement, the characteristics of the bureaucratic process – among others, the predominance of male personnel in the top positions – made (and still make) access particularly difficult. In fact, the women's movement often had to find allies that could act on behalf of women in the representative institutions.

Changes in the women's movement were in fact influenced by changes in the state and in the political actors that acted as "brokers" for the women's demands. In Italy as elsewhere, the women's movement adapted to a reconfigured state. Women's groups learned to deal with the downloading as well as uploading of power and responsibility to respectively lower- and upper-state levels by multiplying their targets of action, intensifying the demands located at the local level, but also using supranational resources (such as funds coming from the EU, as well as the leverage of international norms). The Italian women's groups also took into account the lateral loading of competencies from elected to nonelected bodies, especially by intensifying interactions with the public bureaucracy and increasing recourse to the judiciary. As we are

---

[3] For a summary of Marxist conceptions of the state see Held and Krieger 1981; for a summary of the sociology of the state see Badie and Birnbaum 1979; Birnbaum 1988; Poggi 1990.

going to see in what follows, the offloading of tasks from the state to the market had the strongest impact on the women's organizations, which became increasingly involved in the third sectors, supplying services to women. If these patterns of state restructuring are common to other western democracies (see the introduction to this volume), they were of course filtered by national traditions and institutions, as well as by the very characteristics of the women's movements. In the Italian case, the impact of downloading and offloading of state powers acted upon a patronage model of interest representation, with ideological links between interest groups and political parties, and a clientelistic model of the welfare state.[4] As well as in other Catholic countries with particularly repressive attitudes toward women's rights, the (difficult) alliance between the women's movement and the Old Left was particularly relevant in the Italian case (della Porta, Valiente, and Kousis forthcoming), bringing about a political "protection" of the movement by the party. The specific type of "clientelistic" welfare state developed in Italy had an impact on social movement organizations (the women's groups among them).

THE ITALIAN WOMEN'S MOVEMENT IN THE 1990s: A LONG WAVE

During the late 1970s, a pessimistic mood grew inside the women's movement. Many activists "returned to the private," assessing the failure of the mobilization. Later on, it emerged however that a lot had survived the low ebb of women's protest: "[T]hough it seemed that the era of sensational gestures and mass demonstrations which had so caught the attention of the media was coming to an end, in its wake there frequently remained new forms of political organization among women, a higher profile of women and of women's questions in the public sphere, as well as lively debates among feminists themselves and between them and external interlocutors. In other words, the (apparent) eclipse of feminism as an organized social movement implied neither the abandonment by feminists of the role of political actors nor the disappearance of feminism as a set of disputed and developing discursive practices" (Ergas 1992: 587).

The research on the Florentine case confirms that in the 1990s the movement was alive and well. Many groups were active in Florence on women's issues and many of them were formed by organizational and personal networks built inside the mobilization of the 1970s: Thirteen of the twenty-six

---

[4] The wide scientific production on the welfare state singled out three basic models of welfare: A universalistic model, based on equal access of all citizens to public services, developed in particular in the Scandinavian countries, which was favored by the alliances between the working class organizations and their parties with the peasants' interest organizations; a particularistic model, based on a differential access for different social groups and transfer, developed by conservative parties, supported by the church, typical of central Europe; and a southern European model, weak and a latecomer. For two different typologies, see Esping-Anderson 1990 and Ferrera 1993.

associations interviewed by Valenza (1999) and fourteen of the thirty-two analyzed by Carlucci (1999) have their roots in the women's movement. The women's movement had in fact triggered the blooming of new groups, a tendency that continued well into the 1990s. Nineteen of the twenty-six associations analyzed by Valenza (1999) emerged after 1975 and twenty-one of the thirty-five analyzed by Carlucci (1999: 27) were founded in the 1980s and the 1990s. As we will see, the women's groups of the 1990s had some continuity and some discontinuities with previous mobilizations. The same women's groups in Florence admit a "transformation, expressed in forms of militancy and aggregation that differ from those well known in the rampant years of feminism" (LLF, Progetto 1992, cit. in Valenza 1999: 307). Feminism "is not any more as visible as it was before," since "the time of provocation and street demonstrations is over," even if "the women continue to meet and work, mainly in small groups, on projects and initiatives almost always circumscribed to the city, or even the neighborhood" (ibid.); there is "a net, maybe more underground, but better tied together" (CLD 1998o, in Valenza 1999: 315). Although changes are admitted, and even emphasized, the continuity with the movement of the 1970s is, however, proudly stated, with an optimistic claiming of the success of that movement. Moreover, the continuities in the individual life courses are testimony for such claims. With few exceptions, the women involved in the groups of the 1990s had started their militancy during the protest cycle of the 1970s.

In what follows, I shall single out the main changes in three main characteristics of the movement: discourse, organization, and repertoires of action.

The Women's Discourse: From Liberation to Difference?

Two different definitions of the movement identity have characterized women's movements in the 1970s. Emancipatory strategies emphasized gender equality and liberation strategies stressed gender differences. In Italy, as in other countries, the women's movement of the 1970s was characterized by the claim of autonomy versus the "hegemony" of class conflict. Denying the "primacy of the capital-labor contradiction" and of the sphere of production, the feminist collectives asserted the central role of the male-female contradiction, of sexual difference as opposed to class unity. The women's movement went beyond the traditional discourse of emancipation, elaborating a more innovative one of "liberation." During the 1970s, the feminist analysis shifted from the family as a locus of economic exploitation to the family as the factory of private life (Boccia 1980: 70). In general, the women's movement concentrated on cultural transformation rather than institutional reform. Instead of politics, consciousness-raising groups looked to issues such as reproduction, sexuality, interpersonal relations, and daily life. In the 1970s, consciousness-raising became an alternative mode of doing politics. For many women this involved the abandonment of the

"other" politics, male politics, and consequently withdrawal from the organizations of the Old and New Left. At the end of the 1970s, the attention
given to the private sphere began to be reflected in an ebbing of the movement, a "return to private life," and the predominance of "parzialità" (a
rejection of totality). Besides, the increasing radicalization of the political
climate produced a subordination of more concrete activity to the elaboration of a counterculture, accentuating the pessimism within the women's
movement.

As a direct result of the presence of the (Old and New) Left, however,
the prevalent analyses of women's role in society utilized the traditional categories of "class" discourse: the "exploitation" of women as producers of
services or as sexual objects, the "imperialism" of male values, the "structural
nature" of the "contradiction" between sexes (Ergas 1986: 64). The particular characteristics of Italian feminism emerged in fact above all with the
entry into the movement, from the early 1970s on, of women from the
New Left who, referring to themselves as "Marxist-feminists," proposed a
struggle for "liberation in the revolution" as opposed to "emancipation in
reform." Also from within the women's movement, the attention to political mobilization and outward oriented activities remained present (Valenza
1999). In many factories feminist collectives and "inter-group" organizations
of female "shop stewards" struggled for increased female representation
and the introduction into union platforms of specifically female questions
(the implementation of the "law on equality," the creation of a unified hiring list, more flexible working hours, day-care centers supported by employer contributions, and so on). Moreover, the call for equality came
from the Old Leftist UDI and the unions with even some alliances with
Catholic women's groups and associations of female members of some
professions.

In the 1990s, the discourse of the women's movement changed. In other
countries, a move was noticed from a "politics of ideas" to a "politics of presence" (Phillips 1995: 2). In France, a new mobilization on women's rights
focused on equal representation in elective institutions (see Dobrowolski,
and Jenson and Valiente this volume). Concerned with citizenship, the new
discourse elaborated on a shift from "universal rights" to a "differentiated"
citizenship, with special rights for special groups of citizens (ibid.). Also
in Italy, the 1990s brought about a growing attention toward the presence of women in representative institutions. The Italian chapters of the
women's lobby Emily pushed for parity-based access to representative institutions at the different levels of government, while the female MPs often
made transparty pacts in favor of the implementation of equal treatment for
women.

If we look at the local level, however, the reality is more complex. Side
by side with groups focusing on the political presence of women, others
specialize on other issues, in particular welfare service and culture. Already

during the 1980s, women's groups started to specialize in various topics: from the groups of professional women to the cooperatives in the new service areas, from social services to the elaboration of a new culture (Bianchi and Mormino 1984: 162). Women's groups mobilized in protest campaigns on left libertarian concerns – for peace and the environment, against racism and the Mafia – and for "real equality" in the job market.[5]

If in the 1970s tension had been between emancipation and liberation, in the 1990s, the two poles of women's discourse were parity and diversity. While in the past emancipatory and liberation strategies had been considered as opposed to each other, in the 1990s, a pragmatic approach allowed for the complementarity of the discourse on parity and diversity. In fact, in late 1988, the National Coordination of Documentation Centers, Bookstores, and Women's Houses called for a "composition between feminism and emancipation" (Carlucci 1999: 187). In the 1970s, the refusal of "emancipation" had discouraged participation by the women's movement in the formulation of the first Italian law on "parity of opportunity" (Law 903/77, derived in fact from a European Community (EC) directive, not from the women's mobilization). In the 1990s, the women's groups instead paid attention to the second law on equal opportunity (Law 125/1991).

These characteristics emerge in the analysis of the Florentine case. Some groups (as the Lobby of the European Women, interest groups of women in various professions as well as representatives of the commissions for parity of opportunities inside the various institutions) focus on equal rights for women through positive incentives; other groups seemed to have developed an interest in the parity issues – among them, Giardino dei Ciliegi and Tela di Penelope, which were movement organizations formed by women from the Italian Communist Party (PCI).

Most groups, however, continued to intervene on the same topics that were typical of the women's movement of the 1970s: gender culture and women's problems. First, many groups paid strong attention to culture: the Centro documentazione donne focused on research on female subjectivity, Laboratorio immagine donna on women's activities in the media and film industry, the Librerie delle Donne on women's books, il Teatro delle donne on women in theater, the local section of Società italiana delle storiche on women's history, and Ossidiana on feminine artistic research. Many associations (such as Spazio effe, Giardino dei Ciliegi, Arci Donna) presented themselves as centers of recreational and cultural activities reserved for women with the aim of valorizing gender differences. Other groups intervened on behalf of specific women's problems: Voci di donne on female immigrants,

---

[5] In this sense, the Italian situation seems to differ significantly from that in the United States. In Italy, in fact, the alliance of the women's movement with the unions and the left-wing parties reduced the class-based bifurcation of women's citizenship that Mary Fainsod Katzenstein (this volume) noticed for the U.S. case.

Amandorla on lesbians, Artemisia on violence against women, Il Marsupio on motherhood, and Associazione Donne Insegnanti on education. Some groups, such as the Libreria delle Donne, explicitly affirmed activism both on parity and diversity.

The common discourse that combined parity and diversity was that of a new citizenship with equal rights for different groups. While the discourse on parity was not stigmatized, the theme of diversity was central for the definition of the identity: Women are different from men, but they are also different among themselves. The gender difference was increasingly seen as based less on a biological peculiarity, and instead increasingly defined as a different social, political, and cultural project. The search for identity was located in a "growing consciousness of the self, of one's own role, and therefore of the appropriation of one's own life" (CDD-CCCD, *richiesta contributi*, 1994: 1, cit. in Valenza 1999: 335). Moreover, there is recognition of differences not only toward the outside, but also among women. If in the late 1970s and the 1980s, the emergence of the differences among women had been felt as a challenge to the myth of sisterhood, in the 1990s, instead, it was accepted as a matter of fact, and even appreciated as an enrichment for the movement: "What may appear as mixture, for us is fecundity, the possibility to get to know and respond to the richness of a complex 'feminine society'" (Giardino dei Ciliegi, in Carlucci 1999: 73).

Common to all these groups is a high degree of pragmatism. Ideological divisions are less and less important, while there seemed to be growing optimistic attitudes. In the new groups, women from different backgrounds cooperate: feminists from the small consciousness-raising groups together with women with a "double presence" in the left-wing parties and in the women's movement. Although the women's groups are more heterogeneous, the "historical" ideological splits that had divided the movement in the 1970s have almost been forgotten. Attention to outward-directed action, inherited from the tradition of the Left, has grown since the 1980s. As one feminist stated: "We have transformed ourselves into cooperatives, cultural centers, centers for documentation; we propose to find an audience and support within institutions.... The female world of these new aggregations is a world of pragmatic women, long involved in political circles, giving, on the whole, little importance to the ideological side of the male-female contradiction" (D'Amelia 1985: 124–128, passim). As for the case of Florence, twenty-three groups out of the twenty-six (twelve groups out of thirteen of those with a movement background) present their goals as "concrete" – that meant, they explained, the search for specific solutions to specific problems (Valenza 1999; see also Carlucci 1999). Organizational documents focus on concrete topics, and the very self-definitions avoid the heavily ideologically loaded concept of "feminism" in favor of a less-contested "women's movement" – even in the names of the groups, the word "feminist" is substituted for by the less ideological "women's" (Valenza 1999).

Organizational Structure of the Women's Movement: From Spontaneity to Formal Associations?

In western democracies, women's movements have been characterized by a mixed organizational structure, with formalized organizations working in close coordination with grass-root groupings. In Italy, as elsewhere, the feminist movement of the 1970s was organized in small, informal, decentralized, and loosely coordinated groups. Women-only small groups and consciousness-raising groups were considered the necessary organizational form for the gradual development of awareness of one's oppression ("we are separatist to be autonomous, and autonomous to be free"). Consciousness-raising groups, founded mainly between 1972 and 1974, were considered the instrument for expressing the "most creative aspects" of the movement (Frabotta and Ciuffreda 1976: 12), bringing out the social bases of oppression through a revisitation of daily life with other women. The function of coordination was assumed by organizations within the movement, such as publications, radio stations, or meeting places. The women's movement held periodic municipal-wide assemblies while, at a broader level, flexible forms of coordination were created around certain publications, such as *Compagna, Effe, Sottosopra*, and *Differenze*. Besides, in many cities central premises for the women's movement were opened, serving as meeting places for the various collectives.

In the mid-1970s, with the growth of mobilization on the abortion question and an influx of women from the surviving organizations of the extraparliamentary Left in particular, the small-group structure revealed itself to be inadequate. Divisions began to emerge along generational lines and in particular areas of cognizance; participatory practices sometimes jeopardized decision making. In this situation, a complementary relationship developed between the small autonomous groups, where female identity was formed, and the more structured organizations, providing the necessary resources for mobilization. One of the organizations furnishing material resources to the movement was the UDI: "The difficulties of attempting to realize group goals in the absence of any formal structure are obvious and . . . several feminist collectives in Milan were driven to the 'extreme' of utilizing the UDI offices and network, however compromised by its association with the Communist Party they thought the UDI may be" (J. Hellman 1987b: 197). Resources for the movement were also provided by the trade unions, mostly through the mediation of the women's groups which had already formed within them in the 1970s (Beccalli 1984). In the second half of the 1970s *coordinamenti* (coordinating committees) emerged in factories and unions, attracting women disillusioned with party or movement politics as well as female union delegates (who had even created consciousness-raising groups in some of the bigger enterprises). In all of these cases, the unions offered material resources as the issues arose.

In the 1990s, many of these organizational features changed as women's involvement in the Third Sector constantly increased. Cultural and welfare associations that emerged from the women's movement share some common characteristics. The differences with the past are the product of an ongoing process of formalization of the organizational structure and professionalization. What remains from the past is, however, the prevalence of the decentralized small group, with a strong capacity for networking.

First of all, there is the option of formal structures. A dominant organizational form is the "associazione non a fini di lucro" – that is, (formal) association not oriented to profit. In the beginning of the 1990s, Law 266/1991 started to regulate the sector of the voluntary associations, allowing for public financing of specific activities for those organizations that received that kind of "trademark." Many groups adopted, in fact, a formal statute with the explicit aim of getting access to public funds. In Florence, eleven movement organizations out of thirteen have a formal charter and written rules that define the scope of the organization (Valenza 1999). As for the organizational resources, about 50% of the women's movement organizations own property and one group has a press agent. Delegation of tasks is an accepted principle.

Second, there has been an increase in professionalization – even though there are often conflicts between efficiency and democracy.[6] Looking at the presence of paid functionaries, the selling of services, and the formation of personnel, the movement organizations show a profile similar to that of the other women's groups (with about half of the groups in the highest rank, and only one in the lowest one) (Valenza 1999). Many associations also use external expertise – with the growth "of a competence, a female knowledge that is the result of specific political theories and practices. The feminist reflection developed new knowledge of the body, sexuality, and violence that have become the cultural tools to which the associations refer for single projects. Female associations produce therefore new professional profiles, that are sometimes recognized by the institutions" (Carlucci 1999: 388–389).

Notwithstanding increasing formalization and professionalization, the emphasis on participation has been maintained. Formal rules are not always employed (Carlucci 1999: 50) – to give just one example, in one of the Florentine groups (Libreria delle Donne) the position of president, treasurer, and councilor are chosen by lot. In half of the cases studied by Valenza (1999) (and differently than in the women's organizations that are not part of the movement) the actual division of labor is informal and in eight cases out of thirteen decisions are taken in an informal way, or in the general assembly (two of the thirteen women's groups that are not part of the movement have

---

[6] A similar emphasis on professionalization developed in the shelter movements in the United States, Britain, and Sweden (see Elman this volume).

instead an informal division of labor). In the case of the movement organizations, decisions are decentralized in eight cases out of thirteen (differently than in the other groups where decisions are centralized in eleven of thirteen cases). In the 1990s, the women's movement organizations in Florence remained, moreover, prevalently small in size. In eight cases out of thirteen they have fewer than fifty members, even though there are three organizations with more than one hundred members. Also their budget has usually been meager (in 50% of the cases below five million lira, that is, about $2,000 U.S.), with the exception of the groups that provide external services, and most organizations (fifteen of twenty-six) have had a local range of action (ibid.).

Moreover, the "style" of consciousness-raising persisted in many groups, although with some relevant differences when compared to that of the 1970s. As an activist of the Cooperativa delle Donne in Florence stated, "We believe that starting from the self is the only possible form of innovation in thought and action. The threads of research that we singled out in these years have been part of a process of creation and transformation of ourselves and among ourselves" (quoted in Carlucci 1999: 191). And another confirmed, "The forms of investigation around the object of the discussion aim at keeping a unity of body and soul, life and knowledge. To look into oneself without tricks . . . it is possible only inside small groups, and with the use of a practice of consciousness-raising, in the sense that we start from free associations, from our personal experiences. As far as consciousness-raising is concerned, however, we put some limits to personal experiences and the incontinence of the emotions and projections by focusing on a concrete object of research" (ibid.).

With a decline of mass mobilization, the project of building general coordinating bodies – such as a women's separatist space (Spazio Donne) in Tuscany – failed. There are, however, specific coordinating committees for specific campaigns – in particular for campaigns on specific laws (such as the defense of the abortion law, or the demands of a law against sexual violence) – and, even more important, many networks of local groups active in various regions on the same issues and of women's groups active on different issues in the same town. All the movement organizations active in Florence are linked with each other through a dense net of interaction at the local level; interactions are also frequent with other groups outside Florence, as well as in some cases with groups outside Italy. The group Lilith developed a web site as an "information net for the feminine gender," with links to many women's groups in the country. Occasions for networking are also provided by the local governments. Already in the 1980s, a city councilor with a "double militancy" (in the Communist Party and the women's movement) promoted a Progetto Donna in which several women's groups took part. In the 1990s, most of the movement organizations as well as some of the other women's groups participate in the Consiglio delle Donne of the city of

Florence. This has increased not only the interactions between "the women in the parties" and "the women in the movements," the "feminists" and the "(female) trade-unionists" but also those between the women's groups of various backgrounds. It is worth noticing that, with few exceptions, networking with other women's groups is much weaker for the groups that are not part of the movement area (Carlucci 1999). Many of the organizations of the "bourgeois" parity wing – such as Soroptimist or Fidapa – belong to international organizations but have few links with the women's movement organizations; and the religious women's groups tend to interact more with their own church hierarchies than with other groups outside (Carlucci 1999). Here too, however, there are signs of change, with some of the "bourgeois" and some of the religious groups joining the Consiglio delle Donne.

Women's Repertoires of Action: From Protest to Voluntary Activities?

As far as repertoires of action are concerned, the women's movements of western democracies have been able to combine the more disruptive forms of direct action with traditional pressures. This constellation also characterized Italy. The women's movement introduced new modes of protest into the repertoire of collective action. The search for "nonmale" forms of action led the women's movement to emphasize creativity with art exhibitions, improvised street theater, or the use of comic-strip handbills. Violence was replaced by "imaginative" provocation (Frabotta and Ciuffreda 1976: 14). Protest tactics based on illegal but nonviolent action also flourished. Self-help on abortion added up to disturbance actions such as the occupation of public places and nurseries or groups of militants chaining themselves together to the entrances of public buildings. Italian feminism, however, also organized mass mobilization campaigns, often with the support of women from the Old Left. Alongside more disruptive protest action, the women's movement was also involved at the institutional level, organizing petitioning and referendum proposals (Grazioli and Lodi 1984: 289).

In the 1990s, research in various countries stressed that political action is less and less stigmatized: Many movement organizations focused on pressure politics – with systematic contacts with the media and "entryism" in the parties. In Italy, a main change in the strategy derived from the transformation of women's groups into voluntary associations providing services for associates or clients. Moreover, while recourse to disruptive protest diminished, more attention was paid to various forms of communications, either through mass media or the Internet.

In the evolution of the left libertarian movements there is a proliferation of voluntary associations involved in the Third Sector. Similarly, in Florence, many groups started to offer different types of services. The groups focusing on culture organized conferences, but also training initiatives developed with the aim of transforming "the skills and professionalism, individually or collectively possessed by women, in activities that can break the wearing separation between a frustrating job, needed for survival, and a work that is interesting but underpaid" (Libreria delle Donne, 1992, in Valenza 1999: 363). There are courses on family problems, consultation of archives, legal counseling, homeopathic medicine, music, theater, and photography. In the area of health, the provision of services is presented as a complement to the public duty to intervene (Il Marsupio, 1986, in Valenza 1999: 363). Services like "friendly telephones" are offered on homosexuality as well as violence against women. The group Il Marsupio provides consultations to pregnant women as well as to families; Ossidiana organizes activities for women in prison; Artemisia opened a center for battered women.

In the 1990s, the use of protest – at least, as it was understood in the 1970s – declined. Seven of the thirteen organizations interviewed by Valenza (1999) make sporadic recourse to protest (which is true in the same proportion for the nonmovement organizations); only in three cases do they frequently use protest. While the nonmovement organizations, however, usually limit their protest activities to letters to the press, the movement organizations also use petitions (in seven cases), marches (in five cases), public meetings (in four cases), and leafleting and sit-ins (in three cases). Among the movement organizations, protest activities are used in particular during mobilizations on such issues as peace (as in the case of the Donne in Nero, that organized marches against the Gulf War and later on the Kosovo War), the defense of the environment (as the group De Natura), and antiracism (Voci di Donne is formed by immigrant women). If about half of both types of groups express a positive judgment about protest, the other half are more skeptical, either because they are afraid of public stigmatizing of these activities that may scare women away, or because they believe that "it is not necessary any longer to protest in order to exist." Visibility comes mainly from press campaigns or a skilled use of the Internet, and it is linked to the sponsoring of single projects (Carlucci 1999: 262).

Summarizing, in Italy women's movements emerged in the 1970s with a timing which was quite similar to that of other western European women's movements. As with other women's movements, the Italian one affirmed a new image of women as citizens with full rights, had organizational structures based on direct democracy and small groups, and used noninstitutional forms of political participation to protest against discrimination. The Italian women's movement also showed some peculiarities. First of all, the women's movement developed with some delay and was, at least partially, "imported" from other western democracies. In general, an attempt was made to combine "liberation" discourse with the class discourse of the traditional left; the organizational structure remained very fragmented, with no national organizations present to coordinate action; lobbying activities were virtually absent. During the 1990s, a pragmatic attitude prevailed; associations developed, with a formal structure, but mainly small and mainly present at the local level; most of the activities focused on cultural or social services.[7] Some of the characteristics of the women's movement in the different periods may be explained if we take into account some characteristics of the state and its structuring and the mediatory role played by the main party of the left.

STATE, POLITICAL ALLIES, AND THE WOMEN'S MOVEMENT

At the national level the evolution of the women's movement in the 1970s was influenced by the polarization of social and political conflict. The state reacted to a widespread and long-lasting cycle of protest with a wave of repression that further radicalized the social movements. With centralized institutions and an exclusionary tradition, the Italian state actually pushed the social movements to ally with the left. Notwithstanding moments of tension and internal competition, the complete history of the new social movements in Italy cannot be told without referring to their main allies: the parties of the left and the trade unions. The Old Left influenced the organizational, ideological, and strategic characteristics of the Italian women's movement. At an ideological level, "postmaterialist" claims for "liberation" were intertwined with traditional demands for equality. In its organizational structure, the women's movement combined the decentralized structure typical of new social movements with resources for coordination provided by the parties of the Old and New Left and the trade unions (for similar observations in the Spanish case, see Valiente this volume). As for the repertoire of mobilization, the women's movement invented new forms of protest emphasizing "commitment" over force, but was also able to exploit institutional forms of collective action. The alliance with the Old Left allowed the women's movement in Italy to combine mobilization both within and beyond institutional politics and to link identity-oriented counterculture with policy-oriented mobilization. Women would in fact establish important resources for mobilization in the organizational structures of the left. The daily newspapers of the New and the Old Left alike were used for calls for meetings and demonstrations. The trade unions, too, offered logistical support, becoming more open to feminist demands in the second half of the 1970s (J. Hellman 1987b: 208–209). In the 1980s, the women's movement participated in protest campaigns (in favor of peace, for example, or against

---

[7] A similar evolution was described for other national cases. For instance, an in-depth analysis of left-libertarian movement organizations in Berlin indicated a clear increase in the degree of professionalization, with, however, a lower degree of differentiation and formalization (Rucht, Blattert, and Rink 1997: 125). Although a more systematic comparison would be necessary in order to develop more specific hypotheses, the German case seems characterized by a larger formalization of the interaction between state institutions and movement organizations, while in Italy the left-wing parties still seem to play an important brokerage role between the movements and the public administration.

the Mafia) involving both the new social movements and the Old Left. The women's movement in the call to vote for the left in national (already in 1976) and local elections recognized this complementarity (for instance, Egidi 1985: 108).

Of course, the relations between women and the left were not always easy. This is true especially at the emergence of the women's movement, while the alliance between the women's movement and the left grew more solid in the 1980s: "Though initially slow to respond to the demands of feminism, once the Communists took up a modified version of the feminist project of transformation, the party was able to use its strength to push through parliament a series of more limited reforms that promised to alter – if only gradually – Italian women's conditions" (J. Hellman 1987b: 50). Attention to the issues of women's working conditions, work opportunities, reproduction, violence against women, and social services grew, as did the recognition that sexual oppression was distinct from class oppression (Beckwith 1985: 26–27). In 1986, the party adopted the *Carta delle donne comuniste* whose slogan was "Women's power for women" and which aimed at increasing women's solidarity and women's involvement in culture and political life (Guadagnini 1995: 164). At the local level, autonomous groups often collaborated with the women active inside the left-wing parties and the trade unions.

Party government "Italian style" – what political scientists referred to as "partitocrazia" – reduced the space of an autonomous movement, in part "absorbing" the political demands of feminism. As a leader of the UDI declared: "In the Italian situation, political relations are almost entirely occupied by the parties, to the extent that politics ends up being identified with the parties. The women's movement, but also other movements, exist within the ambit of relations with the parties" (in Guadagni 1985: 17). In their relationship with pressure groups, associations, and social movements, political parties tended to control civil society via *clientela* (that is, the individualistic distribution of public subsidies to clients in exchange for votes) and *parentela* (that is, the distribution of spoils to organizations belonging to the same ideological family) arrangements. For the women's organizations this meant a forced reliance upon their "natural" party ally in their interaction with the state, with very little relationship with the national government – at least until it was under the firm control of the Christian Democratic Party and its allies.

This tendency was probably strengthened by the fact that, with the left outside of the national government, state feminism emerged very late. The two main equality agencies – the Equal Status and Equal Opportunities National Committee and the Equal Status Committee for the Implementation of Equal Treatment and Equal Opportunities for Men and Women in the Workplace – were established only in the 1990s with the task of furthering gender equality, singling out actual instances of discrimination and promoting equality agency within state administration, at the regional, provincial, and municipal level. Only in the 1990s, the Affirmative Action Act (No. 125/91) strengthened the roles of state institutions in favor of women's equality that have the power to select, finance, and monitor affirmative action programs. Equal status advocates were also provided for controlling the application of equal status principles. Here too, although the directive bodies of the two institutions include representatives of women's associations, unions, scholars, and so on, they tended to follow the party composition of the governmental coalition (Guadagnini 1995: 155).

If the exclusionary tradition of the national governments may explain the weakness of lobbying activities in Italy, the long-lasting alliance with the left may account, however, for an easy adaptation to the "restructured" state. If an exclusionary strategy might have pushed toward a refusal of any contacts with public institutions, this tendency was countered by the brokerage role paid by the main party of the left. The increased interactions with the public administration – which, as we have seen, transformed the discourse, organization, and repertoire of action of the women's groups – were made possible by two important changes in the functioning of the state: downloading and offloading of state power. In the 1980s and especially in the 1990s, administrative decentralization developed in Italy (della Porta 1999), allowing for the development of a local state feminism, in particular in the regions where the left was traditionally stronger. In Florence, since the mid-1980s, such local institutions as the Progetto Donna, the Consiglio delle Donne, and the Comitati per la pari opportunità have involved women's organization side-by-side with women's elected representatives in the various institutions. The downloading of state competencies – and local state feminism – developed, however, in a period of fiscal crisis and consequent restrictions on public budgets. In Italy as elsewhere, the offloading of state responsibilities did not go only in the direction of the market, but also strengthened the Third Sector. In search of lower costs and legitimation, the local administrations started to contract services out to voluntary associations; subsidiarity and community became, for left-wing as well as right-wing governments, the solution to budget constraints and citizens' dissatisfaction with traditional politics. For the women's movement, this implied an increasing availability of public funds. The local institutions often became the sponsors of specific projects developed by the movement organizations.

The women's organizations have been quick to adapt to this situation, finding alliance with the state institutions, in particular at the local level. As stated by the president of the Libreria delle Donne in Florence, "In our activities, the kind of autonomy that we call for is an ideational and projectual one, not an economic one: We interact with the institutions and ask for money on specific projects" (in Carlucci 1999: 190). In the movement, the idea developed of a "gendered mediation," that is, of relationships with the institutions mediated by women: "to do things among women, to think among women," "to single out the modality of a political activities not always imposed by external needs and urgency" (Libreria delle Donne 1989: 5, in Valenza 1999: 371). The women in the left-wing parties have been considered important channels of access to the institutions and the presence of women in the institutions has come to be considered "as a new value, because it offers the possibility of improving and innovating them with transversal interventions, that is interventions above political and party-line division" (CDI, Progetto 1987, in Valenza 1999: 338). In general, there is "a growth in the relationships with the institutions, relationships that are based upon collaboration and bargaining, in particular at the local level" (Carlucci 1999: 384). In some cases, women inside the institutions are also members of one or more of the movement organizations (as in the cases of Il Giardino dei Ciliegi and Artemisia, among others).

In Florence, interactions developed with such institutions as the neighborhood council, the city council, the district council, the regional government, the national government and its administration, the university, the prison administration, and the European Union, as well as various research centers, banks, and foundations. The local governments have often sponsored training courses on various topics, prizes assigned by the movement organizations, and conferences, as well as contracting out services. Relationships have been particularly tied with the Commissioni pari opportunità active inside various institutions, but they also involve ministers as different as the Ministry of Justice, the Minister for Home Affairs, the Minister for Education, and the Minister for Health. The groups that intervene on cultural issues have often organized initiatives with the local schools and university, those involved on the issue of violence against women teach to police officers, and those that specialize in women's health have well-structured interactions with the public health system. As many as 92% of the organizations interviewed by Valenza (1999) declared that they present demands to the public administration; all the women's movement organizations analyzed by Carlucci (1999) have looked for and often found a point of reference within the local governments. In particular, the movement organizations have a quite high rate of success in getting public funds. In eight cases out of thirteen they received material support by the local governments (as against four cases for nonmovement organizations). In 65% of the cases, the demands referred to financial support (for the movement organization, in 77% of the cases there was a demand for funding; in 54% a demand for infrastructure). Of the ten organizations that asked for public funding, eight obtained it; moreover, nine organizations had their headquarters in spaces that belong to the public administration (as against six cases for the organizations that were not part of the movement). Half of the organizations belonging to the women's movement declared that they have had frequent contacts with the local institutions and that these institutions have been quite open to their demands. Movement organizations tended, moreover, to be better connected within their environment. They have had contacts with other organizations (in eleven cases out of thirteen, with more than two organizations), as well as with the press (only two groups out of twenty-six do not interact with the media).

In Italy as in other countries (for the German case, see Rucht this volume), therefore, the shift toward more pragmatic and bargaining-oriented relations with the state was facilitated by a parallel shift in the state institutions. It is still unclear if the restructuring of the state and the increasing interactions between the women's organizations and the public administration will increase or decrease the autonomy of the movement vis-à-vis the Old Left. On the one hand, institutional resources may bring about a redefinition of the alliance with the left, with a decline in the patronage activities of the party. In fact, in Florence, if in 50% of the cases the movement organizations feel close to the left, the same proportion declare themselves to be "near to no party," and only one organization admitted having frequent contacts with a party (Valenza 1999).

We have to consider, however, that devolution of public tasks to the Third Sector takes a particular shape in Italy, because of the very characteristics of the welfare state: a particularistic and clientelistic model (Ferrera 1993). In fact, it was the traditional weakness of the left-wing forces that brought about a particularistic welfare state regime, which tends especially to protect some stronger social groups while excluding the weakest ones (Ferrera 1996). Although its level of social spending approximates and even surpasses the European Union (EU) average (Castles 1995), the Italian welfare state – with its disproportional provision of pensions for the previously employed and the lack of a warranty of a minimum salary for the marginal ones (Saraceno and Negri 1996) and the privilege of transfers upon services – relies upon the family as well as charities to balance the exclusion of the weakest. And public funds have been distributed to these institutions without any control on their activities. More recently, the survival of the old and new poor (the immigrants among them) continues to be delegated – with a clear legacy of the traditional logic of "delegated charity" – to the old and new associations active in the Third Sector. The women's groups that enter in the Third Sector may be trapped in these "clientelistic" and "parental" linkages.[8]

A COMPARATIVE SUMMARY

Crossnational comparisons have singled out a "Southern European model" of women's movements characterized by direct action, revolutionary ideology, and very informal organizational structure, with important alliances with left-wing parties and trade unions (della Porta, Valiente, and Kousis

---

[8] Similarly in the Spanish case, state feminist institutions have been accused of selectively financing only ideologically proximate women's groups (Valiente this volume).

forthcoming). This model was contrasted with a U.S. model (Gelb 1989), characterized by emancipatory goals and lobbying strategy. In a diachronic perspective, comparative analysis has identified a process of evolution of women's movements from separatism to professionalization, infiltration of institutions, establishment of alternative institutions, networking, and policy formulation (Lovenduski 1988: 114–120).

In our analysis, the Italian women's movement appeared characterized by double structures of small informal groups and formal associations; the prevalence of emancipatory discourse over "liberation"; and some skepticism about merely countercultural action. The relationships between women's movements, the state, and the party systems explain some of these peculiarities. With their long tradition of alliance with the left, the women's movement seems to be particularly sensitive to the attitudes and behaviors of their main potential ally: the (major) left-wing party. The strong links with the left explain such characteristics of the women's movement as the lack of centralized organizations, the prevalence of a class discourse, and the attention to social activities. The alliance with the left may also have produced a sort of division of tasks, so that women groups "accepted" the delegation of political representation, as well as media work and re-lations with the public bureaucracy, to the (men of the) allied left. The repressive traditions of the Italian state may also have had the effect of pushing the Old Left toward an alliance with social movements, focusing attention on basic civil and political rights, leaving less space for more specific women's issues. The opening of the PCI toward the social move-ments can be explained by the fact that it was contemporaneously a mass party and a party of opposition. Sensitivity to change derived from the internal dynamics of a mass party that found itself profoundly altered (perhaps against its own will) by the waves of collective mobilization of the 1960s (S. Hellman 1987: 133). As an opposition party, moreover, the PCI was amenable to broadening the front of alliances with other extrain-stitutional actors. The alliance with the left was even stronger since, for a long time, the main party in government had been a Christian Demo-cratic one, deeply opposed to women's demands, whom they accused of destroying the family and public morality. The strong power the politi-cal parties acquired after the Second World War, as the main actors of the democratization processes, pushed this need for party alliances even further.

The state restructuring of the 1990s, in particular the downloading and offloading of state power, created resources and constraints for the Italian women's movement; it may have contributed to its survival, but it also pro-foundly changed its strategies. First of all, many women's organizations are active in the 1990s and many of them present strong continuities with their counterparts in the 1970s. The women involved in them are mainly from the 1970s generation, their collective identity originates in the 1970s, and the origins of the movement are (proudly) set in the 1970s. At least at the local level, there seems to be a survival of "second wave" feminism, but with much adaptation to the "restructured" external environment.

If, especially at the local level, dozens of groups continue the struggle of the earlier time, their means are nonetheless different. The old debate between emancipation and freedom is overcome in a discourse that emphasizes a combination of parity and differences – a new citizenship where equal rights come from the recognition of different identities. Women's groups often transformed themselves into formal associations, with the declared aim of getting access to public funding, although with a strong emphasis on participation, and a surprising capacity for networking, even outside the borders of the women's movement. As for their repertoire of action, protest – although still used sometimes – does not have a prominent role, while there is a growing attention to the interactions with old and new means of communication. If most of the groups focus on cultural activities to raise the public consciousness of women's discrimination and oppression, many also offer services to their associates or various groups of women.

Since the 1980s but especially in the 1990s, the development of local state feminism brought about the possibility for many women's groups to get access to public funds. Especially where the left was in government, the interaction with the public administration facilitated a process of growing moderation in strategies and ideology. In Italy, the shift toward an acceptance of state "facilitation" seems to have been eased by the privileged relationships with the Old Left, at least when the Old Left was in power at the local level. The mediation of the party of the left facilitated a kind of political exchange. Faced with the fiscal crisis, the women's voluntary associations facilitate the contracting out of services, with lower cost; faced with the legitimation crisis of the state (and in particular of the political class), the women's movement offered symbolic resources for the building of new collective identities. In exchange, the women's groups received material as well as symbolic resources themselves.

For the women's movement of the 1990s, the state appears less and less as a target, and more and more (especially at the local level) as a sponsor. Against the hypotheses supported by the Marxism theories (or their adaptation), the state is not perceived as the *longa manus* of the capitalist or the patriarchy. Even if the legacy of a tradition of exclusion of the opposition is visible in the Italian case, an administrative decentralization (as yet incomplete), together with a general growth of public transfers to the Third Sector, increased the material and symbolic resources for the women's groups. In this sense, it seems that the "state" is seen as an "enjeu" of the political struggle (Badie and Birnbaum 1979), where "strong" interests ("male" interests among them) have easier access to the decisionmakers but where the women's movement has also been successful in bringing pressure to redress the balance.

On the other hand, however, the growing interactions between state institutions and the women's movement within a strategy of devolution of state powers raise some concerns that take a peculiar coloration in the Italian case. In particular, the risks of a cooptation of the Third Sector, as well as of a decrease in the quality of public services, are increased by the characteristics of the Italian welfare state as well as the peculiar control by the parties over the civic societies. In Italy, in fact, a tradition of a particularistic and clientelistic welfare state, with the protection of "strong" social actors and the clientelistic mediation of political parties, meant the abandonment of the poor to the charity intervention of Third Sector organizations. The weakness of the bureaucracy faced with the strength of the political parties pushed the movement to look for political interlocutors inside the administration. Relationships based on "clientela" and "parentela" developed with so-called "finanziamenti a pioggia" (raindrops sponsorship) where financial assistance was given to ideologically proximate associations with no control extended by the state on the use of this money. The legacy of this tradition is still visible, even if there is an evolution toward a sponsorship linked to the offer of services and public controls on the associations' budgets and functioning. Under these circumstances, downloading and offloading may strongly reduce the quality of public services, increasing the dependence of civil society upon those actors who control, within a clientelistic tradition, public financing. As for the women's movement, the adaptation to the changes in state strategies provides new resources for various activities, but at the risk of taming the movement's potential for disruption and innovation. The "Latin" tradition of direct action and revolutionary ideology seems to weaken when faced with increasing cooperative interaction with the restructured state, especially at the local level, where a long history of overlapping membership with left-wing parties and trade unions eased the interaction between the women's movement and the local administration. Insofar as the restructuring of the state involves a worsening of a welfare model, already particularly unsympathetic to women's demands, the traditional mistrust of the women's movement toward state institutions may yet prevail.

4

Comparing Two Movements for Gender Parity

France and Spain

Jane Jenson and Celia Valiente

In August 1998 the press declared that the Spanish Socialist Party (Partido Socialista Obrero Español, PSOE), the main opposition party, would submit a bill to reform the electoral law. The hypothetical bill, for that is what it was, would have required all electoral lists to limit their candidates of the same sex to no more than 60%. In effect, this was a proposal for a quota of 40% for women. The second largest opposition party, the United Left (Izquierda Unida, IU, ideologically to the left of the PSOE) supported the idea, but the governing conservative party, the People's Party (Partido Popular, PP) strongly opposed it. Such a bill did not pass. Indeed it was never presented to parliament, being considered too risky by leading socialists (*El País*, August 31, 1998; December 27, 1998).

Yet, as the lists prepared for the local, regional, and European elections of June 1999 showed, despite the lack of any legally enforced quotas, the number of women on the lists of the major parties was higher than ever before. Indeed both the conservative PP and the Socialist Party placed a woman in the number one position on the list for the European elections. In addition, in the national elections of 2000, 29% of those elected to the lower house were women as were 24% of those elected to the Senate, while the speakers of both houses are women. Therefore, according to one French observer, parity is "lived in reality," and the debates which have shaken France for a decade about increasing the number of women in elected office, as well as its legislation, has "provoked smiles" if not criticisms (*Le Monde*, March 8, 2001).

France does provide a contrasting story to this one of relatively steady increase in the number of women holding elected office and senior positions in government. In 1998, nine of every ten deputies in the National Assembly were still male. Dominated by the political right, in early 1999 the Senate rejected a bill to enable affirmative action in politics that had already been overwhelmingly approved by the National Assembly. It finally accepted it only under heavy political pressure and threat. On June 6, 2000, France reformed the Constitution of the Fifth Republic, enshrining a legal protection of actions to achieve equal access of women and men to elected office (Article 3). Since then, two sets of elections have been held. In March 2001 local elections increased the percentage of women holding municipal office dramatically from 22% to 48%. However, only 7% took the mayor's office. Moreover, in the elections for governments of cantons (held at the same time and with single-member constituencies), the number of female candidates rose to 20% (from 15% in 1998), but the number elected increased only by 1.5 percentage points, to reach 10% (*Le Monde*, April 22–23, 2001: 6). In September 2001 a first wave of elections to the Senate was held according to the new electoral law. Opposition from senators and machinations by them meant that the number of female senators rose only from twenty to twenty eight in the upper chamber which has 321 members (*Le Monde*, September 21, 2001).

Both these patterns of change were, at least in part, the result of the types of claims made by mobilized networks seeking to change the status of women within their respective countries. In the case of France, these activists proudly bear the name of parity movement (*mouvement pour la parité*) and describe it as a grass-roots movement (Bataille and Gaspard 1999: 32ff). In contrast, for the Spanish case it is we who are naming the loose grouping of feminist activists in left-wing political parties and women's groups mobilized in favor of higher representation of women in state structures the "democratic-parity movement" or "parity movement." Nonetheless, both fit the analytic definition of a women's movement used in this book (see Chapter 1), that is, their definition, content, development, or issues are specific to women and their gender identity. As such, they revive claims advanced by the suffragists of the first-wave women's movement and the actions of the second-wave to feminize political institutions.

The decision to pursue a strategy of reform of the French Constitution was not available to Spanish feminists. In 1996, after fourteen years of socialist government, the conservative People's Party (PP) took over the national government. This successful alternation in power demonstrated (just as it had in France in 1981 when the first left-wing president took office in the Fifth Republic) that constitutional issues of the transition were settled.[1] However, issues of institutional, especially constitutional, change remain difficult in Spain because of the conflicts with Basque nationalists. At this point in time, institutions remain hostage to that issue. No change in the constitution is politically feasible until the issue is settled and therefore most parity activists in Spain do not dare to call for constitutional reform.

But this is only one reason for the differences between the two movements; others are important too. Therefore, this chapter examines and compares

[1] There were, for example, serious discussions in the press throughout the 1970s about whether there would be a hand over of power from right to left, if the candidate of the United Left were to win an election. As late as 1981 a certain sigh of relief occurred as Valéry Giscard d'Estaing moved out of the Elysée leaving it to François Mitterrand; republican institutions had held.

these movements in the following ways. First, it describes the reconfiguration of the French and Spanish states and asks what effects these changes might have for social movement politics. Second, it examines in more detail the actions of these two parity movements, seeking to account for the different strategies and outcomes in the two cases.

RECONFIGURED STATES AND MOVEMENT ACTION

Despite what might appear at first glance to be large differences between the two cases, France and Spain share experiences on several dimensions of reconfiguration of their state institutions, with respect to structural changes within the state, discourses about the role of the state, and changing relationships between the state and civil society (see Chapter 1). We can expect each aspect of reconfiguration to have consequences for the type of mobilization that the two women's movements undertake, although as the next section makes clear, there are also factors in civil society that help to account for differences between French and Spanish women's claims.

With respect to structural changes, both states are committed to the project of building Europe, although for slightly different reasons. In the case of Spain, with its history of Francoism and its more fragile democratic institutions, as well as its economic problems, the European Community (and then Union) was perceived, both from Madrid and in Brussels, as a buttress for the democratization process. After the death of Franco in 1975 all political forces, with much popular support, promoted closer ties with European institutions. Therefore, the governments of socialist Felipe González (elected in 1982) actively participated in the development of a European dimension to their actions and politics, with Spain joining the European Community in 1986. In France, by 1983 the choice of accepting the European monetary regime over any more autarkic solution was made, and in subsequent years, first under the presidency of François Mitterrand and then that of Jacques Chirac, the state was deliberately opened to the influence of European institutions.

These commitments provoked a shift in the institutions of political representation. It became legitimate for citizens, including those who were active in social movements, to seek representation in European institutions and recognition from them. Politics had become multilevel (Liebfried and Pierson 1995).[2] These commitments also brought a change in the very definition of what it meant to be French or Spanish. National identities became more pluralist, more varied, while social rights were realigned.

In addition, in both countries there has been a change in the political discourse about the role of the state, one which blurs distinctions between left

---

[2] This chapter does not address the other way in which politics was becoming multilevel, with the moves toward federal-style arrangements in Spain and stronger regional governments in France.

and right and that has consequences for public policy and service delivery. Both Spain and France have moved away, on the left as well as the right, from the social traditions of the Keynesian welfare state. In part the shift results from the convergence criteria imposed by the European Monetary System, but there have also been, within the domestic politics of each country, forces for neoliberalism, including of a left-wing variety, which would reduce state spending, redirect activities from direct provision to public financing of privately provided services, and seek partnerships with the associations of civil society (Letablier 1996).

In France, François Mitterrand made an historic choice in 1983 to move the economic policy of the socialist governments toward a broad center republican tradition and away from the more left-wing vision of republicanism that placed the goal of reducing inequalities – both social and sexual – front and center (Jenson and Sineau 1995: ch. 5). The goal according to the president and his supporters within the Socialist Party and elsewhere was to "modernize" France by reconfiguring the role of the state and its relationship with civil society. The change in ideological discourses and policy preferences as well as the institutions of the Fifth Republic have led to a weakening of party ties, as the party system itself dissolves in the face of institutional reinforcement of presidentialism and the notion that little separates the social policies of the right from those of the left.

Bringing about such a shift required altering the principles of the political discourses which had underpinned state actions. In the first three post-1945 decades in France, for example, the distinction between social classes and between left and right provided the basis for social and political difference.[3] In the 1980s this link began to disintegrate. While France did not commit itself to the hardy neoliberalism of Reaganism or Thatcherism, equality of opportunity began to replace equality of results as a central goal (Gélédan 1993). France had succumbed to neoliberalism's enthusiasm for competitive individualism.[4]

Child-care services, care for the dependent elderly, and policies for the economically marginal still capture a relatively high level of public funding,

---

[3] Electoral politics of the Fifth Republic became bifurcated. After 1958 the Communists were readmitted to the status of legitimate party and the centrist Christian Democracy folded its tent. Most other forms of politics beyond elections also turned on class distinctions. For example, throughout the postwar period, associations representing any category of the population were aligned with a political family and often with a political party. The latter was the case of the *Union des Femmes Françaises*, a flanking organization of the Communist Party. But there were also parent-teacher associations divided by political family, teachers and professors unions, hunting and fishing associations, and so on. French citizens' political identity depended on their position on the left-right spectrum. Such alignment continues in Spain and is described below.

[4] The goal of achieving equality gave way in these years to struggle against *exclusion*. Rather than seeking to equalize, the idea was simply to make sure no one fell out of society.

but services are being provided outside of public institutions, in the voluntary sector or the social economy. This makes the third sector, nonprofits, and voluntary associations important actors (Jenson 1998; Joël and Martin 1998).

Broad differences in political discourse still separate right and left in Spain. Nonetheless, differences between the major Spanish political families on economic and social policy have also narrowed. Both support monetary rigor and controlling the deficit. The Socialist Party continues to present itself to the electorate as the party most concerned with the maintenance and expansion of the welfare state, rather than abandoning its commitment to social rights. Generally speaking, however, the Conservative Party also tries to look like a center rather than a right-wing party, and so the PP promises not to destroy the welfare state. It has signed social pacts with unions regarding this issue.

Nonetheless, downloading is also occurring in Spain. The conservative government is proposing that people are better cared for by the family and community than by the state. Indeed, the state's financing of services via subsidies for delivery by groups in civil society has resulted in one of the major areas of growth in the women's movement in the 1990s, that is direct provision of services. Whereas in the 1970s such actions were often a form of civil disobedience, with the redesign of social services in the 1990s, women's groups are now involved in front line delivery of state-funded services (see Valiente this book).

Discourses of left and right on class and gender power still distinguish Spain's two political families, then. Parties in the left speak about economic inequalities more often than the Conservative Party, with the latter particularly stressing opportunities for people to participate in the labor market, make a living, take care of themselves, and be able not to depend on the welfare state. Indeed, the notion of "opportunities" is crucial to the PP, which entitled one of the main documents presented to its 1999 Congress, "In favour of a Spain full of opportunities" (*Por la España de las Oportunidades*).

There are two potential consequences of such reconfiguration of the state for social movement mobilizations. One is that as the relationship between state and civil society is altered by governments, the social rights of citizenship lose legitimacy and responsibility is assigned to the family or the community as civil and political rights gain importance. The definition of citizenship may even be narrowed such that it comes to mean only the right to civil and political rights. In such a universe of political discourse, movements still committed to a social agenda and to achieving the social rights of citizenship may find the going heavy, while those whose focus is primarily on civil and political rights may find that their way is smoother. Second, as public services are hollowed out, and provision of services becomes less transparent, social movements may have to adjust their mobilization strategies. The state and its agencies have a less direct – or at least seemingly less direct – involvement in creating solidarity and social equality. The private sector, whether commercial or nonprofit, appears to have a larger role. The result is a challenge to the repertoire of social movements that have traditionally mobilized to face the state and make claim to the state. Finally, as multilevel politics become the norm, patterns of mobilization and interest intermediation will alter.

These observations of the patterns of reconfiguration in states, their institutions, and their practices lead to three alterations in patterns of mobilization of women's movements, and more particularly, the parity movements.

1. The structural change to upload responsibilities to the EU will make mobilization increasingly multilevel, involving the quasi-state institutions of the Union.
2. The greater the shift in political discourse away from its grounding in class analysis, the greater likelihood of crosspartisan or nonpartisan mobilization.
3. The more the principles of postwar, and in the case of Spain post-1975, politics are altered, the greater will be the downplaying of claims in the name of social rights and a rising emphasis on civil and political rights. Those wings of the women's movements that still include a social rights agenda will find themselves in greater difficulty than those that make claims primarily in the name of civil and political rights.

The next two sections of the chapter demonstrate the extent to which the two movements analyzed here follow these patterns. To anticipate the conclusion, we will find that the French movement conforms more to these patterns than does the Spanish one.

LE MOUVEMENT POUR LA PARITÉ IN FRANCE – A STAR ASCENDING

Despite the fact that we now associate the notion of the movement for parity with the widespread mobilization which has marked French electoral and social movement politics and to a lesser extent those of Spain, the first calls for parity were actually organized by the European Community. As early as 1990, the idea of gender parity in decision-making institutions was being advanced in Brussels, and in November 1992 the first European Summit of Women and Decision-Making was held in Athens. A number of French women, from both the right and the left, were actively involved in the summit. For example Simone Veil (a member of a center-right party and former president of the European Parliament) and Edith Cresson (former Socialist Prime Minister of France) were the official French representatives, while Yvette Roudy, Françoise Gaspard, and Elisabeth Guigou (all socialists) were active participants.

The statement of principle signed and named the Athens Declaration asserted: "a democratic system must assure equal participation by its citizens in public and political life. . . . Women represent half the population. Equality requires parity in the representation and administration of countries."

The summit that produced the declaration was organized by the European Network of Women in Decision-Making, which was created and funded by the Equal Opportunities Unit of the European Commission. The latter had, in its Third Action Plan in 1990, identified the absence of women in decision-making positions as a major blockage to the achievement of the equal opportunities guaranteed by Article 119 of the 1957 Treaty of Rome.

At its creation in 1990 the European Network was charged with studying the social and political mechanisms which generate inequality and to collect precise statistical data about women's participation in all domains of decision making. In other words, the task was to provide detailed analysis and to propose concrete actions so that equality could be achieved. While the attention given to gender equality was not new, either for the European Union or for second-wave feminism, there was a slightly different twist. The call was for absolute equality and for mechanisms guaranteed to achieve it.

By the time of the Athens Summit, mobilization was increasing in France. From the beginning, the claim was framed in terms of citizenship. For example, in 1992 Françoise Gaspard, Claude Servan-Schreiber, and Anne Le Gall published *Au pouvoir citoyennes: Liberté, Egalité, Parité.*[5] In 1993, fourteen existing women's associations representing elected women, Catholic women, and the center-right, among others, formed Elles-aussi. Described as dedicated to achieving parity, it would conduct a national campaign to mobilize, support, and prepare women to become candidates in upcoming elections (*Le Monde*, January 16, 1993). Simultaneously, Yvette Roudy created the Assemblée des femmes, as a group within the Socialist Party (Parti socialiste, PS). Despite being an internal body, the group was open from the beginning to interested women who were not members of the party. Academics were included in this category. Among the members of the support committee was Elisabeth Guigou, *ministre déléguée* for European issues. Throughout 1993, colloquia were held, including at the National Assembly and the Senate on March 8, and one at UNESCO organized by Gisèle Halimi's group, Choisir la cause des femmes. The first public demonstration, in front of the National Assembly, also took place in April of that year. Another public event was the publication in the national newspaper, *Le Monde*, of the *Manifesto of 577 persons for parity*. The group was composed of 289 women and 288 men, drawn widely from the political spectrum. Gender parity in electoral institutions was described as being as basic to democracy as the separation of powers and universal suffrage (*Le Monde*, November 10, 1993).

[5] A number of press articles also appeared in 1992 explaining the electoral successes – such as they were – of the French Greens (*Verts*) by their commitment to running lists with equal numbers of women and men.

The basic claim advanced in all these events was the same: There must be an *equal number* of women and men in electoral institutions.[6] The reasons for calling for parity were not always the same, however. As early as 1993 there were a variety of arguments in circulation. One is a republican one, which is perhaps the best known because of being promoted by Françoise Gaspard, one of the most visible activists for parity. It inscribes gender parity in the tradition of the movement for suffrage and identifies the absence of women in politics as a national humiliation. A second part of this argument is that the justification for gender parity is simple: There would be no humanity if there were not two different sexes. Women and men together define and perpetuate the species. Therefore, they must together, and equally, organize social life, not because of any sexual essentialism but because they jointly form the human race. This formulation called for a reformulation of the republican triplet. A true democracy should be based on the real, not false, political equality of all its children, translated into a revised and corrected republican symbolism: liberty, equality, and parity (*Le Monde*, February 19, 1993).

While they sought the same reform, and therefore also mobilized for gender parity in the institutions, other women, especially those coming from the right of the political spectrum, tended to justify it differently. For example, at the UNESCO meeting in June 1993, Simone Veil said, "I believe that men and women are rich in their differences and that they are complementary. It is, moreover, in the name of these differences and of all that women can offer that it is necessary to demand equality in politics."[7]

Many proponents of parity explicitly reject the notion of quotas, preferring instead to promote simple equality, offering several reasons for being wary of them. Probably the most important was the rejection of an earlier quota by the Constitutional Council. In 1982, the socialist government, with the unanimous support of the National Assembly, had proposed a quota of 25% for the lists in municipal elections. In effect, the law would have limited all lists to a maximum of 75% of candidates of the same sex.[8] This timid effort to impose a quota was immediately found unconstitutional by the Constitutional Council, which declared on November 18, 1982 that the law contravened both Section 3 of the Constitution of the Fifth Republic and Article 6 of the Declaration of the Rights of Man and the Citizen. In essence, the argument was that a 25% quota, in the name of affirmative action, interfered with the equality of all citizens before the law, guaranteed

---

[6] For a summary of the arguments, in English, see Gaspard (1998b).

[7] As the journalist Christiane Chombeau remarked, "a few years ago, Madame Veil's views would have provoked protests in a meeting of women. Instead, thunderous applause greeted this claim to a right to equality in difference" (*Le Monde*, June 6–7, 1993).

[8] Do not be fooled by the unanimous vote. Most legislators were confident the Conseil constitutionel would overturn the law.

by these two sections of the constitution.[9] In order to get around the judgment against quotas and affirmative action, activists promoted simple equality, that is parity in the number of women and men (Mossuz-Lavau 1998: ch. 2).

A second reason for preferring parity to quotas was that the word was familiar from existing discourse about representation. While parity itself was a very familiar concept, being used as a basic principle for a variety of employer-employee institutions, use of the term by the European Network and French activists was novel in two ways. It had never before been applied to the composition of electoral institutions and it had not been used to describe the distribution in terms of sex.

The call for a reform of electoral institutions to institute gender parity was quickly linked to broader debates and discursive shifts about the role of the state, one of the elements of reconfiguration of the French state. As the goal of equality of outcome for income distribution gave way to the more liberal search for equality of opportunity, issues of access and fairness came to the fore. Everyone should have her or his chance, but the market (including the political market) would decide the result. Thus, the parity movement with its focus on access and gender equality but its indifference to whether the women elected were right wing or left wing, rich or poor, and so on, fit well with this notion of equality.

Secondly, structural changes within the state, especially those associated with the move to Europeanization, economic reforms, cutbacks, and so on, generated dissent. One of the political spaces in which this dissent was first expressed was in a public debate about the so-called crisis of representation that provoked a good deal of controversy in the winter of 1992–3. By December 1992, the notion was gaining ground that the political world was closed, elites had lost touch and were making decisions that did not reflect their constituents' views, that many were corrupt, and that they clung to outmoded distinctions such as left and right. The time had come, according to the interveners in this debate, to move away from old practices. In this controversy, the Greens, whose positions blurred the usual left-right distinctions, were frequently presented as examples of all that might be good.[10]

The consensus that ultimately emerged from the debate was that it was necessary to replace the old and tired party hacks with a new generation and that the political institutions should be reformed to make them more open

---

[9] Some constitutional experts now wonder whether the Conseil constitutionel would have been able to come to the same conclusion after 1984, when France signed the UN Declaration on the Elimination of Gender Discrimination. It permits affirmative action as a temporary step to promote gender equality (Sineau 1997a: 124, n6).

[10] This description is derived from an analysis of the texts published in *Le Monde* in December 1992 and January 1993. The Verts' proclaimed position was that they were *"ni, ni"* (neither right nor left).

and less likely to be taken over by a small and isolated elite. For example, the holding of multiple offices, which permitted a single person to hold several elected positions simultaneously (for instance, mayor, deputy, regional councillor, Euro-parliamentarian) came in for criticism.

The groups and associations promoting parity that were created in 1992 and 1993 picked up and elaborated precisely such themes. The crisis of representation, in which elected officials were too distant from citizens and there was a need for a new kind of politics, was frequently the point of departure for their claims. Instituting parity would automatically bring a significant renewal of political personnel; the National Assembly in 1993 still was 94% male. The old and tired could be replaced and new politics could begin. For example, prominent socialist and feminist Yvette Roudy justified founding the Assemblée des femmes by the fact that political parties' misogyny – reflected in their failure to nominate women – cut them off from their political base.

As early as 1993, the parity movement exhibited the pattern we have identified as a response to the reconfiguration of the French state. It was heavily influenced by its ties to the European-level Network. The Summit of Athens provided a catalyst to organizing activities in France. The constant back and forth of activists who were active in the European Network meant that funds flowed to French groups, and French political women were among the leaders of the network. Secondly, actions crossed party lines. Initially, it is true that the official groupings tended to reflect the left-right split. The Assemblée des femmes arose in the PS while Elles-aussi was linked to the center-right. Nonetheless, the boundaries were always blurry. The Assemblée des femmes welcomed individual feminists who were not socialists. Moreover, both Simone Veil and Edith Cresson represented France in Athens. Even more telling was the ease with which the earliest demonstrations were organized and crossed party lines. March 8, 1993 was marked by a meeting at the Senate, organized by Yvette Roudy, but including twenty-five women's groups from both left and right, and by a round table at the National Assembly organized by the grouping Reseau femmes pour la parité, again a transpartisan group.[11] In contrast, the feminists active in the popular sector (*le mouvement social*) marshalled only a dozen associations to protest the issue of abortion (*Le Monde*, March 7–8, 1993). Parity was not on their agenda.

These characteristics of the movement intensified over the next years. Actions at the European level continued, French women were involved, and these mobilizations helped legitimate the actions of French groups. For example, on May 18, 1996, thirteen women ministers from the fifteen member states of the European Union signed what has come to be known as the

---

[11] This network included several women's groups, including the Assemblée des femmes, the women's committee of the Verts, the Conseil national des femmes françaises (itself composed of 120 associations), Elles-aussi, and so on (*Le Monde*, April 6, 1993).

Charter of Rome. They had been invited by the president of the European Council to a summit on Women and the Renewal of Politics and Society. While their signature on the Charter did not officially commit their governments, it nonetheless did address a strong statement to the Intergovernmental Conference (IGC) which was about to embark on preparing modifications of the Maastricht Treaty. The Charter identified the principal responsibility of the IGC to be the reinforcement of democracy. In that context, these ministers claimed that democracy requires giving priority to actions with the potential to generate equal participation and a partnership between women and men. Moreover, only with such equal participation will citizens have confidence in their political institutions. In other words, for those who signed the Charter, the next step in the building of European institutions – via the elimination of the democratic deficit – required a radically increased presence of women in all decision-making institutions.

Increasingly, the name CLEF (Coordination pour le lobby européen des femmes) appeared at the head of actions for parity. This grouping of sixty associations was funded (as were similar groups in the other member states) by the EU. CLEF joined, for example, in signing the Open Letter to President Chirac in March 1996 that called on him to live up to his electoral promises on parity (*Le Monde*, March 8, 1996). Another example: CLEF was also in the Network Woman, Man, Parity (Réseau Femme et Homme, la parité) that was formed in November 1998 to assure legislative passage and implementation of a reform.

The fiftieth anniversary of female suffrage (April 21, 1944) provided an excellent occasion for mobilization and several actions were launched. By 1995, however, the best known of the parity activists were seeking to broaden their popular base. They began to name themselves the parity movement. They undertook signature campaigns. They promoted common strategies and joint actions. New networks formed. For example, Demain la parité [Tomorrow Parity] was established in 1995 at the instigation of Françoise Gaspard, who suggested that the largest associations and federations of French women's associations coalesce around a common strategy (Servan-Schreiber 1997: 37). The eight affiliated associations or federations of this network are Action catholique générale féminine (ACGF), Association française des femmes diplômées des universités (AFFDU), Coordination française pour le lobby européen des femmes (CLEF), Elles-aussi, Organisation internationale des femmes sionistes (WIZO), Parité-Infos, Union féminine civique et sociale (UFCS), and Union professionnelle féminine (UPF) (Massé 1996: 4). By 1997, an inventory identified seventy-two associations of all kinds working for parity, forty of which worked almost exclusively on it (Assises nationales 1998: 196). Again, the mobilization and affiliations crossed partisan lines and political families. Indeed, in June 1996, ten female ex-ministers from governments of the right and the left published a Manifesto for Parity in *L'Express* (Sineau 1997a: 120, 3). Again the notion that women and men brought different qualities to politics and that their skills should be respected appeared in this manifesto.

Politicians responded and elections became important moments for debating and clarifying positions, as well as mobilizing. The legislative elections in the spring of 1993 had been a major disappointment; indeed some attributed the surge of mobilization, including the creation of the Assemblée des femmes, to the frustration of that experience.[12] From the beginning of the movement, the overwhelming maleness of the National Assembly and Senate had been described as a French – shameful – exception, a red lantern in the world. Comparisons with other countries (sometimes somewhat dismissive of them) were common. For example, in her overview for the 1993 elections, journalist Christine Leclerc wrote: "[Although a] macho country and an emerging democracy, Spain has three times more elected women" (*Le Monde*, February 19, 1993).

Change did occur, however. In the 1994 Europarliamentary elections, the socialist Michel Rocard ran a list which was – almost – half female and half male.[13] Indeed fully six lists looked as if they were following a parity model. In the 1995 presidential elections, under pressure from the parity movement, the candidates were compelled to reveal their positions.[14] The communist candidate called for a referendum, the Green for constitutional reform, Lionel Jospin (PS) proposed an Estates-General of women to discuss the matter, while Jacques Chirac called on the parties to encourage female candidates. Édouard Balladur, who had forgotten to put the matter in his platform, announced on the 8th of March that he supported minimal quotas for municipal and regional elections.

Following the election of Jacques Chirac in May, the Prime Minister Alain Juppé appointed the most feminized cabinet in French history, at 29%. By November of the same year, he had dismissed eight of the thirteen, provoking an outcry throughout the ranks of women politicians and many parity activists. Such unanimity arose directly from the stance of the movement. While there might be differences in the philosophical grounding of various tendencies, as described previously, there was very little talk of the *policy* content that might follow from electing more women. Moreover, because of the nonpartisanship clearly implanted in the movement, women from the left as well as the right found it logical to defend the *Juppettes*, as the women fired from the cabinet were sometimes termed.

---

[12] The rate of election of women in 1993 was: 17% Communist; 15% ecologists; 8% PS; and 7% UPF. (*Le Monde*, February 18, 1993).

[13] There was a notorious break of the order exactly at the point where the cut-off was expected to be, thereby favoring male candidates. Such alternation was a novelty only for the Socialists; the Verts always had such a list.

[14] An all-candidate meeting was organized by the Conseil national des femmes françaises on April 7.

Consideration of policy content could not be completely avoided, however. The parity activists and the movement itself stumbled for a moment in the fall of 1995. At that time, in response to a call from the CADAC (Coordination pour le Droit à l'avortement et à la contraception), 40,000 women and men, many in family groupings, joined the demonstration in Paris on November 25 in defense of the right to abortion and contraception. While access to abortion had been deteriorating over the years, due in part to the violent actions of the pro-life forces, the precipitating factor creating this large turnout and the support of unions, parties, and women's groups was the legislation produced by an RPR deputy, Christine Boutin. It was hard, in this case, to defend the principle that policy content was not the issue when discussing representation. The problem intensified as the Front National took to nominating women. Nonetheless, activists continued to refuse to enter what they saw as a trap. For example, they used the following argument to explain their principles to those scandalized by the National Front's substitution of Cathérine Mégret, self-acknowledged as having no qualifications for the position, as mayor when her husband was relieved of his duties by the courts:

But in mixing together everything, and using the argument that a "good" male candidate is preferable to a "bad" female candidate, one is quite simply undermining the basic idea of parity. The claim of parity, we should remember, is based on the self-evident assumption that there must be as many women as men in public life, from **all** the political parties that participate in elections. (Servan-Schreiber 1997: 5)

It was finally in 1997 that the situation began to change, on two fronts. Two years earlier the PS had announced that 30% of its candidates in the next election would be female and it would reserve winnable seats for promising candidates (Praud 1998). Its closest competitors took note and when nominations closed, 27% of communist candidates were women, while 28% of those of the Greens and the PS were female. The Right did not follow, although 12% of the National Front candidates were women (*Le Monde*, May 23, 1997). The final results were not as high, of course. Only 17% of socialist deputies were female, but women's presence rose from four to forty-two. The overall average doubled, reaching 11%. Despite this multiplication, only Greece in the EU had a lower percentage.

The second change came with respect to the main demand of the parity movement – that is, for legal action. The government of Lionel Jospin, with the grudging acceptance of President Chirac, decided to propose a constitutional amendment. This had been the recommendation of, *inter alia*, the *Observatoire de la parité*, named by Prime Minister Juppé after the Right won the 1995 elections and reporting in January 1996. The consultative body was headed by Gisèle Halimi, who had in earlier elections stood for the PS, and Roselyne Bachelot, a supporter of the RPR (Rassemblement pour la République, Jacques Chirac's political formation). The original proposal would have located the constitutional legitimacy of actions to achieve parity in Article 34 of the constitution. This would have meant it applied to a wide range of circumstances and might have become a constitutional pillar for affirmative action. After long debates, the cabinet decided to change Article 3, thereby limiting the constitutional permission to elections (*Le Monde*, December 19, 1998). This more limited law was voted by the National Assembly, rejected by the Senate and then finally passed in June 2000.

The debate leading up to the various votes provoked conflict, to be sure. From opponents came calls for everything from instituting quotas rather than changing the constitution, to reforming the electoral law to doing nothing at all. This is not the place to review that debate (among others, for a summary, see Sineau 1997a and Mossuz-Lavau 1998: chs. 3–4). More interesting for our purposes is the conflict *within* the movement for parity about how to achieve it. Immediately after the report of the *Observatoire*, for example, Évelyne Pisier called for a process of nominations which would introduce parity into other political positions than simply elected ones (*Le Monde*, March 11, 1997). For her part, Françoise Gaspard came out *against* the idea of a constitutional amendment, preferring a regular law. She saw the idea of constitutional change as an easy way for male politicians to gain time, as well as to do "damage control" (Gaspard 1998a).

An even more interesting conflict was that about a feminist agenda. After 1995 and the mobilization to defend the abortion law (*loi Veil*) and the eruption of protest throughout France in December, which eventually came to be termed *le mouvement social*, a coalition began to prepare for the National Assizes on Women's Rights, held in 1996 and 1997. Organized in a series of meetings around the country, they involved mobilization of 106 associations, the five main union federations, and seven left-wing political parties, all of whom participated in the preparation of these meetings in the provinces and Paris. Given this composition, it is obvious that the Assizes did not reach very far into the center of the political spectrum; it remained anchored on the left.

Discussion focused on five issues – abortion, violence against women, family policy, work, and politics. However, as the press coverage and the final report both testify, it was only the last two that really received sustained attention.[15] In other words, the issues on the feminist agenda were reduced to these two. The focus on work is hardly surprising, given both the composition of the organizing collectives and the job situation in France, with its unemployment rates hovering around 12% and that of young women substantially higher.

---

[15] For example, the final report of the National Assizes published none of the preliminary studies collected from experts in the fields of family, reproductive rights, or violence, while including several in the domains of work and politics. The section of the report dealing with politics began, as well, with a statement about divergences within the movement about the advisability of legislative change (*Assises nationales* 1998: 175, 183ff)

What is somewhat more surprising is the extent to which the parity movement had come to be seen as the visible face of the women's movement. Overshadowed were issues that had given rise to the women's movement, in the case of abortion, or sustained it through the thin years of the 1980s, in the case of violence against women.[16] It is, of course, not the case that all such issues have been ignored. A campaign in favor of contraception and protection of the supplies of the abortion pill (RU-486) was announced on March 8, 1998, and Prime Minister Jospin eventually got around to appointing an official responsible for women's rights. Fully six months after the election, Geneviève Fraisse, a researcher in philosophy, was named interdepartmental delegate (*déléguée interministérielle*), one of the most minor posts in French public administration. Women's difficulties in the job market have been discussed in the press (*Le Monde*, November 5, 1997) and the 1997 March for Women's Work received some attention.

Nevertheless, none of this competes either in public attention or policy action with the more favored parity movement. It is the social movement that promises to address the institutional crisis by relegitimating political institutions, that gladly accepts the Europeanization of politics, and that attaches no policy conditions, and certainly no social policy conditions, to its claims. It fits well within the neoliberalism of the reconfigured French state.

MOBILIZATION FOR BETTER REPRESENTATION OF WOMEN IN SPAIN

The actions we are calling the parity-democracy movement are not self-named as such, as we have already said. This is one crucial variation among several that distinguishes these two cases. Despite these differences, however, it is helpful to examine the Spanish story for what it tells us about the questions at hand and particularly our expectations about state reconfiguration on social movements. Our argument is that the ways that state reconfiguration has occurred in Spain, while similar in many ways to what happened in France, were tempered by continuing differences between the two political families of left and right. One result is that the movements have not followed the same patterns.

Before moving to that analysis, we will dispose of one hypothesis. This is that the existence and political activity of the groups pressing for the election of more women is due to "need." While France remained at the bottom of the pack in Europe throughout the 1990s, Spain's location was better. The presence of women in political decision making has been increasing in Spain in the twenty years of democracy and has reached the middle of the EU list. In 1995, one in four (24%) representatives in the lower chamber were

---

[16] Family policy, as many other public policies, had never been an important concern of the French women's movement.

women and the increase continued even when the conservatives were elected in 1996 and 2000.[17] Such a continuous increase of women in high-ranked political positions might have, then, weakened the argument that new strategies (especially mandatory quotas for all electoral lists) would have to be tried in order to increase the proportion of female politicians. Opponents can always argue that in some years or decades the number of women politicians will be equal to those of men, if things continue to work in the usual way. The parity-democracy movement, however, seeks faster change.

In part, however, the increase in numbers is due to the quotas established by parties of the left in the 1980s. These, in turn, were the result of mobilizing within parties of the left and the unions even before 1975. Women in the Communist Party (Partido Comunista de España, PCE, later included in the electoral coalition of Izquierda Unida, IU) and in the trade union formerly close to it, the Workers' Commissions (Comisiones Obreras, CCOO), managed to form women's committees at the highest possible organizational level since the beginning. In contrast, women in the Socialist Party (Partido Socialista Obero Español, PSOE) and the union formerly close to it, the General Workers' Union (Unión General de Trabajadores, UGT) initially formed women's units with a lower profile (Threlfall 1996: 119, 138). Feminists were active within the PSOE at least since the beginning of the transition to democracy and sought organizational status within the party. In 1976, a women's caucus (a kind of study group) called Women and Socialism (Mujer y Socialismo) was formed. In 1981, one of its members was elected to the PSOE executive committee, and others followed. In December 1984 the women's caucus was raised to the status of a women's secretariat at the federal executive level (Threlfall 1985).

The left-wing parties established internal quotas. The IU was consistently the third largest party in elections (except in two national elections). It was created by the merger of the Communist Party and other parties to the left of the Socialists, and since 1986 has had a commitment to gender equity and a quota for women in its statutes (*El País*, August 31, 1998). The PSOE, which governed Spain from 1982 until 1996, also established a 25% quota for women in 1988.

Without taking a stand on the claim that change will happen automatically, it seems reasonable to assume that more than "need" was in play. Moreover, several French parties, including the Socialists, have had quotas for many years, without much effect (Praud 1988). Quotas are not sufficient, then, to account for French-Spanish differences. Moreover, Spanish feminists themselves are mobilizing for new strategies and it is their expressed interest which convinces us that more is going on and more attention is needed.

---

[17] This proportion is above those of Belgium, France, Greece, Ireland, Italy, Luxembourg, Portugal, and the United Kingdom, and is very close to those of Germany and Austria, although below the Nordic countries and the Netherlands (Uriarte and Elizondo 1997: 338).

As indicated in the opening paragraph of this chapter, in August 1998 it appeared that the socialists would present a bill to reform the electoral law, thereby instituting a compulsory quota for all parties. This expectation was the product of the on-going efforts of the parity-democracy movement, a very loose set of feminist activists in left-wing political parties and in women's groups mobilized in favor of better representation of women in state structures. Although the announcement was premature, and the bill was not forthcoming, the history leading up to it does reveal the story of the democratic-parity movement.

Issues of representation have preoccupied Spanish feminists for many years. The first democratic elections in four decades, in June 1977, raised expectations among many advocates of women's rights (Durán and Gallego 1986: 208–209). Therefore, on July 13, 1977, at the first meeting of the Congress of Deputies, women's rights activists presented their manifesto in support of the twenty-five women elected to parliament, denounced the fact that there were so few elected, and asked the three feminist MPs to push the feminist agenda in Congress (Escario et al., 1996: 270–272). Through these years, however, the women's movement, albeit weaker than in some countries, pursued an ambitious agenda that went far beyond issues of women's presence in politics. In the 1970s and through the 1980s, among the goals pursued were equality before the law, reproductive rights such as decriminalization of the selling and advertising of contraceptives (achieved in 1978), a divorce law (obtained in 1981), legalization of abortion,[18] criminalization of sexual violence, and equal employment policies. Because in the 1970s the expansion of the welfare state was still seen as a feasible goal by many social and political actors, feminists also concentrated on pressing for social rights which would benefit women.

Since then, as many of the most pressing legal changes (divorce, contraception, violence) had been achieved and as the goals for and spending on social policy have been scaled back, the issue of representation has taken up more of the agenda. Moreover, because the Spanish women's movement in general has involved women within parties, it is not surprising that they have come to focus on matters of access to elected office, both within their parties and more generally.

The current Spanish democratic-parity movement consists of feminist leaders and activists in political parties and in women's organizations,

---

[18] Abortion was illegal in Spain until passage of the 1985 "organic law." Abortion is now permitted under three circumstances: when the woman has been raped, when the pregnancy seriously endangers the woman's life, and when the fetus has malformations. An organic law (*Ley orgánica*) regulates, among other matters, fundamental rights and public liberties. An absolute majority of the Lower Chamber, in a final vote of the whole project, is necessary for approval, modification, or derogation of an organic law. For an ordinary law only a simple majority is required.

primarily from the left.[19] It includes feminists from the Socialist Party and
left-wing political parties to the left of the PSOE, such as the United Left
(Izquierda Unida, IU) and the New Left (Nueva Izquierda, NI).[20] As for
women's associations, the parity movement rose out of well-known women's
groups mainly linked to political parties, including (among others): the
Federation of Progressive Women (Federación de Mujeres Progresistas),
close to the Socialist Party, and the Dolores Ibárruri Foundation (Fundación
Dolores Ibárruri), close to the United Left. Other much less known feminist
groups, that rarely receive mass media attention, such as the Forum of Feminist Politics (Forum de Política Feminista), are also mobilized in favor of
parity democracy.

The conservative PP and women's associations close to it are not mobilized around the issue of political representation, even if their numbers in
elected office have also been increasing since the PP won the elections of
1996 and 2000. As with many other conservative parties (although not, as
we have seen, those in France), women from these parties think that it is
wrong to intervene in the recruitment process in order to elect more women.
For instance, Amalia Gómez, General Secretariat of Social Affairs in the first
PP government, dismissed such efforts as "the wonderbra quota" (*la cuota
del wonderbra*) (*El País* May 18, 1997). Her more restrained colleagues term
quotas a form of discrimination (see Isabel Tocino, PP Minister of the Environment in *Mujeres* 1994, (13) 22–23). Others claim that only their party
gives women real opportunities to gain the centers of power, in contrast to
the artificial quotas of the PSOE (*El País* February 19, 1999).

Conservative women argue instead that the process must be "fair" and
"neutral," so that the "best people" (including women) can be elected. Some
may accept "soft" measures (such as encouraging women to stand for office) but oppose "hard" ones (such as quotas). Therefore, the story of the

[19] The sources for this case study mainly consist of: 1) in-depth semistructured interviews with
women leaders and activists of political parties and of women's organizations conducted
by Celia Valiente in April and May 1999; 2) press articles from *El País* (the main national
newspaper) and *Mujeres* (the publication of the Women's Institute, the main institution at the
central state level in charge of improving women's status); and 3) published and unpublished
documents of political parties and women's organizations. Personal interviews and press
files are more important sources for the Spanish case than for the French for three reasons.
First, there are hardly any academic sources on the topic. Second, press articles are the
only published material. Third, local, regional, and European elections will be held in Spain
in June 1999. At the time of interviewing (April 1999), political parties were elaborating
electoral lists (in Spain there are closed lists). It was especially important to trace the fight
for parity democracy at the moment of making the lists. This could only be done with the
help of press articles and personal interviews.

[20] This movement is feminist, in the sense that its members claim to be so. This is especially important in Spain, where the term *feminist* is usually employed in a derogatory way. Therefore,
many people who believe in the goals of feminism refuse to use the word *feminism* to describe
their beliefs and practices. Yet in this case, the term is used.

democratic-parity movement in Spain is one that tilts to the left, and this is a difference between it and the French movement, characterized by cross-partisanship from the beginning.

Important in Spain, just as in France, is a group formerly called the Spanish Association to Support the European Women's Lobby (Asociación Española de Apoyo al Lobby Europeo), and now named the Spanish Coordination for the European Women's Lobby (Coordinadora Española para el Lobby Europeo de Mujeres). This umbrella organization active in national and EU politics has close ties with the Socialist Party and is the sister organization to France's CLEF.

As the presence of this latter group suggests, multilevel politics has been important to the Spanish story for a decade. International arenas, especially the EU and the UN World Conference of Beijing (1995), were used by Spanish feminists to promote their agenda of equal gender representation in politics. Supranational organizations served as public forums where activists could express demands as well as act as a source of ideas and material resources supporting development of parity demands in domestic politics. Indeed, informants report that even Spanish women from the PP, the conservative party, have become more favorable to the idea of increasing the number of women in political decision-making positions after having attended European-level meetings, where they observed conservative colleagues from other member states promoting that goal (Paloma Saavedra, interview).

The first Spanish moves in favor of parity in the 1990s had a clear European and international dimension. On September 22, 1990, the European Women's Lobby was created, with CLEF from France and a Spanish group soon joining. The European lobby includes Europe-wide women's organizations as well as women's umbrella organizations from each EU member-state. The purpose of this lobby is to promote women's interests at the level of the EU (Hoskyns 1996: 185–186). The Spanish Association to Support the European Women's Lobby was founded in March 1993. It is an umbrella body of women's groups funded mainly with European money. It quickly began to promote parity; in 1994, the Spanish association presented a motion to the General Assembly of the European Women's Lobby in favor of it (*Mujeres* 1994: (13) 23–24).

Spaniards have also been active within the institutions of the EU and through them the UN. In 1994 and 1995, preparation of the Beijing Conference included many events, all of which usually had at least one session related to the topic of equal representation of women and men in politics. These activities were organized, among others, by the Spanish state, the European Union, the UN Committee on the Elimination of Discrimination Against Women, and Spanish women's associations from civil society. The Spanish state, through its Ministry of Social Affairs, was very active in the preparation of the Beijing Conference, because Spain held the presidency of the EU in the second half of 1995 when the conference took place. The Beijing platform of September 1995 described access to political office as crucial for women's well-being and encouraged states to make the necessary provisions for the fulfilment of the aim, including a reform in electoral law (*El País*, November 2, 1998). In addition, the Fourth EU Action Program on Equal Opportunities (1996–2000) was approved in December 1995, when the EU presidency was held by Spain. One of the main objectives of this action plan was the equal participation of women and men in decision making in all fields.

Mobilization also occurred within Spain. For instance, in October 1997 a European congress of political management by women (Congreso Europeo sobre Gestión Política de las Mujeres) was organized in Bilbao by the feminist group Lambroa (Colectivo Feminista Lambroa) to create a women's list for the European elections of June 1999. Female politicians from the parties to the left of the PSOE and regionalist parties were invited to recount their political experiences (*El País*, October 27, 1997). There have also been studies commissioned on the topic of women in decision-making positions, such as the research undertaken by the Dolores Ibárruri Foundation (1998) on the local level. The results were presented in a seminar attended mainly by local politicians from all political parties.

During the campaigns leading up to the elections of June 1999, activists energetically initiated public debates on the issue of women's access to political decision making. However, the proposal to change the electoral law in order to make quotas mandatory for all political parties is under consideration not only in feminist circles (as it is usually the case with gender matters in Spain) but also in the general political arenas.

Just as we saw in France, when the debate about the crisis of representation broke out and involved male as well as female politicians, several people who usually do not participate in debates on gender equality have made significant interventions on the topic. Such is the case, among others, of Gregorio Peces Barba, former president of the Congress of Deputies (a member of the PSOE) and currently president of the Universidad Carlos III de Madrid, and Alfonso Ruiz-Miguel, professor of philosophy of law at the Universidad Autónoma de Madrid. Both men have published articles, the first in *El País*, the country's major newspaper, and the second in *Claves de Razón Práctica*, a leading journal of opinion (Peces-Barba 1999; Ruiz-Miguel 1999). Both articles support parity activists' call to amend the electoral law and develop the claim that such a reform is constitutional.

In addition, in May 1999 the Spanish Coordination for the European Women's Lobby (Coordinadora Española para el Lobby Europeo de Mujeres, CELEM) organized an international conference on the topic including politicians and scholars from EU member states and the European institutions. Parity activists in Spain are fully aware of the danger of Spain finding itself in the same situation as France or Italy, whose constitutional courts have already declared quotas unconstitutional. Moreover, as previously mentioned, activists are not calling for constitutional reform because of the link to the Basque issue. Despite these examples of cross-party activities, however, a major distinction between the French and Spanish actions in favor of parity is that the Iberian actions almost completely respect the left-right divide. Moreover, while women's organizations from civil society play a not negligible role, it remains a secondary one. The initiative has belonged to the Socialist Party.

In general, all individual activists and groups that fight for parity democracy see themselves on the left. The core of the movement is formed by feminist leaders and activists from the Socialist Party and women's associations in civil society but close to the PSOE (Elena Valenciano, interview). The parity movement has been unable – and is probably unwilling – to attract members from the right. The conservative party in government and Women for Democracy (Mujeres para la Democracia), the main women's association very close to the PP, never speak of "parity democracy." They strongly oppose any attempt to make equal representation of women and men mandatory for all political parties and in all state institutions. Indeed, most right-wing parties reject even voluntary quotas.

Even more reflective of the continuing importance of traditional left-right splits in Spain is the fact that there are divisions *within* the left, just as the French (and most other movements) were divided in the 1970s and 1980s. There are groups and activists across the broad left promoting parity democracy, but they do not do so together with PSOE activists. The separation of parity activists who belong or are close to different left-wing parties is not total, of course. Some rather limited joint actions have been undertaken. The most common way such a joint action happens is that a group organizes an event and invites representatives from the other parts of the left. For instance, when PSOE activists organize a debate on parity democracy, they will usually invite a speaker from the United Left and perhaps someone from the New Left. Perhaps only one non-PSOE person will be invited. Moreover, such invitations rarely go to right-wing parity activists. As a result, individual events clearly belong to each party or group; they are not nonpartisan (Pilar Folguera, interview).

Keeping the debate within the bounds of traditional discourse helps to explain the life story of parity in Spain. It also, as we will see, shapes the reconfiguration of the state, where the discourse about the role of the state and the relationship between state and civil society still distinguishes between the two major political families of left and right. Most movement has been in the direction of quotas, rather than parity, and these quotas have been established by the parties themselves. After the defeat of the PSOE government in the 1996 general elections, the party's General Secretariat for Women's Participation (Secretaría de Participación de la Mujer) and the feminist lobby within the PSOE took up the parity democracy issue and provoked a debate. At the Thirty-fourth PSOE Federal Congress (June 20–22, 1997) a resolution passed limiting the presence of candidates of a single sex to no more than 60% in internal party positions and on electoral lists. This was, in other words, an increase of the party's quota from 25% to 40%.

The process of increasing the number of party positions held by women seems to have happened in all left-wing parties (Pilar Arias, Patrocinio de las Heras, and Caridad García, interviews). Indeed, the parity agenda is now being instituted by the newest party on the left. The New Left (Nueva Izquierda, NI) originated from a split of the United Left. Its first congress in 1998 set up a governing structure in which 50% of all decision-making positions were occupied by women.

The actual implementation of quotas for candidates has proven more difficult, however. Indeed, getting the PSOE to respect its own commitment to parity has not been easy. For example, in the regional elections of Galicia (December 1997) and the Basque region (October 1998), the PSOE lists were only 20% and 33% female respectively (*El País*, January 31, 1999). Parity activists in the PSOE mobilized in the spring 1999 to avoid a repetition of this failure to respect the party's position. Key to this action was the fact that two parity activists were members not only of the PSOE executive committee but also of the party committee in charge of the approval of electoral lists: Micaela Navarro (Secretary for Women's Participation) and Carmen Martínez-Ten (a former director of the Women's Institute). The approval of electoral parity lists was controversial, involving as it did rejection of some electoral lists prepared by PSOE leaders for their electoral districts. The committee defined parity lists as those containing at least 40% of women in winning positions.[21] Eventually, however, almost all PSOE lists fulfilled the 40% quota (Micaela Navarro, interview).

There is also another aspect of internal politics that has led feminists to intensify their call for parity and therefore compulsory quotas. The PSOE has a primary system, since 1997, used to designate the candidate for prime minister and to select candidates to other posts including the Basque *Lehendakari*. While some parity activists within the PSOE celebrated the move to primaries, as a mechanism for internal democracy within parties, others soon discovered to their dismay that primaries are very often an exclusively male business. Most of the people who compete in primaries and win them are men. Women tend not to run in primaries and those who dare to compete are usually not elected. There are several reasons for this lack of success, among them, women often lack the backing of important sectors of the party or women are much less known by PSOE members in their districts than male candidates with whom they compete. In the interviews conducted for this chapter no parity activist was openly against primaries, since this position is taboo within many sectors of the PSOE. Nonetheless, all of them confessed

---

[21] Winning positions in a given electoral district were defined as the positions that the PSOE had won in the earlier local, regional, and European elections (Carmen Martínez-Ten, interview).

that they had not foreseen the short-term detrimental consequences of primaries for the representation of women. All of them also declared that other things being equal, quotas would be less effective if primaries continue to be held than in the absence of primaries.

In part to avoid such difficult internal politics, less than two months after being elected Secretary for Women's Participation of the PSOE Micaela Navarro announced her goal of reforming the electoral law to force all political parties to include a minimum percentage of women in their lists (*El País*, August 8, 1997). After what turned out to be a premature announcement of a PSOE-sponsored bill to establish a compulsory 40% quota, the male leadership backed down. Supporters of such a bill mobilized within the party, but could not carry the day. The General-Secretary of the PSOE, Joaquín Almunia, and the candidate for prime minister in the next general election, José Borrell, both agreed that there was a risk that the reform could be struck down by the Constitutional Court (*El País*, December 27, 1998). Thus, convincing the PSOE to move on changing the law proved impossible, despite the expressed support from other left-wing parties. The idea has been revived, however, and is included in the party's platform for the next election (Patrocinio de las Heras, communication).

The Spanish parity movement also differs from the French in that it retains explicit policy goals. Some documents do represent gender parity as an end in itself, as a matter of justice.[22] Parity activists picture themselves as followers of the first suffragists, who fought for the right to vote, while they are fighting for the right of women to be elected. Nevertheless, in the same documents and in the interviews conducted for this study, gender parity is also claimed because activists also maintain a social agenda. The argument goes like this. If women and men were equally represented in the political arena, policy outcomes would be different and more positive. Policy outcomes would better meet the particular needs of women. Policies would be elaborated in a more consensual way. Public measures would include the interests not only of women but also of other, less-privileged groups.

Nor is achieving more women in elected office the principal aim of the Spanish parity movement. It is one among other components of a broader feminist agenda. Equal sharing of family responsibilities is another goal almost always present in parity documents. The argument is that the distinction between the private and the public is fictitious since the personal is political.

---

[22] Since there are no "founding documents" in the parity movement in Spain, we use as the main parity documents five articles on the topic published in *El País* by Cristina Alberdi, Minister of Social Issues, 1993–6 (1998); Inés Alberdi, first Director of the Women's Institute, 1983–8 (1994); Carlota Bustelo (1992) (all three are feminist PSOE activists); Enriqueta Chicano (1999) (President of the Federation of Progressive Women); and María Ángeles Ruíz-Tagle (1999) (President of the Spanish Association to Support the European Women's Lobby).

Responsibilities should be shared: Political decision making should not be the monopoly of men, as family and caring responsibilities should not be the monopoly of women. Spanish parity documents and the women interviewed for this chapter also referred to the need to develop care services in the welfare state, to help women combine their professional and family responsibilities.

In all these regards, the Spanish movement is still promoting the social rights of citizenship. Indeed, parity activists often claim to defend a "new social contract" between men and women, with three dimensions: equal access to political decision making; equal right to paid employment; and equal sharing of caring responsibilities.[23] While political rights come to the fore in interparty debate, social matters still remain a visible part of the feminist agenda.

CONCLUSION

The first section of this chapter suggested that the reconfiguration of the state has had three consequences for patterns of mobilization of the women's movement. Structural changes will make multilevel politics more common. Changing relationships between state and civil society and shifting discourses about the role of the state will blur traditional left-right distinctions, enhancing cross-party actions and giving political rights precedence over social rights. Our analysis reveals that these changes in patterns of mobilization can be observed in both France and Spain, but more consistently in the former than the latter, in large part because the internal party scene remains, as we have already noted, more differentiated in the Iberian case.

Spain has been a major contributor to the politics of the EU, and the democratic-parity movement was actively present in developing and promoting the European agenda as well as using the resources of the EU within Spain. Thus, multilevel politics are present as in France. However, the traditional left-right moorings of Spanish politics have not disappeared as much as they have in France. Cross-partisanship is not the norm. Right-wing parties scorn the PSOE's and other leftist parties' enthusiasm for quotas, although they are nominating women. The left uses the language of parity when calling for quotas, while the PP has coined another expression. It speaks of "equilibrated representation" (*representación equilibrada*) (Rosario Barrios, interview). Moreover, the language of social rights has not been abandoned; increased participation by women is sought *in order to* achieve a broader agenda rather than simply to achieve gender justice. There is a left discourse, coming from both the PSOE and its leftist competitors, defending the welfare state (albeit a retrenched one . . .) while the right displays more interest in shifting responsibility from the state via downloading. Claims for increased representation of women track this distinction; the democratic-parity movement is confined to the left.

---

[23] One might note that the issue of sexuality is completely absent from this agenda.

The French case shows all three patterns reflecting the effects of state re-configuration on the French women's movement. From the beginning, multilevel action was key, and is likely to remain so. Secondly, since 1992 the French parity movement has been decidedly and consistently cross-partisan. This is in sharp contrast to other parts of the women's movement, such as the National Assizes, that traced the more traditional left-right divide. Thirdly, the parity movement has become the acceptable, albeit controversial, face of the women's movement, gaining support from politicians and having at least one version of its claim recognized via constitutional reform. Its agenda of ignoring differences in policy content and focusing only on the gender of candidates has gained favor from politicians across a wide political spectrum.

Therefore, domestic politics influence the ways in which the movement for women's representation is actually inscribed in politics. The left-right divide continues to characterize Spanish politics in general, and the democratic-parity movement, in contrast to that of France, incorporates a policy agenda into its claims for better access for women to elected office. The defenders of the social agenda have not been sidelined.

Interviews for the Spanish Case

Arévalo, Nuria. President of Young Women. Madrid, April 22, 1999.

Arias, Pilar. Coordinator of the Women's Section of the New Left in the Region of Madrid. Madrid, April 19, 1999.

Barrios, Rosario. Parliamentary Adviser on social affairs to the conservative group in the Congress of Deputies. Madrid, April 27, 1999.

Bernard, Norma. President of Socialist Youth of Aragon. Madrid, April 27, 1999.

Candela, Milagros. President of the Association for Feminist Thought and Action. Madrid, April 14, 1999.

Chicano, Enriqueta. President of the Federation of Progressive Women. Madrid, April 15, 1999.

De las Heras, Patrocinio. Local Councillor from the Socialist Party in the City of Madrid. Madrid, April 20, 1999.

Folguera, Pilar. Vice President of the Spanish Association to Support the European Women's Lobby. Madrid, April 14, 1999.

García, Caridad. Secretariat of Women in the United Left in the Region of Madrid. Madrid, April 21, 1999.

González, Lucía. Leader of the Commission on Rights and Liberties in the United Left in the Region of Madrid. Madrid, May 4, 1999.

Martínez-Ten, Carmen. Member of the Executive Committee of the Socialist Party. Madrid, May 4, 1999.

Navarro, Micaela. Secretary of Women's Participation in the Socialist Party. Madrid, April 13, 1999.

San José, Begoña. President of Forum of Feminist Politics. Madrid, April 22, 1999.

Saavedra, Paloma. Chief of the Department (*Jefa de Gabinete*) of the Minister of Social Affairs (1993–6). Madrid, April 28, 1999.

Valenciano, Elena. Director of Foundation Women. Personal interview. Madrid, April 16, 1999.

5

Refuge in Reconfigured States

Shelter Movements in the United States, Britain, and Sweden

R. Amy Elman

States are often credited with influencing the dynamics of women's movements, whereas feminist efforts to end violence against women are infrequently examined in ways that underscore their transformative influence on states. This chapter explores the ways in which shelter movements in the United States, Britain, and Sweden engaged their states in a series of complicated interactions that led to their mutual alterations. In general, shelter movements institutionalized as states developed policies and programs to mitigate violence against women.[1] Over time, the boundaries between movements and states became difficult to delineate, the former professionalized as the latter legitimized, a condition underscored by the eventual development of cooperative "multiagency" initiatives within all three countries.[2]

The question to consider is whether intensified state/movement interaction and the subsequent blurring of boundaries diminished the revolutionary aspirations of these movements and hindered bold attempts at reform. Or, by contrast, did this augmented interplay encourage innovative and well-implemented policies on behalf of battered women?

A comparative overview and appraisal of these developments provides an expanded field from which to contemplate the costs and benefits that movements derive from engaging reconfigured states. The selection of both

---

[1] Meyer and Tarrow portray institutionalization as a process that can "allow dissidents to lodge claims *and* permit states to manage dissent without stifling it" (1998a: 21). My concern is that the state's management of movements can eventually compromise the ability of even moderates within them to launch a credible threat of disruption to "normal politics." Given that any movement's raison d'être relies on its capacity for such commotion, there is cause for concern, though not alarm (see Katzenstein 1998a and note 12 this chapter. As well, see the various chapters in Ferree and Martin 1995).

[2] Multiagency initiatives endeavor to bring all relevant statutory and voluntary sector agencies, including shelters, together to coordinate their services and build a relatively more comprehensive (and preventive) response to violence against women. "Multiagency" and "interagency" will be used interchangeably throughout this chapter.

Sweden and the United States draws on my previous scholarship concerning the differing structure of these states (1996) and my active engagement within their women's movements to counter male violence. Britain, by contrast, furnishes a unique opportunity to extend and refine my analysis by considering a movement whose example inspired U.S. and Swedish women to take action to end male violence. In addition, the composition of the British state rests midway between the fragmentation of U.S. federalism and its highly centralized counterpart, Swedish corporatism. Exploring the mobilization of similar movements within dissimilar state structures encourages an appreciation of the ways in which states differentially affect the access that the women's movements have to authority, political consciousness, cohesiveness, and various strategies. Moreover, focusing specifically on efforts to end male violence provides a lens through which to explore a feminist challenge to one of the most tangible expressions of male power within any state.

This chapter commences with a brief overview of the origins of the shelter movements in all three states. It then considers the intricate interactions of movements in their pursuit of state efforts to enhance the immediate safety of battered women. It concludes with a critical synopsis of recent reforms and suggests that as these states responded to feminist claims, they became somewhat less explicitly patriarchal. In turn, many activists gradually relinquished their most radical inclinations, in ways often imperceptible to outsiders and even, sometimes, to themselves.

SHELTER ORIGINS

If violence against women typified the most brutal aspects of women's subordination, women's shelters epitomized its transcendence. Shelters, thus, became an essential grass-roots component of women's liberation movements. Within all three countries, most shelters provided similar essential functions. Principal among these was a physical space that offered women temporary refuge from the men who abused them and the safety women needed to plan and pursue new lives. They also provided a space within which numerous activists gained invaluable political experience in their struggle for social change.

In Britain and the United States, feminist movements provided the structural and ideological foundation upon which the battered women's movement was built (Dobash and Dobash 1992; Tierney 1982). Feminists in the legal, social service, and health-care professions provided a preexisting network of activists with considerable experience in working on other women's issues. As feminists, most opposed hierarchy and regarded the traditional political system as deeply patriarchal. Movement resources, however minimal, were typically pooled and transformed to assist women most in need.

Britain's first battered women's shelter, Chiswick Women's Aid, was established in 1972 when a woman sought refuge from her abusive husband in a London women's community center. As other women followed suit, the center was slowly transformed into a crowded refuge with an open-door policy until the need for more space necessitated a move. Initially financed by the Hounslow Council (London), the small house was replaced by a large, privately donated mansion. In 1974, newly formed Women's Aid groups from England, Scotland, and Wales held a national meeting and established the National Women's Aid Federation to represent them. Over the next fifteen years, activists in England had established nearly a hundred refuges and those in Scotland and Wales nearly a third as many. During this period, these shelters served tens of thousands of women and children seeking safety. On occasion, however, they were compelled to turn others away. Though local councils housed a majority of refuges, shelters were poor and sometimes lacked space. In consequence, activists relied on volunteer staffing and private donations for basics like food and furniture.

The same year Chiswick Women's Aid was established, a U.S. feminist legal-aid collective that evolved from a consciousness-raising group in Minnesota began a crisis telephone line in a county legal aid office. Like their British counterparts, U.S. activists soon discovered that battered women were essentially homeless if they decided to leave their assailants. Responding to the problem, members of the collective simply took battered women into their own homes (forming "safe-home networks") until they could find them a place of their own and a means of self-support. Two years later, in 1974, these same activists were able to purchase their own house for battered women with donations from numerous individuals, fund-raising events, and grants. Most other shelters across the United States began in precisely the same way, without state funding (see Martin 1976: ch. 10). By 1978 there were approximately 250 shelters throughout the country and the National Coalition Against Domestic Violence (NCADV) was established that year to unite a majority of them. Nearly two decades later, estimates suggest that there are 1,500 shelters offering services ranging from counseling to legal advocacy, childcare, and occupational training (Ms. 1994: 54).

Whatever their dissimilarities and relative limitations, shelters in both the United States and Britain represented women's autonomy. As one British activist remarked, "We ... explode the myth that only men provide security in financial and emotional terms" (in Rhodes and McNeill 1985: 245). The commitment to self-reliance extended well beyond women's individual relationships to men. The state was also at issue; activists in both countries had little faith in "the establishment." Thus, as Betsy Warrior, a founder of the U.S. shelter movement and the editor of the *Battered Women's Directory*, declared:

Laws against wife beating aren't the solution to this problem ... The only short-term solution that is possible is the establishment of houses that could serve as

refuges... Because of the public attitude of apathy – which connotes tacit acceptance of crimes against women – we can't look to social agencies to set up such
refuges but must find ways of establishing them ourselves. (1976: 20–21)

Far from interpreting this and similar positions as threatening, both states
appear to have relished the movements' propensity for self-reliance. For example, when the Parliamentary Select Committee held Britain's first national
hearings on battered women in 1975, shelters received considerable attention and praise. "The committee expressed admiration for the practical work
in refuges, emphasizing volunteerism, the principle of self-help, practical assistance, and the provision of needed services with little financial assistance
from local or national government." (Dobash and Dobash 1992: 122). Em-
bellishing the accomplishments and potentialities of such (private sector)
initiatives provided the ideological scaffolding from which the state could
offload public provision more generally. By the decade's end, ascending right-
wing governments in both countries ardently embraced the rhetoric of private
provision and self-reliance.

By the early 1980s, the success of the U.S. and British movements in reaching battered women had the unintended consequence of making self-reliance
significantly less feasible. As more women were willing to leave their abusive partners, activists were obliged to expand their services. Shelters in both
countries soon discovered that the needs of battered women far exceeded
movement resources, a recognition that came on the heels of reduced public
expenditures which, in turn, made the need for shelter services all the more
urgent.

Under Reagan, U.S. shelters witnessed the state's pursuit of austerity
measures that downloaded the burden of providing social assistance onto
localities. As well, the state offloaded onto the private sector and, by extension, the already limited assets of shelters. For example, in dismantling
the federal job-training program CETA (Comprehensive Employment and
Training Act), Reagan effectively eliminated the major source of funding
for staff salaries within shelters. In frustration, Betsy Warrior proposed that
shelters deliberately place limitations on the services they are willing to provide. She explained: "Instead of allowing communities to shift the burden of
providing medical, legal and economic assistance, and housing onto the meager resources of shelters, communities should be expected to provide these to
all who need them" (1985: 158). In practice, however, the movement found
it difficult to restrict access and utterly impossible to shift responsibility for
such general provision onto a state that had not previously provided it.
Instead, U.S. shelters slowly expanded and vigorously petitioned both the
state *and* the private sector for funding to mitigate the desperation of battered women who sought their assistance.

Britain's shelter movement, by contrast, was relieved of such burdensome
fundraising because it had a significantly more developed welfare state on
which to rely. That is, it retained considerably greater access to affordable

public housing and counted on other sectors as well (for example, a universal health care system and a more generous social security system for women themselves). It would, however, be wrong to underestimate the ways in which the shrinkage in state spending differentially impacted the women who sought their services (Glendinning and Millar 1992). With limited means to purchase or rent new housing, battered women are especially dependent on public provision when fleeing the men who abuse them. And, under Thatcher, the state significantly reduced its stock in public housing through private sales and issued a white paper that ominously predicted an eventual end to public housing. Shelters and other service providers have been coping with the consequences of such offloading ever since. While the shelter movements of both countries approached their states often unenthusiastically, out of fiscal necessity, their differing expectations and outcomes were shaped by the histories of the states to which they turned.

Although state funding solved some problems, it sometimes undermined important movement principles. Several shelters were forced to make organizational changes to fulfill highly competitive funding requirements for government grants. These required, among other conditions, that shelters hire formally trained professionals. According to Andrea Smith, a long-time antiviolence and Native American activist, "This practice excludes most women from full participation, particularly women of color and poor women" (2000–1: 14). Over time, the deeply egalitarian, committed, and collective nature of these movements receded. Shelters began to resemble state social service agencies with professionals employed to serve "clients" (Morgan 1981).

Within a decade, violence against women evolved from a political to a clinical issue and therapy soon supplanted activism in many U.S. and British shelters. The political imperative of collectively challenging male violence (and male power more generally) often came second to the desire of individual women to feel better about themselves (see Kitzinger and Perkins 1993). Eventually, violence was analytically extricated from male power. The heightened visibility extended to "domestic" as opposed to "male" violence obscured the diminished influence of radicals and their analysis.

State funding facilitated institutionalization, professionalization, and de-radicalization in both countries, though less so in Britain where greater access to established social services and affordable public housing assuaged the movement's most cumbersome compromises and fiscal concerns. The British movement thus continued to rely almost entirely on committed feminist volunteers whose original principles and emphasis on autonomy both contributed to and resulted from a preference for grass-roots moderation rather than movement expansion (Dobash and Dobash 1992: 42; Mullender 1996: 3). Under constant pressure to pursue housing purchases and large mortgages, many U.S. shelters bowed to state and market pressures and stressed service provision in ways that minimized social change (Whittier

1995: ch. 3). Still others pursued innovative ways to meet their financial obligations (Elman 1996b: 38). Despite their differing approaches, shelters stress diversified support and are united by a reluctance to accept state financing when it means a consequential loss of their autonomy (Reinelt 1995; Schechter 1988).

Referring to the above movements as "autonomous" may raise some doubt, especially given their growing reliance on state (or even corporate) support. Nonetheless, as the Swedish case makes clear, autonomy is relative. Unlike British and U.S. activists who established shelters with little or no affiliation to political parties or government bureaucracies, Swedish women, at the outset and with little hesitation, worked within political parties. They petitioned the state for public housing and funding with which to establish shelters and services for battered women.

Swedish shelters were established years after those in Britain and the United States. The first opened in 1979 in Gothenburg; later that same year another opened in Stockholm. Birgitta Wistrand, a former chair of the Frederika Bremer Association, a women's rights organization, explains that feminist initiatives were introduced later, in part, because "the ideas behind the movement for women's rights and emancipation have their sources abroad" (1981: 10). In Sweden, activists were more likely to have had experience working within the established political system (through, for example, the women's sections of political parties) than outside of it (within an autonomous feminist movement). Like many of their Italian and Spanish counterparts, most activists were decidedly of the left and the majority of Sweden's first battered women's advocates had neither participated in consciousness-raising groups nor been part of a feminist movement. Indeed, they strenuously objected to feminism. The establishment of one of Sweden's first shelters, the All Women's House, in Stockholm, serves to illustrate this point.

Those who began the Stockholm shelter were indirectly affiliated with the Social Democratic Party, a party synonymous with Swedish governance (Przeworski 1989).[3] The party intervened on behalf of shelter activists to oppose a feminist coalition that had worked for three years to obtain a center for all women, not only for those who were battered. The women who founded the shelter were, by contrast, operating out of a more conventional social-service approach to battered women and objected to the feminist politics and lesbian constituency of the original coalition.

The party eventually secured the house that was to be the women's center and gave it to the heterosexual battered women's advocates. The politicians explained that the advocates' program "was well in line with

---

[3] Indeed, Sweden's Social Democrats have had the longest period of social democratic rule anywhere. They ruled without interruption from 1932 to 1976 and again from 1982 until their defeat in 1991 when the Moderates replaced them for a single term (until 1994).

the municipality's other social welfare efforts and had the qualifications necessary to enable it to become a good complement to the state-run social services" (in Eduards 1997: 129). On the eve of this decision, councilwoman Brit Rundberg despaired that "Stockholm would be the first and only city in the world to have a women's center without a women's movement behind it" (in Eduards 1997: 130).

A tradition of deference to and assimilation within male-dominated political parties (and the Social Democrats more specifically) often resulted in a diminished solidarity among Swedish women. The loyalty that women traditionally extended to the established political parties compromised the effectiveness with which they could otherwise cooperate and mobilize to achieve shared objectives (Hernes 1988). Thus, common undertakings like the establishment of safe home networks were rarely initiated. Still others, such as the founding of shelters, were vulnerable to immediate and unmitigated state intervention. This was typified by the Social Democratic Party's ability to arbitrate the disagreements among activists over women's (shelter) space. One unfortunate result of this bitter struggle was the alienation of many feminists from the shelter movement. In 1984, with limited feminist support, advocates for battered women established the National Organization of Emergency Shelters in Sweden (ROKS).[4]

The relative and persistent absence of feminism within Sweden's shelter movement is most conspicuously evidenced in the circumscribed services it maintains and the reluctance of its activists to assume greater personal responsibility for the battered women in their communities. Indeed, shelter hours are limited and the very term is often misleadingly extended to mere crisis phone lines with sparse and sometimes erratic contact hours. Few activists are available on a twenty-four-hour emergency basis and those that are can be accessed through the police and/or social services.

The apparent reserve of most activists to expand their services may result from a long-standing expectation of favorable state intervention though a comparative consideration of Sweden's undistinguished response to woman battery suggests that such faith may be misplaced (Elman 1996b; 2001a). Like their British counterparts, nearly all of Sweden's shelters receive some support from local councils and/or from social welfare departments, principally to cover rental costs. Aside from this assistance, Sweden's shelters also depend almost exclusively on volunteers, a circumstance as enthusiastically embraced by the Swedish state as by its British and U.S. counterparts. However, in Sweden's shelters, the centrality of volunteerism was hardly an outgrowth of feminist ideology. Rather, it was an economic imperative as refuges lacked the support with which to establish paid staff. Moreover, though Swedes typically view volunteerism

---

[4] ROKS is the Swedish acronym for *Riksorganisationen för kvinnojourer i Sverige*.

contemptuously, no other service provider has depended so thoroughly upon it. This unique circumstance cannot be overemphasized as Swedish authorities otherwise regard unpaid labor as an aberration, unfitting of a social democracy because the state is presumed to provide. Thus, compared to other states, devolution's transnational appeal in privileging volunteerism has – with the notable exception of the shelter workers – been tempered in Sweden.

The potent combination of neoconservative economics and social agenda that, in the 1980s, soared in the United States and Britain had considerably less allure in Sweden. This is not to suggest that Sweden did not pursue austerity measures of its own, like reductions in sick-leave payments and other policies that clearly disadvantaged women (see Elman 1993). Rather, these and other cutbacks were late in coming and marginal by comparison (Sainsbury 1996). "Unlike most other capitalist welfare states, Swedish governments protected and expanded the welfare state during the recession of the 1970s" (Ginsburg 1993: 174). To date, Swedes have maintained a relatively entrenched resistance at the center to the political attack on the welfare state. This was particularly evident when Swedes opted out of the direction in which the conservative Moderates had taken them after only one term (1991–4). In 1994 the Social Democrats resumed power.[5]

Tethered closely to the state from its inception, Sweden's shelter movement differed significantly from both its British and U.S. counterparts whose disdain for and distance from the establishment was once unambiguously expressed. Swedish and British shelters may have shared a relatively more robust welfare state and, thus, a greater reliance on support from local councils and/or social welfare departments; however, there were few similarities beyond this. British shelters, like their U.S. equivalents, remained relatively autonomous from the state and anchored in a distinctive preference for feminist, not party, politics. Nonetheless, shelter activists from both Britain and the United States could ill afford to ignore the conventional machinations of state, particularly as their governments could either dispose or withhold desperately needed resources. Eventually, closer connections emerged and the Swedish shelter movement, once distinctive for its nearness to the state, now seems less an oddity.

What remains at issue is how the differing origins of all three movements and the structure of their states affected the intensified interaction and subsequent adoption and implementation of reforms and policies for battered women. It is especially important to explore efforts that reached beyond the confines of shelters because these are spaces to which women fled but where they could not live permanently.

---

[5] Given the Social Democrats are increasingly indistinguishable from their conservative opposition, caution is needed in this assessment (Elman 1993).

FROM REFUGE TO REFORM

Shelters provide temporary refuge and a condemnation of violence, but they do not possess the means to stop male violence. Because states alone possess the monopoly on the legitimate use of force, shelter activists pursued state power on behalf of battered women to delegitimize male violence. Their efforts further transformed the overtly patriarchal character of states that had indeed once codified such abuse.

U.S. legal doctrine officially declared wife battery an acceptable practice as long as the instrument of assault (for example, whip) was no thicker than the batterer's thumb (*Bradley v. State*, 1824). Similarly, Swedish laws authorized men to beat their wives and, until 1864, imposed no restraints upon them. In Britain husbands retained a legal right to chastise their wives until 1891; thereafter authorities continued to condone woman abuse for decades longer.

Despite the absence of legal sanctions in all three states, the indifference to battered women remained explicitly embedded in their criminal justice systems' response to it. As recently as 1975, the London Metropolitan Police Department reported that:

Whereas it is a general principle of police practice not to intervene in a situation which existed or had existed between a husband and wife in the course of which the wife had suffered some personal attack, any assault upon a wife by her husband which amounted to physical injury of a serious nature is a criminal offence which it is the duty of the police to follow up and prosecute (in Hester and Radford 1997: 83)

Barring those assaults that result in "physical injury of a serious nature," nonintervention was clearly the preferred strategy of police officers; a position similar to that was found in Sweden (Elman and Eduards 1991) and the United States (Ferraro 1989).

What was required in all three countries was a transformation in consciousness, an altered understanding of what constitutes a crime. The movements accomplished this to various degrees, in ways both distinctive and similar.

The United States

The decentralized structure of the U.S. state posed legislative obstacles that pushed many within the shelter movement to seek legal reform through litigation. Though laws could be passed at the state and federal level, lobbying in both instances often proved cumbersome given the bicameral structure of legislatures and the fact that opposition parties sometimes control legislative committees. Instead, courts often eclipse legislatures and bureaucracies in importance as choice channels through which activists pursue social change. Several Supreme Court decisions in the 1960s opened the way for numerous liability suits against public authorities. By the mid-1970s, battered women's advocates successfully argued that the various arrest-avoidance policies of police departments violated the equal protection clause of the Constitution's 14th Amendment (*Bruno v. Codd* 1977; *Scott v. Hart* 1976). In consequence, courts ordered police departments to change their policies to acknowledge the criminal dimensions of woman battery. Orders of protection, first introduced in 1976, to prohibit batterers from further contact with their victims, were more rigorously enforced and soon encompassed broad areas of jurisdiction, including evicting men from their residences.

As the threat of costly lawsuits brought against a municipality or police department increased during the 1980s, a majority of state legislatures adopted proarrest policies to both offset liability and enhance their responsiveness to battered women. In addition, police departments maintained more thorough reports and judges increased the availability and enforcement of protective orders. Victim/witness assistance programs and special prosecution units were also established to elevate prosecution and conviction rates.

Though these measures have been impressive (Elman 1996b; Ferraro 1993), advocates for battered women insisted that without the coordinated commitment of the criminal justice system to their implementation, innovation would languish and women's lives would be lost. In consequence, activists became increasingly involved in multiagency networks with close ties to the criminal justice system. One of the country's first was the Domestic Abuse Intervention Project (DAIP), established in 1980 by feminists in Duluth, Minnesota. In addition to providing educational programs for personnel that stressed male responsibility for violence, they helped authorities pursue proarrest procedures and harsher sentencing policies that acknowledged the serious dimensions of the crime. The results have been impressive: 81% of the women who used the program lived in a violent-free setting within two years (*Ms.* 1994: 35). Similar programs enjoy comparable success in other parts of the country, particularly when shelter activists are accorded the central influence their expertise and experience merits (Dobash and Dobash 1992: ch. 7).

Whatever the benefit of cooperative ventures, some problems persist. As part of the very establishment they once scrutinized, feminists are less apt to be as exacting in their demands and expectations. Indeed, through government funding, activists are now accountable to the state in ways that may compromise the care they are able to extend to battered women. Beth Richie, a feminist scholar and cofounder of the Violence Intervention Project in East Harlem, concludes that the "movement has cut too many deals with people who don't pay us back" (Smith and Richie 2000–1: 25).

With increased state involvement (for example, funding and the expansion of professionals attending to abused women), there is the added risk that more money goes to the salaries and training of professionals (for example, police officers) than to direct emergency services for abused women. Thus, the boast of increased expenditures for and attention to projects concerning violence against women can be misleading. For example, the 1994 Violence Against Women Act authorized federal funding for numerous antiviolence initiatives. Of the $1.6 billion budgeted, $325 million went to projects for abused women and shelters. The rest went to the criminal justice system. Six years later, the Supreme Court determined that the act was an unconstitutional intrusion into state's rights and, furthermore, doubted the need for such legislation. It thus insisted there was little conclusive evidence that male violence posed a significant financial burden on women and, by extension, the nation's economy. The states themselves vigorously disagreed.[6] Several months later Congress revised and passed the act to reauthorize substantial support for federal programs.

The recent attention to the effects of violence on commerce has shifted attention away from a therapeutic emphasis on feelings and the empowerment of individuals to productivity and corporate responsibility. Two key factors conspired to achieve this orientation. First, in its efforts to further politicize the public nature of this seemingly private abuse, the movement emphasized the problems battered women encounter at work (for example, poor concentration and sick leaves), emphasizing a considerable loss to the nation's economy. Second and no less important, feminists established important legal precedent: employers who failed to protect their workers from battery now also risked costly lawsuits (for example, *Yunker v. Honeywell* 1993). In 1997, the U.S. Department of Justice declared that businesses should mitigate violence against women for reasons of health, liability, and safety and "because it makes good business sense" (U.S. Department of Justice, June/July 1997: 1). Intervention, thus, rests on calculations of the company's bottom line and not on the intrinsic value of women. The government also insisted that the corporate promotion of social responsibility through sales advanced the public good. The Justice Department, thus, praised Marshall's clothiers for its sponsorship of an annual "Shop 'till it Stops!" day, an event that is credited with raising public consciousness and profits, some of which go to community projects for abused women (June/July 1997: 2). Other corporations including, but not limited to, Liz Claiborne and Philip Morris have joined Marshall's. Increasingly, activism is inextricably linked to consumerism.

Activists wishing to join arenas to end violence against women now enter a terrain in which past certainties have been relinquished (Taylor and Whittier 1997: 552). There is an elusive convergence of the movement, state, and corporate worlds and the once seemingly distinctive character of feminist politics now seems an either ubiquitous or forsaken presence.

---

[6] Thirty-six states joined a brief supporting the act before the Supreme Court. Only Alabama filed a brief against the law.

Britain

In Britain, the structural conditions that facilitated the easy passage of national law made this option a particularly enticing one for the shelter movement in its earlier pursuit of reform.[7] Indeed, shortly after having established their national network, Women's Aid rapidly pursued the passage of national legislation through a Labour controlled Parliament and witnessed the adoption of two important acts a year apart: the Domestic Violence Act (1976) and the Housing (Homeless) Persons Act (1977). The first allowed for the temporary eviction of the batterer by using a civil injunction and attaching powers of arrest for subsequent violation. The primary purpose of the second act was to prevent the homelessness that results from male violence by establishing battered women as a priority category for public housing.

Laws that seemed easy to pass proved difficult to implement. Courts were particularly reluctant to issue eviction orders. One English judge declared: "I find it difficult to believe that it could ever be fair, save in most exceptional circumstances to keep a man out of *his* flat or house for more than a few months" (in Dobash and Dobash 1992: 187). Scottish courts were equally inimical, insisting that orders be used only as a "last resort" (op. cit.: 188). Yet, even in those instances where courts issued orders, in the absence of rigorous police enforcement, men remained unrestrained in their brutality (Barron 1990).

Early feminist efforts to improve the criminal justice system's responsiveness to battered women proved largely unsuccessful. Of the over two dozen recommendations taken up by the 1975 parliamentary committee on woman battery, none altered police response. Lawsuits remained an unlikely venue to induce reform because of their foundation in individual grievances. British police officers thus remained intransigent in ways their U.S. colleagues could ill afford (Dobash and Dobash 1992: 190–191). Throughout the 1970s, the police insisted that social services and refuges were the most appropriate avenues through which to address the problem (Dobash and Dobash 1992: 151). Eventually, cutbacks in social services made it increasingly difficult for the criminal justice system to cast the burden elsewhere.

When the 1980s concluded, the need to improve their response was seen by police themselves (Grace 1995). In 1990, the Home Office adopted guidelines informing officers that arrest is the preferred strategy of intervention – an approach adopted over a decade earlier in the United States. The emergence of this and similar police reforms has been attributed less to the vigilance of feminists than to an urgent need on the part of police to seek public approval after inner city riots in 1981 and 1985, and the miners' strike of 1984–5 (Radford, Kelly, and Hester 1997: 4). Evidently, complacency

---

[7] This refers to one house that, prior to devolution, effectively considered legislation with committees controlled by one governing party.

concerning crimes against women did not evoke the necessary outrage. Increasingly unable to conceal the "larger" crisis in policing from the public's gaze, the criminal justice system shifted its attention to women and adopted the mantle of protector (Radford, Kelly, Hester, and Stanko 1997: 70).

Unlike its U.S. counterpart, the British movement focused less on enhancing police response through litigation and instead turned their attention to securing safe housing through legislation. Dobash and Dobash explain:

The British were quicker to legislate at the national level, partly because the legislative process provides the party in power with the advantage of leadership on all committees, but also because a more well developed welfare state means that government agencies are generally more active in providing a wider variety of social services to a broader spectrum of the community. (1992: 142–143)

The movement's original pursuit of reform under Labour also meant that activists could effectively emphasize the ways in which welfare provisions could be used in alleviating the suffering of battered women, an emphasis that struck a less responsive chord years later under Thatcher.

The British movement's pursuit of housing and other welfare benefits necessitated their close and early cooperation with authorities. Prior to the institutionalization of multiagency work, shelters liased throughout the United Kingdom with housing departments, social services, and others to provide optimal support to women and their children (Turner 1996: 16). Shelter activists knew that in the absence of cooperative coordination, the implementation of even those laws that they had struggled to pass could be applied in ways that compromised women's safety. For example, housing departments insisted that battered women first seek an injunction against their husbands before requesting rehousing while courts suggested that the women use the Housing Act rather than the protection of an exclusion order. Though these and other problems undoubtedly enhanced the movement's misgivings about conventional agencies, they also underscored the importance of working with them to change.

In 1995, Britain's lateral loading of state responsibility onto nongovernmental actors was evidenced when the government categorically affirmed an interagency response to violence against women (Home Office and Welsh Office 1995). The issue of male violence was now, it seemed, firmly on the national agenda. The government's call for concerted action could have corrected, among other problems, the contradictory implementation of the Housing and Domestic Violence Acts. Instead, shortly after requesting coordinated measures to enhance women's safety, the conservatives adopted the 1996 U.K. Housing Act that frees local authorities from their previous obligation to secure accommodation for the statutorily homeless. A national survey of women rendered homeless through male violence highlights the discrepancy between the 1996 act and the call for measures to deter, if not prevent, violence against women (Malos and Hague 1997: 406).

Multiagency initiatives nonetheless continue to enjoy support from the shelter movement. Enthusiasm may, in part, result from evidence that suggests that such initiatives have led to improvements in policing (Grace 1995; Mullender 1996: 4–5). An alternative and somewhat less appealing explanation is that the movement, unaccustomed to expecting much, has become grateful for so little. Reflecting on nearly two decades of activism, Hannana Siddiqui of Southall Black Sisters, one of Britain's best-known feminist antiviolence groups, notes a positive shift in the public's attitude. She explains, "The very people who tried to close us down in the 1980s . . . are now at least paying lip service to the question of domestic violence, even if they are not doing much about it" (in Griffin 1994: 80).

Activists can sometimes seem easily impressed by those officials appearing to take them and the issues they care about seriously. As one feminist asks in near astonishment:

Who would have thought at the beginning of second-wave feminism that local councils would have Zero Tolerance [public educational] campaigns, that the metropolitan police would have domestic violence units? I think it is quite startling that you've got women like me training police officers, probation officers and magistrates on the politics of sexual violence and giving them the radical feminist line about male power and control. (Sarah in Harne 1996: 245)

It is curious that this otherwise critical activist appears oblivious to the functions she serves in legitimizing the very agencies she seeks to transform and equally unaware of the manner in which she has been altered by the interplay. Having earlier acknowledged that a critique of compulsory heterosexuality was essential to her understanding of male violence, it was a perspective that became increasingly difficult for her to use (ibid.). This difficulty is not hers alone. Other feminists have observed that with the state's increased acknowledgment of women's oppression came a diminished emphasis on the role of sexuality in and gender specificity of crime (for example, MacKinnon 1989: ch. 8).

Whatever conclusions may be reached concerning the significance of British reforms to mitigate male violence, for many the underlying motivations of the state remain at issue, particularly given the escalating importance of transnational contexts such as European integration. Some within the movement emphasize the state's need for redemption in the wake of rioting (for example, Radford, Kelly, and Hester 1997); others observe that cutbacks in social welfare swiftly followed multiagency initiatives (for example, Malos and Hague 1997). Competing assessments aside, the pursuit of a single European currency (requiring that member states have deficits below 3% of GDP and outstanding public debts below 60% of the GDP) has, in part, legitimized the chorus of post-Keynesian calls for cuts in social welfare programs. Together these factors underscore the utility of the cooperative enterprise for the state in its pursuit of legitimacy in difficult times. The question remains whether the movement's interests and those of the state can coincide, a query complicated by the added strains of devolution and European integration, processes that could enhance the state's receptivity to innovative projects precisely when it is least able to execute them (Elman 2001).

Sweden

For structural reasons similar to those of their British counterparts,[8] Swedish activists relied on legislation, not litigation, to improve the responsiveness of the criminal justice and social service systems to battered women. Their first efforts concerned the inadequacies of existing rules of prosecution. Together with the women's sections of various parties, they specifically requested that violence within the home be subject to public prosecution, thus enabling third parties to file formal complaints against batterers while absenting those they victimize from pleading in court. The new law, adopted in 1982, passed with ease as it required no additional expenditures and mandated neither arrest nor prosecution. Instead, it simply enabled police officers to investigate and detain batterers, which police previously could not do unless the woman herself reported her assailant and requested prosecutorial assistance. Yet, in the absence of mandating arrest, procedural reforms, or additional training, the law seemed more symbolic than sincere.[9]

Women's advocates soon turned their attention from the successful prosecution of batterers to women's more immediate need for police intervention and protection. Together with the women's sections of various parties they proposed orders of protection which were adopted by the Riksdag in 1988, over a decade after their initial use in the United States and Britain. Soon after, a government study found that nearly 40% of women who sought protection were denied it (BRÅ, PM 1989: 2). This may be attributed to the wording of the reform, which explicitly discourages the use of the orders. The law states that "conflicts" between men and women "should be solved in another way than through a restraint" and that orders are to be issued only under circumstances "where the general *threat* of punishment is not enough" (SFS 1988: 688).[10] Moreover, unlike both British and U.S. orders,

---

[8] The relative centralization and strength of Sweden's state is reflected in its legislative process. Legislation is adopted solely at the national level and reforms are channeled through the state's bureaucracy. When the Riksdag considers a bill, parliamentary majorities are relatively easy to obtain as governments emerge from disciplined party majorities that can ensure that preferences are translated into policy.

[9] While Swedish authorities attribute the escalation in reported assaults to this law, a study conducted years after its adoption showed that most battered women lacked a general familiarity with the criminal justice system and did not even realize that their assailants had committed a crime (BRÅ, PM 1989: 2, 32). It is, therefore, unrealistic to attribute the increase in reported incidents to this act.

[10] Interestingly, the wording of this Swedish law would violate U.S. standards of equal protection.

those in Sweden may not exclude men from the residences they share with those they abuse. The majority of battered women who live with their assailants are thus disqualified from seeking the protection such orders could afford.

Eager to portray itself as a champion of women's concerns, though reluctant to directly confront the shortcomings of existing legislation, the conservative government took office in 1991 and increased funding for the provision of security alarms and, in some cases, bodyguards. Such action appears impressive. But, rather than limiting the mobility of men (through, for example, protection orders and mandatory arrest), these paternalistic measures have women reliant on security systems and bodyguards. Not surprisingly, then, few women sought this particular assistance.

Ironically, it was precisely the adoption of these questionable initiatives and reforms that provided the conservative government with ammunition for its assertion that "efforts to prevent various forms of violence against women have high priority in Sweden" (Swedish Institute 1993). Despite the subsequent shift to Social Democratic governance, this statement appears in all state literature pertaining to women (for example, Arbetsmarknadsdepartmentet 1998). Indeed, such literature was essential to Sweden's international self-image as a staunch advocate of sexual equality, especially as it approached European membership in the mid-1990s.

Having resumed power in 1994 with the promise of greater receptivity to women's issues, the new Social Democratic government called for its own antiviolence initiatives and emphasized interagency cooperation (SOU 1995: 60). With increased funding for such efforts, the government entrusted established authorities (for example, the National Police Board and the National Board of Health and Welfare) to develop internal progress reports, training, and educational programs (Regeringskansliet 1998: 6).[11] By contrast, the shelter's role in monitoring or providing (additional) educational support was not emphasized. Rather, they were asked to continue their direct, "practical" assistance to battered women and received additional funding only for this purpose (Arbetsmarknadsdepartmentet 1998: 11). Thus, their expert contribution to an expanding arena of official concern was circumscribed.

The state's marginalization of the shelter movement has been partially concealed by its "greater acceptance of the feminist definition of assault as an expression of men's control of women" (Eduards 1997: 165). In fact, in sharp contrast to both Britain and the United States, Swedish public discourse evolved from "domestic violence" to "violence against women." Prioritizing

---

[11] This is discouraging, as battered women were critical of the assistance they received from them. Social workers were, for example, the least inclined of all professionals to stress the criminal nature of battery and, instead, took a therapeutic approach (Elman and Eduards 1991). A follow-up survey suggests little change nearly a decade later (Elman 2001a).

violence against women rhetorically has not, however, been manifested in enhancing women's safety on a concrete level. This point is clearly exemplified
through a critical examination of recent legislation.

In 1998, the government enacted two legislative reforms with serious
implications for battered women. One attempts to mitigate the systematic
abuse of women by no longer requiring separate proceedings for each abuse
(Regeringskansliet 1998: 2). Whether this provides an incentive to prosecute
abuse more tenaciously remains at issue, especially given that legislation
adopted the same year concerning child custody and visitation undermines
the limited protection this and other reforms could provide. According to the
second law, women who do not actively support their children's contact with
their fathers risk losing custody. Even battered women at women's refuges are
thus expected to maintain contact with their batterers to guarantee ongoing
visitation for their children – a policy that clearly places women's lives at
risk (Nordenfors 1996). Refuges that refuse to reveal the whereabouts of
battered women and children seeking safety from abusive fathers risk lost
state funding and police intimidation. The current chair of ROKS declares,
"I've worked on this issue since 1979 and it has never been worse than it is
today" (Beausang 1999).

Recent Nordic research into the shelter movements observed an increase
in general hostility to women's movements and a trend away from political action and an increased emphasis on service provision (in Eduards
1997: 153). This is also the direction in which the state traveled when
it elected to rely on its own professionals and not shelters for service
provision. In all state/movement engagements, movements run the risk of
being marginalized. That this swiftly happened to Sweden's shelter movement suggests that its close and early cooperation with the centralized
state may have, in the long run, facilitated its decline. Eventually, the state
could effectively dismiss the very actors whose efforts had enlarged and
legitimized its standing, both within Sweden and throughout Europe and
elsewhere.

CONCLUSION

Shelter movements politicized male violence so that our conceptions of the
political have expanded to include what was previously private. In addition, state endeavors to end such abuse are equated with democratization
and "first world" status. The connections made by the British, U.S., and
Swedish movements provided their states with the incentive to side with
women against the men who abuse them. The legitimacy of each of these
three states is determined, in part, through their ability to subdue, subvert,
or conceal the most explicitly patriarchal of their (past) inclinations. This
shift signals one of the greatest triumphs of a social movement and one of
the most significant transformations of states.

The power of states, like that of movements, is evidenced by their capacity to adapt to changing circumstances. With diminished influence and affluence in the 1970s, all three states emerged from recessions with an appreciation for social movements whose knowledge and energetic emphasis on postmaterialist values, autonomy, and volunteerism helped provide cost-effective and creative solutions to a bewildering array of social problems. Among other things, this included the downloading of tasks from state authorities to nonstate actors, as described in the introductory chapter. Unable to effectively subvert shelter movements, the state enlisted their support and selected to transform in ways the movements demanded. All states abandoned their earlier, explicit affirmations of male privilege regarding male violence and established agencies, programs, and policies that provide women with opportunities for redress and protection from abusive men. Even the European Union, to which Britain and Sweden belong, abandoned its noninterventionist position on male violence. In 1997, the European Parliament designated 1999 as the "European Year Against Violence Against Women" and the European Commission proposed funding for educational efforts (through Daphne), to promote zero tolerance for violence against women throughout member states. Nonetheless, the state's (and the Union's) rhetorical support of and fiscal assistance to shelter movements often precipitated cutbacks in public provision more generally, a politics suggesting that the state's (and Union's) interest in violence against women was not necessarily motivated by a concern for women.

Though the shelter movement's efforts to end male violence failed to provoke an unabashed and well-organized opposition, feminist principles were nonetheless frequently undermined by a proliferation of professionals. Writing from Britain, Jill Radford, Liz Kelly, and Marianne Hester explain: "What was in the 1970s a feminist struggle for recognition of the prevalence and social meaning of sexual violence has in the 1990s become an arena of increasingly individualized frameworks and practices. Sexual violence has become...a multitude of syndromes and disorders, all of which require 'treatment.'" (1997: 11). The transformation of shelters and crisis centers into relatively professional service organizations was not the problem of British feminist activists alone, nor is it an issue only for shelter activists. As other chapters in this volume make clear, the professionalization of women's movements has occurred in a variety of contexts cross-nationally.

In the states examined in this chapter, professionalization can be traced to a variety of factors but key among them was the call of activists themselves for increased state intervention. Unable to meet the needs of an increasing number of women who came forward in atmospheres of raised consciousness, shelters sought state support. The state obliged and, in turn, made its requests. Its promotion of a relatively conservative, social service approach to violence against women is evidenced in the projects and groups it chose to support. The combined influence of a forceful Social Democratic Party and a centralized state informed the Swedish movement's conception (via the establishment of the All Women's House) and hindered the subsequent development of a grass-roots movement. In Britain and the United States, financially strapped shelters were forced to make organizational changes in their structures to meet the hierarchical funding requirements of governmental agencies. Protest became a less prominent "repertoire of action" for U.S. and British activists than it had for Italian women (see della Porta this volume). It is likely that the European Union's recent interest in efforts to end male violence will have a similar outcome (Elman 2001).

While state intervention deradicalized significant segments of the movements under consideration, it also contributed to environments in which meeting the needs of battered women became less alien. This was particularly evident in the United States where the state encouraged the corporate community to address the issue of violence against women at work. Driven by profits and/or the fear of costly litigation, businesses developed internal sensitivity programs and external ad campaigns. To some, such mobilization trivializes woman abuse while to others it seems a step forward in legitimizing feminist concerns. Regardless, these and numerous other initiatives like Britain's new housing act or Sweden's provision of bodyguards frustrated some activists into withdrawal while inspiring still others to cooperate with the very authorities whose positions alarmed them.

Paradoxically, it was precisely the disappointing response of authorities to battered women that moved interagency (and lateral) initiatives forward. Yet, determined to change the state, feminists who endured were often unaware of the ways in which they had themselves been altered through the exchange. Hence, self-identified radicals could boast of their influence over those authorities that they trained and not appreciate the way they had been changed in the process. While the centralized structure of the Swedish state could inhibit dissent through the threatened withdrawal of all funding, within the decentralized contexts of Britain and the United States, with a plethora of avenues of alternative support and authorities to influence, the suffocation of dissent was to a greater degree self-imposed.

While the state's recognition does have conservatizing consequences, its shortcomings can also inspire radical reactions (Katzenstein 1998b).[12] Movements and states are now engaged in an intricate and sometimes awkward embrace that results from and, in part, encourages the gradual release

---

[12] Katzenstein's persuasive analysis of women in the church and the military provides a corrective to panic for those quick to equate recognition by or entrance into the mainstream with eschewing challenging claims. Her cases centered on women who were not necessarily connected to the feminist movement prior to their political debut. By contrast, our focus is on those whose experience of feminism often originated in *relatively* autonomous habitats (for example, women's shelters) – those spatially situated outside of the institutionalized environments (for example, church and the military). The difference may account for our sometimes contrasting perspectives concerning institutionalization and deradicalization.

of carefully defined roles and expectations. In Britain and the United States, the once antagonistic relationship between the shelter movements and their states has been replaced by a cautious collaboration. In both states shelter workers are now a crucial link between battered women and the legal system and also frequently the child welfare and social service systems (Schneider 1994: 47).

After years of selecting to be "outside the system" it is seemingly incongruous that British and U.S. activists sometimes find that, relative to their Swedish counterparts, they have assumed a more prominent position in the state's adoption, execution, and monitoring of policies and programs for battered women. The significance of movements is no longer discerned in their ability to marshal visible demonstrations against the state or business communities, but instead as carriers of ideas that influence states to alter their agencies in ways that make such protest unnecessary.

Interviews

Beausang, Angela. Director, National Association of Battered Women's Shelters. Stockholm, Sweden. May 19, 1999.

6

Shifting States

Women's Constitutional Organizing across Time and Space

Alexandra Dobrowolsky

Constitutional revision is arguably the most obvious and profound example of state reconfiguration given the monumental scope of constitutional settlements, which not only formalize political priorities but also articulate a nation's political aspirations and their enduring nature. The repercussions of constitutional change are felt, both directly and indirectly, not only within states, but also in civil society, in various communities and even within families. With such wide-ranging implications, it is no wonder that constitutional change has been, and remains, a challenging terrain of feminist state struggle.

This chapter describes, analyzes, and assesses women's movement/state relations in the realm of constitutional politics in Canada and the United Kingdom in light of the reconfiguration processes presented in the introductory chapter. It explores not only the different structural but also conjunctural contexts that shape feminist strategies. More importantly, I argue that, stemming from women's movements' diverse and changing strategic repertoires, feminist organizing has the potential to modify political landscapes, propel alternative discourses, and promote particular identities. In the sphere of constitutionalism examined in this study, women's movements have not only advanced an extensive policy agenda and more expansive political discourses, but have challenged, and often attempted to alter, relations between political forms and actors, broadly conceived. Through an array of tactics women have worked to insert themselves into states' constitutional discussions, often aware of the risks involved, but with the realization that otherwise they would be excluded from the debate.

Canada's efforts to "patriate" (that is, bring home) its constitution from Britain in the early 1980s, along with subsequent efforts at Canadian constitutional reform in the late 1980s and early 1990s, shed substantial light on state reconfiguration by constitutional revision. Similarly, the significant constitutional developments that have occurred within the United Kingdom since the end of the 1990s are illuminating. Both offer illustrations of political possibility, even in the midst of periods of neoliberal ascendancy/ consolidation where one would assume that many opportunities would be foreclosed. In certain respects, these constitutional reform conjunctures could certainly serve to accelerate neoliberalist tendencies, formalizing downloading, uploading, offloading, and lateral loading. At the same time, however, this constitutional revisioning could also conceivably open up the reconfiguration process. These diverse experiences across time and space highlight the variegated interaction between women's movements and states.

The Canadian and U.K. cases also constitute an intriguing comparison given the multiple affinities between the two nations. Canada shares a colonial history with Britain and many political institutional and cultural features including the Westminster parliamentary model, cabinet government, and the office of prime minister. Both use single-member plurality (SMP) electoral systems and currently have multiparty systems, albeit with a tendency for one party to dominate. In Canada, the Liberals have traditionally dominated party politics, but have been successfully challenged by the Progressive Conservative (PC) Party. While the Liberals and Conservatives have historically interchanged government and opposition positions, there have been a number of "third party" challengers (for example, the New Democratic Party (NDP), the Bloc Québécois (BQ), and the Canadian Alliance (CA), formerly Reform). In Britain, the Conservative Party historically has dominated, trading seats with the Labour Party, but now both compete against various "third parties," most notably the Liberal Democrats but also the Scottish National Party (SNP) and the Plaid Cymru in Wales. Finally, Canada and Britain both turned to neoliberal programs in the 1980s with Conservative governments initiating reconfiguration policies, and then respective Liberal and (arguably) Labour governments carrying on these macro-economic-political projects.

To be sure, Britain and Canada also differ on important grounds, including the fact that the former retained an unwritten constitution, whereas Canada opted for a written one with its Constitution Acts of 1867 and 1982. Recent changes have filled the gap somewhat, with Britain's 1998 Human Rights Act (Morrison 2001: 347–350; Wadham 1999). Another major distinction is that Canada adopted a federal system at its inception, assigning the provinces specific jurisdictional authority. These provincial powers are also undergirded by unique linguistic, ethnic, cultural, and regional identities (epitomized by the province of Quebec). Over the last few decades, the trend has been toward ever more dramatic decentralization with extensive downloading from the federal government to the provinces. At first blush, here Britain provides the obvious contrasting case, given its reputation as a unified, highly centralized state. Nonetheless, post-1997 (after the May 1 Labour victory) constitutional developments have precipitated greater convergence. For instance, Tony Blair first ventured onto the constitutional reform road via differentiated degrees of downloading to Northern Ireland, Scotland, and Wales (Boyle and Hadden 1999; Leicester 1999).

To simplify this intricate hybrid of shared and divergent experiences, the chapter is organized on two planes: spatial and temporal. Because of the recently shifting locus of constitutional change in the United Kingdom, here I will concentrate on transformations across space. In Canada, despite the federated nature of the Canadian state, space is underplayed in favor of time. The temporal focus is useful given that Canadian feminists have had profound constitutional experiences over a more prolonged period and thus we can learn from modifications in contexts and strategies. Moreover, Canadian women have national and/or umbrella organizations that have co-ordinated campaigns focusing on the central state's agenda, which will be emphasized rather than the regional, provincial, or local variations of feminist activism. In contrast, women in the United Kingdom have not had con-certed, protracted experiences with state-sanctioned constitutional reform, as the dominant Conservative Party in recent decades upheld the status quo. Moreover, British feminists, historically, have not worked through national organizational structures (Gelb and Hart 1999: 151) to the same extent as has the Canadian women's movement. As time comes to the fore in Canada, shifts in strategies become apparent. As space comes to the fore in the United Kingdom, the particularities of feminist constitutional mobilization in three chosen areas – England, Scotland, and Northern Ireland – come into relief,[1] highlighting enlightening variations in activism within a comparatively small territory subject to a centralized British state.

When discussing the movement/state interactions on constitutional is-sues, I focus on two aspects: 1) political opportunities/constraints and state reconfiguration, and 2) identity politics. However, the former cannot simply be treated as independent variables because new or modified opportunities can be created by social movements. Conversely, identity cannot be treated solely as dependent; identity can shape the political opportunities of social movements. Put differently, collective identity can affect strategic choices which, in turn, can affect movement outcomes and future political struggles. Thus, both political and identity politics contexts can be both facilitating and constraining.

---

[1] To keep the length of this chapter manageable, Wales is not included in this study, although it is part of my larger research. My first round of interviews took place in London, Edinburgh, and Belfast in the spring of 1997. Follow-up interviews were carried out in all these cities, as well as in Glasgow and Cardiff in June 1999. The Canadian case is a condensed version of two more detailed accounts (Dobrowolsky 2000, 1998). Interviews for these pieces were conducted in late 1995 and early 1996. Most interviews were conducted in person and tape recorded, although a few were done over the phone. All participants, save one, agreed to full disclosure of their names. I sincerely thank all of the interviewees. Any errors, misinterpretations, or omissions rest with me.

THEORETICAL AND PRACTICAL CHALLENGES

State reconfigurations that come as a result of constitutional change have provided a window of opportunity for women and other collective actors. Once again, constitutional adaptations may include downloading, offloading, uploading, and lateral loading, but in whatever shape or form the changes come, constitutional reform involves some retooling of the political status quo. Hence, women's movements seize the moment, and try to refashion an agenda usually defined and dominated by white men. However, they can do more than react in these situations: Women's movements have also worked *proactively* to shape and expand political practices and discourses. Therefore, this chapter seeks to uncover the complex and contingent forms of feminist/state interactions by comparing not only how different political opportunities and constraints influence women's movements, but also how women's movements have influenced the state, as well as political practices and discourses. This serves to shine a spotlight on some of the limitations of leading political process models.

More specifically, my aim is to transcend the narrow purview, unidirectional causation, and lack of dynamism in analyses where traditional political structures dictate the shape and forms of social movement strategic choices. For example, Sidney Tarrow's concept of political opportunity structure is widely used to explain social movement mobilization (Tarrow 1998, 1996b, 1994, 1989) and is often employed to explain or differentiate women's movements' strategies. Political institutions (Katzenstein and Mueller 1987) and/or political cultures (Bashevkin 1998; Vickers, Rankin, and Appelle 1993) are used to justify the strategies disparate women's movements embrace. The political opportunity structure includes a range of considerations from more stable institutional arrangements, such as constitutional tracts and political systems, to more flexible aspects, including changing party patterns (Young 2000: 13). It has been increasingly recognized that political opportunities/constraints also include more provisional and potential openings and supranational contingencies (Gamson and Meyer 1996; Klandermans 1997; Kriesi, Koopmans, Duyvendak, and Guigni 1995). Recent proponents of political process models also incorporate more movement influence by recognizing that movements may create opportunities (Klandermans 1997; Kriesi et al. 1995; Meyer and Staggenborg 1996; Tarrow 1998, 1996b, 1994).

Nevertheless, in the final analysis, the causal arrows still run from a collection of established political considerations onto social movements. More-or-less conventional political variables "provide the most important incentives" and ultimately dictate the shape and forms of movements' strategic choices (Tarrow 1998:7). Thus, a movement's organizational repertoire "is constrained by the requirements of various political arenas" (Meyer and Staggenborg 1996: 1649). The political determinism of this approach leaves little scope for social movement agency, innovation, and influence. What is more, these models seldom reflect a more expansive notion of what constitutes "the political," whereby formal and informal political domains overlap and influence one another.

The case studies that follow demonstrate this more complicated relationship. Recent state reconfiguration clearly has had deleterious effects on women's movement organizing. For instance, Margaret Thatcher's Conservative government's elective dictatorship and even John Major's kinder, gentler Conservative regime provided a profoundly inhospitable political and economic environment. Yet women continued to mobilize for change and even responded to neoliberal reconfigurations. For instance, lateral loading meant that women could make inroads in quasi-state bodies, offloading meant that others concentrated their efforts in the voluntary sector, and uploading meant that women targeted the supranational organizations like the European Union (EU) and European Courts (Bashevkin 1998; Meehan and Collins 1996). At the same time, still other feminist interventions were cultivated and aimed at fundamentally changing the political status quo, where women not only seized but made opportunities in an effort to open up conventional politics.

Similarly, after Canadians elected a Conservative government in 1984, the state downloaded state responsibilities to the provinces, and engaged in lateral loading, all in efforts to "streamline" the state. While offloading also occurred, the state's neoliberalism mostly manifested itself in the form of cutbacks, including in-state funding for women's organizations. This not only contributed to more antagonistic movement/state relations, but political-process models would lead one to assume that this would stultify mobilization, that is, this would *not* appear to be a fluid moment of opportunity. And yet, under these seemingly inopportune circumstances, women's movements challenged the state. Movement coalition building and oppositional mobilization grew. For instance, feminist organizations forged alliances with other equality seekers, especially those opposing neoliberal policies such as free trade, extreme downloading, and limitations on social spending. In turn, these coalitions created their own political opportunities and sometimes constraints. In spite of an unfavorable economic climate and decidedly cool political relations, the women's movement persevered and realigned its strategies, forging alliances to construct a more inclusive constitutional agenda.

A broader conception of politics, then, helps us to understand how women could organize even under circumstances of conventional political constraint. While constitutional openings certainly provide a spark, other considerations explain how women could fan the flames to spread more expansive political practices and discourses. Here, the incorporation of identity politics becomes pivotal. Identity is constructed and deployed as a basis for making claims and achieving strategic change (Bernstein 1997). Different forms of identity politics are promoted by different women's movements over time and space and the politics of identity influence their strategies

(Buechler 2000: 195). Whereas political process models have concentrated on states and the conventional political, new social movement scholars have tended to focus on collective identity and civil society (Melucci 1996: 76, 1996b: 33, 1995: 44–47, 1989: 34; Touraine 1997, 1981). Women's constitutional mobilization clearly involves both (Dobrowolsky 2000). Indeed, a careful consideration of the intricacies and implications of collective identity (Bondi 1993: 96) sheds light on our understanding of women's constitutional interventions.

Identity politics can be understood as efforts to deconstruct and reconstruct multiple and intersecting identities in order to resist and contest dominant power relations and socioeconomic, political, and cultural discourses and practices. They encompass a much larger field of politics than formalized political arenas and so efforts at categorization are fraught with difficulty. For instance, some make the distinction between "traditional" cleavages (center-periphery, class, religion, among others) and "new" cleavages or new social movement identities, such as gender (Kriesi et al. 1995: 25). This typology is problematic not only for its new/old distinctions (which are particularly faulty in relation to women), but also because contemporary constitutionalism exhibits not only the coexistence, but the intermingling of these collective identities. The push toward devolution, the rise of Scottish nationalism, and the battles in Northern Ireland have resulted in clashes between complex collective identities, which has significant implications for women's movements' constitutional reform platforms. Canadian feminist organizations harnessed pan-Canadian nationalism (for example, the antifree trade mobilization which coincided with constitutional change initiatives of the late 1980s) and have had to contend with the conflicting nationalist demands of both Quebec and Aboriginal peoples; they have had to factor in women's regional and provincial identities and struggles, as well as those based on race, ethnicity, ability, and sexual orientation (Dobrowolsky 2000, 1998).

In underlining the multiple dimensions of identity, complementary and contradictory outcomes become evident (Bernstein 1997; Brown 1995; Butler 1990; Minow 1995). Given these diverse manifestations and repercussions, it is crucial to trace how women's movements challenge, or fail to challenge, connect, and disconnect, multiple, interconnected identities; how identity is both strategically used *and* serves to affect strategies; and how these struggles change over space and time. In sum, an understanding of more expansive political processes and discourses (Koopmans and Statham 1999), including the changing political texture, context, and influence of identity, becomes crucial.

These claims will be borne out in the sections that follow. In the next section, I provide a longitudinal overview of Canadian women's movements' constitutional interventions. The second section turns to the United Kingdom and three internally differentiated settings: England, Scotland, and Northern Ireland. In the third section, I consider political opportunities/constraints and identity politics, and their two-way relationship with women's movements. The fourth section concludes with observations concerning the ways in which state–women's movement interactions create new possibilities for thought and action, as well as potentially new political arrangements.

FEMINIST CONSTITUTIONAL ACTIVISM IN CANADA:
CHANGES OVER TIME

In Canada, three distinctive constitutional struggles spanned three separate periods (for a more detailed account see Dobrowolsky 2000, 1998). The first period in the early 1980s represents the culmination of longstanding women's equality struggles, where Canadian feminists concentrated on what would become an expanded Canadian (as opposed to British tied) constitution and a completely new Charter of Rights and Freedoms. The Constitutional Act of 1982 patriated Canada's founding constitutional document (the Constitution Act of 1867) and contained amendment provisions whereby changes to Canada's constitution no longer required the consent of the British Parliament. The 1982 Act also included a new Charter of Rights and Freedoms: an entrenched, judicially reviewable bill of rights. The latter "changed dramatically (some might suggest irreparably) the character of one of Canada's founding constitutional principles: the supremacy of federal and provincial parliaments . . . [given that the] Charter establishes the rights and values that are to be the normative standards for evaluating state action" (Hiebert 1999: 185). A subsequent round of constitutional contestation was set off in 1997 by the Meech Lake Accord, a document drafted by political elites to assuage Quebec as it had not consented to the earlier 1982 constitutional resolutions. When the Accord failed to be ratified by all the provinces (in 1990), a new round of constitutional wrangling ensued (1990–2). This culminated in yet another agreement, the Charlottetown Accord, which was drafted in the summer of 1992, and was subsequently rejected in a national referendum in the fall of that year.

Time: The Early 1980s

Through Canadian feminists' efforts in the early 80s, Section 15 of the Charter of Rights and Freedoms was reworded to provide a more secure, substantive response to earlier, procedural equality provisions. A new equality rights clause, Section 28, was also added then freed from a last-minute addendum, Section 33 (which constituted a legislative override to certain enumerated grounds in the Charter). Feminist activists were the driving force behind the formulation and inclusion of these more expansive equality provisions and their representational strategies changed over time.

Given their continued underrepresentation in traditional political arenas, women were compelled to mobilize from "without" to affect constitutional outcomes. However, in the early 80s, there also was room for feminists to maneuver from "within." This opportunity stemmed from the fact that, since the 70s, the federal government had appointed feminist women's advisors in the state and acted on certain policy initiatives in response to women's movement concerns (Burt 1990; Findlay 1987; Geller-Schwartz 1995). There were also a few sympathetic women in the political parties, and as party positions vis-à-vis the Charter and constitutionalism either were not firmly fixed or were contestable, inroads could also be made here (Burt 1988; Haussman 1992; Hosek 1983; Kome 1983; Roberts 1988; Vickers 1993). While feminist activists were by no means professional lobbyists, they did work, nonetheless, to influence conventional political actors and were able to gain some ground (interview with McPhedran).

Of course, these state/party targets were not obstacle free, nor were they free from political manipulation (interview with Anderson). In certain cases, government funding to feminist organizations was withheld, in another, a state-sponsored women's constitutional conference was canceled, and in the final stages of this process, in a concession to the provinces, the federal government weakened the equality provisions with Section 33. However, women used the federal system to their advantage. They put pressure on provincial premiers, shored up the support of partisan women, coordinated mass-based opposition by way of phone and letter campaigns and, in some cases, protested, with the federal government finally succumbing.

Initially responsive, but ultimately ambivalent, state relations were frustrating but not unanticipated. Women's movement representatives were aware that, although useful, the state could not be targeted using only the tactics of conventional lobbyists (presenting briefs and meeting with political officials, supportive bureaucrats, and party members). Accordingly, women's movement representatives combined these efforts with social movement strategies, particularly intra-movement (within the women's movement) networking. Feminist umbrella organizations and national women's organizations mobilized their member groups and local contingents in order to have their constitutional concerns voiced and recognized (Gotell 1990; Kome 1983; Razack 1991). Conferences and meetings were held, and constitutional issues were debated in newsletters and in the feminist press.

Despite various outreach efforts in and outside the women's movement, pivotal feminist mobilizers reflected the tenor of the women's movement at the time, which was that it was predominantly white, Anglophone, and middle class (interview with Baines). There was some recognition of more diverse claims, for instance, those of Aboriginal women, yet these issues fell off of the agenda as activists pragmatically narrowed their sights, settling for an undifferentiated notion of women's equality. This meant that a unidimensional identity of woman was promoted and differences between women were not emphasized. In the end, the form and priorities of the movement, as well as a conducive political and socioeconomic environment, contributed to the "success," and the limitations, of the struggle. That is, the nature and forms of political struggle (both within and outside the state) would soon be subject to change.

Time: 1987–1990

Five years later, because Quebec rejected the early 1980s pact, a new deal was struck in June of 1987. The prime minister and leaders of the provincial governments (known collectively as the First Ministers) hastily hammered out the Meech Lake Accord behind closed doors and then declared that this document was meant to welcome Quebec back into the constitutional "family." For many feminists, especially those outside of Quebec, the Accord constituted a threat to their equality rights. Whereas the Accord raised issues for different women, most women's groups critiqued the closed process and a provision circumscribing the federal government's spending power and ability to create new social programs by downloading. Groups outside of Quebec also questioned the Accord's recognition of Quebec as a "distinct society." This distinct society clause, and another that clarified its scope, seemingly set up a hierarchy of rights where certain enumerated rights (and not women's rights) appeared to have precedence over others. Again, women drew on multiple strategies to have their concerns heard, but this time, because the political context had changed, the emphasis shifted.

Given the secretive nature of this deal, women were caught unaware and had to react rapidly to a document that they believed jeopardized their hard-won equality rights. Key actors had little time to network and consult with a larger and more diversified Canadian women's movement. Women's movement representatives, many part of the earlier campaign, once again prepared briefs and tried meeting with politicians. The growth of feminist legal expertise produced technical and legalistic responses, but these failed to convince politicians. Unlike in 1981–2, feminist analyses in 1987 were discredited and their political maneuvering stymied (interviews with Baines; Hacker; McPhedran; Ruth). Due to an all-party agreement on the Accord, the upcoming 1988 general election, and a hardening neoliberal consensus, with dwindling state support and a tighter rein on a slimmer bureaucracy, "inside" routes were constricted. Previous political openings appeared sealed.

"Outside" organizing also was circumscribed as women did not have the time to ground their complex analyses and bolster their efforts with grassroots support. Moreover, a growing rift developed between feminist organizations in and outside of Quebec. Quebec women's groups supported the distinct society clause due to Quebec's nationalist aspirations, while leading feminist analyses formulated outside of the province saw this concession as detracting from existing sexual equality rights.

Because there was a three-year ratification period for the Accord, feminists could work on their networking and their outreach efforts over time, and so a more considered, new direction developed (interviews with

Cameron; Rebick). Women's groups intensified not only their intra- but also their intermovement organizing (between other social movements). National feminist organizations critical of the Accord made linkages with provincial women's groups that were opposed to the deal and forged alliances with social policy advocates, trade unionists, and left liberals. For example, the centerpiece of the Conservative government's neoliberal agenda, and the 1988 federal election, was the Canada/U.S. free trade agreement (FTA). Feminists, leftists, and Canadian nationalists banded together to oppose FTA (Bashevkin 1989; MacDonald 1995). These anti-FTA policy linkages and movement connections were redeployed in the constitutional context as the costs of neoliberalism and the dangers of a shrinking social safety net were underscored (interview with Rebick). At the same time, the prioritization of certain collective identities (that is, Quebec) over others was problematized, given coalitions with groups based on race, ethnicity, and ability as well as Aboriginal peoples organizing against the Accord.

With a strategic shift in emphasis, national women's organizations like the National Action Committee on the Status of Women (NAC) simplified the legal jargon, backed away from the "distinct society" critiques, and stressed what they perceived to be the democratic deficiencies in the Accord's process and substance via intra- and intermovement networking. Promoting the discourse of the inappropriateness of "eleven white men in suits" determining the future of the country, publicizing the Accord's potential threat to social programs, and questioning the status of women's equality rights, all by a coalition of diverse identity-based groups, helped to discredit the Meech Accord. In the end, the Accord failed to meet the June 1990 ratification deadline.

Time: 1990–1992

As a result of this fight waged by women and their allies, the next effort at accommodating Quebec constitutionally, during the next (1990–2) round of negotiations that would lead to the Charlottetown Agreement of 1992, could not ignore demands for open, consultative procedures. Federal and provincial governments bombarded the citizenry with committees, commissions, and task forces. However, given prior constitutional interventions, particularly on the part of women, the federal government also worked to discredit collective action. For example, in arenas such as the Spicer Commission and in consultations staged across the country, the government denigrated what it termed "special interests" and emphasized the input of "ordinary Canadians" thereby marginalizing collective identity (especially women's) mobilization (Dobrowolsky 1998).

Feminists continued to work to heal the wounds of Meech, and thus, unlike in the previous round, were more prepared and proactive. Early on, NAC and Equality Eve (formerly the Ad Hoc Committee of Women on the Constitution) engaged in networking and outreach. The focus was on informing women, getting them talking about constitutional options, and building a grass-roots consensus. This time, in an even harsher economic and political climate, with even fewer funds available and more political backlash, lobbying was only selectively used. Targets were few and well defined. For example, there was work on influential, sympathetic politicians, such as the federal Intergovernmental Affairs Minister Joe Clark and the Ontario New Democratic Premier Bob Rae. Later, advocating gender parity in the Senate, women received support from Premier Harcourt of British Columbia, another New Democrat, and Premier Cameron of Nova Scotia, who was by no means on the left, but was amenable to a more representative Senate. However, the real thrust of feminist mobilizing during this period was to target civil society and cultivate a critical consciousness through media work, educational outreach, coalition building, and protest.

Women's movement activism included not only traditional political sites, but the opening of new and different political spaces. Women's groups demanded representational parity in conventional political institutions. Calling for a 50/50 male/female based Senate elected on the basis of proportional representation (PR) and a gender-balanced Supreme Court, they also pushed for constitutional deliberations beyond elitist, closed-door First Minister Conferences, advocating constituent assemblies and encouraging diverse women across the country to meet in their organizations, or simply over lunch, and around their kitchen tables (Equality Eve printed placemats with points of constitutional discussion on them). In these ways, the movement encouraged constitutional debate that included an array of actors beyond traditional political confines.

Feminists had been instrumental in problematizing the secretive deal making of the past, and although politicians responded with conventional committees and commissions, these standard political devices fell short of the mark, with one joint house committee even disbanding because of public skepticism and lack of involvement in it. In an attempt to save face, the government came up with an innovative alternative, staging five regional conferences, which actually reflected prior demands on the part of feminists and their allies to create more open, discursive fora. While the government still used the rhetoric of hearing from "ordinary Canadians," these conferences nonetheless provided an opening for collective mobilization. Women's movement representatives worked with other activists, including members of the Action Canada Network (ACN) and the Canadian Labour Congress (CLC), to bring varied perspectives and new proposals to the table. The President of NAC later recounted the progress that was made, from victories like proportional and gender representation in the Senate, to the wider recognition that there could be a different constitutional agenda (interview with Rebick). While many of the specific gains did not survive later negotiations, feminist activists had politicians and the public discussing issues such as the need for a recognition of difference – from asymmetrical federalism to an affirmation of Three Nations (the Canadian nation, plus Quebec and Aboriginal nationhood) and multiracial and cultural realities, as well as gender. Moreover, through such discussion fora, creative possibilities for citizens' participation had emerged. Finally, as a result of such alternative political arrangements, the final Charlottetown Agreement reflected aspects of a more progressive agenda, (for instance, in the inclusion of a social charter) in addition to the state's neoliberal priorities.

Nonetheless, because many of the conditions desired by feminist organizations did not appear in the Agreement, key women's groups decided to oppose the deal. The choice was a difficult one, and came in response to concerns raised by a prominent Native women's organization and other groups that felt marginalized by the Agreement (interview with Rebick). Through multipronged efforts, many of which were coordinated by NAC and the Native Association of Women of Canada (NWAC) (interview with McIvor and Nahanee), prominent elements of the women's movement staged a convincing "No" campaign in the referendum on the Agreement and, in the end, it also failed to pass.

Lessons over Time

In the early 1980s, women made greater "insider" gains and were less confrontational, with the state and political parties more amenable to their claims. They relied on an undifferentiated identity of "woman" based on sameness not difference. Lobbylike activities were the preferred strategy, but these were bolstered by efforts at mass mobilization. During the Meech Lake Accord interlude a reactive response and reversion to these tactics were followed by a strategic turn that emphasized both intra- and inter-movement networking. In the Charlottetown round, lobbying was limited and there was much more work on grass-roots initiatives, coalitional and various identity politics linkages. As a result, organizing was both more inclusive and more oppositional. Adverse conditions under a reconfigured state clearly intensified the struggle as compared to the early 1980s.

By the late 1980s and early 1990s, there were fewer concrete political gains, for with both Meech and Charlottetown, what women's organizations ultimately succeeded in doing was jettisoning agreements. Identity politics shifts changed the nature of the movement and its strategies affecting both the number of actors involved and the issues addressed. With a women's movement more attuned to diversity and with a wider array of alliance partners, concerns grew in scope and complexity making coordination and consensus difficult, and affecting both practices and proposals. While it failed in securing key formal provisions, as had occurred in the early 1980s, the movement succeeded in opening up the debate and ensuring that constitutionalism in Canada was not a rarefied discussion reserved for institutional political elites. In the end, while feminists had fewer direct, tangible, and quantifiable effects, they certainly exercised more dispersed, discursive, and qualitative influence.

WOMEN'S CONSTITUTIONAL ORGANIZING IN THE UNITED KINGDOM:
CHANGES OVER SPACE

In the United Kingdom, there have been recurring calls for constitutional renewal; however only in recent years as a result of growing doubts about the legitimacy and democratic viability of formal British political institutions have serious and substantive discussions and support for new proposals grown. Women have not only added their voices to the constitutional discussion, raising concerns about access, equality, and proportionality, but in some cases they have launched debates regarding the nature and forms of representation and democracy. As will become apparent when regional variations are examined, certain combinations of strategies and identities have resulted in more political and discursive change than others.

Space: England

In England, feminists have mobilized for constitutional change in the parties, various think tanks, organizations specifically geared toward constitutional reform, and numerous women's groups. Although the Liberal Democrats were the first to commit to constitutional reform, the reticence of Labour and the intransigence of the Conservative parties began to wane in the late 90s. New Labour's embrace of constitutional reform has been especially noteworthy given years of ambivalence on the matter. Women's activism within the party has contributed to this change of heart. For instance, the Labour Campaign for Electoral Reform (LCER) was spearheaded by women such as Mary Southcott (Georghiou) who published countless pamphlets and reports and swayed influential Labour MPs on the merits of PR in general, and for women in particular. LCER women staged events, portraying themselves as "new suffragettes," and worked to mobilize Labour women in women's sections, branches, wards, constituencies, and unions.[2] Organizations such as the Labour Women's Network (LWN) and Emily's List were established to increase women's representation through support, training, lobbying, and fundraising.[3] Beyond

---

[2] For example, see the flyers: New Suffragettes. No date. *Votes for Women*; and Labour Campaign for Electoral Reform. No date. *Women need Electoral Reform*. See also Linton and Southcott 1998; Southcott 1996, 1993. A number of significant Labour ministers have been LCER supporters, such as Mo Mowlam, Clare Short, Tessa Jowell, and Janet Anderson. See LCER, 1996–7. *Political Report*.

[3] LWN was established in 1988 to address the low numbers of Labour women in the House of Commons and Emily's List United Kingdom was founded in 1993 to introduce funding schemes to boost women Labour Party selections.

the parties, feminists have advocated constitutional change in movements, think tanks, and research institutes not specifically geared to women.[4] For example, within the Charter 88 movement women organized a forum on "Feminising Politics" and discussed altering electoral laws; changing the adversarial nature of the House of Commons (making it more "woman friendly"); and devolving power to create more political openings for women.

Improving women's standing in traditional political institutions and enhancing women's equality have been clear objectives for longstanding women's groups like the Fawcett Society (established in 1866 but revitalized in the 1990s; Gelb and Hart 1999: 157) and newer organizations like The 300 Group (interviews with Stephenson; Swain). The latter concentrated on training women candidates, with the target of 300 women in Parliament, whereas the former promoted various equality campaigns, including electoral reform, through educational materials, media outreach, and networking (Fawcett Society 1997: 18). The Fawcett Society networked on issues of constitutional change organizationally, through the Women's National Commission (WNC), as well as interpersonally through contacts with Charter 88 and research groups like the Constitution Unit (Fawcett Society 1995/96; interview with Smith; interview with Stephenson). The state-tied WNC and Equal Opportunities Commission (EOC) also encouraged political activism for an equality agenda.[5]

This focus on conventional political arenas constituted a dramatic shift in the once state-averse British women's movement's orientation (Gelb and Hart 1999), as substantial feminist energy was directed toward the political parties, especially those supportive, or at least sympathetic, to women's concerns. In addition, state networks via the WNC and EOC were consolidated. Therefore, a premium was placed on fostering insider connections.

This approach was not far removed from the early constitutional organizing of Canadian feminists, which involved lobbying and traditional political contacts. However, in Canada these constitutional reform efforts were bolstered with grass-roots support. The emphasis in England, however, was on creating conventional political gains. This meant that much of women's constitutional mobilization was not infused with grass-roots organizing nor was it oriented toward diverse communities (interview with Stephenson). By moving away from inter- and intramovement mobilization, less inclusive, traditional forms of politics were legitimized. However, the lack of a diversified

---

[4] For instance, feminists are active in the center-left Institute for Public Policy Research (IPPR) and the nonpartisan DEMOS, the Constitution Unit, an independent inquiry into constitutional reform, as well as Liberty and Charter 88.

[5] The WNC, as a state-tied umbrella group, tended to have more of a conservative orientation. However, its work on equality, representation, and democracy showed more promise as it underscored the limitations of traditional political forms.

movement base to support "insider" women made it harder to challenge partisan priorities and state directives.

As a result, constitutional reforms to date have come from the top down with close governmental control of their shape and substance. Modifications of British institutions (Blackburn and Plant 1999) involved tinkering with less powerful or anachronistic bodies, such as reforming the House of Lords (White 2000). Attempts to modernize Parliament in general have been "dull, unambitious and painfully slow" (Beetham and Weir 1999: 133). Proportional representation was instituted for European elections and the new regional assemblies, but the prime minister would not embrace Lord Jenkins' Electoral Commission proposal of a hybrid Westminster system (Berrington 1998: 23–24; Cole 1999). Eagerly anticipated new measures like the Human Rights Bill and Freedom of Information Act have met with disappointment at their narrow scope. Constitutional restructuring has taken place, but modifications have been careful and tightly controlled providing little challenge to centralized decision making (Evans and Hencke 1999; Kavanagh 1998: 38–39).

While women helped to propel these winds of change, they appear more swept up than rooted in the process. To be sure, record numbers of women entered Parliament in 1997 (121 MPs, 101 Labour women), yet these gains proved difficult to sustain as many of the seats won by women were not safe. Labour created a Ministry for Women, plus a Women's Unit, headed by Baroness Jay of Paddington, whose mandate was to assess the impact of policy on women and formulate policies that promote equality (Women's Unit 1999). The Unit sponsored studies on women's earning and violence against women and teenage girls, and instigated a government road show "Listening to Women" whose findings were summarized in glossy booklet form. However, because the Women's Unit was "in policy terms, far from the epicentre of decision making" (Perkins 1999: 6), the concern was that it involved more image than substance. There was the distinct impression that the prime minister was "simply waiting for the unit to wither away from neglect" (ibid.). Having these new structures and more women in government did not forestall controversial policy decisions such as Labour's Social Security Bill, which cut benefits to lone parents, 90% of whom were women. Only one female Labour MP, Maria Fyfe, voted against the bill, prompting the remark: "It is clear from this that women's interest will not necessarily be advanced by more women in Parliament unless women have enough power to influence party policies more effectively" (Robertson 1998: 2).

Labour also took pains to defuse potential opposition (interview with Power, 1999). This is well illustrated in the case of the WNC, which joined the Women's Unit in the cabinet office. Since the WNC was an advisory non-departmental body set up and funded by the state, Labour moved to make it more "accountable" to the state (not necessarily to the women's movement).

Thus, the government changed the WNC's orientation from representing "member" groups to contracting with "partners" in the community. The WNC's head became a public appointment and the executive was replaced with a steering committee approved by the Minister for Women (interview with Evans and Taylor).

In sum, English women concentrated their constitutional efforts on reforming traditional British political institutions and the resulting political changes have been at best modest, at worst worrisome. As one journalist remarked at the end of Labour's first administration in May 2001:

The suffragettes chained themselves to railings outside No. 10 to give women the vote. To give them power we might have to resort to more drastic measures: naked hunger strikers surrounding Millbank, perhaps; or gun-toting feminists hijacking a Concorde. Nothing else seems to work: the election of 101 women MPs failed to give women clout; so did the Ministry for Women. [This and more]... failed to change the macho mood in politics. (Odone 2001: 19)

Hyperbole aside, the point is that women's strategies have been conventional and their discursive claims have been, for the most part, limited to promoting an undifferentiated gender identity through increases in women's representation. To date, results have been disappointing, especially compared with the forms of, and responses to, Scottish women's constitutional activism.

Space: Scotland

In Scotland women targeted conventional political institutions, focusing on the same traditional democratic forms as their English counterparts. Yet here the possibility, and then reality, of a new Scottish Parliament resulted in a unique dynamic with the potential for broader political inclusion. It provided not only inspiration, but room for political innovation. Here, the successful formalization of Scottish identity was bolstered by a greater degree of community, and especially women's, involvement. While English women's groups tried to add their issues to a constitutional and democratic reform agenda, gender equality in Scotland became "an intrinsic part of the broader debates on democracy, accountability and representation" (MacKay 1997: 9).

The umbrella organization the Scottish Convention of Women, women's representatives in political parties and the trade union movement, and women's organizations set up a Women's Issues Group in the Scottish Constitutional Convention as early as 1989 (Coote and Pattullo 1990: 271, 273–287; Lindsay 2001: 172; MacKay 1997: 30). Wide-ranging discussions were held and information was collated on women's representation in a new Scottish Parliament and on the political obstacles women face. Other groups formed – some party tied (such as the Woman's Claim of Right Group[6] and the Scottish Labour Women's Caucus), others not (such as Engender and the Women's Coordination Group (WCG)).

Engender was launched as a research and campaign organization, whereas WCG comprised representatives from Scotland's major women's groups, including church associations and the Women's Forum Scotland (a group tied to the European Women's Lobby). Both Engender and WNC mobilized women and men in the campaign for equal representation in the Scottish Parliament (interview with Robertson, 1997). They lobbied the Scottish Office and the parties on the 50/50 option, but also collected and distributed information about women in Scottish society and politics, networked, and built coalitions. This outreach was more routine in Scotland than in England. Not only were there solid connections between Engender and WCG, but intermovement linkages were crucial. For example, WCG worked closely with women in the Scottish Trade Union Congress (STUC) as the latter had put forward the 50/50 option in the Scottish Constitutional Convention (Engender 1995; Lindsay 2001: 173) and "extended this principle into their [union] organizations"(Brown, McCrone, and Paterson 1996: 184). Through work on the Scottish Civic Assembly women promoted the view that "It is important that if a Scottish parliament can achieve 50/50 representation, so should the Assembly."[7]

As in England, there were partisan connections. The Scottish Labour Party (SLP), for instance, promoted "twinning" in elections to the new Parliament where each constituency was matched with another in terms of location and winnability and two candidates, a male and female, were chosen (*New Statesman* 1998). This, plus the fact that SNP agreed to put women high on their party lists, meant that the first Scottish Parliament contained a record 37% women. While this fell short of their 50% goal, Scottish women still made inroads by infusing a grass-roots sensibility, "import[ing] into the mainstream of representative democracy the political culture of the margins – those campaigns, social movements and community actions where women were already strong"(Coote and Pattullo 1990: 275). Women's constitutional mobilization resulted in not only a Minister for Women's Issues, but also a Women's Advisory Group and a Scottish Women's Consultative Forum (SWCF) in the new Scottish Parliament, both providing access points for diverse women within civil society.

Still, the extent to which difference – not only between women and men, but also among women – can be incorporated remains to be seen. Although the Scottish Parliament had substantial numbers of women, expressed a

---

[6] This group is both a multi- and nonparty group, but with significant Scottish Green Party influence.

[7] These views were expressed in the following: 1996. "The Importance of the Civic Assembly in the Democratic Process in Scotland." *Engender Newsletter* 12: 2.

commitment to being "woman friendly," and created the SWCF, the fact that it contains no people of color, male or female, is a major representational gap (Kelly 1998). Further, as one Engender member pointed out, the relationship between women activists and the new political insiders remained contentious: "[t]he tendency for the former to turn into the latter is very real: we need to focus on keeping channels open." (Henderson 2000: 5). Nonetheless, efforts at valorizing women's movement and collective mobilization, that is, the unconventional political, are marked compared to the more conventional political focus in England, and thus the Scottish case may hold more hope for democratic expansionism.

Space: Northern Ireland

The importance of multiple open channels of political communication is even more apparent in Northern Ireland. Here women hope to use gender to bring about a compromise between conflictual identities: nationalist and unionist; republican and loyalist; Catholic and Protestant; left and right. While in England and Scotland the focus has been on traditional political institutions (more in the former and less so in the latter), the representational strategies in Northern Ireland, given the exceptional context, break traditional molds. This is partly because women in Northern Ireland were almost totally excluded from the conventional political domain.[8] Women's activism, therefore, did not revolve around conventional political institutions, but was rooted in the community. However, the creation of the Northern Ireland Women's Coalition (NIWC) crossed the institutional/noninstitutional political and other divides.

In response to frustrations with the peace process and their absence from the negotiations (Aretxaga 1997: 4; Sales 1997: 199), the Northern Ireland Women's Coalition was formed in 1996. At an open meeting, women's groups and individual women were invited to field women candidates for elections to all-party peace talks and the newly constituted Northern Ireland Forum (Hinds 1999; Roulston 1997: 65; Wilford 1999). This opportunity was created on April 18, 1996 by the passage of the Northern Ireland Entry into Negotiations Bill and the Ground Rules for Substantive All-Party Talks in the British House of Commons. It called for a May 30, 1996 election with talks to begin in June and adopted a peculiar list system, a modification of the single transferable vote with a regional top up,[9] for this exceptional

---

[8] When it operated, Stormont Parliament had only nine women. By the 1990s, women continued to be chronically underrepresented in all the parties, especially in the Unionist Party (Sales 1997: 171).

[9] It was suggested that the most interesting context was "for the five additional negotiating teams after the 'big five.'" See 1996 "With or Without You," *Fortnight* 350: 5. The big five refers to the main parties: the Ulster Unionist Party (UUP); Democratic Unionist Party (DUP); the Social Democratic and Labour Party (SDLP); Sinn Fein (SF); and the Alliance Party (SP).

event. NIWC formed as a party with a grass-roots campaign and a platform
of human rights, equality, and inclusiveness. It garnered 7,731 votes, 1% of
the poll, and secured a place at the talks, choosing a Protestant (Pearl Sagar)
and a Catholic (Monica McWilliams) as representatives.

Although a registered political party, NIWC combined party politics with
lobbying and grass-roots activism. As the NIWC attended all-party and peace
talks, it ensured that not just party-political issues, but citizens' interests were
negotiated. The Coalition lobbied, pressing for equal opportunity measures
in other parties, met with British politicians, including the prime minister,
and produced position papers (Sharrock 1997: 7). Still it continued to stress
that developments within the formal political arena were only one aspect
of politics in Northern Ireland. In so doing, it introduced a new dynamic[10]
that shaped the rules of procedure, promoting dialogue and understanding
(McWilliams 1996: 9–10). This alternative approach stemmed from NIWC's
cross-community foundations, a result of women's movement organizing and
work done in women's centers (Cockburn 1998). The Coalition organized
open conferences and discussions "in an effort to take advice from as many
women and social activists as possible about how to fashion a new form of
participative politics, politics that women, in particular, can relate to as having clear meaning for them" (Northern Ireland Women's Coalition 1996: 1).
Holding monthly community meetings, publishing a newsletter for members, and working to extend public debate and a more diverse consultative
base were NIWC preoccupations (McCabe 1997: 19; NIWC 1996). Through
networking and consultation, the Coalition brought together women with
various identities from homes, businesses, unions, community groups, the
voluntary sector, and educational institutions.

The NIWC's mark was discernible on the historic Belfast (Good Friday)
Agreement of April 10, 1998. This ambitious multiparty accord contained
many innovations, among them the forging of consociational relationships through an internal government for Northern Ireland and the establishment of a North-South Ministry and a British-Irish Council (Boyle
and Hadden 1999). It also included "successful amendments from the
NIWC ... [including] ... policies for advancement of women ... ; special initiatives for young people particularly affected by the conflict; recognition of
the links between reconciliation and mixed housing and integrated education, and the promotion of a culture of tolerance" (Fearon 1999: 116–117).
Due to NIWC efforts, the Agreement also contained commitments to equal
opportunity in relation to gender, class, creed, ethnicity, and disability and
provided for a new Civic Forum intended to represent the community and

Beyond these, the parties that made it into the running were: the Progressive Unionist Party
(PUP); the Ulster Democratic Party (UDP); the Labour/No Going Back; and the NIWC. On
women in the traditional political process, see Miller, Wilford, and Donoghue 1996.
[10] Still the NIWC experienced a lot of gendered backlash (Fearon 1999; Sharrock 1997).

voluntary sector, trade unions, youth and student sectors in the Assembly (Whitaker 1998: 8). The Agreement was put to a referendum on May 22, 1998 and received 71% support (O'Neill 1999: 171). Subsequently, two NIWC members – Monica McWilliams and Jane Morrice – were elected to the fledgling Northern Ireland Assembly (Fearon 1999: 157–158). Now, as one of them admits, the challenge facing the Coalition is to keep up the pressure as "outsiders inside" (interview with McWilliams).

Summary: Spatial Variations

Constitutional reforms and remedies within the United Kingdom vary, reflecting different priorities and strategies for women's movements in England, Scotland, and Northern Ireland. Nevertheless, in combination, they demonstrate, as does the Canadian case, that women's movements can affect state reconfigurations, both quantitatively and qualitatively. Women's most distinctive contributions, perhaps, come from criss-crossing formal and informal political domains and attempting to forge democratic hybrids.

EXPLAINING VARIATIONS

To understand why strategic emphases differ over time, as in the Canadian example, and across space, as in the United Kingdom, two interrelated explanations are advanced: modifications in political opportunities and constraints; and transformations in identity politics patterns. Once again, these variables are not deterministic, rather they are influencing as well as *influenced* by women's movements.

Political Opportunities/Constraints and State Reconfigurations

As neoliberal imperatives took hold in the United Kingdom and Canada, there was less sympathy for various "impositions" on the state. Under Thatcher, local and institutional women's organizing suffered a staggering blow with the closure of the Greater London Council and broader measures taken to strengthen central government control, discredit local council initiatives, and withdraw support from women's and other community projects dubbed the "loony left." In Canada, from Brian Mulroney's Conservative administration to Jean Chrétien's Liberal government, funding for feminist organizations dissipated. Even the prominent, state-tied Canadian Advisory Council on the Status of Women (CACSW), which had fostered women's constitutional advances and "insider" networks, was ultimately dismantled by the Liberal government in 1995. Thus, state reconfiguration certainly had an effect upon women and on feminist organizing.

There are, however, variations between neoliberal priorities in Canada and the United Kingdom (Savoie 1994). Since 1979, the ideological commitment and continuing reach (Bonefeld, Brown, and Burnham 1995;

Sheldrick 2000) of neoliberal ideas in the United Kingdom have limited spaces in which to maneuver. In Canada, neoliberalism has always been more pragmatic and brokered (Bashevkin 1998). Moreover, neoliberal initiatives that were given rhetorical force by the Mulroney Conservatives were not fully realized until the Chrétien Liberals came to power. There were also different emphases across Canada's ten provinces and two territories, rendering more political "permeability" (Jenson 1990).

In light of our concern with "space" in the United Kingdom, there are also variations within its boundaries. For example, in Scotland, numerous institutions and ideas tempered the neoliberal agenda: from the Scottish Office and the presence of strong trade union influences, to ingrained ideas of equality and social justice with historical and contemporary resonance (Brown, McCrone, and Paterson 1996; MacKay 1996–7). Scotland's reliant economy, the decline of its heavy industrial base, and the closure of manufacturing plants had resulted in economic vulnerability. Northern Ireland was even more economically dependent (Ruane and Todd 1996:158–160), and, like Scotland, suffered from a limited industrial base and high unemployment rate (Collins and McCann 1991: 116). These difficulties were compounded in Northern Ireland by religious-based economic discrimination (Ruane and Todd 1996: 150). Here it was even more difficult to impose a neoliberal agenda, as the fear was that withdrawal of state largesse would cause chaos. Nonetheless, given politico-economic constraints trickling down from Thatcher and her successors, both Northern Ireland and Scotland were compelled to turn to wider markets, gradually directing attention away from Britain to new opportunities in the European Union (EU). As a result, Scotland and Northern Ireland were more amenable to EU political arrangements than England. Combined, these factors suggest more opposition to neoliberal reconfigurations and more willingness to counter them in Scotland and Northern Ireland. This resistance and the consideration of alternative options provided a more porous context for activism.

While Thatcherism and its legacies affected all women in the United Kingdom, their impact differed by race, ethnicity, religion, class, and location. London-centerd feminist activists, especially white and middle class ones, were better situated in relation to economic opportunities and, of course, in political location, being within striking distance of Parliament. The greater economic disadvantages of women at the peripheries may have contributed to more oppositional organizing. This also explains, in part, their willingness to seek out coalition partners that also experienced marginalization and were critical of neoliberal economic dictates. The fact that Scotland and Northern Ireland were more distant, literally and metaphorically, provided further maneuverability, whereas women's constitutional organizing closer to the English hub took more limited and conventional routes.

For Canadian women, the early 80s constituted a time of flux, a period that marked the end of the Keynesian welfare state but not quite the start of neoliberalism, which left space for feminists to work with the state and parties and establish equality provisions. The women involved were mostly white and middle class. As state reconfiguration occurred the women's movement was compelled to focus on jeopardized national social programs and direct its attention to women on the bottom rungs of the socioeconomic ladder, such as Aboriginal, racial minority, and disabled women. More extensive alliances with greater emphasis on coalition work with social policy advocates and neoliberal opponents ensued.

Overall, conventional politics were more "closed" in the United Kingdom than in Canada. The most obvious example here is the Thatcher administration's program of centralizing authority in what was already a highly centralized state. Despite Blair's moves toward devolution in Scotland, Northern Ireland, and Wales, there has been far less sharing of power than exists in the Canadian federal system. Historically, Britain's bureaucratic politics and culture have been closed as well. With no written constitution and now only a limited Bill of Rights, and with European-inspired court-based challenges only a recent phenomenon, it has traditionally been harder for British women to make gains from within (Bashevkin 1998; Lovenduski and Randall 1993: 17–56). Thus, up until 1997, the proportion of women in the Canadian Parliament was double that of Britain's.[11] Some would suggest this difference is also attributable to Britain's historically more ideological, or closed, class system (Berrington 1987; Dunleavy, Gamble, Holliday, and Peele 1993; Ingle 1989: 223–224) which contrasts with Canada's brokerage system that appeals to various constituencies to attain electoral success.

The closed political system in the United Kingdom created a sharp division of feminist strategies between grass-roots mobilization and mainstreaming in the 1970s, with a preference for the former. Especially in England, with Labour in Opposition providing sustained critiques to Thatcher's authoritarian regime and striving to open up and democratize the party (Perrigo 1996: 116–129) and with new parties more willing to embrace women's issues, many feminists chose to work from inside oppositional parties (Gelb 1995). There were also efforts to affect state structures and agencies, especially via local councils (Coote and Pattullo 1990: 230–251). While some of these, like the Greater London Council, were subsequently shut down, or cut back, cuts and squeezes on state agencies created new opportunities as political officials

---

[11] In 1995, there were 9.7% women in the United Kingdom Parliament. In Canada, as of 1993, there were 17.9% women in the House of Commons and 15% women in the Senate. However, after Canada's June 1997 election, 21% of the Canadian House of Commons was female. With Labour's landslide victory in May 1997, plus given the short-lived, but nonetheless effectual, all-female short lists, the number of female MPs rose from 62 to 121; 101 were Labour women, 13 were Conservatives, and there were 3 Liberals and 2 SNP female MPs. This means that in 1997, the British percentage has doubled; the House is 18% female, not far from Canadian levels.

looked to community groups to service needs. At the same time, with lateral loading there was a paradoxical increase in quangos offering other possible political openings.[12] Still, with so few potential entry points overall, women in England identified select routes to bring about change and their political strategies narrowed.

In Scotland and Northern Ireland, however, there was not only a greater sense of frustration and/or injustice, but also potential for more fluid politics. The concern was that the Conservative Party was "willing to rule from a southern English power base and ride roughshod over those who did not support it"(Ruane and Todd 1996: 218). For example, many Scottish citizens were incensed at having to undergo Conservative rule after the 1992 election, when the party received only 14% of the vote in Scotland (Bonefeld, Brown, and Burnham 1995: 99). Here the SLP could take more risks than its English Labour counterparts. The latter had to do electoral battle with the traditional forces of the Conservative Party, whereas the SLP defined itself in relation to a more radical SNP, requiring a distinctive nationalist and leftist stance. In Northern Ireland, there was also a sense that the "'top-down' concept of sovereignty implicit in the British constitution imped[ed] the search for radical forms of local democracy which might permit greater communal equality" (Ruane and Todd 1996: 230); hence the push for more porous politics.

In Scotland and Northern Ireland, the ground was more fertile to cultivate different kinds of politics, allowing structures to take root that could accommodate difference. In light of their critical distance from British institutions, creating reticence if not outright hostility toward them, and their local political dynamics, there have been more variegated political institutional and community-based interactions. In Scotland, the idea of an entirely new institution, the Scottish Parliament, provided a significant political opportunity. The ability to start from scratch inspired women to demand distinctive institutions, such as the 50/50 split and more consensual, community-informed politics.

In Northern Ireland, given British rule, citizen participation in traditional political institutions and debate was generally minimal. In its place was a strong and vital community-based political life. The politics of the ceasefire, however, created a unique opportunity for greater community involvement in both traditional and less conventional political arenas, prompting exceptional political arrangements: different electoral systems and new institutions for dialogue and deliberation. These unique circumstances fostered democratic experimentation. Both contexts provided an opportunity for women's constitutional activism, one which women exploited.

---

[12] This is particularly evident in Northern Ireland where "the state increasingly interacts with more specific community representatives [and] ... may even turn over aspects of state, social and economic activity to those groups" (Morison and Livingstone 1995: 146).

While these political opportunities enhanced the potential for feminists to influence both traditional and new forms of politics, they were not all determining. In other words, feminists not only seized existing opportunities but also created their own political openings. In the Canadian case, women expanded the opportunity provided by the Charter by adding *new* equality clauses and closing existing loopholes. At times, such as the initial stages of the Meech Lake Accord, reactive organizing took place, but at other points *proactive* organizing was more apparent, as with the grass-roots education and action and coalition building in the Charlottetown round. Institutions that were un- and underrepresentative, from elitist First Ministers' conferences, to the Senate, and the courts were challenged. Alternative political arrangements from 50/50 PR-based Senate and constituent assemblies to the discussion of constitutional politics around kitchen tables were advocated.

In England, some women created opportunities for change by lobbying and highlighting democratic gaps in traditional institutions, but at the risk of cooptation. In Scotland, and even more so in Northern Ireland, women challenged the shape and direction of various representational forms, conventional and otherwise, striving to accommodate their movement experiences. These struggles took place in a context of opportunity and constraint, but women did not just react to these political conditions, they struggled and also acted to create strategic openings. This becomes particularly apparent when one considers the dialectical influence of identity.

Identity Politics Challenges and the Challenges of Identity Politics

Identity politics are crucial when considering the different strategic emphases of feminist constitutional organizing. In Canada, during the early 1980s, the women's movement did not sufficiently acknowledge the existence or legitimacy of a plurality of identities. By the mid- to late 80s, given criticisms of the lack of diversity in the women's movement by women of color, immigrant women, disabled women, and others, the movement could no longer ignore the implications of intersecting identities. With the Meech Lake Accord focusing on Quebec and a dualistic recognition of French and English founding nations, the government refused to deal with a plurality of issues and identities, whereas the women's movement could not. Obviously, certain women's movement initiatives faltered, particularly initially, with respect to understanding Quebec feminist positions. Then, some women's groups tried to shore up women of color, immigrant women, and disabled women's organizations to counter the groups calling for more sensitivity to Quebec's aspirations. This resulted in serious divisions within the movement but reparations were made in the next round, where there were concerted efforts to consider a wide range of identities. Feminist organizations spoke of three founding nations and they acknowledged the effects of race, ethnicity, and ability

as never before. Still, the volatile context within and between communities
made the positions taken by some feminist organizations, particularly during
the referendum campaign, problematic. Through all this, however, identity
politics did not preclude consensual politics and compromise (Dobrowolsky
2000, 1998).

In England, women's constitutional organizing, in general, was channeled
and funneled. With some exceptions, feminists active in raising representational and equality issues were primarily white, middle class, and able bod-
ied. Like the Canadian women's movement, the British women's movement
has also had to respond to questions of diversity; however, women's groups
in England concentrated their constitutional efforts in seeking greater representational access for women in traditional political arenas, and in so doing
underscored an undifferentiated notion of "woman." Although they were
not advocating sameness, neither were feminists celebrating difference.

The fact that identity politics have been considered to be highly problematic in England goes a long way in explaining this situation. Class identity
has historically held priority here with gender claims, let alone those of
race and ethnicity, only haltingly accepted (Phillips 1997: 145). However,
increased nonwhite immigration and the rise of racism have raised basic
questions about identity and citizenship in Britain (Messina 1989), coming
to a head under Thatcher (Mason 1995; Hesse et al. 1992). On the right,
identity politics concerns were linked to the "loony left," and castigated as
expendable politics that overloaded government, wasted public resources,
and detracted from legitimate, centralized government control. On the left,
the fear was that the politics of difference had displaced materialist politics (Phillips 1997: 146). Moreover, from the late 70s onward, the British
women's movement itself experienced significant upheavals as a result of
divisions over class, gender, race, ethnicity, and sexual orientation (Mirza
1997). Thus, many considered identity politics to be fragmenting, politically
explosive, and something to be avoided (Lovenduski and Randall 1993).

In contrast, Scottish identity politics produced a catalyst for change. Instead of being a problem, here identity politics was used for empowerment, as a goal and as a tactic. As the distinct Scottish identity became
more pronounced in the contemporary context, it intersected with women's
senses of identity and allowed for the formation of new alliances and networks. Gender and Scottish identity combined in interesting ways, where
women's contributions to the constitutional debate were seen to reinforce
a progressive, civic-minded, forward-looking Scottish nationalism. This encouraged broader community linkages as different communities sought to
bring about innovative, equitable Scottish institutions. Whether these institutions can include diversity in terms of multiracial and multicultural realities,
or issues of disability and so on, remains to be seen. However, some have
suggested that the combination of conventional and innovative democratic
forms, to which we can add feminists' consensual and coalitional efforts, are

"primed to exploit a new pluralism" (Walker 1995: 163) allowing more diverse representation.

In Northern Ireland, there have been deep and tragic conflicts from the "clash of ethno-national, cultural, religious and political identities" (Wilson and Nolan 1996: 16–17). However, the NIWC has attempted to use gender to bridge these polarizations and bring about compromises between rivaling identities. This is not without fundamental difficulties. For example, in establishing itself as a party of women with multiple identities, the Coalition was accused of detracting from different positions, whether party, political, religious, nationalist, or other, by "poaching" women from various sides (interview with Hinds). Moreover, to build a consensus, some highly contentious issues were sidestepped in favor of issues on which women could unite, such as childcare or employment. The danger was that "[a]ttempts to build a common agenda in which women can bury their differences may bring limited gains"(Sales 1997: 201). Still, because the Coalition expanded the boundaries of the "political" in terms of both the issues it raised and its forms of organizing, there was also more hope for the recognition of multiple, intersecting identities, as was evident in their contributions to the Good Friday Agreement.

There is no denying that the politics of identity are complex, fluid, and contingent. They can be essentialist and reductionist, as well as conflictual and divisive. However, the point here is to emphasize how identities *both* are used by and influence women's movement mobilization. While they can prove fragmenting, as was evident in the English example, they also have the potential to offer integrative political expressions and struggles, as was apparent in Scotland. There is also the danger of exclusive deployment, for example, emphasizing differences between men and women, and not among women. Still we have also seen how shared identities can be harnessed, in Northern Ireland and Canada for instance, to work across diversity in not reductionist but expansionist ways. In short, women's identity politics can be used as strategies for change, potentially transforming and creating political spaces.

CONCLUDING COMMENTS

Women's movements are influenced by formal political opportunities/ constraints, that is, a reconfigured state, or constitutional change, as well as more informal and identity politics predispositions. Yet women's movements not only respond and react to these opportunities/constraints; they also mobilize proactively, forging new political relationships, promoting alternative discourses, and fostering innovative representational forms. As the foregoing constitutional change chronicle attests, they do this with a wide, adaptable strategic repertoire.

Of course, not all women's movement strategies are effective or beyond reproach. There are often miscalculations, tensions, and multiple constraints indicated in all of the strategies and struggles recounted in this chapter. Advances are often tenuous and retreats are common. Despite these risks, in the realm of constitutionalism, women's movements in Canada and the United Kingdom, with their respective forms of mobilization that shift in time and over space, have clearly had an effect on state reconfiguration and on civil society. In fact, their efforts (in some cases more than others) attempt to fuse the two. Thus, women's movements have had a unique impact on political practices and discourses broadly conceived.

Interviews

Sincere thanks to those who agreed to be interviewed for their time and resources. Any errors, misrepresentations, or omissions rest with me.

Anderson, Doris. November 15, 1995.
Baines, Beverley. April 13, 1996.
Breitenbach, Esther. February 23, 1997.
Brown, Alice. June 1, 1999.
Cameron, Barbara. April 12, 1996.
Corrin, Chris. June 1, 1999.
Evans, Valerie and Moira Taylor. June 17, 1999.
Fearon, Kate. February 25, 1997.
Fearon, Kate. June 8, 1999.
Follett, Barbara. March 4, 1997.
Forsyth, Fiona. February 28, 1997.
Hacker, Pat. November 16, 1995.
Hinds, Bronagh. February 24, 1997.
Mackay, Fiona. February 23, 1997.
Meehan, Elizabeth. February 24, 1997.
McIvor, Sharon and Teressa Nahanee February 5, 1996.
McPhedran, McPedran. November 22, 1995.
McWilliams, Monica. June 8, 1999.
Power, Greg. February 17, 1997.
Power, Greg. June 21, 1999.
Rebick, Judy. November 15, 1995.
Robertson, Sue. February 27, 1997.
Robertson, Sue. June 2, 1999.
Russell, Meg. June 17, 1999.
Ruth, Nancy. November 16, 1995.
Smith, Nicole. February 20, 1997.
Stephenson, Mary-Ann. March 4, 1997.
Sutherland, Leslie. June 1, 1999.
*Swain, Ann. February 20, 1997.
Wilkinson, Helen. March 4, 1997.

* telephone interview

7

The Women's Movement Policy Successes and the Constraints of State Reconfiguration

*Abortion and Equal Pay in Differing Eras**

Lee Ann Banaszak

INTRODUCTION

In all European and North American countries, there are signs that the women's movement has influenced politics and policy since the early 1970s. Women's representation in parliaments, cabinets, and executive branches of government has risen considerably, particularly in the 1980s (Beckwith this volume; Bystydzienski 1995; Darcy, Welch, and Clark 1994; Lovenduski and Randall 1993; Randall 1987). In Norway, for example, the percentage of women in the Norwegian parliament, the Storting, rose from 16% in 1975 to 26% in 1985 and then to 36% by 1990 (Bystydzienski 1995: 14). Increasingly, political parties and some nations are considering specific quotas for women in elected office (Jenson and Valiente this volume; Lovenduski and Norris 1993: 9–11). The number of individuals who accept nontraditional roles for women has also increased since the early 1970s (Black 1980; Klein 1987; Monk and García-Ramon 1996). Moreover, some policies supported by the women's movement – reproductive rights, affirmative action, equal pay, support for domestic violence victims – have been implemented in every country.[1]

However, as these changes occurred the nature of nation-states underwent fundamental changes. As women have sought more state control over hiring and wages to reduce sexual discrimination, the globalization of the economy and market competition has reduced the willingness of states to regulate firms. Sharp cuts in some nation-states' social expenditures have coincided with increased demands for state support of childcare, victims of

---

* The author would like to thank Karen Beckwith, Mary Fainsod Katzenstein, Eric Plutzer, Dieter Rucht, and Theda Skocpol as well as several anonymous reviewers for comments on earlier drafts of the chapter. A previous version of this chapter was presented at the 2001 American Political Science Association annual meeting.
[1] However, countries vary greatly in their adoption of such policies and, in all cases, the policies do not go far enough by the standards of the women's movement.

domestic violence, and poor women. Women have entered national legislatures as decision-making power is being limited by international agreements,
downloaded to local governments, and usurped by nonelected governmental bodies. Thus, the major characteristics of state reconfiguration appear to
be obstacles that hinder women's movements from achieving many of their
goals.

In this chapter, I examine how the ability of feminists to achieve policy
goals is affected by the reconfiguration of the nation-state. I explore two
questions. First, I investigate whether their ability to achieve policy goals is
influenced by the degree to which an issue is essential to neoliberal ideology. Individual policies may be more-or-less central to the economic globalization and free market ideology that accompanies state reconfiguration
(see Banaszak, Beckwith, and Rucht this volume). In this chapter, I focus
on women's movement policy success in two issues: abortion reform and
equal pay. Equal pay policies, because they require restrictions on the employment market, directly contradict free market ideology. Kessler-Harris
(1988) argues that equal pay laws are largely opposed by entrepreneurs
who see such laws as questioning the fairness and constructed nature of the
market. On the other hand, opponents of free access to abortion are largely
motivated by religious values, which makes it a highly contested moral issue
but one unchanged by the increased emphasis on neoliberal ideology.[2] Thus,
Lovenduski (1986) argues that these two policies reflect very different policy
goals. Abortion policy develops regulatory policies that assure open access
and safety of legal abortions while equal pay involves economic redistribution. Given the centrality of free market values to reconfiguration, we would
therefore expect to find that equal pay policies, because they are more central
to neoliberal ideology, are most likely to be altered by the reconfiguration
process. However, as we shall see below, state reconfiguration has a much
more nuanced affect on women's movements' policy achievements.

Second, I examine whether feminists' policy effectiveness is shaped by
the degree of reconfiguration that has occurred in a particular country. If
reconfiguration has a negative impact on feminist movements, we should find
feminists in states that have undergone greater restructuring to be suffering
more policy setbacks than those in states that have fewer characteristics
of reconfiguration. To examine the effect of reconfiguration on policy, I will
compare equal pay policies in Great Britain and France and abortion policies
in Ireland and Germany.

Within each policy area, each of the two countries I selected had continued
debates on the policy through the 1990s and represents a different degree of
reconfiguration (see Table 7.1). Between the two countries in the equal pay
case study, the United Kingdom has undergone more state reconfiguration

[2] For example, see Klatch (1992) and Luker (1984) for the ideological bases of support for
conservative and antiabortion activists in the United States.

TABLE 7.1. *Country Categorization According to Degree of State Reconfiguration*

	Equal Pay Case Study	Abortion Case Study
More reconfigured	United Kingdom	Germany
Less reconfigured	France	Ireland

than France. As Banaszak, Beckwith, and Rucht (this volume) argue in detail, the French state, in part because of the electoral success of the left throughout much of the 1980s, did not reduce national state power and offload to private individuals, especially when compared to its British counterpart. Although France has been a stronger supporter of the European Union (EU) than Britain, it has not ceded much responsibility to local authorities and remains committed to strong state welfare policies and state ownership of economic enterprises.

In the case of abortion policy, I compare Ireland with Germany. While Germany may not have engaged in the same degree of reconfiguration as its British counterpart, it can still be classified as more reconfigured than the Irish state. Particularly under Helmut Kohl, the German government became a strong supporter of the EU and also engaged in some reduction in social policy – particularly in the area of health care. Although unification increased overall state spending, attempts were made to increase Länder control over many areas, and to reduce the range of policy areas over which the national government has competence (Jeffery 1996). More concern was also given to the degree to which the national government intrudes on the market (Dyson 1996).

On the other hand, Ireland, like France, has been slow to abandon the ideology of state interference and reduce the responsibility of the state. State and party ideology continues to emphasize the state's role in reducing inequality and poverty (Hardiman 1998: 123). Ireland also continues to embrace state-owned enterprises; Haughton (1998: 46) argues that these institutions "are more important now" than in the 1960s. Similarly, Ireland has moved toward more centralization rather than increasing the responsibility and power of local governments (Ardagh 1994: 48–51; Keogh 1994; Schmitt 1998). For example, the national government discouraged regional participation in the EU until 1992 (Keogh 1994: 330). The one area, in addition to participation in the EU, where Ireland has moved toward reconfiguration is in granting increased political power to nonelected state bodies. For example, since 1987 the National Economic and Social Council (where representatives of trade unions and employers sit) has increasingly determined social policies (Hardiman 1998: 124). Nonetheless, these changes reflect a move toward the corporatist structures that already exist in Germany and many other European countries.

Thus, for the purposes of this chapter, Germany and Britain will serve as examples of countries that have moved further toward state reconfiguration and France and Ireland will serve as examples of countries that are less far along in the reconfiguration process. While a true test of the effect of state reconfiguration requires examining a wider range of issues and countries, this chapter represents a preliminary assessment of state reconfiguration's effect on policy making.

The chapter proceeds as follows. First, I discuss the relationship between reconfiguration and women's movement achievements, focusing on the four countries that will serve as case studies. I then examine abortion policy in Ireland and Germany from the 1970s through the 1990s, and, in a fourth section, equal pay legislation in France and Great Britain during the same time period. In both sections, I focus explicitly on the degree to which the four dimensions of state reconfiguration – uploading to the EU, downloading to local government, offloading to the private sector, and lateral loading to nonelected state bodies – have affected policy outcomes. The final section draws some preliminary conclusions about the role that state reconfiguration has played in the achievement of feminist policies.

STATE RECONFIGURATION AND PUBLIC POLICY ACHIEVEMENTS

Because the reconfiguration of states has been associated with conservative governments, scholars have generally argued that these changes limit the types of policies that can be and are achieved by the women's movement (Bashevkin 1998). Yet the relationship between reconfiguration and women's movements' policy outcomes is more complex than this simple hypothesis suggests. First, reconfiguration is not a uniform process; countries may experience more reconfiguration in one area than another, and a country may move in opposite directions along different dimensions. Given the complexity of form and direction that reconfiguration can take, each dimension must be discussed separately. Second, the effect of each dimension of reconfiguration on women's movements' achievements may differ. For example, feminists have viewed the expansion of EU authority more positively than the privatization of state responsibilities. Thus, we need to develop separate hypotheses for each dimension of reconfiguration in order to capture potentially conflicting influences.

Uploading Authority to the European Union

The transfer of power to the European Community has been a mixed blessing for the women's movement. On the one hand, women are better represented in the European Parliament than in many national parliaments and women members of the European Parliament (MEPs) have actively supported feminist policies (Beckwith this volume; Vallance and Davies 1986). On the other hand, the European Parliament has limited powers to affect European law. Despite recent reforms of EU institutions, the Council, which has ultimate decision-making power in most cases, and the Commission, which controls the policy agenda, continue to dominate decision making. In this sense, the shifting of state authority to the European Community represents a loss of influence by national parliaments and an increase in the power of nonelected state bodies (that is, the Commission). Since women are more likely to be represented in parliaments than cabinets, women's movements are likely to be disadvantaged by the shift. Nonetheless, Vallance and Davies (1986) argue that feminist MEPs have excelled at using informal powers of persuasion to influence policies toward women. By coordinating efforts with the Commission offices in charge of women's issues and using the European Parliament as an arena for raising issues, their influence has been greater than the degree of their formal decision-making power would suggest.

Because the EU has instituted only limited policies toward women, uploading authority has not advantaged women's movements. The EU offices responsible for women are located in the Directorate General in charge of employment and industrial relations. Consequently, the Action Programmes for Women's Equality have concentrated on equal pay, equal opportunity in education and training, a reduction of barriers to women's employment, and equity in social security benefits. Only recently has the Action Programme called for increasing women's representation in EU institutions. This limited focus is a result of the EU's limited mandate as an economic institution; priorities of the women's movement, such as violence against women and abortion politics, have traditionally not been under its purview (Elman 1996a). Although the EU's mandate has expanded in the last few years, the social policies that include these issues continue to remain underdeveloped.

Moreover, the effect of EU policy on individual women's movements depends largely on their previous achievements. For those countries that have greater inequality between men and women in education and employment, EU policy may represent tangible gains for women's movements. However, in countries like Sweden, where women have already made greater strides in achieving social equality, increased power to the EU potentially represents the loss of previously achieved gains. Even when the EU does not require a uniform policy, governments and political parties feel pressure to reduce social programs in order to remain competitive with other EU countries.

All of the countries included in this chapter are EU member countries. However, they do vary in the types of policies they had upon entering the EU, and in the degree to which they have opted out of particular parts of EU treaties (for example, the United Kingdom opted out of monetary union). In the case of abortion policy, Ireland's constitutional amendment prohibiting abortions places it as the most repressive of abortion rights while German women have more extensive rights. In the case of equal pay policies, France has the most egalitarian policies while the United Kingdom has largely fallen behind EU standards.

Downloading Authority to Local Governments

Not all states have shifted power to local governments, but in the United States, Canada, Italy, Germany, and more recently Great Britain (under Tony Blair), local governments are increasingly empowered to control social policy. Here too, the effects of local control on women's movements' policy achievements have been mixed. The downloading of state authority and responsibility reduces the power of national parliaments just as women are ascending into these arenas. Yet women's representation has traditionally been higher in local governments, meaning that women's opportunity to affect policy is probably greater at the local level (Lovenduski 1986; Randall 1987).

Similarly, the ability of local states to affect policies allows both women's movements and their countermovements to have control over policy. On the one hand, local control enables local authorities to introduce less feminist policies or implement existing policies in ways that reduce the feminist potential.[3] On the other hand, in some local governments, such as the Greater London Council, the women's movement has managed to gain representation. Yet, even these governments have been increasingly constrained by their new responsibilities. As local governments acquire more of the duties that traditionally belonged to the national state, particularly under tight economic conditions, their ability to finance existing policies is reduced.[4] Thus, we might expect to see more variation in the type and implementation of policy as countries download responsibilities to local governments.

Lateral Loading: Increasing Power of Nonelected State Bodies

In addition to the transfer of state power and responsibilities to local governments and the EU, power has also shifted away from the elected institutions of the state to nonelected bodies. For example, in Great Britain quangos became increasingly responsible for implementing policies beginning in the 1970s (although Thatcher did attempt to stem the tide). Again, this change has mirrored the rise in women's representation in elected institutions, suggesting that the increase in women in parliaments occurred as real power transferred elsewhere (see, for example, Bystydzienski 1995: 62).

[3] In the United States, for example, after a period of increasing federal influence on abortion policy in the 1970s, conservative countermovements have managed to use state governments to introduce stricter abortion policies (Goggin 1998; Staggenborg 1991).
[4] For example, in many German Länder spending on local women's projects has decreased in recent years (Kamenitsa 1997: 65–66 but see Blattert 1998 on Berlin).

How the rising power of nonelected state bodies affects women's movements' policy achievements depends on the degree of women's, and particularly feminist, representation in these institutions. Trade union activists and business leaders have generally dominated such bodies. Traditionally, both groups have few women in leadership positions and are unsympathetic to the goals of the women's movement (Randall 1987; Stetson and Mazur 1995; Young 1996). Where unsympathetic unions and business groups determine appointments to these institutions, women's movement influence will be low. Women's movements are rarely represented on nonelected state bodies and then only when the appointed body deals specifically with "women's issues" (Heenan and Gray 1999; Stämpfli 1994 on Switzerland). Since few policies are considered to fall under this rubric, women's groups are usually not consulted. For this reason, Stetson and Mazur (1995: 8) argue that "the state has empowered the very areas of participation... where men dominate."

Despite the lack of feminist representation, in some countries women's representation is stronger on appointed boards and commissions than in elected institutions. For example, in 1988 women held about 20% of the seats on boards and commissions in Great Britain, while their representation in Parliament was only 6.3% (Lovenduski and Norris 1993: 46, 166). Heenan and Gray (1999) find a similar pattern in Ireland, although representation on boards unrelated to traditional women's issues of education and equal rights was much lower. They also note that women's representation is influenced by trade unions' and business enterprises' role in the appointment process.

We might therefore expect that an increase in the authority of nonelected state bodies would be most detrimental to women's movement's interests where these conflict with trade union or business politics and where women's representation in these organizations is low.

Offloading to Nonstate Bodies

Perhaps most damaging to women's movement policy success is the growing tendency for states to recategorize certain issues as totally outside the purview of the state. Increasingly, states have mandated that private groups – corporations, civil society, or the family – are responsible for certain types of policy. This offloading of policy responsibility has two negative effects on women's movements' ability to achieve policy. First, it reduces the amount that states spend to redress women's problems. Bashevkin (1998) notes that programs benefiting women have particularly suffered under these reductions. Policies focused on reducing inequalities between the sexes that are seen as impeding market forces (such as employment programs) have been cut extensively. Second, many women's movement policies (for example, equal pay, domestic violence, sexual harassment) require the regulative arm of the state to ensure enforcement. To the extent that state regulation is reduced by offloading, it becomes difficult to guarantee that such policies are being implemented. As we shall see, private sector groups differ among themselves in how they implement policies. Thus, offloading does not always involve a change in government policy; when regulatory agencies are weakened and implementation is offloaded to the private sector, policies may become unenforceable or determined by private interests.

On the other hand, privatization provides more freedom for women's movement projects to operate without the constraints of state regulation. State support is usually predicated on compliance with certain rules and regulations. Often these rules and regulations can change a movement's character, altering its organization and structure (McCarthy, Britt, and Wolfson 1991) or molding its activities to fit prevailing cultural norms. For that reason, radical women's movements insist on autonomy from the state, preferring instead to struggle against existing cultural and political institutions that oppress women and avoid "the contamination of conventional politics" (Jenson 1987; Lovenduski 1988: 114). In that sense, the reduction of state activity might create opportunities for new forms of movement activity or organization.

Thus, overall the reconfiguration of the state is likely to hurt women's movements' abilities to make concrete policy gains. However, there are several caveats to that general rule. In countries where women's movements had made few policy gains, the uploading of decision-making power to the EU may force concrete changes. Moreover, to the extent that reconfiguration shifts political power to areas where women have greater representation – such as the local levels or the EU – it creates opportunities for feminist policies. In the cases of the downloading and offloading of state policies, reconfiguration may also produce variation in the actual policy or its implementation.

STATE RECONFIGURATION AND ABORTION POLICY

Abortion has been a highly salient issue, unifying the different strands of the women's movements (Randall 1987), and inspiring their most visible acts of protest (Rucht 1994: 210–211). In West Germany[5] and Ireland as in many other western European countries, liberal, socialist, and radical feminists support the liberalization of abortion laws (Galligan 1998; Outshoorn 1988). Struggles over abortion policy occurred in Germany and Ireland throughout the 70s, 80s, and 90s – the same time period as major state reconfiguration was occurring within Europe and North America.

---

[5] Throughout this chapter the term "Germany" refers to the Federal Republic of Germany. Until 1990, this constituted the area commonly called West Germany. From 1990 on, it refers to this geographic area and the five new Länder as well as the former East Berlin.

In Germany, women's movement protest against the criminalization of abortion and a social democratic government led in 1974 to legislation legalizing abortions during the first trimester, which was invalidated by the German Constitutional Court. A new law, adopted a year later, allowed women to have abortions only when there were medical, eugenic, or social hardship reasons, or when the pregnancy was a result of rape or incest. The unification of Germany in 1990 again intensified the abortion debate because East German law allowed abortions during the first twelve weeks. Both East and West German women's organizations organized massive protests calling for a liberal abortion law (Rucht 1994: 384), but the final unification treaty only allowed the continuation of separate policies in the two regions for a year, until an all-German parliament could decide the controversy. After unification, the women's movement began a coordinated action for the freedom to choose an abortion during the first trimester. However, in the end the German Bundestag adopted a law that combined the "trimester concept with mandatory counseling" (Mushaben 1997: 78). Women could decide whether or not to have the abortion after receiving counseling. Again, the German Constitutional Court overturned this legislation, resulting in a new abortion law in 1995. This law requires mandatory counseling and states that most abortions are to be considered illegal but not punishable (*rechtswidrig aber straffrei*),[6] meaning that they are not covered by medical insurance except in cases of financial need.

In Ireland, while abortions had been illegal based on the British Offenses against the Person Act of 1861, in 1983 "the absolute right to life of every unborn child from conception" was enshrined in the constitution by referendum (Randall 1986; Yishai 1993: 212). In the late 1980s, the Irish Supreme Court interpreted this amendment as forbidding even the distribution of information about abortion clinics in other countries. Liberalization of abortion policy began in 1992, when the Supreme Court ruled in the *X case* that abortion is permitted when the pregnancy constitutes "a real and substantial risk to the life of the mother" (Connelly 1999: 20). Later that year, two constitutional amendments codifying women's right to information about abortion and to travel to other countries were adopted by referenda. A third amendment, which would forbid abortions in the case where the pregnancy affected the health (as opposed to the life) of the mother failed. Although the Irish women's movement was not very active on the abortion issue prior to the 1983 referendum (Randall 1986; Yishai 1993), since that time women's movement organizations have mobilized for referenda campaigns, staffed underground information sources, and engaged in numerous acts of protest against the strict abortion policy (Galligan 1998; Smyth 1996).

---

[6] Only abortions that are considered medically necessary or abortions for rape and incest victims are considered legal. Such abortions are covered by medical insurance.

How have different aspects of state reconfiguration affected abortion policy in these two countries? Despite the potential compatibility of liberal abortion laws to free market liberalization, state reconfiguration has not worked to increase women's access to abortion. The growing power of the EU has left national abortion policies untouched or, as we shall see, even reinforced existing national policy. Increases in local government power permit greater inequality in abortion policy, allowing both liberalization and decreased access simultaneously. The offloading of state responsibilities to regulate abortion has also strengthened discretionary control over abortion access. Let us look at each of these in turn.

Uploading: The European Union

In the late 1970s, German and particularly Irish abortion policy was on average more restrictive than that of the other seven EU countries (see, for example, Ketting and van Praag 1986: 160–161). While equal pay legislation by the EU forced a minimum standard for all countries, no legislation creates a similar standard for abortion access, despite the increasing emphasis on building a common European social policy. Only the European Parliament, which has adopted several resolutions calling for increased access to abortion, has discussed an EU abortion policy (Outshoorn 1988: 213–215; European Union. European Parliament 1999: 7). Yet the Commission has ignored these resolutions. On the other hand, EU inaction has not simply allowed individual nations to choose their own policies. If anything, the activities of the EU have reinforced restrictive national policies, even contradicting some of its own principles to further other EU goals.

Although the EU has actively promoted the free movement of people, goods, and services through regulation and judicial proceedings in the European Court of Justice, both Ireland and a few German states (notably Bavaria) have abortion policies that contradict these principles. Until 1995, Ireland prohibited the distribution of information on overseas abortion services and travel to other countries to receive an abortion. Irish women's organizations attempting to provide such information were hurt by the 1991 European Court of Justice ruling that this prohibition did not contradict the European Community's single internal market policy (*SPUC v. Grogan* 1991). The court justified this ruling by calling abortion a service protected by EU treaties but denying that the provision of information about abortion was covered as part of the service. Four years later, in the famous *X case*, the attorney general of Ireland got an injunction prohibiting a fourteen-year-old girl from traveling to Great Britain for an abortion (O'Brien 1998: 113). Although the Irish Supreme Court overturned the injunction, this decision was not based on the EU laws requiring the free movement of people. Rather, it relied solely on the Irish constitutional amendment that permits abortion if the life of the mother was in danger. The court argued that the girl's potential suicide threatened her life, thereby justifying the abortion without denying Ireland's right to prohibit travel in the case of abortion (Ardagh 1994: 191). Some German Länder also limited women's right to travel for abortions or to provide information about clinics in other European countries before 1990 (Friedrichsen 1989: 70; Krieger 1987: 78). Thus, EU principles of freedom of trade and movement have not been applied in the case of abortion policy.

The EU has also traded acceptance of restrictive abortion policies for member states' support of other policies. In attempting to ensure the Irish government's support of the Maastricht Treaty, the European Council included a special protocol stating that the treaty would not invalidate the Irish abortion law in any way (Smyth 1996). This action reduced the opportunities of the Irish women's movement to appeal to Community law and constrains future policy making at the EU level. This protocol in the Maastricht Treaty meant that changes to Ireland's abortion policy can only be effected by national legislation. Ireland's recent rejection of the Treaty of Nice by referendum, partially because antiabortion forces argued that the treaty reduced national control over abortion policy, has stimulated French officials to request an addendum recognizing Ireland's "right to ban abortion" (Marlowe 2001). Thus, to gain Ireland's support for integration, the EU has limited the ability of the Irish women's movement to appeal to EU institutions.

Nonetheless, the Irish women's movement has utilized other European-level opportunities, particularly coordination with women's movements in other EU countries. In 1992, Irish feminists worked with British feminists to protest the ban on information by sponsoring a demonstration that transported pamphlets naming British abortion contacts across the Irish border (Taylor 1998). In June 2001, Irish feminists organized a visit from a Dutch ship intended to provide Irish women with abortions in international waters ("Women on Waves" 2001).[7] While these demonstrations have provided mainly media exposure, they indicate the Irish movement's willingness to work outside of national institutions.

Despite the Irish women's movement's transnational mobilization and the contradictions between Irish abortion policy and EU doctrine, EU institutions have refused to protect the "free movement of goods, services and people" principle in the case of abortion. As we shall see, its hands-off policy contrasts greatly with its active role in the case of equal pay policy.

Offloading to the Private Sector

As is the case with equal pay policy, implementation of abortion policy often is influenced by private sector decisions. The availability of abortion

---

[7] In the end, the boat failed to get a license to perform medical procedures from the Dutch government and no abortions occurred.

procedures, as well as the character of support services for individuals seeking abortions, is determined by nonstate organizations. In Germany, the abortion counseling mandated by the 1995 law is provided largely by charitable and church organizations. Although the German Constitutional Court mandated that counseling inform women that "the unborn life has its own right to life" (Mushhaben 1997: 83), there remains leeway in the content of the counseling. The law allows groups like Pro Familia to have a very different emphasis than Donum Vitae, the Catholic organization involved in abortion counseling (Rechnungshof Baden-Württemberg 2000: 13). Thus, the character of abortion counseling varies by provider and, as we shall see, local states encourage different private providers.

Recent events in Germany have further indicated the power that private groups have over policy. In 1998 the pope forced the German Catholic church to abandon its counseling of abortion seekers, despite requests from the German Christian Democratic Party and local church leaders that it continue ("Germany: Catholic church to end abortion counseling certificates" 1998). While Catholic laypeople formed a private organization, Donum Vitae, to continue the counseling, in the short term some German Länder were left with a shortage of counseling centers. For example, Niedersachsen had thirty fewer counseling centers in the year after the church abandoned their counseling (Waschbüsch 2000). Thus, just the choice to enter or leave abortion counseling affects women's access to abortion.

Because states choose how, and to whom, they offload social policy functions, some of the specific characteristics of offloading are influenced by the state. In Germany, the national and Länder governments (as we shall see in what follows) not only license counseling centers but they also encourage particular types of groups. For example, after unification, the Kohl government established counseling centers in East Germany (since they did not exist). Despite the overwhelming secular or Protestant population in the five new Länder, the Kohl government chose to fund more Catholic church–run centers than those run by Pro Familia – the German chapter of Planned Parenthood (Reimer 1996: 175). When the most recent German abortion law mandated counseling for women, many Länder offloaded much of the abortion counseling by providing financial support to these private organizations rather than expanding government counseling offices. In the state of Brandenburg, for example, over 85% of the budget for abortion counseling centers goes to private organizations (Brandenburg. Ministerium der Finanzen 2000). As we shall see in the next section, Länder decisions about which private organizations to support create inequality in abortion services.

Downloading to Local Governments

Although Germany has seen some increase in local government authority and responsibility in the 1980s and 1990s, these changes have not manifested themselves in abortion policy. Moreover, local governments have not been involved in the development or execution of Irish abortion policy. Hence, one cannot discuss whether the devolution of power to local governments alters abortion politics in either country. However, contrasting the federal system in Germany with the more unitary Irish system provides some evidence of how devolution might alter abortion politics. Therefore, this section discusses Länder involvement in German abortion politics.

In Germany, local governments have always had some freedom to determine abortion policies. Before the 1992 revisions in abortion policy, Länder differed considerably in how they enforced the requirement that a medical, eugenic, criminal, or social (for example, psychological problem) reason be given. While states like Berlin easily granted abortions under the social criterion, abortions for social reasons were largely unavailable in Bavaria and Baden-Württemberg (Reimer 1996). Rucht (1994: 378), for example, notes that in 1989 only eighteen abortions were registered in Stuttgart compared with over 4,000 in Dortmund, a similar-sized city.[8] Several German states reduced the number of abortions not only by limiting the acceptable criteria for a legal abortion but also by restricting the number of abortion facilities. Under the current law, German Länder continue to enforce very different abortion policies by determining which independent organizations receive state support as abortion counseling centers (*Schwangerschaftskonflikberatungsstellen*). While some women's movements organizations have held demonstrations in an attempt to gain funding for liberal counseling centers, they have not been very successful (Rucht 1994: 388). For example, in 1998 the state of Baden-Württemberg gave DM 4.7 million to Catholic counseling centers and only DM 3.1 million to Pro Familia although the latter organization counseled many more women (Rechnungshof Baden-Württemberg 2000). Thus, by consciously funding some types of counseling centers over others, states choose how much emphasis is put on antiabortion values.

Local states in Germany, particularly Bavaria, are also independent actors in battles to determine national abortion law. After the Social Democratic/Free Democratic government legalized abortions in the first trimester in 1976, several Christian Democratic Union–controlled Länder challenged this legislation in the Constitutional Court, eventually leading to its invalidation (Reimer 1996). Moreover, Reimer (1996: 179) states that before the onset of unification, the Bavarian state government was preparing to contest the use of health insurance funds for abortion and other Länder's permissive implementation of existing abortion law before the Constitutional Court. Bavaria also spearheaded the drive to overturn the 1992 abortion law in the Constitutional Court, and adopted "supplementary" laws in 1996 requiring women to state a reason for seeking an abortion and

---

[8] Rucht (1994: 378) argues that the reduced numbers reflect widespread "abortion tourism," that is, women traveled elsewhere to get abortions.

prohibiting doctors from earning more than 25% of their income from abortions.[9]

Thus, the example of abortion politics in Germany indicates that downloading should influence abortion politics. In the case of Germany, local autonomy has been used both to liberalize a stricter abortion law and to increase restrictions.

Lateral Loading: Nonelected State Bodies

Of all the dimensions of reconfiguration, lateral loading has been the least significant in large part because very little abortion policy has been transferred to nonelected state bodies. However, several authors argue that nonelected state bodies tend to delay reforming restrictive abortion laws (Outshoorn 1986; Randall 1987). For example, Outshoorn (1986: 19) notes that when Dutch politicians finally dealt with the abortion issue, they convened a government expert commission to study the question, which both postponed and depoliticized the question.

The conservative role of nonelected state bodies is seen in the current abortion debates in Ireland. The Irish Medical Council was established by law in 1978 to register and discipline doctors and provide guidance on professional standards and ethical conduct. Thus, the Irish state empowered the Council to regulate the medical profession. The Medical Council's ethical guidelines include a strong statement against abortion: "The deliberate and intentional destruction of the unborn child is professional misconduct" (Houston 2001: 7). These guidelines are more conservative than Ireland's actual abortion policy, especially since 1992. Yet only in 2001 did the Medical Council revise these ethical standards in line with the new policies made in 1992. The new guidelines would allow termination of pregnancies "when there is a real and substantive risk to the life of the mother" and "when the foetus is nonviable" (Houston 2001: 7). However, as of this writing these changes are likely to be reversed as a result of legal challenges from within the medical community. Thus, the Medical Council – the designated regulatory agency of the medical profession – hinders abortion access through ethical guidelines. Because medical ethics is considered a professional matter, elected officials, political parties, and most importantly, the Irish women's movement are excluded from the debate despite the fact that abortion policy is otherwise considered a political issue.

Reconfiguration and Abortion Policy

The discussion above suggests that state restructuring has not aided women's movements' attempts to increase access to abortion. Yet it has also not had

[9] In 1998, the German Constitutional Court found that Länder were not entitled to write such supplemental laws, invalidating this legislation.

an overwhelmingly negative effect. The increased power of the EU has not liberalized abortion policy, even where the economic imperatives of the EU clash with prohibitions against abortion. That Ireland's policy of restricting information about abortion services was not considered market restriction suggests that such definitions are influenced by political concerns (that is, the desire to maintain Ireland as a member of the EU) or by traditional views that such concerns fall in the realm of the private rather than the public sector. The example of the Irish Medical Council also indicates how nonelected state bodies can serve as a conservative force on feminist policies.

Offloading to local governments or downloading to nongovernmental institutions affects abortion policy in both positive and negative ways. Federalism and the increased power of private institutions makes it more difficult for women's movements to translate strong mobilization into practical policy. Federal systems require mobilization in multiple geographical areas and mean facing multiple and varying opportunity structures. Although occasionally this fractionalization of policy and power structures allows some liberalization of abortion policy where this is not possible on a national level, it also means that other geographical areas may introduce restrictive policies. In short, federalism is good for innovation but not for achieving universal rights. Even more problems are faced when power is offloaded to private institutions. There are no clear mechanisms for influencing these institutions, which, depending on the organization's ideology, are more-or-less amenable to women's movement concerns.

In order to understand whether the relation between state reconfiguration and abortion policy is unique to a particular policy, we need to examine a policy closer to the heart of state reconfiguration: equal pay policies.

STATE RECONFIGURATION AND EQUAL PAY POLICY

While equal pay has not been as prominent an issue in European women's movements as abortion, it has also been a focus of feminist activity. Both the French and British women's movements included equal pay among their initial demands (Byrne 1996; Jenson 1982). Most of the feminist activists involved in the equal pay issue during the 1970s worked within trade unions and political parties. In France, socialist feminists were active supporters of women's equality in employment (Mazur 1995; Stetson 1987); the women's organization of the Confedération Générale du Travail (CGT) encouraged multiple conferences on working women and equal pay (Cockburn, Beccalli, Piva, and Ingrao 1984). In Great Britain, women within the Trades Union Congress (TUC) mobilized support for equal pay among working women (Mazur 1995; Meehan 1985). TUC also organized several equal pay rallies in the late 1960s, including one that drew 30,000 people. The women's movement – both older established organizations and the newly mobilized women's liberation groups – also fought for equal pay: creating organizations specific to the issue, conducting demonstrations, and petitioning and lobbying Parliament to adopt legislation (Jenson 1982: 367; Lovenduski and Randall 1993: 181; Meehan 1985: ch. 2).

Moreover, women's movement support for equality in employment increased over time in both countries. Mazur (1995) argues that by the mid 1970s subgroups within the French women's liberation movement (MLF) were mobilizing for antisexist legislation. Although in the 1980s many of the feminist groups disappear, "one of the most active visible post-MLF feminist groups, the Association Européene contre les Violences Faites aux Femmes au Travail...has focused on sexual harassment in the workplace" (Mazur 1995: 192). Within the Greater London Council, feminists fought to create equality officers to enforce equal pay legislation and discourage sexual discrimination in the workplace (Lovenduski 1988). Although initially skeptical of the British Equal Opportunity Commission (EOC), women's movement organizations increasingly worked with it in the late 1970s and early 1980s (Lovenduski 1988; Meehan 1985). Starting in the mid-1980s in Britain and the late 1970s in France, unions also spearheaded battles on the equal pay issue as women increasingly penetrated union leadership (Healy and Kirton 2000) or the union felt a need to address women's movement demands (Cockburn et al. 1984: 57–58; Daley 1999: 201–202; Jenson 1987a: 550; Short 1996: 18).

Controversy over equal pay issues in Great Britain and France has occurred along three dimensions. While early legislation in France and Great Britain demanded only equal pay for men and women in the *same positions*, more recent policies have moved toward equal pay for women in positions of *equal value*. Equal pay for equally valued work alleviates some of the structural differences in employment: Many women work in occupations that employ only women, which pay less than jobs in male-dominated professions. A second concern is the proportion of the population and benefits covered by these provisions. In many countries, equal pay provisions covered only some employees, for example, applying only to public employees or encompassing only firms of a particular size. Recently coverage of part-time workers has been debated. Controversies surround the question of which benefits, such as pension plans, are included in equal pay provisions. A third dimension of debate is how equal pay legislation is enforced. These questions include whether the burden of proof is on the plaintiff or the employer, what sorts of evidence indicate discrimination, whether unions or women's associations can file suits on behalf of women, and whether complainants must utilize traditional collective bargaining procedures first.

State reconfiguration affects the way that each of these issues are addressed. As before, let us examine each of the dimensions of reconfiguration separately.

Uploading to European Union

Unlike abortion policy, the offloading of power onto the EU had some positive effect on equal pay policy until recently. Article 119 of the Treaty of Rome, the basis for equal pay in the EU, was adopted as a result of France's concern that the equal pay statute in its constitution would hamper French competitiveness in the EU's open market (Mazur 1995). Although it was originally to be put in force by 1962, it was not until the 1970s that the EU began enforcing Article 119 because of resistance from other member countries.[10] Of the original six signatory states to the Treaty of Rome, four were subject to actions by the EU Commission because of insufficient enforcement of Article 119. The European Court of Justice also helped women by deciding in *Defrenne v. Sabena* (1976) that individuals could bring suit against individual employers for violating Article 119 even where no national laws existed.[11]

While Article 119 initially was narrowly construed as equal pay for the same work, the EU also widened the scope of Article 119 in the 1970s. In 1975, a Directive (75/117/EEC, Article 1) broadened interpretation of Article 119 to include pay "for the same work or for work to which equal value is attributed." Warner (1984: 150) ascribes this directive to growing pressure from women's movements and trade unions. In addition, although pensions and bonuses were initially excluded from the definition of pay, later rulings enlarged the meaning of equal pay to include these aspects. The Equal Treatment Directive of 1976 (76/207/EEC) also expanded the principle of equal pay to equal treatment in other aspects of employment such as hiring, firing, promotion, and working conditions.

European Union actions, particularly in the late 1970s, helped French and British women's movements advance the cause of equal pay. A 1965 Commission report argued that all member countries had failed to implement Article 119. Although French Law required equal pay for equal work, it was not until the 1972 Equal Pay Law that procedures were implemented to enforce this principle. Inspectors of Labor were charged with investigating complaints and levying small fines (Stetson 1987: 144). When the EU introduced the Equal Pay for Equal Valued Work Directive in 1975, France already had this principle enshrined in the 1972 Equal Pay Law. However, the

---

[10] Several authors argue that EU institutions became more progressive than the EU's member countries because of connections to the women's movement. Warner (1984: 161) argues that the Commission maintained a stronger stance on equal pay policy because it sought support from the women's movement. Mazey (1988: 78) argues that women's strong representation in the European Parliament advanced equal pay policy because many female members of the European Parliament were committed to equal rights for women.

[11] However, the ruling also argued that individuals could not sue for back pay. Warner (1984: 148–149) cites several sources who argued the later ruling was a result of pressure from national governments particularly the United Kingdom and Ireland.

law did not provide any mechanism for evaluating job classification schemes for discrimination (Mazur 1995).

The influence of the EU on British legislation has been even stronger. Although Britain passed its Equal Pay Act in 1970 (long before the EU began enforcing Article 119), the act only applied to women in companies where job classification schemes were used (MacLennan 1992). The European Court ruled in 1982 that selective enforcement of Article 119 was prohibited and demanded that the United Kingdom amend its Equal Pay Act (Kenney 1992; Landau 1985). Britain was also forced to adopt equal pay for work of equal value in 1983 (Kenney 1992; MacLennan 1992). EU provisions provided new opportunities for British feminists. In 1993, for example, feminists in the British Equal Opportunities Commission even considered using EU equal pay provisions to sue the British government for increasing income inequality with its trade union bill ("Equal Pay for Women" 1993).

While the EU continued to push equal pay and equal treatment policies into the 1990s, its policies have become more mixed. On the positive side, a 1997 directive (97/81/EC) calls for equal treatment of part-time employees, although it explicitly allows some benefits to be limited by "period of service, time worked or earnings qualifications" (European Union 1997). Several European Court of Justice (ECJ) cases have also granted equal protection to part-time workers in promotions[12] and pensions.[13] On the other hand, the Court permits companies to dismiss part-time workers first (*Kachelmann vs. Bankhaus Hermann Lampe* 2000). Meulders (2000) also argues that the EU's policies encouraging a "flexible" work force increase part-time work in the low-paid sectors already dominated by women, preserving income and occupational inequalities.[14]

Recently, the European Court of Justice has limited member states' use of legislation to encourage the hiring of women. Although the EU has stated that positive action is necessary to assure equal opportunities (Directive 76/207), in *Kalanke v. Freie Hansestadt Bremen* (1993) the ECJ ruled that women may not be automatically hired above men of equal qualifications. In *Abrahamsson and Anderson v. Fogelqvist* (2000) the ECJ also prohibited national laws that set aside positions to increase the proportion of women or allow the appointment of women over men with better qualifications. However, some forms of positive action against inequality are still permitted. In *Marschall v. Nordrhein-Westfalen* (1997) the court ruled that affirmative action policies are permitted when they do not make the promotion of women over men of

---

[12] See the European Court of Justice's decision in *Hill and Stapleton v. Revenue Commissioners* (1998).
[13] See the European Court of Justice's decisions in *Preston et al. v. Wolverhampton Healthcare and NHS Trust and Fletcher et al. v. Midland Bank* (2000), *Deutsche Post AG v. Elisabeth Sievers* (2000), and *Deutsche Telekom AG v. Agnes Vick* (2000).
[14] Jenson (1988) makes the same argument for France.

equal qualifications absolute (that is, other criteria could lead to male candidates' selection). The ECJ's rulings have reduced the scope of affirmative action, especially in those countries where feminists had already made the greatest gains.

The European Union also relies heavily on individual nation states to implement its policy. As a result, the Equal Pay and Equal Treatment directives have been applied differently in the various member states. One problem is that the Equal Pay for Equal Work directive of 1975 "provides no guidance as to how work of equal value might properly be measured. In consequence, different Member States have adopted different criteria" (Mazey 1988: 71). For example, the Equal Pay Directive allows sex-specific hiring for jobs where sex is a determining factor (for example, wet-nurse, actress). Great Britain allows sex-specific hiring under this provision "if the holder provides personal services" (Kenney 1992: 87), while France does not. Similarly, many countries have been loath to examine job classification schemes. In France, it was not until the 1983 antisexism legislation that "[u]nnecessary employment policies that are facially neutral and have a disparate effect on one sex, such as height and weight requirements" were prohibited (Stetson 1987: 149) and this legislation remains largely unimplemented (Laufer 2000: 232).

Thus, despite the centrality of the equal pay issue to aspects of state reconfiguration (indeed because of it), the EU has had a positive influence on equal pay legislation. However, that positive effect has been limited in scope. In the late 1970s and early 1980s, the equal pay policies were modest, but the actions of the EU encouraged greater equality for men and women. In the late 1980s and 1990s, the EU's performance has been more mixed: pushing equality for part-time employees in some areas but not others, limiting the use of positive discrimination by member states, and leaving untouched the ability of nations to define categories of work (within limits).

Downloading to Local Governments

France has not downloaded much authority to local government, and under Thatcher, Great Britain actually dissolved many local governmental authorities. While Tony Blair introduced policies to recreate local governments, these institutions are too new to analyze. Hence, I have only indirect evidence on how downloading affects equal pay policy.

Local-level government authorities in Britain were active in equal opportunity policy. Between 1978 and 1986, approximately 40% of the local authorities adopted equal opportunity policies designed to influence their own hiring practices and those of firms that did business with local governments (Byrne 1996: 63; Lovenduski and Randall 1993: 192–196).[15]

---

[15] Lovenduski and Randall (1993: 192) note that local authorities constitute the largest employer of women in Britain. As a result, local policies could have great implications for women.

Lovenduski (1995: 123) argues that women's movement activists focused on local programs because they found the national Equal Opportunity Commission (EOC) too hierarchical and tied to status quo interests. Indeed, local equal opportunity policies surpassed national policies, often involving attempts to alter structural disadvantages caused by employment segregation. Such local policies included strong affirmative action programs, the provision of child care, education and training programs, and contractor compliance policies that granted subcontracts to companies with records of equal employment and "equal opportunities hiring and promotion programs" (Lovenduski and Randall 1993: 196).

However, at the end of the 1980s, many of these programs had disappeared, in part because of Thatcher's abolition of the Greater London Council (GLC) and because the 1989 Local Government Act prohibited the use of contractor compliance to implement equal opportunity for women (Lovenduski and Randall 1993).[16] Despite these setbacks, local government women's committees continue to exist. In fact, new committees were established in Scotland early in the 1990s. The elimination of the GLC even had some positive effects; the national EOC, which had largely been ignored by feminists, attracted some of the GLC's feminist activists. For example, Valerie Amos, who worked for the London government, later became chief executive of the EOC (Lovenduski 1995).

Thus, as was the case in abortion, local governments provided opportunities for innovation in equal pay policy. While these innovations promoted greater affirmative action and increased both the pay and employment of women, opportunities were also limited. Innovation occurred only where political alliances allowed it (in Britain, largely where the Labour Party controlled local authorities). This means that innovations do not become widespread policy. Another consequence is that these policies are constrained by local political parties and trade unions which provide financial and political support only where these policies do not intrude into their traditional domains (Lovenduski 1995; Lovenduski and Randall 1993; see also Ferree 1995 for Germany). These limitations suggest that even as local government authority expands under the Blair government, equal pay policy achievements will be limited.

Lateral Loading: Nonelected State Bodies

Nonelected state bodies play a large role in both the development and the implementation of equal pay legislation. Because equal pay issues are central to the concerns of trade unions and employer organizations, these groups developed equal pay legislation along with women's organizations. For example,

---

[16] On the other hand, local authorities were still permitted to use contractor compliance policies to enforce racial equality (Lovenduski and Randall 1993).

both the Trades Union Congress and the Confederation of British Industry engaged in government sponsored negotiations over the final wording of the British Equal Pay Act of 1970 (Meehan 1985). In France, the two largest unions helped to determinine the character of both the 1972 Equal Pay and the 1983 Égalité professionelle laws. In both France and Great Britain, major union organizations – Confédération Générale du Travail and the Trades Union Congress – opposed attempts to eliminate legislation that protected women from certain types of work (Kenney 1992; Mazur 1995). Employers fought against the imposition of additional costs from equal pay provisions (Mazur 1995: 215; Meehan 1985: 65). Thus, both trade unions and employer organizations slowed the initial pace of equal pay legislation.

Equal pay laws also created nonelected state bodies responsible for implementation, and trade union and employer representatives compose the majority of these bodies. In Great Britain, the Equal Opportunities Commission (EOC), created by the 1975 Sex Discrimination Act, is composed of representatives from trade unions and employers. These are nominated by the Trade Union Congress and the Confederation of Business Industry as well as government representatives (Kenney 1992). While evaluations of the EOC vary (cf. Corcoran 1988 and Kenney 1992), researchers agree that it has not been very supportive of individuals filing complaints. Kenney (1992) argues that this is a result of the tripartite nature of the EOC and the norm of British bureaucratic neutrality that has tended to exclude feminists from the organization. Corcoran (1988) and Bashevkin (1998) argue that the EOC has not been granted enough funds to adequately support their mission.[17] Under the Blair government, other nonelected state bodies also influenced equal pay policy. In 1999, the Better Regulation Task Force – created by the Blair government and composed largely of business representatives to streamline government regulation – called for no further improvements in discrimination law. In response, the government decided to continue a voluntary approach to eliminating inequality begun under the conservative government (Ward 1999).

Unions and business play similar roles in France. Although France adopted equal pay legislation earlier, it was slower to develop independent agencies to oversee the legislation. The Comité du travail féminin formed in 1965 of representatives of labor, business, and women's organizations was an administrative committee subsumed under the Ministry of Social Affairs. Nonetheless, Mazur (1995: 85–86) argues that the agency was a strong advocate for equal pay policy, and even a bastion for state feminism in the early years. However, only in 1983 was a state agency, the Conseil superieur de l'égalité professionnel (CSEP), created to oversee implementation of equal pay legislation. This conseil is composed of labor and business representatives,

---

[17] For example, Thatcher cut the Equal Opportunity Commission staff from 400 to 148 (Bashevkin 1998: 106).

but is closely tied to the labor ministry. The CSEP is much weaker than its British counterpart, largely providing information and assisting in the development of positive action plans within businesses. Moreover, as in the United Kingdom, the scope of the CSEP was reduced during periods of conservative rule; between 1986 and 1993, the CSEP met only sporadically and all its subcommissions were disbanded (Mazur 1995: 219).

The influence of nonelected state bodies is also seen in the adjudication process of equal pay cases in both France and Britain. Industrial courts or nonbinding arbitration bodies rather than the judicial system serve as the primary locus for such cases. In Britain, complaints are handled by 1) the Advisory, Conciliation, and Arbitration Service, which negotiates settlements but has no enforcement power; 2) industrial tribunals and the Employment Appeal Tribunal, which do not create case law and are relatively informal (although lawyers may represent each side), and 3) the Central Arbitration Committee, which monitors collective agreements for discrimination (Nandy 1980). These bodies are composed of representatives of business and labor although a judge presides over the Employment Appeal Tribunal. Kenney (1992) and Corcoran (1988: 64) argue that these tribunals are often uninformed about equal pay law and advantage employers. Although industrial tribunals are informal, employers often utilize legal counsel while plaintiffs usually have no legal representation and are not offered legal aid because of the tribunals' informal nature (Kenney 1992).

In France, equal pay cases are usually adjudicated by prud'hommes (labor courts), where the judges represent major unions and employers. However, until 1983 work inspectors from the Ministry of Labor had to investigate a complaint and find the employer in violation of equal pay statutes before the case could be heard (Mazur 1995). Mazur (1995) argues that the labor courts rarely were sympathetic to equal pay cases because the judges came from male-dominated industries. Moreover, she argues that work inspectors did not do an adequate job of investigating or forwarding equal pay cases because the administration "was overloaded by the demands of complex labor law and was understaffed, poorly paid, and generally entrenched due to the hostility of a right-wing government to business regulation" (Mazur 1995: 103).

Thus, in both France and Great Britain, corporatist institutions representing labor and business limit the implementation of equal pay legislation. Even where unions have been supportive of equal pay laws, as French unions were in the late 1970s (Mazur 1995: 190), enforcement of equal pay has been uneven at best, reflecting unions' other interests and the variation in support for equal pay by local unions.

Offloading to the Private Sector

Compared to abortion policy, the implementation of equal pay legislation relies even more heavily on the activities of private organizations, especially in periods when the EOC and CSEP were targeted for budget reductions. Consequently, the private sector has played a large role in determining the character of equal pay legislation in France and Great Britain.

One example of offloading to private groups is the government's use of business initiatives to advance equal treatment of women workers. In Great Britain, John Major developed the "Opportunity 2000" initiative to increase the number of women in high-level occupations. Although designated a British government initiative, "Opportunity 2000" was completely privately sponsored and business driven (Forbes 1997). In France, offloading occurred of the 1983 Egalité professionelle law, which left implementation largely in the hands of business and unions. The law mandated that employers provide works councils made up of trade union representatives with annual information on pay differentials to allow them to monitor progress toward equality (Jenson and Sineau 1994: 255; Laufer 1998: 57). It also allowed individual complaints of discrimination to be settled without penalty to corporations if they created a workplace gender equality plan (Jenson 1988: 162). In addition, the government encouraged gender equality plans among businesses in the early 1980s by offering financial aid of up to 50% of training costs and 30% of employee salaries (Laufer 1998: 58). Yet, only twenty-five firms created gender equality plans and most failed to provide useful reports on pay differentials (Laufer 1998). The French government has chosen not to push the enforcement of these provisions further (Laufer 1998, 1994).

The primary area where private groups have assumed state decision-making roles is in the determination of what constitutes jobs of "equal value." Although equal pay laws require that jobs of equal value receive equal pay, states have relied on existing job classification schemes to determine equal value. These job classifications are created by unions as part of the collective bargaining (Rubery, Bettio, Fagan, Maier, Quack, and Villa 1998) or by corporations (Lanquetin 2000). Governments have been slow to interfere in the creation of these classification schemes. Only in 1997 did the French court rule that employers must justify classifications that produce pay differentials between men and women (Lanquetin 2000: 248). In the United Kingdom, there is local flexibility in job classification systems (Rubery and Fagan 1995: 107), and considerable evidence for gender discrimination. For example, Munro (1999) demonstrates that even in the late 1980s women who cleaned for a living were almost always classified at a lower job classification than men performing the same tasks.

Offloading has also indirectly decreased equal pay between men and women. Because governments embraced equal pay principles relatively early, offloading, which reduces the size of the state's workforce, increases pay inequality. In Britain, for example, the contracting out of public sector jobs to private firms has increased pay differentials between men and women, and unemployment rates for women (Munro 1999). Private firms are also subject to fewer regulations about minimum pay and benefits, leading to worse pay and benefits for individuals in positions that are contracted out. The off-loading of state jobs has also revived arguments that public sector benefits and pay should be reduced to match the market. Offloading affects women more than men since positions contracted out tend to be in the service sector, which is dominated by women (Rubery and Fagan 1995: 105).

However, the offloading of state responsibility provides some opportunities for women's associations to become more directly involved in the implementation process. In France, trade unions and women's associations have been able to serve as advocates for women plaintiffs in equal pay cases although few have done so (Mazur 1995: 141). Between 1975–83 no trade unions supported equal treatment cases and in only one case was a feminist organization (Choisir) involved (Mazur 1995: 142). A 1985 antisexism law also allows women's organizations to intervene in discrimination cases on hiring and firing but gives unions the monopoly over questions of pay, training, and promotion (Stetson 1987). In Great Britain there are more signs of change. In the 1990s, unions have increasingly engaged in legal actions on equal pay and sexual discrimination issues; for example, in 1998 British trade unions spearheaded equal pay claims of women in the National Health Service (Milne 1998).

Overall, then, offloading has tended to reduce the enforcement of equal pay policies. Regulatory agencies, already relatively weak in both countries, have been even more impaired by budgetary cuts. Because offloading occurs where equality is greatest (for example, government jobs) or in female dominated sectors (for example, service jobs), the contracting out of government work has also increased pay inequality between men and women. Moreover, trade unions and business organizations have benefited more than feminist organizations from the offloading of state power in the case of equal pay. Where the state has allowed private groups to implement equal pay legislation, it has most often relied on unions and industry. These actors serve their own interests, pursuing pay equity only where they benefit.

Equal Pay and State Reconfiguration

In the 1980s and 1990s, equal opportunity programs, offices, and training programs have become much more commonplace despite their potential interference with a free marketplace. Yet, as Table 7.2 shows, the equalization of salaries has stalled in recent years[18] (see also Clarke 2001; Walby 1997). Indeed, the most recent figures in Great Britain indicate that pay inequalities

---

[18] As many authors have noted, the harmonized data collected by the European Union are not good measures of pay equity because they focus on earnings in areas where few women are employed and because countries differ on the inclusion of part-time workers (see, for example, Meulders, Plasman, and Stricht 1993: 109–112 and Rubery, Smith, and Fagan 1999: 224). Nonetheless, the data presented in Table 7.2 represent the only possibility for examining long-term changes in pay equity.

TABLE 7.2. *Women's Hourly Wages as a % of Men's (for Manual Workers in All Industries)*

Year	1977	1980	1983	1985	1989	1990	1993	1998
France	77.4%	78.3%	80.1%	80.8%	80.7%	80.8%	80.8%	80.6%
United Kingdom	71.6%	69.6%	69.5%	69.3%	67.6%	67.2%	68.4%	69.9%

Sources: 1977–85: Eurostat. 1987: 129; 1989–90: Eurostat. 1996: 54, 102; 1993: Rubery, Smith, and Fagan 1999: 225; 1998: Eurostat. 2000: 37, 41.

between men and women have increased since 1997 (Odone 2001a). Moreover, even under leftist governments, women's movements find it difficult to institute or implement additional equal pay policies on the national level since the 1980s. Although the EU continues to be a source of advancement of equal pay issues, even there the results have become more mixed in recent years. One reason may be that initial changes, which required regulation against overt pay discrimination, fit more easily with a free market economy than those that require positive action, such as quotas for women, affirmative action, or the revision of job classifications to reflect comparable worth.

Offloading is the biggest obstacle to equal pay policies. Contracting out work eliminates feminist equal pay policies achieved in governments. When businesses and employers implement equal pay policies, little progress is made (see Forbes 1997 in the United Kingdom and Mazur 1995 in France). Trade unions are only slightly better at implementing equal pay policies. Only where trade unions see such policies in their interest (as they have in recent years in Great Britain) has the offloading of responsibility to unions led to better enforcement. Herein lies the difference between France and Great Britain. Since the mid-1980s, French unions (with the exception of the Confédération française des travailleurs chrétiens) have been unwilling to embrace womens' and pay equity issues (Daley 1999: 202). Feminists have found a less inviting reception in French unions than in British ones (Cockburn et al. 1984; Daley 1999; Milne 1998). Moreover, because French trade unions are themselves divided, they have been less able to respond to state reconfiguration. As a result, the offloading of equal pay policy in France has largely allowed employers to take the upper hand.

Similarly, since nonelected state bodies are also dominated by employers and unions, much also depends on the stance of unions. Labor courts have tended to be less sympathetic to equal pay claims and the actions of equal pay commissions – the EOC in Great Britain and the CSEP in France – hinge on union support. Thus, as in the case of offloading, lateral loading's effect on equal pay policy is influenced by factors such as women's representation in unions or unions' perceptions about the usefulness of women's movement support.

Not all aspects of reconfiguration diminish feminists' abilities to abolish pay inequities. As was the case with abortion policy, existing local governments' activities suggest that downloading may increase innovative equal pay policies in some local authorities.

CONCLUSION

The analysis of equal pay and abortion policies illustrates how women's movements' accomplishments are affected by state reconfiguration. In the introduction I posed two major questions: 1) Is it harder for feminists to achieve policies that contradict free market principles, and 2) how does state reconfiguration influence feminist policy achievements? The answers to both questions are complicated.

One original hypothesis of this chapter was that state reconfiguration would make equal pay policies harder to achieve than advances in abortion rights because solutions to pay inequalities conflict with market concerns. In fact, this does not appear to be the case, at least initially. Rather, equal pay legislation made great progress in both countries, particularly in the early years. Why is this so? It may be that the conflict with neoliberal concerns, even while inspiring greater opposition, insures that the issue is always on the agenda. The centrality of the issue to the concerns of major political actors (that is, trade unions and business) may create stronger and more focused alliances than an issue such as abortion, which is less related to these actors' concerns and divides their constituents. Hence, only rarely do unions or employers consider abortion issues and then they are always secondary in importance. This lack of centrality also allows the EU to use abortion policy as a tool in gaining other policies. Few member states and few organizations (outside of feminist groups) objected when the EU traded off reinforcing Ireland's strict abortion policy for the Maastricht Treaty.

However, while the initial equal pay policies were made without too much conflict with market principles, more recent policies – positive action, increasing the pay, benefits, and bargaining power of part-time employees, and regulating job classification schemes – impose more on both business and labor. This may explain why in the 1980s and 1990s the pace of reform slowed, and the European Union began to vacillate on the issue. Although women's movements are now better represented in the EU and national governments than in the 1970s, they have gained influence as equal pay policies have become much more threatening, particularly to business interests. If the pace of reform continues to slow, a reassessment of equal pay policies in ten years time may indeed conclude that the initial hypothesis – that such policies are harder to achieve – is indeed correct.

How has state reconfiguration influenced the ability of the women's movement to make and implement policies? Here again, the answer is complicated. Some dimensions of state reconfiguration have positive impacts on movement policy achievements, others have overwhelmingly negative impacts. Moreover, the impact varies depending on the type of policy.

The previous discussion of the differences between abortion and equal pay policies suggests that overall the uploading of responsibility and authority to the EU is likely to limit the women's movement's future policy gains. Few feminist concerns (for example, violence against women) are central to the economic issues that drive the EU, and hence, most are likely to receive the same treatment as abortion: ignored by policymakers or worse still used as a bargaining chip to acquire policies more central to other actors' concerns. The only positive aspect to uploading is the increasing influence of the women's movement in the EU and their use of transnational mobilization. The European Parliament's willingness to press for more abortion rights in 1999 reflects women's movements' growing influence in this body (see Beckwith this volume; Vallance and Davies 1986). Women's movements have organized to lobby the European level (Helfferich and Kolb 2001) and are increasingly using transnational connections to influence national policy, as my discussion of abortion indicates. Unfortunately, a lack of access to those institutions with greatest decision-making power may limit women's movements' abilities to translate these newfound strengths into concrete policy gains.

The lateral loading of responsibility to nonelected state bodies also reduces women's movements' influence. These bodies often include representatives of those major nonstate actors perceived to have a vital interest in the policy area. In the examples of nonelected state bodies discussed here women's movement organizations were never officially represented. Equal pay fell under the purview of trade unions and employers and even abortion was defined as an issue of the medical profession. When women's movements were able to influence these nonelected state bodies it was through their ability to infiltrate other organizations (for example, trade unions) or the state itself (Stetson and Mazur 1995). However, women's movement influence depends greatly on the receptiveness of these other bodies. As the discussion of equal pay suggests, receptivity arises from a complex interaction between the initial state of the institutions and the factors that might make them open to women's movement claims. For example, the fragmentary nature of the French unions reduces their responsiveness to women's claims. On the other hand, unions in both countries saw a need to incorporate women as they operated in increasingly difficult political and economic conditions. Thus, even as nonelected state bodies are exclusionary, women's movements can gain entrée into these bodies under favorable political conditions.

Women's movements have benefited most from the process of downloading tasks to local governments and offloading to nonstate actors. Local governments may serve as innovators, permitting women's movements to achieve positive changes in smaller geographical areas when national changes are impossible (Elman 1996b; Kriesi 1995). Similarly, offloading to private groups provides greater opportunities for the women's movement to directly affect the implementation, and thereby the character, of policy. However, much then depends on the movement's ability to mobilize and control resources, and on the extant political opportunities. In localities where movements lack allies or face opponents, where local governments are closed to women's movement influence, or where other groups dominate policy implementation, opportunities to affect policy disappear. Moreover, the disadvantage of offloading and downloading is the creation of inequality among women. Feminists in some geographical locations may make great gains while others suffer under conservative policies. Similarly, offloading increases inequality among women in the same geographical area; women with knowledge about service providers or who chance upon more profeminist providers receive quite different treatment from those who lack information or who chance upon antifeminist providers. As Katzenstein (this volume) suggests, state reconfiguration may therefore hurt lower-class women more than their middle-class counterparts, who have information and the resources to choose providers.

The analysis here represents only a first step in determining how the changes in state structure influence women's movements' policy successes. Two policy areas and four countries do not provide enough evidence to make firm conclusions about how continuing state reconfiguration will affect women's movements' influence. Moreover, the evidence here suggests that different dimensions of state reconfiguration work in contradictory ways, although overall the reduction in the nation state's authority and capacity has come at the expense of the women's movement. In the case of abortion, the move toward the EU, toward more local government control, and toward increased power of nonstate entities has reduced opportunities for and increased constraints on women's movements. While the increased power of the EU has had a more mixed effect on equal pay policy, the rise of nonelected state agencies has crippled the achievement of equal pay policy. Overall, then, state reconfiguration does not bode well for the future ability of women's movements to achieve feminist policies.

8

The Gendering Ways of States

*Women's Representation and State Reconfiguration in France, Great Britain, and the United States**

Karen Beckwith

[E]veryone has an interest in participating in the construction of choices in the policy areas that... affect them. Thus, being the subject as well as the object of policy is a critical aspect of women's... interests. (Orloff 1996: 70)

INTRODUCTION

As postindustrial welfare states have reconfigured their powers and policies, how has women's parliamentary presence been transformed, and how, if at all, have these changes been related to feminist movements? This chapter examines the relationship between major state transformations and women's representation in three nations, from the early 1970s to the early 1990s, and considers the ways in which gender representation and practices are changing, in part, in response to reconfigurations of each state and to the feminist movements in each state. The nations under examination – Britain, France, and the United States – are particularly useful cases for examining the pattern of women's electoral representation. In each nation, a vibrant, multifaceted feminist movement revived in the 1960s and 1970s, and endured across major state and party system changes in the 1980s and into the 1990s. Attention to women's electoral chances and to the policy representation of organized women has been evidenced in public agendas in all three nations and a public discourse about women and about gender developed in response to feminist movement organizing. Concomitant with the persistence of feminist organizing into its third decade, the states in which

* To the following colleagues and friends, I extend my gratitude for their assistance and their support; they include Lee Ann Banaszak, Marilyn Beckwith, Fitz Beckwith Collings, David Farrell, Mary Fainsod Katzenstein, Peter Katzenstein, Jeffrey Lantis, Joni Lovenduski, Ulrike Liebert, Amy Mazur, Jocelyn Praud, Donley Studlar, Sidney Tarrow, Susan Tarrow, and Nicholas Colannino of the European Commission. A special thanks to Lee Ann Banaszak, Dieter Rucht, Mary Fainsod Katzenstein, Jeffrey Lantis, David S. Meyer, and Joel Wolfe for their careful readings of an earlier version of this chapter.

feminist movements found themselves were in the process of considerable transformation, reconfiguring state powers, relocating state authority, and relinquishing many of the policy commitments of the social welfare state.

As locations of state power – and the extent of state powers – shifted, did the feminist movement find political opportunities for entering state venues, particularly parliaments, as decisionmakers? As states multiplied the locations in which state power is exercised and in which state policies are developed and/or implemented, did these movements redirect their efforts and their agendas? What strategies did feminist movements employ in response to state reconfiguration? In addressing these questions, I present each of the national cases, detailing specific patterns of reconfiguration and summarizing the activities and targets of the feminist movements in each state. Second, I analyze the pattern of women's election to political office. Finally, I conclude with 1) an assessment of the relationship between state reconfiguration and women's electoral presence and 2) a range of research hypotheses concerning women's movements' strategies in the face of state reconfiguration.

A concern with women's electoral representation may require some justification in the context of state reconfiguration and feminist movements. First, feminist political thought has identified the state, variously defined, as problematic for organized women. Although some feminist theorists have envisioned the state as inherently hostile to women, sufficiently to render it a site of women's disempowerment (for example, Brown 1995; MacKinnon 1982), more recent feminist scholarship has challenged these claims by pointing to the state's lack of coherently expressed interests; its multiple and conflicting discourses, powers, and venues; its historically contingent nature; and its inefficiencies and changeabilities. Shirin Rai (1996), for example, understands "the state" as a "network of power relations existing in cooperation and also in tension [situated] within a grid which is composed of economic, political, legal, and cultural forms all interacting on, with and against each other" (5), seeing the state as "[embodying] complex gendered relations that work against women, as well as providing resources for negotiation and struggle" (14–15). Rai's vision of the state suggests the importance of the "state" as a venue for women's representation (even within parliaments) and influence (if only through collective action).[1] Sonia Alvarez (1990), writing from the Brazilian case, argues that "*the State is not monolithically masculine* or antifeminist. If we 'unpack' the State and examine its multiple institutional and ideological instances, we may find points of access, points where concerted gender-conscious political pressure might make

---

[1] Rai (1996) argues that, "for the majority of [Third World] women, the question is not whether or not to approach the state. *It is they who are approached by the state*, in many instances in a brutal and violent way" (18); this again suggests that the "state" is an arena of compulsory importance for women, even if its content and practice lack coherence.

a difference" (272; emphasis in original). To the extent that points of access may be shifting, closing, or opening for different sets of actors as states reconfigure their formal powers and policy responsibilities, organized women may be positioning themselves in parliaments, and elsewhere, to take advantage of these potential opportunities – or they may be failing to assess these as opportunities or failing to act upon them, even if so recognized. If the patterns of state reconfiguration that we identify and analyze in this volume constitute a "distinct historical conjuncture," then it may be, as Alvarez argues, that "the State is potentially a mechanism . . . for social change . . . in women's lives" (Alvarez 1990: 273). Georgina Waylen (1998) makes a similar point, identifying "the state [as] a site of struggle" rather than as a venue clearly and unambiguously invested in "male" interests (7). This, again, suggests that women's access to the site of struggle, as it were, including to elected positions in governments, is an important consideration for feminist movements.

Second, there is an obvious conceptual distinction, partially embodied in political practice, between "feminist movements" and "elected women." Feminist movements have not always prioritized the election of feminists to office; there have been various disputes about the wisdom of supporting female candidates, feminist female candidates, and feminist candidates for elective office;[2] certainly not all elected women are feminists and the lack of (indeed, impossibility of) a subset of universally acknowledged "women's" issues makes congruency between elected women and women's issues unlikely, if not impossible. Furthermore, the link between women's isomorphic representation and women's substantive representation is not yet underpinned by scholarly consensus about distinctive policy choices of female, compared to male, legislators (see, for Britain, Childs 2001; Cowley and Childs 2001; for the United States, Dodson forthcoming; Dolan 1997; Thomas 1991; Welch 1985).

Nonetheless, in the absence of detailed crossnational longitudinal data on feminists' access to office, and given an empirical base that is not yet conclusive about elected women's distinctive support for feminist legislation, it is reasonable to ask what the current aggregate patterns of women's legislative presence are in the context of major state reconfiguration and a concern for opportunities to advance feminist agendas. Although the attention in this chapter to women's elective presence in different state venues, as states reconfigure their powers, may appear to conflate women's electoral participation, women's issues, and feminist movements, I want to hold, if in some tension, the recognition and understanding that these are distinctive concepts that are nonetheless empirically related, even if problematically, in temporally specific, nationally bounded cases.

[2] See, in the United States, the distinction between Emily's List and the NWPC; see efforts by the 300 Group and by Labour Party activists in Britain.

Third, this chapter evinces no empirical concern with feminist policy agendas within formal state venues, although clearly this would constitute another possibility for investigating the relationship between feminist movements and reconfigured states. This absence should not be read to indicate a lack of concern, or even a prioritizing of women's electoral activism over or in preference to feminist movement mobilization outside and/or against state institutions. The assumption that feminist policy results offer more scholarly insight into feminist movement successes than does a seemingly more conventional assessment of women's entry into state elective bodies begins with an understanding of "the state" as something that does things for (or against) women, rather than as a location *where women are*, or *where women might be*, positioned to advance (or to protect and to defend) a feminist agenda. To paraphrase Waylen (1998), "The state therefore is not to be avoided" nor the potential for women's presence within it (8).

MAPPING STATE RECONFIGURATION AND FEMINIST MOVEMENTS: PATTERNS OF INTERACTION IN THREE NATIONS

Britain, France, and the United States, like Canada and other West European nations, have undertaken substantial reconfiguration of their state powers and policy responsibilities since the 1970s. The cross-case pattern of state reconfiguration is evidenced: 1) in the transfer of some state sovereign powers, particularly in economic terms, to supranational authoritative bodies or to international treaty arrangements (uploading); 2) in the transfer of formal state powers and/or social policy from national to subnational state arenas (downloading); and 3) in relinquishing traditional social welfare responsibilities to nonstate associations or actors (offloading). These three forms of state reconfiguration have occurred in Britain, France, and the United States, varying only in degree (see discussion in Banaszak, Beckwith, and Rucht this volume).

For organized women, state power has shifted to two locations. For Britain and France, partial state sovereignty has shifted from the central state to the European Union (see Mather 2000) and, to the extent that real power resides in the EU, it may serve as a location of real political opportunity for feminist movements (see, however, Bretherton and Sperling 1996). Beyond this, for all three nations, state power remains within state boundaries, relatively unchanged in terms of state sovereignty but reconfigured in terms of delegation of policy responsibilities.[3] In the United States, powers remain divided and shared between the federal and state governments; in Britain and in France, parliaments maintain their preeminence, especially in France, and therefore retain their status as target arenas for feminist movements.

[3] With the exception of devolution of powers to Scotland, discussed in detail elsewhere.

The extent to which feminist movements have redirected their efforts and have relocated themselves within these state reconfigurations can be evidenced: 1) by changes in the movements' strategies and 2) by women's electoral success in different state venues. The impetus to move into specific state locations, and women's success in being elected to state office, are most likely to be effected through the availability of sympathetic political parties that serve to facilitate, although not to guarantee, feminists' efforts to advance their candidates and their policy preferences. A feminist movement able to employ a political party as a carrying agent for its candidates will have met a necessary condition for placing women in locations of state power.

Although recognizing the impact of structural and other factors on women's electoral success, this chapter's central concern is not how women succeed in winning elections.[4] It examines instead the linkages between feminist movements and enhanced opportunities for women's electoral success, where organized women have identified (or failed to identify) changing locations of state power and have moved strategically in response to, or anticipation of, increased opportunities for representation. In considering these possible relationships concerning state reconfiguration, I turn first to a discussion of state reconfiguration and women's state presence in Britain.

Britain: Strong State, Less State?

Among the three nations, Britain has experienced the greatest and most extensive changes in state powers, best understood as occurring in two distinct periods. The first period encompasses the Thatcher and parts of the Major governments, from 1979–97; the second period includes the Blair government and parts of the Major government, from 1992 to the present. Although these periods are distinct, they are not perfectly congruent with governments, and they are distinctive on different reconfiguration elements. The first period is marked by a concentration of national state power, a resistance to the transfer of power to supranational institutions, and, concomitantly, a radical offloading of state policy responsibilities. As

---

[4] That other factors are also related to women's electoral success is indisputable and an impressive literature addresses these factors, particularly in regard to West Europe. These include the extent of party alternation in government, where predictable and persistent one-party dominance of government may close women's opportunities for election and may deflect feminist efforts elsewhere. Where a feminist movement and other actors, such as parties, anticipate that governing power is not secured by a single party, where the opposition has a chance to replace the governing party, a movement may find ways of opening access within parties and may direct most of its efforts to electoral work (see, for example, Darcy and Beckwith 1991). The availability of internal party quotas (Matland and Studlar 1996) and a proportional representation electoral system (Norris 1985) with party lists in districts of large magnitude (Engstrom 1987; Matland 1993; Rule 1987) have been identified as structural conditions facilitating women's access to office, although these factors have not necessarily been related to feminist movement activism supporting women's candidacies.

the Conservative government increased and further centralized its national state powers, it also hollowed out the state in terms of its policy responsibilities, resulting simultaneously in a strong state which was also less state (see della Sala 1997). The absence of competing institutions, such as an empowered and autonomous national judiciary, facilitated the concentration of national authority and permitted the advance of the policy agenda of the Conservative governments.[5] The second period is marked by a continuation of offloading of policy responsibilities but also by the devolution of formal state authority from the House of Commons to a Scottish Parliament and a Welsh Assembly, and by a limited commitment to selected European Union (EU) policies.

Less State for Which British Women?

As Britain moved toward privatization and offloading, the unitary state retained its formal powers and persisted as a crucial venue for exercising state policy and coercive powers. It also was a losing ground for feminist issues and for issues of crucial importance to women, as the state systematically downloaded and offloaded responsibilities for health care, unemployment protections, public education (including government support for university education), and child welfare, with adverse results for all women, both because women and children are major beneficiaries of these policies and because women are disproportionately represented among public employees in healthcare and education. The sale of public enterprises to private owners under the Thatcher and Major governments led to widespread unemployment among the working class (particularly in steel, auto, coal, and shipping), the impacts of which were concentrated among working-class women. With unshakable Conservative majorities in the House of Commons from 1979 to 1992, the feminist movement and the working class were excluded from state influence and could not protect social welfare policies from concerted state changes. As a result, reconfigurations of state powers in Britain created different (negative) political opportunities for middle-class and for working-class women.

Between 1979 and 1992, the Conservative Party governed with substantial majorities in the Commons.[6] Out of power, the Labour Party, in the early 1980s, struggled internally over policy issues and the party's ultimate direction, provoking an internal split that gave rise to the Social Democratic

---

[5] Studlar (1996) identifies "the operating principle of the unitary state – devolution when politically and, especially, administratively convenient, with a reversion to centralization when political forces dictate. Under parliamentary sovereignty, all it takes to reverse decentralist moves is a simple majority vote in the House of Commons, with the attendant procedures in the House of Lords" (60).

[6] Such absolute Conservative Party dominance was curtailed with the 1992 election results, which provided John Major's government with a modest 336-seat majority, dependent upon the good health of all Conservative Party members and upon the votes of the Ulster Unionists.

Party. Although Labour began, after the 1987 elections, to resolve what had been highly bitter internal conflict by revising its program, moving toward the center, and restructuring its relationship with the trade union movement (and attempting to modernize its relationship to other constituencies, including women), it was not until the mid-1990s that this program of renewal was completed under the leadership of Tony Blair.

During the 1980s, part of the feminist movement responded to the government's absolute closure to feminist issues by refocusing its efforts within the Labour Party and by militating for increased representation by elected women in the House of Commons. Feminist organizing focused on the Labour Party as more sympathetic to feminism and on the establishment of Women's Action Committees (WAC) in the early 1980s (Byrne 1997: 120). These were active at the local council level where the Labour Party still had governing powers, such as the Greater London Council (which had a particularly active committee). By the late 1980s, feminists had successfully argued for an Equal Rights Department in the Trades Union Congress (1988) and had persuaded the Labour Party to create a Shadow Ministry for Women (1989); in the early 1990s, Emily's List was initiated, following its U.S. counterpart, to raise money to support campaigns of feminist candidates. The Labour Party also adopted a variety of quotas for increasing the selection rate of female candidates for Parliament.

Efforts by organized feminists to gain access to elective office through the Labour Party were also directed toward the European Parliament (EP). As Britain tentatively moved toward Europe, and as European institutions such as the European Court of Justice issued decisions concerning employment practices, the European Parliament emerged as a suprastate venue of political importance for organized feminists in Britain. Working within the Labour Party, organized feminists sought internal changes that would increase the number of female candidates and women's chances of being elected to the EP.

Other feminists focused their efforts on the creation of autonomous women's spaces (Elman this volume; Rowbotham 1996). Autonomous women's refuges and shelters for battered women and rape crisis centers proliferated in the mid-1970s, and in 1975, the National Women's Aid Federation was founded to coordinate their efforts and communication (Byrne 1997: 112). Disputes over issues of race and identity politics helped to create new feminist groups, such as the Organization of Women of African and Asian Descent in 1978, but also served to fragment others, such as the National Abortion Campaign, from which the Women's Reproductive Rights Campaign split, acrimoniously, in 1984. As autonomous feminist groups proliferated, British feminism experienced multiple solidaristic and separatist campaigns throughout the 1970s and into the 1980s. The Women's Peace Camp at Greenham Common attracted women from across Britain, who stayed at and supported the camp for varying lengths of time; the camp organization, however, was also fragmented by internal feminist, working-class, and lesbian politics, reflected in camps at individual gates to the military base (Roseneil 1995). The movement struggled in solidarity to defend a liberal national abortion policy, with massive demonstrations in 1975 and 1979 and, in 1987, with the Fight the Acton Bill mobilization against an antiabortion bill in the Commons; within the same years, the National Women's Liberation Movement Conference, created in 1970, held annual meetings, until 1978, after which it disbanded (Randall 1992: 83).

Randall (1992, 1998) and Lovenduski and Randall (1993) suggest that British feminists, with a hostility to the state, were late to recognize changing political conditions, and focused their efforts outside the state, missing an opportunity to defend women's policy issues against the Conservative governments' attacks on the British welfare state. By offering little resistance within state institutions and by an unwillingness to engage with electoral and party politics, British feminism may have facilitated state reconfiguration in terms of downloading and offloading policy responsibilities. Ruggie, in contrast, argues that the British state, whose apparatus was almost completely captured by Conservative governments, was rendered inhospitable to feminism (Ruggie 1984, 1987; see also Bashevkin 1998). Nonetheless, as political opportunities for the feminist movement closed at the level of the unitary British state, one component of the movement remained autonomous and separatist, as another – joining liberal and socialist feminists in concert – walked the long road within the Labour Party to bring that party to power, attempting to recast the political opportunity structure for feminists within the state by employing the Labour Party as a carrying agent for female candidates and, it was hoped, feminist policy preferences. A third group of organized women, nonfeminist working-class women, responded to British state reconfiguration by direct disruptive action.

From the mid-1980s to the mid-1990s, British working-class women undertook a remarkable mobilization, involving direct action and mass protest in response to the class-specific reconfigurations of British state power. Given that the Conservative government's programs of privatization created burdens borne primarily by the working class, and given the fragmentation of the British feminist movement, working-class women mobilized separately, in their own organizations. Beginning with the 1984–5 miners' strike against the state-owned and operated National Coal Board, women in mining communities organized National Women Against Pit Closures (NWAPC) to support striking miners and their families. Mass demonstrations organized by NWAPC in Barnsley and in London in May and August of 1985 involved hundreds of marchers and NWAPC held its first national conference in July 1985. Cross-class hostility and suspicion precluded NWAPC from soliciting the participation of organized feminists; similarly, class-based assumptions about sexism among miners and the National Union of Mineworkers made organized feminists reluctant to provide active support. By 1992, the British government proposed another round of mass pit closures, projected to result in unemployment and redundancies for 70,000 miners and for 30,000 workers in related industries and services. NWAPC remobilized in response, by establishing a series of pit camps modeled on the Women's Peace Camp at Greenham Common, by holding mass rallies in the coal communities, and by organizing mass rallies and petitions in London (Beckwith 1996, 1997).

As privatization programs continued, and as corporations unilaterally changed work practices, working-class women in Liverpool mobilized in defense of dockworkers. With the abolition of the National Dock Labour Scheme and an assault on working agreements between the Mersey Docks and Harbour Company (MDHC) and the Transport and General Workers Union (TGWU) in September 1995, Women of the Waterfront (WOW) emerged in October as a community-based support group of "wives and partners of the Liverpool dockers" (Lavalette and Kennedy 1996: 54). "Initially their main activities included collecting money, attending the demonstrations and organising events for the dockers and their children" (Lavalette and Kennedy 1996: 50); these early efforts extended, in 1996, to engaging in mass picketing at dock gates, to petitioning Prime Minister John Major, to speaking to other groups and to the mass media, and to picketing the private residences of MDHC management and of "local Liverpool scabs" (Lavalette and Kennedy 1996: 53). Although there were few links between WOW and the feminist movement, organized working-class women from NWAPC provided advice to WOW activists (Lavalette and Kennedy 1996: 50; Pye 1996). Despite the extent of working-class women's organizing and resistance, they were unable to change British state policies of privatization, and of defunding and relocating social welfare responsibilities. In the absence of a working-class, socialist, or Labour Party in government, and in the absence of organized women within the House of Commons, working-class women had no allies within the state structure, and an inside-outside strategy involving elected women within the Commons was unavailable during these years.

Women in the British State

Among European societies, Great Britain has most resisted including women in the political elite. (Lovenduski 1994: 300)

Given changes in the British state and changes within organized feminism, where is the feminist movement in the state? More specifically, as part of the feminist movement has sought to advance women in elective office, targeting the House of Commons and the European Parliament as useful venues for advancing (or at least protecting) social welfare and equal opportunity policies important to women, have these efforts succeeded?

Table 8.1 indicates the range of elective success for women in the House of Commons from 1974 to 1997 for the Conservative and Labour

TABLE 8.1.   *Number and Percentage of Women Elected to the House of Commons, by Party, 1974–1997*

Year	Conservative Women	Labour Women	Total
1974 (Feb.)	3.0%	4.3%	3.7%
	(9)	(13)	(23)[a]
1974 (Oct.)	2.5%	5.3%	4.3%
	(7)	(18)	(27)[b]
1979	2.4%	4.1%	3.0%
	(8)	(11)	(19)
1983	3.3%	4.8%	3.5%
	(13)	(10)	(23)
1987	4.5%	9.2%	6.3%
	(17)	(21)	(41)[c]
1992	6.0%	13.7%	9.2%
	(20)	(37)	(60)[d]
1997	2.0%	15.3%	18.4%
	(13)	(101)	(120)[e]

[a] Includes one woman elected for a regional party (Plaid Cymru/ Scottish National Party; Norris and Lovenduski 1993: 46).
[b] Includes two women elected for a regional party (Plaid Cymru/ Scottish National Party; Norris and Lovenduski 1993: 46).
[c] Includes one woman elected for the Liberals, one for the Social Democratic Party, and one for a regional party (Plaid Cymru/ Scottish National Party; www.parliament.uk/commons/lib/ womenmps.htm).
[d] Includes two women elected for the Liberal Democrats and one for a regional party (www.parliament.uk/commons/lib/ womenmps.htm).
[e] Includes three women elected for the Liberal Democrats, two elected for other parties, and the Speaker (www.parliament.uk/ commons/lib/womenmps.htm).
Source: Calculated by author from Inter-Parliamentary Union (Margets 1997, table 1: 185).

Parties. Bluntly put, electoral politics has not welcomed British women. From 1979, with a low of 3.0% women in the Commons, to 1992, with women constituting 9.2% of all MPs, women have had little presence in the Commons, in either of the two major parties, regardless of which party held a governing majority.[7] Only in 1997, with the election of a Labour government, does the percentage of women in the House of

---

[7] Women's parliamentary inclusion varies little with party control of government; that is, women in the Conservative Party did not hold substantially more seats in the Commons than did Labour women, when the Conservatives were in the majority. In Britain generally, women's electoral chances have not improved with their party's overall electoral performance.

Commons reach double digits. Although the representation of elected women in the Labour Party increased after 1983, Labour women still accounted for less than 6% of Members of Parliament, and for less than 14% of their party's parliamentary delegation by 1992.[8] From 1974 to 1997, the Labour Party contributed substantially more, however, to women's representation within the Commons; the difference between the percentage of women in the Labour Party and in the Conservative Party is statistically significant at $p \leq .0144$. The effects of internal party efforts to nominate more women are modestly evident in the increases in women's electoral success in both parties since 1987; the Labour Party's success in 1997 did not bring with it a substantially larger female delegation, in percentage terms, than was the case in its loss in 1992 (15.3 versus 13.7%).

Given that Parliament is still a crucial venue for legislating on women's issues, liberal feminist efforts to advance women's policy issues by increasing women's presence in Parliament cannot yet be identified as successful. Nonetheless, these data suggest that organized women, including the electorally oriented British feminists of the 1980s and 1990s, have managed to move into the state's parliamentary arena. The presence of more than one hundred Labour women in the Commons can be attributed to the organized efforts of feminists within the party to increase women's nominations, to ensure their placement in likely constituencies, and to engage the Labour Party in making internal changes that positioned it for electoral success by 1997.

Feminist efforts have not had much more success at the European parliamentary level, the other state venue useful for advancing British women's policy interests. Unlike the case for many EU member states, women's representation in Britain's EP delegation is not significantly higher than it is in the Commons. As Table 8.2 shows, women's EP presence did not substantially increase, after the first European parliamentary elections in 1979, until the most recent elections in 1999. Eleven women (or 13.8% of the British delegation) were elected to the EP in 1979, increasing to sixteen women (or 18.4%) in 1994 (Corbett, Jacobs, and Shackleton 1995: 54), constituting a 3.6% increase across fifteen years. By 1999, twenty women were elected to represent Britain in the EP, constituting less than a quarter of the British delegation. The contrast with other nations' representation of women in their EU parliamentary delegations in 1994 is striking: almost 44% of Denmark's delegation consisted of women; more than a third of the German delegation was female; and a third of the Spanish delegation was female. Britain ranks among those countries with the lowest representation of women at the European parliamentary level, including Greece (16%), Italy (12.6%), and Portugal (8%; Corbett et al. 1995: 51).

---

[8] In the 1997 general elections, Labour won a 418-seat majority in the Commons, and 101 women were elected; 120 women were elected by all parties, constituting 18.4% of the Commons, still far from the 325 women necessary to reach a representation mark of 50%.

TABLE 8.2.   *Number and Percentage of Women in the*
British European Union Delegation, by Party, 1979–1999

Year	Conservatives	Labour	Total*
1979	10.0%	23.5%	13.8%
	(6)	(4)	(11)
1984	13.3%	15.6%	14.8%
	(6)	(5)	(12)
1989	12.5%	15.6%	14.8%
	(4)	(7)	(12)
1994	11.1%	19.4%	18.4%
	(2)	(12)	(16)
1999	8.3%	31.0%	23.0%
	(3)	(9)	(20)

* Totals include women elected for minor parties (not shown). In the
1999 elections, eight women were elected on minor party lists: five
Liberal Democrats, 2 Greens, and 1 Plaid Cymru.
Source: Calculated by author from *Times Guide to the European
Parliament* (1979, 1984, 1989): 60, 66, 86; "Women in Decision-
Making" Butler and Westlake 1995: 174; see also Corbett, Jacobs
and Shackleton 1995: 51–54.

Given that the European Parliament is a relatively new institution, it might
have been expected that British women would have been more successful in
advancing their representation within the EP. Under conditions where new
political institutions are being constructed, more opportunities for women's
influence and inclusion may be available. In Britain, however, limited uploading (and limited reconfiguration) meant that EP elections constituted less of
an opening for organized women than they did, for example, in France.
Three facilitating components for exploiting this limited opening were missing in Britain. First, as suggested earlier, the election of women to national
(or international) office was not on the agenda of the British feminist movement in the late 1970s; British feminism was still grappling with issues of
autonomy and reluctance to engage the state at a moment in which advancement of women's candidacies within the EP might have been easiest.[9]
Second, the British national electoral context worked against women's representation. When the European Parliament held its first elections in 1979,
the Labour Party was in disarray and the Conservative Party had succeeded
in winning governing power, with 339 seats (or 53.4%). The Conservatives
controlled the national electoral and governing context; as a unified party

[9] British women's candidacies might have been advantaged not only because of the opportunity
offered by a newly constructed state venue, but because the rules for candidacy established
by the Labour Party for the 1979 EP elections foreclosed candidacies for those candidates
(mostly men) already standing for elections to Westminster.

unreceptive to women's candidacies (with one notable exception), Conservative success closed electoral opportunities for British feminists.

Finally, the internal party context, for Labour, within which British feminists might have organized for representation in the EP, was also discouraging. After the 1979 parliamentary elections, the Labour Party began to undertake internal organizational restructuring, bringing the Parliamentary Labour Party under the control of the mass party, where trade unions controlled a plurality of the vote, radicalizing the party's program, and leading to a split within the party leadership and the founding of the Social Democratic Party in 1981. In short, Britain's reconfiguration of limited uploading meant limited openings for women's candidacies in the EP elections in 1979 and 1984, openings that were closed by the British national context.[10]

Britain: Less State, More States?

Recent events suggest that Britain is becoming "less state," by devolving governing powers to Scotland and Wales. Two Scottish referenda and elections to a new Scottish Parliament in May 1999 indicate that formal state powers, formerly the purview of the House of Commons, have been relinquished to Scotland and would be exceedingly difficult to recover by Britain (Bogdanor 1999). Although a detailed history of devolution and the Scottish feminist movement is precluded in this chapter, it is worth noting that Britain's experience with state reconfiguration by downloading formal state authority served directly to empower organized women (see Brown 1998; see also Dobrowolsky this volume). The Scottish feminist movement anticipated devolution and was instrumental in raising equity issues in democratic representation, in shaping the electoral system to develop an inclusive body of election law, and in nominating female candidates for election to the first Scottish Parliament since 1707. By positioning women in a newly constructed venue of state power, Scottish feminists were able to elect an impressive number of women to the new Parliament: 46 (or 35.9%) of the 128 new Members of the Scottish Parliament (SMP) were women. As a result, the Scottish Parliament ranks sixth, among parliamentary democracies, in its percentage of female members.[11] Of the newly elected women, the preponderance were elected on Labour Party nominations or lists (twenty-six, or more than 20% of all SMPs); more than 95% of all elected women had been candidates of left or left-leaning parties: Labour, the Liberal Democrats, or the Scottish

---

[10] The Conservatives won thirty-six seats; Labour won twenty nine. It is interesting to note, but will not be developed here, that the success of women elected to the EP has not been dependent upon the overall electoral fortunes of the party nominating them.

[11] Nations that have higher percentages of women among national legislators are Sweden (42.7%), Denmark (37.4%), Finland (37.0%), Norway (36.4%), and the Netherlands (36.0%); ("Women in National Parliaments" 1999).

National Party (more than 10% of all SMPs are SNP women). Organized women in Scotland succeeded in identifying and employing these parties successfully to carry women into the new Scottish Parliament. The construction of a new specific state arena offered an opportunity for Scottish women to participate in its building, to shape it to create electoral opportunities, and the possibility, therefore, of policy opportunities as well.

France: Same State?

France has undergone less change among the dimensions of reconfiguration than has Britain. France remains a highly centralized nation, with decision-making powers located in the national state. The French have not devolved major decision-making powers to regional or local governments (downloading), and have retained the unitary nature of the French state, in marked contrast to Italy and Spain. Nor have the French relinquished – either through explicit transfer or by refusal to pursue policies – responsibilities for the traditional social policies of the welfare state, such as control of public education or child welfare.

The French engaged in a series of privatization of industries in the 1980s but, as suggested earlier, privatization has not been unidirectional, has oscillated with changes in party government, and has lacked the ideological underpinnings of radical free market neoliberalism (Maclean 1995; Zahariadas 1995: 122–123). Zahariadas argues that state presence was strongest in France in the late 1980s, among six selected OECD (Organisation for Economic Co-operation and Development) countries, "with 100 percent state ownership in six of eleven economic sectors" (Zahariadas 1995: 11). In marked contrast to Britain's unidirectional program of privatization of national industries, the French state, in the first Mitterrand government, introduced a program of bank nationalizations (1981–2), assuming additional state public policy responsibilities that had previously been private. The Chirac government, in 1986, initiated a privatization program that "proposed to change the rules of the economic game" (Maclean 1995: 274) and that encompassed industrial groups, banks and finance companies, insurance companies, and communications groups.[12] Nonetheless, the Chirac government's privatization program did not involve an attack on the principle of state ownership of economic enterprises, was not antistatist in its intentions or rhetoric, and constituted a "privatization that began with reinforcing state power" (Zahariadas 1995: 132). The 1986–8 privatizations are more rightly characterized as reprivatization, given that those enterprises privatized by the Chirac government were those that had only been most recently nationalized by the Mitterrand government. When the Socialist Party resumed power as a minority government in 1991, privatization abated

---

[12] For a list of French privatizations, see Zahariadas 1995, table 5.1: 118).

although it did not completely cease, and the return of the center right to government in 1993 marked a resumption of privatization that was "budget-driven and ideologically spent" (Maclean 1995: 273).

The recent policy history of France does not give evidence of a systematic transfer of policy-making responsibilities to nonelected quasi-state bodies, nor is there a pattern of defunding in regard to traditional social welfare support, as in Britain. The French state, on these dimensions, has held on to its powers and has maintained the primary social responsibilities of the traditional welfare state. On other dimensions, however, France has similarly experienced a reconfiguration of power. Since 1957, France has had long-standing political commitments to Europe as a unified entity, commitments which have been evidenced in a transfer of state power to the European Union through the Single European Act (1987) and the Treaty of Maastricht (1993). Powers to determine permeability of national boundaries, to regulate migration across EU member states, to set currency valuation, to determine monetary policy, and to determine some specific market and employment policies have been transferred from the French state to the European Union to the extent that autonomous state decision making in these arenas has been diminished. France has not reserved specific state powers for itself as a condition of EU monetary union or, obviously, as a condition of EU membership; to the extent possible, France has transferred major state powers to the EU. In addition, French national policy making has been more constrained, since the 1970s, in economic policy terms, by its status as a G-7 nation (now G-8) and by its involvement in other supranational treaty arrangements, such as the General Agreements on Trade and Tariffs (GATT).

For the feminist movement, the French pattern of minimal transfer of policy responsibilities within France and the maintenance of state powers at the national level suggests that the French state continues as an important venue for feminist politics and that organized women seeking to make and influence French state policy should be best positioned by continuing a focus on the national parliament. In addition, the French commitment to the EU suggests that the European Parliament is also an important venue for French feminist political influence.

Unitary State, Fragmented Movement?
The richness and complexities of the French feminist movement and its relationship to the French state have been chronicled and analyzed by multiple scholars within and outside France; to do justice to this complexity and history is beyond the scope of this chapter. The following is a modest summary of a movement that arose in a single wave but in multiple manifestations; whose struggles over equality, difference, sexuality, psychoanalysis, and socialist and trade unionist ideology and politics resulted in reified segments of the movement in the 1970s (Jenson 1996: 79); and whose focus by the

1990s had become electorally centered in a unity unpredictable in 1970, the marking year of the origin of the French feminist movement.

The rise of French feminism in the early 1970s was quickly evidenced by the formation of small groups, public meetings, and organizing around issues of equal employment and pay, sexuality, and abortion. Various autonomous groups and groups within parties and the labor unions provided the basis for the revolutionary and syndicalist wings of the emerging movement, which also embraced a third wing concerned primarily with equality issues (Jenson and Sineau 1994; Jenson 1996). Feminist organizing focused primarily on abortion and employment issues in the 1970s. The mid-1970s saw syndicalist feminists organizing with labor unions and left parties around work issues and women's profession- and trade-based groups emerged (for example, associations of female lawyers as in the Ligue du Droit des Femmes; Jenson and Sineau 1994: 252; Jenson 1996: 82–87).

At the same time, the feminist movement turned to abortion reform. In 1971, petitions supporting abortion reform were printed in the mass media, one signed by 343 women, many of whom were celebrities who had had illegal abortions, and another signed by 331 doctors who had performed illegal abortions, bringing the problematic nature of the abortion law fully onto the public agenda. Shortly thereafter, Choisir la cause des femmes, advocating abortion reform, was founded, and, in 1973, the Mouvement pour la Liberté de l'Avortement et la Contraception was established (Duchen 1986: 12–15). In concert with others, these groups succeeded in achieving limited reforms (for a five-year time frame) in French abortion law. By 1979, abortion reform had been extended and confirmed in response to mass mobilizations of women, neighborhood abortion counseling centers, and organized flights to countries where abortion was legal. In October 1979, for example, the mass March of Parisian Women, involving 50,000 participants, evidenced public support and pressure for abortion services (Jenson and Sineau 1994: 254).

Abortion reform, mass protest, and local autonomous feminist organizing characterized the 1970s in France; by 1979, however, the feminist movement fragmented. The syndicalist feminists associated with and within trade unions demobilized and the rise of Psychanalyse et Politique confirmed the split of a formerly revolutionary, now separatist, feminism concerned with issues of women's space and culture. Psyche et Po also legally seized the *mouvement de libération des femmes* as its exclusive trademark, confirming a hostile break with the remaining components of the movement. As the separatist feminists abandoned the public arena and with abortion rights secured, equality issues in employment and electoral access were foregrounded. Although "improved state policies never served as the primary goal of [the revolutionary wing of] the movement" (Jenson and Sineau 1994: 251), by the 1980s, with the accession of the Parti Socialiste (PS) to government, the feminist movement turned to an emphasis on access to state institutions and to political parties.[13] PS proposals requiring candidate parity provisions in parties were passed by the National Assembly in 1982, only to be declared invalid by the Constitutional Court (see Jenson and Valiente this volume).[14] The Socialist government also proposed changes in the electoral system, from a first-ballot majority with second-ballot plurality provisions to proportional representation, which helped to focus feminist efforts on equality and state access issues (see Jenson and Sineau 1995; Jenson 1996; Mossuz-Lavau 1998; Sineau 1988).

Within political parties, particularly the Socialist Party's Mouvement Démocratique et Féminin (MDF), feminists had been advocating quotas for women in all levels of the party, including candidacies. A 10% internal quota was initiated in 1973 and raised in 1977 to 20%; feminists' efforts and criticisms of the party managed to achieve a 30% quota in 1991 (Appleton and Mazur 1993: 103). Similar pressure was brought upon the PS externally, by the Mouvement pour l'Integration des Femmes à l'Action Sociale (MIFAS) in the late 1970s. Other feminists within the PS proposed a women's group (*courant*) within the PS as a venue for feminist representation and a launching point for women's candidacies, election, and policy proposals.[15] By the early 1990s, French feminism had focused on representational parity issues across all parties, with the emergence of groups like Au pouvoir citoyennes, Elles-aussi, and Assemblé des femmes, Women for Parity (1993), and Parity Tomorrow (in 1996; see Jenson and Valiente this volume; see also Haase-Dubosc 1999), at a time when the French state appeared to offer considerable opportunities to women. In 1993, the "Manifesto of the 577 for a Parity-Democracy" was published in *Le Monde*, asking that "all local and national elected assemblies will be made up of as many women as men" (Haase-Dubosc 1999: 186). It was not until 2000 that the French government, in a campaign supported by the PS and by Prime Minister Lionel Jospin, enacted parity legislation.

French feminism's turn to parity constituted a feminist issue, according to Haase-Dubosc (1999), insofar as it was a "political strategy, a move for greater civil equality for all women and, as such...a means but not an end" (206). It offers the possibility of increased electoral access for all female candidates, regardless of party, and hence includes a potential for the election of nonfeminist women representing parties hostile to feminist

---

[13] This constituted a considerable change in the movement, according to Sineau, who argues that "Le féminisme français...refusé tout rapport avec les institutions établies....Au moment même où le mouvement des femmes en tant que mouvement social est si puissant, le MLF prône un antiparlementarisme militant. Il a donc sa part de responsabilité dans la sous-représentation actuelle des femmes en France" (Sineau 1997b: 100).

[14] The provision was reinstituted in 2000 with the parity law (Daley 2001).

[15] None of these ventures was successful within the PS. According to Appleton and Mazur (1993), "Existing quotas have never been respected within the party, either at the national or the local level" (109).

goals and issues (see also Jenson 1996: 105–108; Jenson and Valiente this volume).

In the context of parity organizing, especially in the mid-1990s, the French state still possessed considerable state sovereignty and policy responsibility. Alternations in power by the Center-Right and the Socialists suggested electoral opportunities for feminists and for female candidacies, particularly through the left parties, offering openings at the level of the French state for women's entry. In addition, reconfiguration of state power relocated some state authority in the European Union, similarly suggesting an increase in electoral opportunities for French women in that venue. Given these locations for feminist influence, as a result of modest state reconfiguration, where were French women?

Women in the French State

[In France], the electoral route is seemingly barred to women, [given its] legacy of exclusion. (Jenson and Sineau 1994: 244)

In 1999, the Inter-Parliamentary Union placed France fifty-fifth among nations, ranked according to the percentage representation of women in lower houses of national legislatures ("Women in National Parliaments"). Table 8.3 shows the pattern of women's representation in the National

TABLE 8.3. *Number and Percentage of Women in the French National Assembly, by Party, 1973–1997*

Year	PCF	PS	UDF-RPR	Total
1973	4.1%	–	1.1%*	1.6%
	(3)	(0)	(2)	(8)
1978	13.9%	0.9%	1.5%*	3.7%
	(12)	(1)	(2)	(19)
1981	9.0%	6.6%*	2.6%	5.5%
	(4)	(19)	(4)	(27)
1986	8.5%	9.8%*	2.8%	5.9%
	(3)	(21)	(8)	(34)
1988	4.0%	6.2%	5.0%*	5.7%
	(1)	(17)	(13)	(33)
1993	8.7%	5.2%	5.9%*	6.0%
	(2)	(3)	(28)	(35)
1997	13.5%	16.3%*	3.5%	10.9%
	(5)	(40)	(5)	(63)

* Indicates majority governing party in the National Assembly.

Source: For 1973 and 1978, Charlot 1980: 184, table 6.10; 1973 figures include RPR only. For 1981–93, Jenson and Sineau 1995, Annexe 7. For 1997, calculated by author from "Presentation," www.parité.asso.fr, July 6, 1999; includes RPR only; and "Women in National Parliaments."

Assembly, from 1973 to 1997, by party.[16] Although women's presence in the National Assembly improved substantially in 1981, with a Socialist president and a Socialist majority in the National Assembly, increasing by more than 40%, women remain seriously underrepresented in the French national legislature. Only in 1997 did women pass (barely) the 10% mark, as was the case for women in Britain, although women in the United States managed to surpass the 10% mark five years earlier. Women's representation in the French Assembly varies considerably across major party groupings, with the PS and French Communist Party (PCF) promoting women's candidacies and, in 1997, substantially increasing the percentage of women within each party's delegation. Women's representation is also affected by the parties' overall electoral success; that is, as the proportion of seats won in the Assembly increases for a party, women candidacies generally increase. Given the parity attempts within the PS since the 1970s, French women have succeeded in gaining access to an important state site for advancing feminist policy issues. Despite cross-party parity organizing in the 1990s, outside of left parties, however, French women have been confined to very modest representation, even within the center-right parties that held majorities in the National Assembly. A difference of means test between the PS and the UDF-RPR in their election of women shows, however, that party differences miss statistical significance at $p \leq .0743$.

As is the case for many member states of the EU, the French EP delegation has a higher representation of women than does the National Assembly (see Table 8.4). French women's representation has increased substantially across recent European Parliamentary elections, although women already constituted a fifth of the French EP delegation in 1979, a proportion that it has consistently maintained and eventually exceeded. By 1994, French women constituted just under a third of the French EP delegation, and by 1999, two fifths of all French MEPs were women. This record easily surpasses that of Britain, and, as early as 1994, France ranked among those nations with the highest female representation, exceeding the EU mean of 26% (Corbett et al. 1995: 51).[17]

The pattern of party support for women's election to the EP, despite small numbers for some parties (for example, Communists, Verts), suggests that all parties have advanced women's candidacies, and that left parties have been most successful in advancing women within the EP. Table 8.4 shows that, for the various center-right combinations, women's representation within those party coalitions has increased proportionately across the past twenty years; similarly, the PS and the PCF have increased the percentage of women within

---

[16] For a visual representation of this pattern, see Appleton and Mazur 1993, figure 5.1: 94.
[17] Denmark's delegation has the highest percentage of women MEPs at 44%, followed by Germany (34.3%), Spain (33%), Luxembourg (33%), the Netherlands (32.3%), Belgium (32%), and France (31%) (Corbett et al. 1995: 51).

TABLE 8.4. *Number and Percentage of Women in the French European Union Delegation, by Party, 1979–1999*

Year	Party or Party Group						Total
1979	UFE 19.2% (5)	DIFE (RPR) 20.0% (3)	Socialists/Rad. 28.6% (6)	Communists 21.2% (4)			22.2% (18)
1984	Union Opposition 19.5% (8)		Socialists 30.0% (6)	Communists 20.0% (2)		FN 10.5% (1)	21.% (17)
1989	UDF/RPR 11.5% (3)	Centre 28.6% (2)	Socialists 27.3% (6)	Communists 42.9% (3)	Verts 44.4% (4)	FN 10.0% (1)	23.5% (19)
1994	UDF/RPR 17.9% (5)		l'Europe Sol. 26.7% (4)	Communists 57.1% (4)		FN 9.1% (1)	31.0% (27)
1999	UDF/RPR 38.1% (8)		Socialists 45.4% (10)	Communists 50.0% (3)	Verts 44.0% (4)	FN – (0)	40.2% (35)

Source: Calculated by author. For 1979–89, Pascal 1990: 343–344. For 1994, Gaffney 1996: 101, table 5.2. For 1999, "Women in Decision-Making."

each party's delegation across the past two decades. Second, the left parties have the highest percentage representations of women within their EP delegations. In the 1990s, the Socialists (1999) and les Verts (1994) approached parity, while the PCF met parity in 1999 and actually exceeded it in 1994. These successes, Haase-Dubosc (1999) suggests, reflect the efforts by organized women to advance women's candidacies within these parties in the context of the parity movement. She claims that "by 1994, six French lists of candidates for the elections to the European Parliament reached or almost reached parity between women and men.... The socialist list was a parity list up to the eighteenth candidate, and the Communist Party presented a slight majority of women" (188).[18] Sineau, however, reminds us that the PCF is now marginalized within French politics and hence can no longer promote women's representation as had once been the case, either nationally or within Europe (Sineau 1997b: 101). Table 8.4 reveals the absolute numbers of female communist MEPs that, in the context of overall EP electoral marginalization, provide strong percentage representation of women within the small PCF delegation.

Although French feminists have not succeeded in gaining substantial representation in the French parliament, they have thus far been successful in acquiring and increasing their representation in the European Parliament. Given the importance of both venues for exercising state power and for shaping policies important to women (and to feminists), French feminists are better positioned in Europe than they are at home but these are gains to be defended, especially as the EU moves power from the European Commission to the Parliament. As EP powers increase, French female MEPs may find themselves vulnerable to electoral defeat, especially given particularly high turnover and low average length of service among French MEPs generally (Corbett et al. 1995: 51). Nonetheless, French women have moved into the EP in increasing numbers, primarily through the agency of parties of the left. To the extent that the PS and, with their smaller numbers, the PCF and les Verts support feminist issues in this supranational venue, French feminists will be well positioned for the next five years to advance their policy agenda.

The United States: Same State, Less State

Because the United States has a federal arrangement of state powers, it has undergone less apparent structural reconfiguration than have Britain and France, in terms of redistribution of formal decision-making powers. In the United States, individual states maintained a constitutionally undergirded set of specified and implied sovereign powers that have provided them with

---

[18] For additional discussion of nomination patterns, see Jenson 1996: 113n83.

considerable autonomy in policy making. In this regard, the United States exemplifies an extreme version – in the context of West Europe and Canada – of the devolution of national power, although this "devolution" is obviously not the result of changes since the 1970s and was constructed constitutionally by shifting powers from the individual states to the national government rather than the reverse. U.S. federalism has directed political movement activism to at least two levels: the national government and the individual state governments. The U.S. feminist movement, throughout its history, has moved across these levels in response to political changes, as specific struggles, party balance, or configurations of power have indicated that one arena is more useful than another for advancing a particular policy issue.[19]

Although the United States has not devolved new formal decision-making powers to the states (for example, the national government still maintains its ability to regulate interstate commerce),[20] a major change since the 1970s has been the downloading of national governmental policy responsibilities to the individual states.[21] Welfare policy is the prime example of a policy arena where, although formal powers have not been relinquished by the national government, implementation and regulation of welfare and poverty policy have been downloaded at the national level and shifted to the states. Social welfare provisions including unemployment benefits, medical care benefits for the indigent, and school lunch programs for poor children, for example, are funded at lower levels in the 1990s than in the 1970s, are less inclusive in terms of categorizing recipients, are more subject to individual state regulation, and are implemented through individual state agencies. Although the authority of the national state remains unchanged from the 1970s to the 1990s, social policy responsibility has been devolved to the individual state governments. Beginning with the Reagan and Bush administrations and continuing under Clinton, reconfiguration of responsibility for traditional social welfare state policies has marked a major relocation of policy struggle in the United States, a policy arena of particular importance to women and to the feminist movement (see Katzenstein this volume; also Goodstein 2001; Mink 1998).

In the United States, state welfare policies have been few and modest in scope in comparison with those of Britain and France. Downloading

---

[19] For a discussion of women's mobilization across federal and state levels in the suffrage movement, see Banaszak 1996; for a discussion of women' mobilization at these different levels in regard to the struggle for legalized abortion, see Staggenborg 1991.

[20] Note, however, the series of U.S. Supreme Court decisions in the 1980s and 1990s that have staved off further assumption of local powers by the federal government and that have returned some national power to the state level (for example, *U.S. v. Lopez*, 115 *S.Ct.* 1624 (1995). See also the Unfunded Mandates Reform Act of 1995.

[21] Retiring Senator Phil Gramm (R-Texas) was quoted as saying, "Never in American history has so much power been passed back from the federal government to the states and counties and cities and the people than in the last 25 years" (Mitchell 2001).

responsibilities for nationally directed policies has meant less change for U.S. feminists than has been the case, for example, for Britain. Similarly, British governments have engaged in extensive offloading, locating some former social welfare state powers thoroughly outside the state. The U.S. national government has had few welfare state commitments to relinquish and hence has not engaged in comparable offloading or privatization.

In comparison with Britain and France, since 1990, the United States has transferred relatively little of its authority to supranational institutions. The United States has longstanding membership in NATO and the United Nations (as have Britain and, since 1966, France), which preceded post-1970s reconfigurations of state authority and policy responsibilities and hence marks a continuity of military and foreign policy authority to these international treaty organizations across the post–World War II era. The North American Free Trade Agreements, however, are evidence of the relinquishing of U.S. national authority in regard to limited economic powers, such as setting import and tariff policies, and shape the beginnings of an integrated international market in North America whose authority is not unilaterally subject to its individual member nations. In addition, the role of the U.S. national government in the World Trade Organization (WTO), in the International Monetary Fund (IMF), and in GATT indicates that organized women should also focus their efforts and their presence in these organizations, nonelective though they be.

By the 1990s, these limited reconfigurations of state authority and policy responsibility confirm the dual importance of national and individual state arenas for feminist movements. As the national government relinquishes its (historically limited) welfare state commitments to the individual states, policy struggles over issues highly salient to feminist movements are relocated in state governments, an important arena for women's electoral representation. If it is the case that the feminist movement's emphasis on electing women to office has also opened electoral opportunities for conservative women at the state level, issues of feminist electoral and policy activism within state governments are heightened. This reconfiguration, by downloading policy, however, is not matched by a shift in formal state authority; the national government retains its policy-making powers, which it is structurally empowered to reemploy and hence persists as a crucial venue for organized feminism. If the policy implementation struggle has shifted arenas, it has done so at the direction of the national government, which is free to resume social welfare policy responsibilities and could do so with a change of government.

Moreover, to the extent that global economic forces encourage international economic agreements and the construction of supranational economic institutions and given that the U.S. national government remains the arena for the development of U.S. membership and involvement in these institutions and for influencing their policy direction, the importance of the national government as a venue for the feminist movement and for the election of women is reinforced. Finally, the supranational policy agreements located in GATT and the WTO suggest that feminist movements will be disadvantaged in these venues even if they have strong national legislative presence.

U.S. Feminism and Electoral Politics

In its post–World War II reincarnation, the U.S. feminist movement was evidenced in three major branches: socialist, radical, and liberal, whose emergence reflected class, race, and generational origins and prior experience in other social movements. Predominantly middle class, white, and young in its core activists in the late 1960s and early 1970s, some components of the radical and socialist branches of U.S. feminism can be traced to the U.S. civil rights movement (Evans 1979; King 1987; McAdam 1988) and to the anti-Vietnam war movement (Ferree and Hess 1994: 68–75). The mid-1960s were marked with nondiscriminatory employment legal advances for women, but also by the development of feminism within other progressive movements. Young white women's experience in the black civil rights movement was summarized in the Student Nonviolent Coordinating Committee's (SNCC) position paper on "Women in the Movement" in 1964 (Evans 1979: 233–235). The autonomous Chicago Women's Liberation Union was founded at the end of the decade in 1969. In 1973, the National Black Feminist Organization and the First National Lesbian Conference were organized; in 1972, the National Conference of Puerto Rican Women was founded, followed in 1974 by the Mexican American Women's National Association and by the National Alliance of Black Feminists and the Organization of Pan Asian American Women in 1976. The 1970s saw extensive mobilization and activism on the part of socialist feminists and radical feminists in autonomous collectives and local feminist service provision. In 1972, feminists founded Bay Area Women Against Rape and the first rape crisis hotline opened in Washington, D.C. Across the decade, rape crisis centers, shelters for battered women, and abortion counseling clinics (such as Jane, in Chicago; see Staggenborg 1991) proliferated. A rich preponderance of feminist bookstores, reading groups, collectives, restaurants, cultural spaces, publications, take back the night marches, women's studies centers, women's music groups, and radical and socialist feminist conferences and public meetings across the 1970s matched the concurrent state-oriented activism of liberal feminism. The U.S. movement, in its various socialist, radical, and liberal branches, flourished, even with opposition, through the 1970s and into the 1980s; Brenner (1996) argues that "there is still a thriving women's culture closely tied to and supported by urban lesbian communities and by feminists in the countercultural 'Left' milieu" (57).

Unlike the cases of the British and French feminist movements, the liberal branch of the U.S. feminist movement was a powerful force from the outset, had longstanding commitments to women's access to elective office, and was experienced in dealing with – and had frequently targeted – the national state for policy change. The relationship between liberal feminists and the U.S. state has been long standing. Costain argues that the national government invited the emergence of liberal feminism in the early 1960s, laying the foundation for the second wave of the movement (Costain 1992; Hartmann 1998). In 1961, President Kennedy appointed his President's Commission on the Status of Women; in 1963, Congress passed the Equal Pay Act. The following year, the 1964 Civil Rights Act, including sex discrimination protections in Title VII, was passed, and, in 1966, the National Organization for Women was founded. In 1967, President Johnson issued Executive Order 11375, establishing affirmative action provisions in federally contracted employment, and by 1968, the National Democratic Party had proposed inclusive quotas for women (as well as for African-Americans and young people) as national convention delegates (see Kirkpatrick 1976). By the 1970s, liberal feminists were actively supporting women for elective office, were mobilizing to influence Congressional policy making, and were organizing themselves into autonomous profession- and work-based groups, such as Federally Employed Women (FEW), Women Employed (in Chicago), 9 to 5 (an organization of clerical workers), and the Coalition of Labor Union Women (CLUW), and into equality-oriented organizations such as the Women's Equity Action League (WEAL). In 1972, the National Women's Political Caucus was founded to support feminist candidates for office and Congress proposed the Equal Rights Amendment (ERA) to the Constitution, which thirty states ratified within the first year of its passage.

Liberal feminism experienced a major defeat, however, in 1982, with the states' failure to ratify the Equal Rights Amendment. Space constraints preclude a discussion of the history of feminist mobilizing around the ERA and a rich and sophisticated literature debates its failure (Berry 1986; Boles 1979; Hoff-Wilson 1986; Mansbridge 1986). The amendment process, and the ERA failure, underscored the two-tier strategy necessary for national feminist policy success, and taught second-wave feminists the importance of individual states, as well as the federal government, as locations for mobilization and struggle.

What is particularly striking about the U.S. feminist movement, in comparison with those of Britain and France, is the early rise and longstanding presence of organized liberal feminism and its emphasis on women's election to office. Still mobilizing in the 1980s, liberal feminists founded Emily's List in 1985, a campaign group whose purpose is to identify and to finance feminist candidates for office by bundling contributions from individual List members. In 1987, the Fund for a Feminist Majority was established to support feminist congressional candidates. Across the 1980s, National Organization for Women membership continued to increase

(Ferree and Hess 1994: 224–230). Promoting women's candidacies and election and targeting the state for policy change were not the result of socialist feminist disenchantment, as in Britain in the 1980s (Randall 1992) or the fragmentation of the movement over separatist/double militancy disputes, as in France in the 1980s (Jenson and Sineau 1994), but were embedded in U.S. second-wave feminism at its emergence. The liberal feminist agenda, at least in regard to electoral politics, evidences a remarkable persistence in the face of ERA failure and internal movement struggles over lesbianism, racism, and identity politics.

Given that the liberal wing of the U.S. feminist movement has always targeted electoral politics, and given its two-level state target strategy, how successful has the movement been in placing women in state and national elective office?

Feminism in the U.S. State

Table 8.5 shows the percentage of women elected, by party, to the U.S. House of Representatives from 1974 to 1998, including "The Year of the Woman" in 1992.

Given the pattern of women's electoral access to the House of Representatives, it should come as no surprise that the National Organization for Women discussed the possibility of forming a third party in 1990. Few women have been successful in winning election to the House across the twenty-year span shown in Table 8.5. Fewer than ten Republican women gained access to the House in any election between 1974 and 1980, when ten Republican women won office; from 1984 to 1992 these numbers do not improve substantially. There is an increase to seventeen Republican women for 1994, 1996, and 1998, and Republican women reach their summit at eighteen representatives in the 2000 elections.

Democratic women actually lost seats between 1974 and 1986; it is not until 1988 that more than fourteen Democratic women sit in the House in any single year.[22] Note that this period of Democratic women's low representation within the House was concurrent with Democratic Party majorities in the House, indicating that the party's overall electoral success did not extend to women. Indeed, in both parties, women's electoral success did not vary with party success in winning House seats. Although half again as many women won House seats in 1992 as they did in 1990, the base numbers are so small that a sixty-eight percentage increase in elected women is required to move women's House presence above (barely) 10%. Women's greater presence in the 103rd Congress is attributable to the relatively high numbers of Democratic women who won office; Republican women's representation,

---

[22] In 1986, more women were nominated for election to the House of Representatives by the Republican Party than by the Democrats (Brenner 1996: 38).

TABLE 8.5.   *Number and Percentage of Women Elected
to the U.S. House of Representatives, by Party, 1974–1998*

Year	Republican Women	Democratic Women	Total
1974	3.5%	4.8%	4.4%
	(5)	(14)	(19)
1976	3.5%	4.5%	4.1%
	(5)	(13)	(18)
1978	3.2%	4.0%	3.7%
	(5)	(11)	(16)
1980	4.7%	4.1%	4.8%
	(10)	(11)	(21)
1982	5.4%	4.9%	5.1%
	(9)	(13)	(22)
1984	4.9%	5.1%	5.3%
	(11)	(12)	(23)
1986	6.2%	4.7%	5.3%
	(11)	(12)	(23)
1988	6.3%	5.4%	6.7%
	(13)	(16)	(29)
1990	5.4%	7.1%	6.4%
	(9)	(19)	(28)
1992	6.8%	14.0%	10.8%
	(12)	(35)	(47)
1994	7.4%	15.2%	11.0%
	(17)	(31)	(48)
1996	7.0%	16.9%	12.4%
	(17)	(37)	(54)
1998	7.6%	18.5%	12.9%
	(17)	(39)	(56)

Source: Calculated by author; "Women in the U.S. Congress, 1917–
2001;" Ornstein, Mann, and Malbin 1998.

although higher in 1992 than in 1990, remains substantially the same.[23] As organized U.S. feminists have pursued elective office across three decades, the House of Representatives, as a major venue of state power undiminished by state reconfiguration, is strikingly resistant to women's election to office.

[23] For a discussion of the feminist movement's relationship with the Democratic Party, see Brenner 1996: 38 and also 30, where she argues that "contesting for influence within the Democratic Party apparatus and electing sympathetic Democratic Party candidates to office has left them dependent on this party and powerless to counter the Democrats' abandonment of the New Deal." A difference of means test shows a statistically significant difference between the percentage of women elected to the House by Democrats and Republicans between 1974 and 1998 ($p \leq .0184$).

TABLE 8.6.   *Number and Percentage of Women Elected to U.S. State Legislatures, 1975–1999*

Year	Lower	Upper House	Total House
1975	9.3%	4.5%	8.1%
	(521)	(89)	(610)
1977	10.4%	5.2%	9.2%
	(594)	(102)	(696)
1979	12.0%	5.5%	10.3%
	(662)	(108)	(770)
1981	14.0%	7.0%	12.1%
	(770)	(138)	(908)
1983	15.0%	8.7%	13.3%
	(818)	(173)	(991)
1985	16.5%	9.9%	14.8%
	(904)	(197)	(1101)
1987	17.3%	11.1%	15.7%
	(946)	(222)	(1168)
1989	18.4%	13.0%	17.0%
	(1005)	(260)	(1265)
1991	19.5%	15.0%	18.3%
	(1066)	(299)	(1365)
1993	21.7%	17.2%	20.5%
	(1182)	(342)	(1524)
1995	21.9%	17.2%	20.6%
	(1191)	(341)	(1532)
1997	22.8%	18.4%	21.6%
	(1238)	(366)	(1604)
1999	23.5%	19.6%	22.4%
	(1276)	(388)	(1664)

Source: "Numbers of Women in Office."

U.S. feminists have also targeted state legislative elections as a venue for women's access and influence. Table 8.6 shows the percentage of women elected to state legislatures from 1975 to 1999. As Wilcox (1994) argues, women's access to state legislative office shows "a steady, incremental...increase" (3). Across twenty-five years, the percentage of women in state legislatures increased from less than 10% to more than 20%, with considerable variation across individual legislatures (Wilcox 1994: 9; see also Thomas 1994, table 8.1: 142).

Several reasons have been identified to explain women's better electoral record at the state legislative than the congressional level (for example, see Thomas 1994: 144–146). Anticipating or responding to the federal government's downloading of social welfare policy responsibilities has not been suggested and, given a slow and steady increase in women's access (rather than a punctuated increase in the mid-1980s and thereafter), it is also unlikely that women's increasing presence in state legislatures is related to national state reconfiguration. Rather, women's steady assumption to state legislative office is concurrent with efforts of the liberal wing of the U.S. feminist movement to advance women's candidacies at the statehouse level.

This slow and steady increase in women's election to lower state houses is evidenced by summary statistics. The mean increase between 1975 and 1999 is 62.9 seats, with a fairly large standard deviation (30.1 seats; range = 116–9). This is accounted for by a leap in the number of women elected to lower houses between 1991 ($n = 1066$) and 1993 ($n = 1182$; see Table 8.6). Regressing percentage of seats in lower houses held by women on year, the R-square value equals .998, an almost perfect linear relationship indicating the slow and steady progress of women's election to lower state legislative assemblies. The slope indicates an annual seat increase of 0.6%.

As the U.S. state has reconfigured, the U.S. feminist movement has persisted in its pattern of a proliferation of organizations and groups, a combination of autonomous and state-involved strategies, and the focus of its liberal wing on the election of women to office. Because most of the state reconfiguration in the U.S. has concerned the jettisoning of policy responsibilities, either through policy downloading or through complete policy offloading, it is surprising that the pattern of U.S. feminist strategy and focus has not shifted to include increasing resistance to state policies and to an increasingly autonomous stance. The national and state governments remain clear arenas of power and policy making, and hence an electoral strategic emphasis may be a rational continuity. Reconfiguration alone, however, is an unconvincing predictor of such continuity at the state legislative level.

CONCLUSION

As formal state powers have been reconfigured and as policy responsibilities have been shifted from national governments to lower state levels (or abnegated altogether), feminist movements have responded by identifying those arenas of state power that, despite the transfer of policy responsibilities, still retain formal authoritative powers. During the 1980s in Britain, France, and the United States, formal powers of the national state persisted and, in Britain's case, intensified. The British and U.S. movements, excluded by and large from government influence from within the state, mobilized around electoral strategies designed to support women's election to the national legislature. The French movement, with Socialist dominance of state governance, took until the early 1990s to mobilize to increase women's representation. By the end of the 1990s, major components of all three feminist movements were organizing around issues of women's access to governing power at the state level, recognizing the importance and persistence of national state power in shaping policies relevant to women, in feminist directions or otherwise. As formal state powers retained their location and force at the national level, feminist movements mobilized for women's entry at that level and sought to create political opportunities for women's candidacies.

Feminists' organized efforts have also had similar effects. In all three nations, left parties have served to increase the numbers of elected women, both internally, within the parties, and externally within parliaments across time.[24] All feminist movements can claim to have had success in increasing women's legislative representation through left-wing parties, however problematic the policy ramifications and regardless of a variety of additional contributing factors.

The struggle to increase these numbers and the modest size of the increase across a decade are evidence of the difficulties the movements face in launching a campaign to increase their position within state institutions. Not until 1992 did the total number of women, regardless of party, exceed 10% of all members of the U.S. House of Representatives; not until 1997 did that number exceed 10% for the British House of Commons and the French National Assembly. Only in France did women's representation increase proportionately with (left-wing) parties' overall electoral success. For Britain and the United States, the proportion of elected women did not increase when the proportion of party seats increased. Given the variety of strategies employed by all three feminist movements, within parties, within electoral laws, and within constitutional provisions, the low numbers of women's representation in national legislatures bespeak a resistance on the part of the state to women's direct access to legislative power.

Reconfiguration and Representation

Where states have engaged in extensive reconfiguration, women's electoral opportunities and presence have increased. Extensive uploading, for example, increases electoral opportunities for organized women, who generally act on them. France has experienced the most state reconfiguration in terms of uploading, by transferring select sovereign state powers to the European Union, primarily concerning monetary and employment policies. Organized women in France have targeted the European Parliament to increase women's representation which, at the outset in 1979, was relatively high in comparison

---

[24] For all three nations combined, the differences between left and right parties in their election of women across all nations for all years in the dataset are statistically significant at $p \leq .0002$.

to women's representation in the National Assembly; and women's representation within the French EP delegation has continued to increase.[25] Uploading of formal state powers has increased women's electoral opportunities at suprastate levels.

Britain's most dramatic reconfiguration was the downloading of formal state powers to Scotland (see previous discussion). Like reconfiguration by uploading, devolution opened major opportunities for Scottish women, who then prepared for state changes, organized an electoral strategy, and gained an impressive presence in the new Scottish Parliament. More than a third of the new SMPs are women (35.4%), placing the SP among the ranks of Scandinavian nations in terms of female representation. In this case, downloading of formal state powers has increased women's electoral opportunities in the new state arena.

In the United States, policy downloading constitutes the major state reconfiguration from the 1970s to the 1990s. Organized women in the United States targeted and intensified their electoral efforts, already in place, as the national government downloaded policy responsibilities to state governments, without relinquishing formal governing powers. Although the liberal wing of the U.S. feminist movement was already actively advancing and supporting women's candidacies, their success increased dramatically in the early 1990s. In the United States, where policy responsibilities for social welfare have been shifted to the individual states, women have increased their presence in state legislatures across the past dozen years, exceeding the 15% mark in 1987, and are positioned better in the 1990s than they were in the 1970s to influence policy making at this level. As in the cases of France (uploading) and Britain (downloading of state power), where the United States engaged in its most extensive reconfiguration (through policy downloading), women have had the most electoral success. In short, where states have reconfigured the most, organized women have had the most opportunities and the most success.

Conversely, where states have engaged in less reconfiguration, organized women have generally had less state presence. In France, the state that has least reconfigured its powers at the national level by downloading, women also have the least parliamentary presence. Despite feminist mobilization for parity, French women have received a symbolic rather than substantive response from the state. In Britain, the state that has least engaged in uploading state powers to the European Union, organized women are poorly represented, particularly in comparison with EP delegations from other nations. In the United States, where there have been few welfare state policies to offload, organized women have not been active or engaged. In general, less state reconfiguration has meant less representation for women.

---

[25] Impressively in the 1999 elections, where 40.2% of the French EP delegation are women; see Table 8.4.

TABLE 8.7.   *State Reconfiguration and Movement Response: Strategic Interaction*

When the State:	The Movement:
anticipates uploading	prepares a state-involved, electoral strategy at the supranational level to create opportunities and (depending on the nation) encourages reconfiguration
uploads	employs a state-involved, electoral strategy at the supranational level
anticipates downloading	prepares a state-involved, electoral strategy at the local or subnational level to create opportunities and (depending on the nation) encourages reconfiguration
downloads	employs a state-involved, electoral strategy at the local or subnational level
anticipates offloading	employs a strategy of resistance and disruptive protest
offloads	employs a strategy of autonomy

Reconfiguration and Strategies of Women's Movements

What do these cases suggest about the relationship between state reconfiguration and the strategies of women's movements? The results of three national cases are hardly dispositive; nonetheless, I suggest the following as research hypotheses for testing in additional cases (these are summarized in Table 8.7).

First, feminist movements' strategic choices respond to opening and closing opportunities (and to no opportunities) at the state level. As formal powers are relocated or dispensed with, political uncertainty increases for all actors, expanding the potential scope of political participation and conflict in new or reconfigured arenas of power (Schattschneider 1960). State reconfiguration, through downloading and uploading, creates a major opening of opportunity for feminist movements to gain access to and influence within the state. Barring mistakes, women's movements will respond to these particular openings by adopting a strategy of electoral mobilization, legislative access, and policy influence. Second, where state reconfiguration has been modest (or where state reconfiguration is anticipated), women's movements will also adopt a strategy of creating opportunities by encouraging and shaping state reconfiguration (see Table 8.7).[26] As the reconfiguration

---

[26] To reiterate, examples of feminist movements encouraging reconfiguration are those of, first, Scotland, with devolution approaching, where women organized to support an electoral system conducive to electing women and to mobilize for women's candidacies within the Scottish National Party and the Labour Party (see also Dobrowolsky this volume). Second, in Britain, women organized within the Labour Party knowing that internal party renovations

of state powers progresses, feminist movements will target arenas that are opening or that can be opened to women's elective access. Where states have already reconfigured, movements respond to the signal that openings exist by turning toward the state and state-affiliated groups, such as political parties, and by employing a strategy of state involvement and electoral orientation. The appearance of openness, marked by uploading and downloading, leads women's movements to an electoral strategy.

Where states have not reconfigured, or where reconfiguration has primarily involved offloading of state power, women's movements are more likely to employ strategies of autonomy or protest. States that have not shifted powers upward to transnational organizations or downloaded powers to regional or local governments offer no new electoral access for women; states that offload state powers similarly foreclose electoral opportunities. Where no openings for influence in the state appear to exist for organized women or where openings appear to be unlikely in the foreseeable future, the strategic response of women's movements is to organize autonomously – independently of parties, by targeting the movement's own projects, outside the scope of the state (for example, *consultori*, rape crisis centers; see della Porta, Elman this volume) or to engage in disruptive protest (for example, Women Against Pit Closures). In regard to state reconfiguration, offloading signals closing opportunities for electoral influence. Autonomy (which can facilitate state reconfiguration through offloading) and disruptive protest (which can potentially forestall offloading) are women's movements' strategic responses to closedness.[27]

Wendy Brown observes that "the central paradox of the late modern state [is that] its power and privilege operate increasingly through disavowal of potency, repudiation of responsibility, and diffusion of sites and operations of control" (Brown 1995: 194). In the three nations examined herein, organized feminists have recognized that even if one were to accept that Britain, France, and the United States can be characterized by governmental

initiated in the 1980s could be employed to advance women's interests. Third, in France, the parity movement was an attempt by the women's movement to create electoral access in a state that had limited reconfiguration, primarily restricted to uploading.

[27] Again, examples include the protests in Britain in response to proposed restrictions on access to abortion, under conditions of closedness, as the national state reassumed local governing powers, and the mass protests by women as Britain offloaded state-owned industries (particularly coal). The exception to this claim is the U.S. case. With high levels of offloading and policy downloading by the U.S. national government, the U.S. feminist movement has not become increasingly disruptive or autonomous in its organizing. In part this may reflect the comparatively minimalist social welfare statism of the U.S.; the increase in offloading has occurred in a state with notably fewer social welfare commitments than is the case in West European nations generally. In addition, the U.S. feminist movement's persistent electoral strategy may reflect its political cultural context (see Banaszak, Beckwith and Rucht this volume), a context which emphasizes electoral involvement, discourages (or at least routinizes) protest, and favors a limited state.

claims of state impotence and inability, these states are reconfiguring real powers – both structural and policy powers – that continue to exist and to offer governing possibilities in new locations. As states have "diffused sites and operations of control" but have not irrevocably relinquished state powers, organized feminists have mobilized, sometimes inadvertently and sometimes intentionally, with greater or lesser success, to locate elected women in these new sites of power. The state – in Britain, in France, in the United States – understood as a set of "sites" or "arenas" (Pringle and Watson 1990: 229) of political struggle has, in the process of reconfiguration, offered opportunities to organized women to enter political contestation over issues crucial to feminists. Feminist movements in Britain, in France, and in the United States recognized the costs of nonengagement with the state as well as the opportunities offered by state reconfiguration and, despite considerable resistance, have seized these opportunities to increase their presence within the state as one site of feminist struggle.

9

Re-Dividing Citizens – Divided Feminisms

*The Reconfigured U.S. State and Women's Citizenship**

Mary Fainsod Katzenstein

However much academics profess skepticism about any unidirectional path of social progress, there is a strong tenor of optimism among those who argue that legally established rights are on the whole expanding and that social movements staking out such claims are able to build on the successes of their predecessors.[1] In this chapter, I separate myself from such intimations of progress through time and provide grist for the skeptics' mill. In the United States, the legal entitlements of poor women have been contracting, not expanding. With the post-1980s' reconfiguration of state institutions in the United States, economically privileged women have been able to hold their own – to organize, to defend, and even to enlarge on previously established entitlements. The same can not be said for women in or near poverty. For poor women in the United States, the second wave of feminism can be said to have crashed on the shoals of a polity where the rights of political and social citizenship are not conferred but must be captured by organized interests and movements.

---

* I refer here to Suzanne Mettler's *Dividing Citizens: Gender and Federalism in New Deal Public Policy.* Ithaca and London: Cornell University Press, 1998.
[1] The work of John W. Meyer at Stanford and his colleagues/students is most noteworthy for the extensive documentation of the world-wide spread of legal entitlements. Their studies address the global diffusion of women's suffrage (Ramirez, Soysal, and Shanahan 1997), of women's economic rights (Berkovitch 1999), and of women's access to higher education (Bradley and Ramirez 1996). They are careful to note that, "Decoupling policy and implementation, legislation and action, allows nation-states to adopt 'progressive' programs and structures and at the same time to continue oppressive practices" (Meyer, Boli, Thomas, and Ramirez 1997 – the quote is from Berkovitch 1999: 2). A recent study of gender equality in the United States that portrays an ineluctable march toward women's advancement is Robert Max Jackson (1998). Sidney Tarrow's discussion of cycles of protest (1989, 1998) and Leila J. Rupp and Verta A. Taylor's work on the ascendance of the women's movement in the 1960s out of the doldrums that followed the first wave of the women's movement can be read as a sanguine interpretation of the opportunity for movements to build on previous movement repertoires, claims, and successes.

In *Dividing Citizens: Gender and Federalism in New Deal Public Policy*, Suzanne Mettler argues with great persuasiveness that the New Deal created two classes of citizens. Social programs of the 1930s forged gendered and racialized categories through which national entitlements were extended to white men; it was left to the different states whether to embrace or repudiate claims to social benefits that others might make. Federalism fueled a divided citizenship:

Men, particularly white men, were endowed with national citizenship, incorporated into policies to be administered in a centralized, unitary manner through standardized, routinized procedures. Women and minority men were more likely to remain state citizens, subject to policies whose development was hindered by the dynamics of federalism and which were administered with discretion and variability. (Mettler 1998: xi)

Given how deeply a divided citizenship was inscribed into law and social policy in the 1930s, it is remarkable that thirty years later, in the course of the 1960s and early 1970s, this bifurcation was largely reversed. But this reversal was to be long enduring for some women and only momentary for others. By the mid-1990s, it became clear that women of economic means had been permanently settled into national citizenship; not so poor women. The question this chapter poses is how movement politics enters into this account.

How national citizenship comes to be first restored to women and then once again bifurcated – this time by class (which in the United States is also about race) – is best told through a narrative of state-movement dynamics. The story develops in two phases. In the first phase, on the heels of the 1960s civil rights upheavals, women (irrespective of economic status) came to be recognized as finally entitled to social citizenship. This was not for the most part a triumph of feminist activism. In fact the dawn of the feminist movement's second wave resulted in no small measure *from* the extension of citizenship rights proffered by politicians vying for electoral power who sought to appeal to women's groups (Costain 1992). But activists were quick to take advantage of the state's responsiveness and well into the 1970s feminist and other civil rights organizations successfully pressured Congress, government agencies, and the courts on behalf of women across the socioeconomic spectrum to churn out legislation, policies, and judgments that promoted women's interests. But by the 1980s, a change had set in. An overinflated economy, the oil crisis, the growing deficit, and the election of Ronald Reagan ushered in a retreat of the state – a retreat that was both a conservatizing regime change as well as a more fundamental reconfiguration of state institutions. It was this process of state reconfiguration and the differentiated social movement politics that ensued that opened the way to the class-based bifurcation of women's citizenship. Feminist activism among middle-class women was able to survive the state's reorganization and political retrenchment in large part because middle-class feminists had become *insiders* and were able to make their power felt through workplace and institution-based associational politics. But associational politics served poor women far less effectively. Associational politics could not stem the tide that swept the rights of poor women once again beyond the perimeter of national regulation and government-mandated federal standards.

A "DIVIDED CITIZENSHIP" REUNITED: THE RIGHTS REVOLUTION

As the United States entered the 1960s, little had happened to unsettle the New Deal's institutional reorganization that, as Mettler's study records, extended the social benefits of national citizenship to white men and that consigned social programs for all others to the purview of the different states. The New Deal revolution that placed the force of the national government on the side of the "ordinary" worker, providing protection against the vagaries of the market and the ravages of unregulated capitalism, left whole categories of the *most* ordinary of workers unprotected by national regulation. As Mettler documents, agricultural laborers and domestic workers were omitted from minimum wage and insurance schemes and social security, the "centerpiece" of New Deal legislation, provided largely for the male breadwinner or, in the event of his death, his widow. Left to state discretion, the regulation of social programs and the protection of fair wages for nonwhite men and most women was undermined by interests of local powerholders.[2] The state reconstruction of the 1930s bequeathed a gendered and racialized legacy that endured well into the 1960s. The programmatic bequest of the 1930s, as Nancy Fraser elaborates it, was "masculine" and "feminine" social programs. The first (unemployment insurance, social security or retirement insurance, supplemental social security insurance or disability), were contributory programs provided to those with paid work records and were seen as earned benefits not government handouts. By contrast, the other "feminine" programs – Aid to Families with Dependent Children (AFDC), food stamps, Medicaid, and public housing assistance – were generally administered by the states, financed out of both federal and state tax revenues, means-tested, and absent any contributory component, were depicted as government largesse (Fraser 1989: 150–152).

The 1960s went some distance to remedy the segmentation of citizenship rights inherited from the 1930s. Partly, this was a correction driven by market forces. As women moved into paid occupations, joined the organized sector

---

[2] Lucy A. Williams writes: "For example, Georgia closed AFDC cases in certain counties with seasonal employment whenever the county board designated the period one of full employment, whether or not the mother was employed. The Georgia regulation also provided that earnings from full-time employment would not be supplemented by a partial AFDC grant, regardless of how low the earnings were. African-American AFDC mothers were denied benefits during harvest season in rural counties, forcing them to work in the fields for substandard wages (in Kairys 1998: 573).

of the labor force, and acquired education that placed them in increasingly higher-waged positions, women acquired some of the governmental protection (unemployment and disability insurance and retirement security) that had been "neutrally" accorded white, male citizens.

But the process was also driven by legislative reform. Even before the emergence of national-level women's movement organizing in the mid-1960s, Congress passed the 1963 Equal Pay Act and the 1964 Civil Rights Act (Title VII) to be followed by the 1965 and 1968 presidential executive orders (11246; 11375) that assigned national government agencies the task of monitoring equality in wages and discrimination-free hiring and promotion. Only later, toward the end of the 1960s and early 1970s, did the numbers of newly formed, Washington-based feminist organizations burgeon, unleashing a wholesale crusade by activists bent on making the promises of federal citizenship real. And indeed a burst of legislative activity and litigation in Congress in the 1970s was the result. But, as Charles R. Epp's study of the "rights revolution" vividly depicts, the 1970s and 1980s explosive growth of formal organizations in the second wave of feminist activism succeeded rather than anticipated the first major legislative reforms of the mid-1960s and early 1970s (1998: 53).

Indeed, there should be no mistake about the sequence of movement claims. This was not a case of middle-class reforms expanding to include other marginalized groups. Quite the reverse. This early legislation that legitimized the subsequent rights claims of middle-class feminists was the offshoot of a far broader democratic upheaval. Ironically, given the importance of the 1960s legal reforms to middle-class feminists in the next decades and the reversion of citizenship rights for poor women to its earlier tiered status, these 1960s legislative reforms were the fruit of the mobilizational momentum that had grown out of the antipoverty and antiracism politics of the 1950s and early 1960s (Evans 1979).

For the period of the 1960s and early 1970s, it seemed that poor women were on the way to being incorporated as participants in the social citizenry of the nation. The Fair Labor Standards Act was amended in 1966 to include agricultural workers and in 1974 to provide for domestic laborers and others working in the unorganized sectors of the economy (Mettler 1998: 223). Litigation in the federal courts also promised at first to secure poor women nationally recognized rights that had been earlier denied under a multitiered system of social citizenship. Although the courts had not (nor do they now) generally recognize economic need as the basis for constitutionally protected claims, active litigation by legal advocacy groups came close to establishing welfare as an entitlement. Numerous challenges accosted particular provisions. Requirements that limited benefits to households where parents were "ceremonially married" or to illegitimate children were struck down (Mink 1998: 71). In *King v. Smith*, the "suitable home" qualification that made families with "substitute fathers" ineligible for benefits was struck down; but more fundamentally, in a series of subsequent cases and as a result of political organizing, as Lucy Williams summarizes, welfare came close to being declared an entitlement:

> ... the Supreme Court interpreted the amorphous language of the Social Security Act ('Aid . . . shall be furnished with reasonable promptness to all eligible individuals') as creating a *statutory categorical entitlement* to benefits. This interpretation meant that, as long as Congress did not rescind this language, the states were required to provide AFDC benefits, albeit in amounts determined by each state, to certain categories of eligible individuals. And in *Goldberg v. Kelly*, the Supreme Court ruled that an AFDC recipient was entitled to a fair hearing prior to the termination of benefits. The jurisprudential effect of *Goldberg* was to designate welfare as a right, or entitlement, triggering procedural due process, rather than a mere privilege. (Kairys 1998: 574)

Activists, most prominently the National Welfare Rights Organization, pursued the promise of these "entitlements," recognizing in the right to a pretermination hearing an important instrument with which to empower welfare recipients. Through a variety of strategies, organizational leaders helped to organize the poor to claim the benefits to which they were legally entitled (Piven and Cloward 1979: 264–363).

The repairing of a divided citizenship that would be class inclusive actually seemed to be within institutional reach for this brief period. The prevailing state discourse (that promised a "war" on poverty and that called for citizens to "ask not what your country can do for you but what you can do for your country") provided justification rather than censure for a movement politics that would challenge the inequities still built into legislation and policy. And although the national government was the target of much of this organizing, it was also the agent of much advocacy work as well. Independent middle-class legal advocacy groups were an important catalyst in these reforms. So too were activists drawn from low-income neighborhoods and poor communities. And as long as the "Great Society" legislative provisions were extant – those that funded the Legal Services Corporation and that in support of "maximum feasible participation" put neighborhood activists on the government payroll – challenges to the bifurcated system of social citizenship promised to be actually institutionalized, with the ongoing dangers of cooptation but also the possibilities of incorporating within the state itself an engine for social reform.

THE 1980s AND THE CLASS-BASED RE-FORMATION OF WOMEN'S CITIZENSHIP

But these promises were short lived. With the reconfiguration of the state that evolved most dramatically from the 1980s on, feminist activism that had never successfully bridged class divides saw this separation further institutionalized and with it a reconstituted class-based bifurcated citizenship.

The reconfiguration of the state was multifaceted. *In no small way, it was linguistic.* With Ronald Reagan's election to office, the parlance of individualism supplanted the language of governmental responsibility. Sylvia Bashevkin quotes from Reagan's book, *An American Life*, which castigates "big government" ushered in by the New Deal:

FDR in many ways set in motion the forces that later sought to create big government and bring a form of veiled socialism to America. . . . One of his sons, Franklin Roosevelt, Jr., often told me that his father had said many times his welfare and relief programs during the Depression were meant only as emergency, stopgap measures to cope with a crisis, not the seeds of what others later tried to turn into a permanent welfare state. Government giveaway programs, FDR said, "destroy the human spirit," and he was right. (1998: 29)

State reconfiguration from the 1980s also meant the offloading or progressive privatization of governmental activities. Right from the outset, sharp lines were drawn to limit government responsibility. *Harris v. McRae* (1981) upheld the Hyde Amendment, which barred federal government funding for abortions. Over the years, child-care provisions in both the tax code and welfare policy were designed to support privatized solutions to family child-care needs (Michel 1999); and increasingly private management and contracting have made inroads into several of the most important public institutions that have structured the lives of the poor – low-income housing, and the welfare[3] and prison systems (President's Commission on Privatization 1988; on prisons, see Bowman, Hakim, and Seidenstat 1993).

State reconfiguration from the 1980s onward further entailed the restricting of access to state institutions (designated in this volume as "lateral loading"). Right from the start of the Reagan administration (indeed already by the late 1970s), it was clear that these reconfigurative measures would have stark implications for the poor. Massive tax cuts were accompanied by policies calling for cutbacks in expenditures on poverty and welfare programs. Tom Edsall, then a *Washington Post* reporter, described the drive to cut taxes under Reagan as of momentous importance in that it "submerged the fifty year commitment to an expanding federal government" (1988: 149). Analyzing the 1981 Economic Recovery Tax Act, Edsall writes:

The legislation lowered the capital gains rate, sharply cut the top rate on unearned income, and shrank enormously the power of the sole provision in the tax code designed to restrict a concentration of wealth in the hands of the few, the inheritance tax. As the legislation passed the House, Thomas P. (Tip) O'Neill, Jr., one of the few remaining politicians whose roots remained firmly in the Democratic party of Franklin Delano Roosevelt, sat slumped in a chair far to the rear of the House floor (1984, 18).

---

[3] In Texas, corporations such as Lockheed and IBM, Joel Handler writes, "are bidding to privatize the entire welfare system" (Handler 1997: 12n26).

From the defunding of legal services under the Reagan administration and the dismantling of community boards to the more recent (1996) prison reform act that prohibits "trivial" suits against prison administrations together with the dismantling of prison educational programs, the attenuation of access to the state has been continuous. As Paul Pierson writes, indirect strategies may be the most transformative. Cutbacks, that is, may be less significant in the longer run than "... institutional reforms that strengthen the hands of budget cutters, policies that weaken the government's revenue base, and efforts to undermine the position of pro-welfare state interest groups" (1994: 7).

What has been the implication of this reconfiguration for women's citizenship? Much has been made of the "backlash" and of the struggle that feminist organizations have had to wage merely to hold onto the policy measures and litigation successes achieved in the prior decades of the 1960s and 1970s. No doubt this captures a part of the story. Defending reproductive rights has absorbed vast energies and resources. By contrast, proceeding with the 1970s efforts to pursue comparable worth, for example, is in such a period of political retrenchment largely futile. The presidency of George Bush, Sylvia Bashevkin writes, records a sharp decline in feminist influence when "... among twenty-four actions, two-thirds went against feminist positions (and) more than 75 percent of Supreme Court decisions and more than 40 percent of legislative actions between 1988 and 1992 were inconsistent with (feminist) group claims" (1998: 75).

Nevertheless, the story can be told in very different ways depending on the "class" lens through which the record is viewed. The 1960s restoration of social citizenship for women of economic means was not undone. The right to equal pay, to merit-based employment and promotion, to reproductive choice, to credit, and to insurance (free of provisions that discriminate based on sex) are all still fundamentally in place assuming the "means" are there to make women competitive applicants and economically viable clients. The point is that national-level regulations that brought resource-endowed women into the orbit of state protection are fundamentally unaltered.

For poor women, the story is very different. As the most recent welfare reform act amply demonstrates, social provisions for welfare recipients are no longer regulated in any meaningful way through national standards or uniform federal provisions. Already evident in the Reagan administration's Family Support Act of 1988, the sabotage of national regulations came to full fruition in 1996. Known as the Personal Responsibility and Work Reconciliation Act, the reforms abolished AFDC, JOBS (Job Opportunities and Basic Skills Training, the work and training program for welfare recipients), and Emergency Assistance to Families with Children. These national programs were replaced by block grants of federal funds to the states called Temporary Assistance to Needy Families (TANF). Although the states are supposed to maintain spending at no less than 80% of past spending levels, the entitlement to assistance has disappeared. Indeed, the national legislation sets a lifetime, five-year limit on welfare and a two-year time limit which sets work requirements for much of a state's caseload. Thus, the rights of many poor women formerly on AFDC are now curtailed by reforms that neither set uniform eligibility requirements nor guarantee any minimal level of assistance. The only national "standard" that is established insists on welfare recipients fulfilling work obligations and leaving the rolls after a specified time period (The Personal Responsibility and Work Opportunity Reconciliation Act of 1996-PRA).[4]

What has been called "the New Federalism" by the Urban Institute[5] has far-reaching implications for the lives of poor women in the domains of health, housing, legal services, and many other arenas. Some examples:

- The 1996 PRA's restrictions on legal immigrants' rights to benefits (some of which were restored in 1997) severely limits the access of immigrants to Medicaid and TANF benefits, giving extensive power to the states to determine eligibility for particular programs and assistance (Fix and Tumlin 1999).
- For poor families not on welfare (bound to increase as many leave the rolls) it is harder to gain access to needed services (child care, child support, employment, and training) since the points of access provided through welfare assistance are now less readily linked. Declines in welfare caseloads, for example, risk leading to declines in Medicaid enrollment (Burt, Pindus, and Capizzano 2000: 20; Ellwood and Lewis 1999).[6]
- Medicaid coverage has declined particularly severely for adults and slightly for children as well (Ku and Bruen 1999).
- In 1996, Congress continued funding for the Legal Services Corporation but barred lawyers from bringing class action suits against the government (Brennan Center for Justice 2000; Norton 1997) – legislation ruled as unconstitutional by a majority of one vote on the Supreme Court.[7]

---

[4] Food stamps and Medicaid were not included in this wholesale abandonment of the welfare federal entitlement. The Republican Congress, Craig Volden writes, endeavored to alter the structure of both federal entitlements to food stamps and Medicaid. "Only after Congress agreed to abandon these other changes – Medicaid reform in particular – did President Clinton end his opposition to the [TANF] legislation" (1997: 68). Saundra K. Schneider writes that although the Personal Responsibility and Work Opportunity Reconciliation Act (PRA) left "much of the previous medicaid system intact" and "provided the same set of health care services ... as they did before welfare reform was enacted," the state government now plays a much larger role in determining how individuals and families qualify for Medicaid services (1999: 202).

[5] The Urban Institute has undertaken a vast project assessing the consequences of fiscal and political devolution onto the states. See their website: http://newfederalism.urban.org/html.

[6] PRA increased funding for the Child and Dependent Care Tax Credit in 1996 but reduced funding for Title XX (Long, Kirby, Kurka, and Waters 1998).

[7] In a 5–4 decision on February 28, 2001, the United States Supreme Court held that a congressional restriction on legal services programs was unconstitutional. The restriction, enacted by the U.S. Congress in 1996, prohibited programs which receive funding from

- While increasing allocations to some agencies such as Veterans Affairs and the Federal Emergency Management Agency, Congress shrank Housing and Urban Development (HUD) housing programs for low-income families (Healey 1996: 2762).
- As women's rates of incarceration are growing, the rights of prisoners to bring "frivolous" suits was severely curtailed by the 1996 Prisoner Litigation Reform Act (Riewe 1997).

How did movement activism figure in this bifurcation of women's citizenship? Why is it that middle-class feminists were able to withstand the assault on the social provisions of the 1960s that afforded them national citizenship and activists representing poor women were not? The answer does not lie in the differential resources of Washington-based lobbying or interest groups. Few if any feminist organizations in Washington are particularly well endowed with funds or personnel. Anne Costain, in fact, begins her much-respected study of the women's movement by posing the question of how a seemingly ill-staffed and resource-poor organizational presence in Washington in the 1970s could have launched such a massive political movement.

Part of the explanation lies, I propose, in the strength, established by the 1980s, of middle-class feminist "insiders." I do not mean to suggest that the feminist insider was someone who became "one of the boys." To the contrary, middle-class feminist insiders have been people who have sought out positions inside institutions only to bring their disquiet and their nonconformity with them. These insiders are feminists who have fought to enlarge opportunities for women from within newfound (to women) occupational or institutional environs. In the course of so doing, they have organized networks and associations that now pervade the institutional spaces of government, the church, the media, athletics, the military, the professions, commerce – the mainstream institutions of both state and society.

This feminist associationalism mushroomed in the 1970s across the entire workplace environment. White-collar workers in the federal government joined Federally Employed Women (FEW). Women lawyers, engineers, computer programmers, mathematicians, sociologists, historians, and biologists (to name only a small number of the professional and academic disciplines) joined women's associations and caucuses. Black social workers and journalists and African-American military personnel formed specialized associations. Lesbian nurses joined Cassandra. Military women pilots organized WMA-military women aviators. Navy officers joined WOPA- Women's

the federal Legal Services Corporation (LSC) from representing clients who seek to challenge or reform welfare laws and regulations. Justice Kennedy, writing for the majority in *Legal Services Corporation v. Velazquez*, held that the First Amendment does not permit Congress to "define the scope of the litigation it funds to exclude certain vital theories and ideas."

Officers Professional Association. Policewomen and firefighters formed women's associations.

The highly localized character of these work-related associations was evident in the specialization of organizations within a single institutional or workplace environment. Take simply the print and broadcast media. At *The New York Times,* according to Nan Robertson's arresting account, *The Girls in the Balcony,* The Women's Caucus, born over a luncheon in 1972 initiated, first, a series of meetings with the paper's management and, then, a lawsuit. In 1978, the paper settled the class action suit just as the case was to have gone to trial. *The New York Times* was not alone. At *The Washington Post,* even as the Washington-Baltimore Newspaper Guild had filed charges with the Office of Human Rights alleging race, sex, and age discrimination at the paper,[8] women's networks at the paper were operating at a less formal level. At the *Post,* the Mother's Group, for instance, started as a support network in 1985 and continued to meet off and on for a number of years. It gathered for lunches, exchanged memos, and initiated planning meetings with newsroom management to facilitate part-time options and greater sensitivity toward family issues. For the most part, women's associations served simultaneously as support networks, data and information gathering clearinghouses, networking agencies, as well as the organizational base for lobbying and news-generation. The Women's Institute for Freedom of the Press, which described itself as "promoting the radical restructuring of the communications system," collects data, publishes articles on women and the media, and puts out an annual directory of women's media organizations and publications; The American News Women's Club is a Washington-based networking organization; American Women in Radio and Television is an umbrella group for women in the broadcast media; Women in Communications, Inc., is a much older association dating back to presuffrage days with over 11,000 members and 186 professional and student chapters. It describes its mission as "Leading Change" and its objective as, in part, uniting "members for the purpose of promoting the advancement of women in all fields of communication." JAWS (the Journalism and Women Symposium) is a much smaller network of journalists that meets in an annual forum in Colorado. A newer organization, the International Women's Media Foundation, started in 1989, made its debut with a large conference in November 1990. Many of the groups, such as the Association for Women in Sports Media and WISP (Women in Scholarly Publishing) have a specialized membership. Others – such as Women Against Pornography, itself the subject of much media attention; Action for Children's Television, whose aim is to encourage diversity and eliminate commercial abuses in children's programming; and the Prison Reading Project which sends material to women

---

[8] Charges were filed with the Office of Human Rights of the District of Columbia on July 13, 1988. The Guild (AFL-CIO) is at 8611 Second Ave., Silver Spring, MD, 20910, (301) 585-2990.

in prison – are engaged in particular, largely feminist-run, media endeavors. And this list does not count the explosion in the 1970s of feminist presses, journals, and magazines that aimed particularly at a feminist audience.

Such associations were not limited to the workplace. The localization of feminist activism was more generally institution based: In churches, in athletics, among charitable organizations, and in philanthropy, women's organizations seeking equality and gender-aware policies and practices proliferated.

Why this eruption of localized, institution-based middle-class feminist associationalism? There is nothing in U.S. culture – joiners that American men and women may be – that makes the unfolding of feminist associationalism inevitable. Were that true, there would be a continuous history rather than intermittent swings, cycles, or eruptions of women's associationalism. Its origins in the 1960s and 1970s are, rather, in an important sense *state derived*. The incorporation beginning in the second half of the twentieth century of equal opportunity norms within the state through legislation and judicial action created two conditions for this kind of associationalism. First, state-authorized equal opportunity norms opened up social and economic institutions previously restricted to a far more homogeneous elite legitimizing the presence of diverse groups in these new institutional locales and second, it encouraged through the language of equal opportunity itself a "parochial" politics that required one group to compare itself to the group most like itself. The emergence of feminist claims making, I have argued elsewhere, is part of a larger historical process in which the domination of social and economic institutions by white, protestant, and male elites is by the mid-twentieth century disrupted (Katzenstein 1998a). Two processes precipitated the change: white "ethnics," women, and nonwhite groups begin (through education and economic mobility) to move out of segregated institutional spaces (Irish parishes, Jewish law firms, Black and women's colleges) into social and economic institutions long dominated by Protestant, white men. Equally important, rather than silently adapting to existing institutional norms as the few nonelite individuals admitted into elite domains had long done, these newly mobile groups (white ethnics, women, African Americans, Jews) began to see institutional domains – *with the validation of the law on their side* – as open to contestation (Katzenstein 1998a).

Beginning in the 1950s and gathering momentum in the 1960s and early 1970s, legislatures and courts enunciated principles of equal rights and backed these promises up through a massive number of court decisions that struck down discriminatory laws and barred discriminatory practices. Legislation providing for equal opportunity in employment (Title VII of the Civil Rights Act of 1964) and in education (the 1972 amendments) gave women access to new occupational and institutional spaces. But what underwrote the localization of activism most strongly, I believe, was the judicial interpretation of equal opportunity legislation which required that plaintiffs show that the law failed to treat those who were *similarly situated* the same. The logic of equal opportunity language impelled women to compare themselves to men in their exact situation: retail saleswomen to their male counterparts, women lawyers to male lawyers, women officers in the Navy to male officers in the Navy. The law thus invited organizing in highly localized institutional spaces. And because the courts proved remarkably receptive to the explosion of feminist litigation, associationalism at the localized institutional level was rewarded.

Associationalism was not solely dependent on the specific authorization of the law. Had it been, this associationalism would have been more vulnerable to the attack on civil rights that fanned out within the Congress and the courts during the Reagan and first Bush administrations. Civil rights legislation fell off (Costain 1992) and numerous civil rights initiatives in hiring and educational admissions suffered setbacks in the courts. But by the 1980s the *discourse* of equal rights had become broadly legitimated both within the state and within society at large. The associational activism of feminists inside institutions was sustained in part because equal opportunity had become part of institutional culture and middle-class feminists could make use of equal opportunity norms as tools to challenge institutional practices (Swidler 1986). Women's studies programs, military women's groups, organizations of women coaches, and female athletic teams demanded an institutional justification of the numbers of women hired and promoted and of resources expended on programs important to women's concerns. Middle-class women endowed with leadership and organizational skills could invoke a discourse that had diffused outward from the state to institutional spaces.

As feminists have pointed out on at length, equal opportunity discourse was not entirely unproblematic for reasons that are both unrelated and germane to the bifurcation of a class-based gendered citizenship. Equal opportunity discourse generated at least three kinds of problems: First, by focusing debates specifically on comparisons of "similarly-situated groups," it muted debate over difference. Concretely, this meant that it was easier to challenge the denial of a promotion to women who aspired to male jobs than to question the deficient pay of women in women-dominated occupations – daycare, social work, secretarial jobs, and nursing. Equal opportunity language made it difficult to question androcentric institutional norms and structures. Equal opportunity norms in the military made it possible for women pilots to claim the right to fly combat aircraft but provided no legal basis for challenging the practice of their male counterparts bonding through fraternal expeditions to strip joints and prostitute-frequented barrooms (Katzenstein 1998a). Second, equal opportunity as I have earlier suggested encouraged narrowly focused claims making rather than alliance building. To draw on the military for another example: Uniformed women activists ready to brave the opposition to sex equality were reluctant to forge coalitions with gay and lesbian activists lest the addition of another controversial cause encumber their own chances of success (Katzenstein 1998a).

Third, and most important to the discussion of this chapter, equal opportunity doctrine in some ways subverted the links between activists of different class backgrounds that might under some conditions be forged. The different and more favorable constitutional status accorded race- and sex-based claims (as compared to class-based ones) led in part to the divided character of associational politics. If you could make your case successfully based on race- or gender-based claims, why forge an alliance with others whose case was likely to be repudiated in the courts of law? The incorporation of equal opportunity as a state-sanctioned norm did undeniably affirm the legitimacy of middle-class women's associations pursuing a wide range of claims tailored to the specific exigencies of their own institutional and occupational situations. Equal opportunity norms did not offer poor women the same protection.

To return to the role of middle-class feminists as institutional insiders: Debra Dodson's interesting essay on the Partial Birth Abortion Ban Act of 1995 reveals what difference a politics of insiders' "presence" can make in institutional change. She asks whether the presence of women has a bearing on how the issue was dealt with in Congress – whether "descriptive ('stand for') representation of women does affect substantive ('act for') representation of women" (1). Her answer is that women's presence resulted in different arguments being made from those that were ventured by male legislators. "The results of this study," she says simply, "suggest that even in the aftermath of the 1994 elections, women members of Congress remained more likely than their male colleagues to 'act for' women in ways consistent with the policy agenda of the contemporary women's movement" (1995).

Transpose this argument from gender to class. The *absence* (or invisibility) of poor women in many institutional environments means that some arguments are not getting made or heard however much we may think that others can speak "for" them. It is worrisome that activism among the poor appears to have declined relative to the rate for the nonpoor. Based on a coding of GSS data, Robert Wuthnow notes a decline in association membership that was significantly more pronounced among the less privileged than among the advantaged: "For example, among those raised in lower-income families, 72 percent were members of associations in 1974 (8 percent fewer than among people raised in above-income families); but by 1991, those from low-income backgrounds had declined in association memberships by 7 percentage points whereas those from high-income backgrounds had declined by only 3 points. Among the *most marginalized*, there was an 18-percentage-point drop" (Wuthnow 2002: 26). The importance of this is notable given the different issues which are raised by different groups within the population. In their study of political participation, Burns, Schlozman, and Verba note that in their survey, issues of basic human need were mentioned by African American and Latino activists much more frequently than by others. "One can only wonder," they note "if they were better endowed with participatory factors – and therefore, were more active in politics – if welfare might have gotten some of the kid-glove treatment being accorded to another category of government benefits, Social Security?" (1998: 37).

CONCLUSION

Different from Scandinavia where women's citizenship rights are to a large extent state conferred rather than movement won, in the United States the contours of social citizenship have been fashioned out of the interaction of social movement activism and state direction. Distinct, that is, from national contexts where the course of policies is shaped largely by debates and decisions located within the bureaucracies and ministries of the state, in the United States the evolution of women's citizenship has been played out institutionally at the intersection of governmental and societal arenas. Theda Skocpol said it well when, in her analysis of the growth of a maternalist welfare state in the United States, she emphasized the "fit – or lack thereof – between the goals and capacities of various politically active groups, and the historically changing points of access and leverage allowed by a nation's political institutions" (1992: 41).

The class-based bifurcation of women's citizenship in the last two decades unfolded at just this junction. The turn toward privatization of governmental services, the discursive shift away from collective to individual responsibility, the offloading of government programs to state and local communities, the narrowing of access to the courts and legislature resulted from and in turn shaped the character of movement activism. As the relationship between the state and the women's movement changed, the gap between the disadvantaged position of those groups organized by and on behalf of poor women and the insider position of activist middle-class feminists became ever more distinct.

For middle-class feminists in the 1980s, state reconfiguration did not undermine the force of political mobilization. Middle-class feminists in the 1980s came into their own as institutional insiders. This did not mean they were "power brokers" but it meant that their presence, often their contentiousness, came to be expected whether in the halls of Congress, in the corridors of military bases, in university buildings, in the suites of law offices, on the basketball court, in the pulpit, or on the morning news show (Katzenstein 1998a). In these new, widely dispersed, institutional locales, middle-class feminists formed associations – informal networks and formal organizations – through which they worked to ensure that the rights to equal opportunity which had been recognized in the legislature and the courts would not be dismantled and indeed might be further extended. From these institutional niches, middle-class activists were able to pressure for the enforcement of federal protections in jobs and employment (whether of the Equal Pay Act, Title VII of the Civil Rights Act, or Title IX of the education bill).

Associationalism has served poor women far less well. Less well equipped with the resources to organize and to represent themselves, and far less favorably positioned in terms of access to influential positions in government, in the media, and in the workplace, poor women benefited considerably less from the processes of institutionalized feminism than did middle-class activists. With state reconfiguration, the legal foundation on which the poor or those who seek to represent the poor can mobilize has been severely weakened. The downloading of state responsibilities (PRA and block grants), the offloading of activities to private organizations (the privatization of job training and placement, the privatization of prisons and detention centers), and the lateral loading (so termed in the book's introduction) of access to federal protections (the weakening, for instance, of legal services for the poor, including the incarcerated) have served to recreate, albeit in a different form, the divided citizenship of earlier times.[9]

The reconfiguration of the state and the class-based bifurcation of women's citizenship has not, of course, entirely disabled the political involvement of poor women or activism by others on poor women's behalf. At the national level, *organizational* momentum *does* certainly endure. Three sources for optimism bear consideration. First, a number of autonomous advocacy organizations, heavily dependent on foundation support (and also on corporate donations and government contracts), are active providers of informational resources, scholarly research, legal briefs, and the personnel who do the face-to-face lobbying for legislative reform.[10] What Margaret Keck and Kathryn Sikkink (1998) note to be true of international advocacy networks is also true "at home." With opportunities for activism diminishing in Washington, advocacy networks that "...are not powerful in a traditional sense of the word...must use the power of their information, ideas, and strategies to alter the information and value contexts within which states make policies" (16). Second, the law (and Constitution) is sufficiently pliable such that when some discursive possibilities for securing rights are foreclosed, others can be located in alternative conceptual locations. Even as poverty is not a constitutionally recognized basis for protection under the fourteenth amendment, those who are poor have

---

[9] Some federal entitlements do remain: food stamps and Medicaid, though perhaps in somewhat weakened form; and the Earned Income Tax Credit, of crucial importance to the working poor, in strengthened form. For a discussion of the broad array of federal entitlements during an earlier period preconfiguration, see Howe and Longman (1992).

[10] The Institute for Women's Policy Research gets 60% of its funds from foundations. They average about one government grant/contract a year (conversation, Jill Bronstein, 5/17/99). Organizationally, IWPR and others, such as Wider Opportunities for Women (WOW), the National Women's Law Center, the National Black Women's Health Coalition, the Urban Institute, which has received major funding to examine the impact of block grants, and the National Partnership for Women and Families, to name only a few of the many nonprofit organizations in Washington that devote much of their time and resources to issues of poverty, have for the most part grown in size over the last decade.

found protection in guarantees of privacy or other protected liberties. Just recently, for example, legal advocates for women on welfare were successful in winning a decision from the court that declared unconstitutional a state law that sought to withhold their own state's higher welfare payments to migrants from states with lower benefits for the first year of residency on the grounds that the law infringed on an individual's right to travel. Finally, the divided character of social entitlements relocates rather than simply forecloses opportunities for activism. Faith-based organizing, union activity, and less formal networks and projects run by women seeking to take advantage of state or block-grant funding for daycare or housing or other social supports have been widely documented in accounts of local politics (Albrecht and Brewer 1990; Bookman and Morgen 1988; Naples 1998; Smith 1999). But such sanguine possibilities are unlikely, in the end, to overcome the dual reality of a "redivided citizenship" and divided feminisms.

10

Cultural Continuity and Structural Change

The Logic of Adaptation by Radical, Liberal, and Socialist Feminists to State Reconfiguration*

Carol McClurg Mueller and John D. McCarthy

In assessing the impact of the "reconfigured state" or "neoliberalism" on "second-wave" women's movements one of the most interesting questions for students of social movements is whether and how the form in which they had become institutionalized influenced their responses to these changes in the established democracies of West Europe and North America.[1] Social movement analysts have generated a variety of theoretical accounts that privilege variation in the structure of political arrangements over other factors in accounting for the ebbs and flows of citizen collective action. The several case studies included in this volume, then, follow a well-worn analytic path with their focus upon how national women's movements confront reconfigurations in the structure of large, powerful states. We wish to focus our primary attention here upon the lessons these case studies can teach us about how different women's movements respond to the threats and opportunities posed by state reconfiguration. We particularly are interested in how the familiar internal differentiation into "radical," "socialist," or "liberal" branches of contemporary feminism may facilitate and/or constrain their ability to shape and adapt to the processes of state reconfiguration.

The extensive body of rich empirical materials provided in the preceding chapters provides the basis for addressing neglected issues regarding differentiation within a movement's structure and culture and for understanding their

* The authors wish to acknowledge the insightful comments on a previous version of this chapter by Myra Marx Ferree, the editors of this volume, and anonymous readers.

[1] We do not attempt to resolve the issue here of what constitutes a "feminist movement," a "women's movement," a "movement by women," or mobilization around "women's issues." We consider all of these forms of mobilization empowering; however, feminist movements seeking various realizations of women's equality characterize the three major branches of the contemporary women's movement that form the empirical base of discussion in the present volume. In basing our comments on the present chapters, we also ignore the important variations in women's movements in other geographic locations and in response to other important challenges such as democratization in Latin America and the former Soviet Union.

variable resilience and capacity for response given different patterns of institutionalization. We suggest that national women's movements in particular, and social movements in general, can be characterized by their structuration of axial elements. We imagine that these patterns may constrain and/or facilitate the ability of mobilized movements, when faced with fundamental changes in political structure, to shape and adapt to changes in political opportunity or threat. The literature on social movements has been unclear on which social movement elements are more likely to be adaptive over time. It was our initial assumption that stably institutionalized configurations of elements would play a decisive role in how resilient women's movements were in response to the threats and opportunities posed by state reconfiguration. At the same time, we recognized that the complexity of contemporary women's movements suggested the possibility of far more variable outcomes.

We begin by developing the idea of movement "clusters,"[2] by which we mean relatively distinguishable and more-or-less coherent constituent segments of ongoing movements. We associate these clusters with familiar distinctions among radical, socialist, and liberal branches of second-wave feminism in the established democracies of Europe and North America of concern to the authors here.[3] Distinct mixes of structural and cultural component elements can be used to characterize such branches or clusters distinguishing the important features of more-or-less institutionalized social movements in general and second-wave women's movements in particular. National movements, in general, and women's movements, in particular, differ from one state to another in terms of the existence, viability, and/or resilience of radical, socialist, and liberal configurations. The features have been widely employed to explain the timing and the spatial and social location and success of ongoing collective action (J. McCarthy 1997). We group the elements into the two broader categories of movement structure and movement culture. We define a social movement's structure as a more-or-less loosely coupled set of more formally organized groups linked in a variety of ways with less-structured networks of activists intersecting with more-or-less spontaneous public actions (Oliver 1989). Western movement cultures draw on taken-for-granted assumptions of liberal democracies (Boli and Thomas 1999) and, in some cases, carefully articulated ideologies (Oliver and Johnston 2000) as well as strategically oriented collective action

---

[2] Our actual preference is for the term "configuration," but in the present context, such a designation would create confusion with the key theme of the volume built around "state reconfiguration." Our concept of "clusters" is similar to Melucci's (1996, 1989) broad interpretation of "collective identities." That is, we see a delimited set of social movement elements that show continuity over time and space as a total gestalt even as they are renegotiated and reconfigured.

[3] Although we recognize that other, more encompassing, typologies have been proposed (see, for instance, Bryson and Campling 1999; Lorber 1998), we restrict our concern to the three that have figured most prominently in the cases discussed in this volume.

frames (Snow, Rochford, Worden, and Benford 1986) that are linked to time-sensitive campaigns and events (Snow and Benford 1992).

We suggest that specific historical instances of these several structural and cultural elements display considerable coherence over time in more-or-less recognizable patterns, and that transpositions resulting from negotiations as movements respond to internal shifts in recruitment, leadership, and resources and external threats and opportunities. Our major concern is what patterns of elements show the greatest resilience in response to external opportunities or threats from state reconfiguration.[4] We return to the question of how best to describe second-wave feminist movements' patterned responses in the next section. Here we provide a brief discussion of the axial elements, calling attention to important variations across the diverse women's movements chronicled in the preceding chapters.

CLUSTERS WITHIN INSTITUTIONALIZED SOCIAL MOVEMENTS

Despite the enormous variety of possible combinations of social movement elements, the stable patterning of elements into distinct clusters commonly occurs as movements evolve. In addition to the clusters within contemporary feminism, the United States saw a "civil rights movement" give birth to a movement for "black power"; the recent peace movement encompassed the "freeze movement" and the "peace and justice movement" as well as the "movement for nuclear disarmament." These clusters, segments, or tendencies are sometimes associated with specific social movement organizations, but, more frequently, they are patterned around a comprehensive set of mobilizing structures and movement cultures that both legitimate and frame their collective identities and claims. A set of key axial elements can be used to characterize social movement clusters in structural (mobilizing structures,

---

[4] David Meyer's parallel analyses of the foregoing chapters may appear, at first reading, orthogonal to our own. The disjunction is a result, however, of the contrasting sets of assumptions we adopt and the different lenses they offer for interpreting the materials. Political opportunity theorists in general, and David Meyer in this volume in particular, imagine social movement actors to be nimble and primarily political actors, relatively unencumbered by their own cultural and organizational histories. Consistent with that imagery, Meyer claims that "Social movements are generally opportunistic...(this volume)." He goes on to claim that "It is clear that activists gravitate to the places where they can mobilize safely, or toward open spaces" (this volume). Sociologists of social movements, on the other hand, are more likely to emphasize that movements of some maturity are likely to be constrained by internal factors that stem from their own previous efforts. Having previously invested extensive efforts in specific movement identities and well-worked-out repertoires of collective action, especially those including organizational structures, can make adaptation to new opportunities both psychically and materially costly. As a result, our analyses focus most attention on factors internal to the several clusters of women's movements in assessing how those clusters differentially respond to variable political opportunities. Meyer focuses his primary attention, instead, upon political openings, shifting alliance structures, and other exogenous factors.

resources, repertoires, and targets) and cultural terms (ways of identifying injustices, movement goals, and coherent activist identities).

Movement Structure

The multiple *mobilizing structures* that link people together, and therefore, upon which movements may build in fielding collective action, are as diverse as the forms of human interaction. They range from the more-or-less formally organized routine life patterns constituted in, for instance, neighborhood associations, religious organizations, and friendship groups to the formal organizations that have been developed for broader social purposes, but devote some of their effort to supporting movement-related collective action. We see many such organizations playing a role in national women's movements as described in these chapters, including associations of professional women (for example, the Spanish Association of University Women, Women in Scholarly Publishing in the United States), as well as women's divisions of political parties (for example, the Women's Action Committee in the British Labour Party). We also see such organizations in trade unions and in religious denominations. There are government agencies devoted to women's issues, such as the British Equal Opportunities Commission. Central for institutionalized social movements at the end of the twentieth century are the many social movement organizations (SMOs) that have been formally constituted to pursue movement goals. The rich diversity of such groups is seen throughout the preceding chapters. The shape of a movement's mobilizing structure may be used to characterize any national social movement (McCarthy 1996).

Institutionalized movements typically include a number of SMOs. Like organizations with other purposes, an SMO must devote some of its resources to organizational maintenance and it also must establish a stable pattern of *resource accumulation*. Such resources may be material, human, informational, and moral (Cress and Snow 1996). Local organizations are more dependent upon volunteer human resources, while organizations with a wider geographic scope tend to be more dependent upon material resources. All groups depend upon moral and informational resources. We see institutional material resource flows of various kinds to women's groups in these chapters. They range from the European Union's funding of the French group CLEF, which brought together sixty associations in an alliance supporting parity, through the Spanish Women's Institute that has subsidized a wide variety of women's groups.[5]

Repertoires are the mixes of strategies and tactics typically employed by a movement's clusters in any time or place. Some repertoires are embedded

---

[5] The potential unreliability of government subsidies of this kind is seen in their dissipation during the last several decades in Canada as described by Dobrowolsky (this volume).

in organizational routines and to the extent that a movement's mobilizing structure is dominated by SMOs, repertoires and mobilizing structures can be expected to be more tightly coupled. Repertoires are probably more loosely coupled at the level of local, grass-roots movement organizations. Of particular importance here is the mix of insider/outsider tactics employed as feminists engage governments, unions, and service agencies as employees, appointees, officials, supplicants, and antagonists (see origins of this distinction in Eisenstein's work on Australian feminism, 1995; see also McCarthy, Smith, and Zald 1996). Movement repertoires, as with mobilizing structures, can be thought of as more-or-less flexible or adaptable to circumstances and more-or-less complex or diverse.

Movement Culture

We use the rubric "movement culture" to capture the dominant goals of a movement, the way in which those goals are framed as solutions to injustices, and the collective identity that both precedes individual identities and is negotiated in terms of strategic efforts to align individual identities with those of the larger movement.[6] *Framing* typically refers to systems of meaning that identify causes of injustice and link them to specific goals and targets of mobilization (Snow et al. 1986; Snow and Benford 1988, 1992). Analysts of collective action have come to view the success of such framing efforts as crucial to understanding the trajectory of social movements. Gamson and Modigliani (1989) cast such efforts into a broader context by conceiving of them as part of ongoing framing contests within states that may differ dramatically between states (Ferree et al. 2002). The process of strategic framing and the evolution of activists' *collective identities* can be expected to be, to a certain extent, a reciprocal one. Although mobilizing structures and repertoires of contention need not necessarily be tightly prefigurative, activist identities are likely to be embedded in the ways in which movements do collective action. As well, activists' self-conceptions can be expected to hinge on what they believe their activism is, most fundamentally, about. Activists' identities are typically forged in struggle; historically, specific struggles are waged with certain tactics, frames, and structures in pursuit of specific goals. Collective identities come to be associated with groups and organizations, so we would expect that collectivities would have stakes in defending their organizational selves. As a result, it seems reasonable to suggest that both collective identities and individual activist identities that are forged during one period of struggle are likely to be resistant to being recalibrated when

---

[6] The concept of collective identity is commonly used to clump strategic frames and collective identities for purposes of analysis (della Porta and Diani 1999: 83–109). Melucci's (1996: 68–77) conceptualization of collective identity, at its broadest, encompasses these and also what we call movement structure.

environmental circumstances change. Thus, there are multiple reasons for expecting considerable inertia in the links between social movement culture and structure when political opportunities and threats transpire as a result, for instance, of state reconfiguration. Yet we also know that the elements combined into social movement clusters are continually subject to challenge and renegotiation. Old alliances break down; state repression drives activists underground; internal divisions result in fragmentation; leaders are replaced by new recruits who rise to leadership on the basis of a new framing of opportunities and threats. As numerous observers of contemporary feminism have pointed out, radical feminism, for instance, has undergone repeated reinvention within a broadly accepted set of assumptions (Echols 1989; Ryan 1989; Whittier 1995).

Clustering of Movement Structure and Culture

While it has commonly been observed that many social movements tend to cluster together in time (Tarrow 1989) and that repertoires of collective action tend toward modular forms across multiple social movements at any given historical juncture (Tarrow 1998; Tilly 1995), the stability of the element clusters as we conceive them has received relatively little theoretical attention, although it is one of the chief means of distinguishing various strands within a social movement. Complex, long-lasting movements, like the women's movements described here, tend to develop several relatively stable configurations of elements that incorporate the diverse possibilities of the political culture and mobilizing structures within a given state or polity. A diversity of clusters within a polity offers survival value for the movement as well as the potential for factionalism and self-destruction (McAdam 1982; Mueller 1994).

How modern movement configurations, strands, or clusters form and evolve through time is shown to be a result of the possible frames within the political culture as well as the pattern of births and deaths of SMOs. Ferree (1987), for instance, shows the likelihood of liberal and "autonomous" feminisms in the United States and Germany respectively as to some extent a reflection of the political cultures in the two countries. On the other hand, Brulle (2000) argues that the clustering within the U.S. environmental movement is anchored in distinct birth cohorts of organizations that share similar structure, goals, frames, and resource dependencies and whose supporters embrace similar identities. Similarly, Minkoff (1999, 1995) shows that the change toward the dominant repertoire of liberal advocacy within the U.S. women's and racial-ethnic movements is shaped more by the emergence of new groups than shifts in strategy by existing groups.

Further, elements combine in a variety of ways to create an overall movement cluster under a variety of conditions, some of which are unique to specific states and/or locales (see, for instance, Ray 1999, on differences between women's clusters in Bombay and Calcutta). Using a cultural approach, for instance, Lofland (1996, 1993) has argued that the peace movement of the 1980s had a two-tiered cultural "profile" which was sparse at the national level but highly variable at the level of "clusters" differentiated by six main "forms of seeking," each representing a different theory of how to accomplish social change (1996: 212).

Our approach is both more and less ambitious than Lofland's. On the one hand, we seek to encompass all of the elements described above that we believe define a social movement cluster. On the other, we accept the self-designations of movement participants as to the major lines of demarcation in contemporary women's movements, including the labels that have assumed critical importance to participants in designating and claiming collective identities (Bashevkin 1998; Bryson and Campling 1999; Ferree and Hess 1994; Hellman 1987a; Lovenduski 1986). These clusters or movement segments center on unique patterns of social movement elements that differ in terms of their mode of seeking social change. In addition, they are associated with more global frames and collective identities based in both the unique and general options available in the political cultures of modern democratic states and the repertoires of contention associated with existing traditions of both protest and electoral mobilization. Despite their stability over time, movement segments also have the potential to develop or change in the face of opportunity or threat. Social movement theory has traditionally failed to address which of these cluster elements are more stable and under what conditions. The present volume offers case material for posing such questions more precisely.

ELEMENT CLUSTERS IN CONTEMPORARY FEMINISM

From the beginning of second-wave feminism in North America and western Europe, at least three main clusters (or tendencies, segments, or branches) have been apparent in alternative modes of seeking to bring about change in women's condition: *radical* forms of feminism, which have placed patriarchy or women's oppression by men at the heart of their analysis; *socialist* feminism, based on a materialist analysis and ambivalent alliances with parties of the left; and *liberal* feminism, which pursues equal rights claims making, primarily through various forms of pressure on the state. These clusters have combined variously with greater or lesser strength in the women's movements described here. In North America, for instance, the liberal tendency has been stronger than in western Europe where both radical and socialist tendencies have had greater importance. In the aftermath of state socialism, women in eastern Europe have generally disavowed labels associated with the discredited language of "equality" and/or "liberation"; this leaves them with a circumscribed political space and vocabulary for mobilization (Jaquette and Wolchik 1998).

These segments represent not only particular types of mobilizing structures, but also the movement culture evidenced in framing, collective identities, and claims that typify the major tendencies in the states represented here. While such a typology greatly simplifies the diversity of tendencies within each state, it facilitates the isolation of dynamic responses to the changes in political threats and opportunities of state reconfiguration.

Radical Strands of Women's Movements

Students of women's movements have observed that, although these three tendencies have varied greatly from country to country, European feminism has primarily taken the form of radical or autonomous movements and, secondarily, of socialist feminism which has aligned to varying degrees with labor unions and parties of the left. Although radicals supporting an autonomous course have been important actors in both the U.S. and Canadian movements, they have been much less important as a tendency than in European feminism.

Radical tendencies have reflected a framing of feminism that takes the oppression of women as the root of all oppression. Radical or women-centered feminists see a fundamental opposition of interests between men and women, represented by the theory of patriarchy in which the state, the law, marriage, and other institutions historically dominated by men universally oppress women (Greer 1971; Millett 1970). As described here in chapters on Italy by della Porta, on Britain by Beckwith, and on movements for battered women in Sweden, Britain, and the United States by Elman, mobilization centered originally in consciousness-raising groups that turned to projects organized at the local level by nonhierarchical collectives seeking to empower individual women while addressing specific issues of women's oppression, for example, rape, domestic violence, abortion, pornography, and support for lesbians, single mothers, prostitutes, and immigrant women (Bryson and Campling 1999: 25–28; Ferree 1987; Hole and Levine 1971: 240–241).

The emphasis of radical feminism has been on the creation of separate women's institutions and the rejection of ties to state and political parties. Dispersed local groups have been linked through a variety of means other than hierarchical organizations. Elman, for instance, refers to hotlines linking women's shelters in the United States. Beckwith describes one of the most dramatic examples of a women-only strategy of radical separatism, the peace encampment established in Britain at the Greenham Common nuclear weapons base, where over 30,000 women demonstrated their opposition to the deployment of U.S. cruise missiles in 1981. In addition to national or regional encampments, local groups may be linked as they were in the former West Germany through publications, conferences, and travel (Ferree 1987; see also Briët, Klandermans, and Kroon 1987 on the Netherlands).

This form of mobilizing structure has been described by Gerlach and Hine (1970) as "decentralized, segmented and reticulate."

The great strength of radical movements has been their grass-roots efforts in building women's communities by providing feminist services to women (see Buechler 1990; Ferree and Hess 1994; Whittier 1995) and their contributions to feminist theorizing (Echols 1989; Ryan 1992). Nevertheless, they have been plagued by several vulnerabilities: the lack of material resources that accompanies isolation from male centers of power; the limits of volunteerism in providing local feminist services to meet the accelerating needs of women (see Ferree and Martin 1995); what Jo Freeman (1975) has termed "the tyranny of structurelessness," and the factionalism that Beckwith finds, for instance, at encampments like Greenham Common (see also Ryan 1989); and the difficulties in coordinating and sustaining regional or national campaigns (Beckwith this volume; Staggenborg 1991 for the United States).

The lack of material resources has led radical movements in Europe to turn sometimes to progressive parties on the left; in Italy, for example, the state's repression of progressive forces during the 1970s led women's liberation groups to turn to unions as well as progressive parties for meeting rooms, copying facilities, and other practical needs (della Porta this volume). Such alliances are not universally available to autonomous feminists, however, as Elman indicates for Sweden, where radical women remained largely independent of left parties that dominate the political space. Beckwith describes the importance of resources made available to radical groups through the Greater London Council in the early 1980s before the Thatcher government assumed control of the GLC (see also Bashevkin 1998; Bryson and Compling 1999). Turning to the male-dominated state for funding or to parties and unions for allies represents a major compromise for proponents of a radical critique of patriarchy. On the other hand, radical feminists might not be expected to fare well under the privations of state reconfiguration. Yet a history of greater autonomy from material resources and allies in male-dominated institutions might make them more resilient when state resources have been withdrawn.

Liberal Feminism

Despite strong radical tendencies in North America (see particularly Taylor 1989; Whittier 1995), the most visible political face of the women's movement has been "liberal feminism" because of its embrace of the forms of representation associated with liberal democracies and its strong reliance on the state to achieve an agenda based on equal rights for women (Bashevkin 1998; Bryson and Campling 1999; Costain 1992; Ferree 1987). Liberal feminists have relied disproportionately (but not exclusively) on lobbying for legislation, bringing court cases, and seeking public office. The repertoire of liberal feminism has been much less central throughout

Europe than in North America. Yet reconfiguration has recently raised issues like electoral "parity" to prominence in France and Spain (Jenson and Valiente this volume) and in the states of Britain where constitutional issues have assumed new importance (Dobrowolsky this volume). Liberal feminists assume that men's historic abuse of power can be remedied through legislation, court decisions, and women's equal representation in the institutions of governing. From the campaign for suffrage in the nineteenth century through the demand for abortion framed in terms of "a woman's right to choose," the liberal feminist agenda has been couched in terms of individual rights.[7]

The primary mobilizing structures of liberal feminism are the familiar formal, hierarchical organizations committed to lobbying and drafting legislation, recruiting and supporting candidates for office, and litigating cases on behalf of women as described in detail by Beckwith and Katzenstein (this volume) on women's associational presence in the United States and by Dobrowolsky (this volume) on Canada (see also Bashevkin's comparison of Canada, Great Britain, and the United States 1998).

Although sensitive to the radical feminist critique of bureaucracy and hierarchy in their formal structures, these organizations have depended on their memberships primarily for dues that support a national office and professional staff, newsletters, and web sites and, periodically, for participation in letter-writing campaigns and protest demonstrations (Gelb and Palley 1987; McCarthy 1987). Both Beckwith and Katzenstein (this volume) point to the creation of liberal feminist organizations and caucuses across differences of race and ethnicity, as well as strictly professional and work-related organizations throughout the organizational structure. In addition, Katzenstein (this volume) details the degree to which women's associationalism reaches into a wide range of more specialized occupational niches in "government, the church, the media, athletics, the military, the professions, commerce – the mainstream institutions of both state and society."

Although these authors do not retrace the legislative successes attributed to this organizational presence and to the increasing preponderance of women at the polls (see Mueller 1988), Costain's (1992, 1988) accounts indicate the massive legislative breakthroughs for women under the mandate for equality during the 1970s in the United States, and Bashevkin (1998) argues for even greater success in Canada (see also Dobrowolsky this volume). As Beckwith and Katzenstein describe here, liberal feminists in the United States had already achieved a well-established interest representation for middle-class, employed women by the time neoliberalism became entrenched with Reagan's election in 1980. Liberal feminists in Canada faced a greater threat

---

7 More recently, the rights frame has been embraced as a powerful framing device for pursuing women's concerns through transnational advocacy networks (Bunch 1990; Keck and Sikkink 1998).

to core interests from state reconfiguration and moved to reconstruct both their mobilizing structures and their movement framing (Dobrowolsky this volume; also Bashevkin 1998).

In terms of its mobilizing structures, the weaknesses of liberal feminism reverse those of radical feminism. The strength of a national presence provides a coordinating mechanism with constant oversight and input vis-à-vis the state in relatively open political systems such as those of the United States and Canada (Bashevkin 1998; Gelb 1989), but fails to provide the grassroots support that radical feminists achieve. This "infrastructural deficit" (McCarthy 1987) in the United States accounts, in part, for the successes of the prolife countermovement at the state level as well as the loss of the Equal Rights Amendment when it failed to achieve ratification by 1982. In terms of framing, liberal feminism is susceptible to the individualistic claims of the Conservative Party in Great Britain and the even wider appeal in the United States of arguments that fail to recognize the structural sources of inequality (Bryson and Campling 1999).

When faced with state reconfiguration, framed in terms of neoliberalism, liberal feminists' close, though contested, relationship with the state would be problematic. On the one hand, strong national organizations might seem a formidable resource against cuts in resources to programs for women in state downsizing. On the other, liberal feminists largely share a political culture that fails to attack structural sources of inequality; this leaves them without the cultural resources to attack neoliberalism's individualistic ethic.

Socialist Feminism

The framing of socialist feminism is materialist in analysis and in its programmatic agenda. Many socialist feminists tend to see the origins of women's subordination in class exploitation, with women allocated the tasks of reproducing and tending the labor force while periodically serving as a reserve of unskilled and low-paid labor. Although socialist feminists oppose dogmatic assertions that the end of capitalism would automatically result in women's liberation, they do see women's emancipation as closely linked to the class struggle (Deckard 1975: 341–342, 374). Other socialist feminists, like Heidi Hartmann (1981) tend to see class and gender oppression as resulting from two rather than one dynamic force at work in history. Socialism offers its major appeal outside North America with its lack of viable socialist parties. Like liberalism, it supports equal rights and opportunities for all, but, unlike liberalism, it views oppression as systemic and embraces a collectivist approach (Bryson and Campling 1999: 16–24). Despite the variety of analytic frames, socialist feminists tend to endorse a social agenda that seeks to alleviate the class differences of women and their families that exist under capitalism.

The mobilizing structures of socialist feminists correspond roughly to those of the unions and parties with which they are allied. Like the liberal feminists of North America, they work through left-dominated governments in the European states. They tend not to develop the independent, freestanding national organizations typical of liberal feminists in the United States or the state-supported women's advocacy groups of Canada. They are more likely to participate in party- or union-sponsored activities explicitly devoted to women's issues. With the support of the Labour Party in Britain, they supported "municipal feminism" at the local level. With their Labour allies, they campaigned for transport, childcare, housing, and health, demanding women's committees within the appropriate authorities to address these issues (Bryson and Campling 1999). The most influential of these women's committees was set up by the Greater London Council in 1982 and included radical women as well as socialist feminists.

In the countries under study, socialist feminists have tried a wide range of relationships with parties of the Old and the New Left. Given many feminists' suspicion of male-dominated hierarchical organizations, including unions and parties of the left, maintaining these ties has been problematic. Even before reconfiguration, however, in many European countries, the left offered powerful allies, material resources, and a concern about women's social agenda. Della Porta's account (this volume) of the advantages associated with such compromises by otherwise radical Italian feminists has already been described. Valiente's discussion (this volume) of post-Franco Spain, beginning with the period of democratic consolidation, shows one of the strongest relationships between feminists and the parties of the left. She found the collaboration, however, as "troublesome as in other Western democracies...." (51) where the choice is between political marginalization and the possibility of cooptation. In this case, the strong alliance with unions and socialist parties by most feminists in Spain has had implications for the form of feminist organizing, for repertoires of collective action, and even for the divisions that have threatened the movement. There have also been multiple advantages for Spanish feminists: establishing "state femocrats" (Eisenstein 1995) in bureaucracies of the state such as the Women's Institute, emphasizing gender equality policies at the national level, and offering services to women and families that the state does not and has not provided. In other European countries, the relationship was more problematic, especially when the feminists in question were defined by a more radical identity, as Elman found in Sweden.

Socialist feminists, then, would seem to have a unique advantage when faced with state reconfiguration. They have had years of experience in negotiating complex alliances with unions and parties of the left – if they choose to resist or mitigate the effects of state downsizing and the increasing reliance on market forces for the allocation of goods and services as the state withdraws from traditional responsibilities. Alternatively, the left has traditionally treated women's concerns as those of a little sister and failed to recognize their interests or accord them full participation.

DIMENSIONS OF STATE RECONFIGURATION AND POLITICAL OPPORTUNITY THEORY

What structures of the state are being reconfigured and what is the trajectory of those changes? Along with the editors of this volume we place heavy emphasis upon the scope and volume of state responsibility as constituting core dimensions of state reconfiguration.[8] First, the scope of authority of nation states is seen as being reduced as authority is redistributed to alternative territorial levels.[9] Devolution, or the decentralization of power to subnational geographical units, is conceived as occurring sometimes in punctuated fashion in democratic transitions (for example, in Spain power to the regions) and constitutional revisions (for example, in the United Kingdom the establishment of regional parliaments with enhanced authority). And, it is seen in more gradual ways in the transfer of certain governmental responsibilities (for example, welfare in the United States). The globalization of authority is more abrupt for clusters of states choosing to cede authority upward as in the European Union and North American Free Trade Agreement. It is more gradual in the increasing authority vested in global institutions such as the United Nations Human Rights Commission, the World Bank, the International Monetary Fund, and the World Trade Organization. These several routes, then, can lead to fundamental reconfiguration of the scope of authority, reversing the long trend of its having been increasingly vested in nation-states, the process that shaped the emergence of the standard features of the national social movement (Tilly 1995).

Second, the volume of state authority declines as a result of the shifting scope of authority. But the transfer of traditional state responsibilities of education, health, and welfare to private actors exacerbates that decline. And the increasing interpenetration of state and private actors that result in reducing state control over a wider range of public policies facilitates it (Banaszak, for example, describes required abortion counseling being performed by private groups like the Catholic Church). These processes are more difficult to specify than the more punctuated changes in the scope of authority and are

---

[8] Another pattern of reconfiguration focuses not on changes in the scope and function of state authority, but rather on rules of access. The French and Spanish women's movement campaigns for parity represent calls for the reconstitution of the rules of their respective electoral regimes.

[9] We ignore, in this discussion, the transition to democracy in Spain, since it is a form of state reconfiguration that has received extensive attention by scholars elsewhere (Hipsher 1998; Mainwaring 1992; Pagnucco 1995) and is not a central focus of the essays in this volume.

much more difficult to aggregate across national systems in order to assess the extent of a nation's decline in volume of authority.[10]

We expect that the institutionalized features of movement clusters and their relative strength in a nation are important in understanding how women's movements respond to state reconfiguration. Political opportunity theorists, however, have strongly argued that key elements of social movements, goals, and tactics, for instance, are shaped by the most stable aspects of a nation's political system such as the strength of the party system, proportional representation, and the strength of the judiciary (Kriesi 1995; Kriesi et al. 1995; Ray 1999). Koopmans argues that these dimensions of "political opportunity structure will generally provide more powerful explanations for cross-national comparisons than for longitudinal, single-country studies" (1999: 100). These arguments also imply a lack of movement flexibility in the face of shifts in the scope and volume of state authority.

In general women's movements have not been primary proponents of devolution. For instance, the forces that originally set a quest for constitutional revisions in motion in Canada and the United Kingdom did not, for the most part, include women's movements (Dobrowolsky this volume). But in both instances, organized women's groups became deeply involved in taking advantage of the opportunities that such revisions were seen to offer, having a role in shaping the process. The general thrust of both of these instances of constitutional reform took the form of demands from culturally distinct territories for the decentralization of political authority. In the United Kingdom devolution has resulted in important shifts in authority to representative bodies in Scotland, Wales, Northern Ireland, and London. Once the basic charter of a nation-state comes open for consideration, however, other kinds of structural change in political institutions can easily be raised.[11] In the case of the Canadian and several regional women's movements in the United Kingdom, these importantly included formal political representational formulae and women's equality rights. The ability of movements to affect public policies in the shorter run, however, is shaped by the structure of their alliances with other political actors – especially political parties and, where they are strong, labor unions (Kriesi 1989) – as well as their access to the state (Costain 1992). Access and impact are importantly shaped by whether a movement's party allies are in

---

[10] The views of some serious political opportunity analysts about the importance of these trends, however, suggest caution. "National political institutions and national political coalitions will continue to shape in characteristically different ways the issues on which people mobilize, the ways in which they organize and act, and the outcomes their mobilizations are likely to have" (della Porta and Kriesi 1999: 4).

[11] It was just this possibility that led many groups to oppose the proposed convention to amend the U.S. Constitution that was motivated by advocates of school prayer, but many critics saw as inevitably expanding its concerns once the opportunity to restructure U.S. political institutions presented itself.

or out of power and analysts of second-wave women's movements have typically seen greater opportunities for access and impact with left parties in power (della Porta and Rucht 1995). In the United States for instance, the expanded agenda of second-wave feminism contributed to a partisan realignment in which Republicans embraced a profamily social program and Democrats became the party of women's rights (Wolbrecht 2000). This line of argument leads to the expectation that women's movements will have greater access and impact when responding to state reconfigurations carried out by regimes under the control of their allies – usually parties of the left. Whether or not the strands of a women's movement take advantage of such opportunities, we expect, should be shaped by their various patterns of institutionalization.

CLUSTER RESPONSES TO STATE RECONFIGURATION

Institutionalization is the process by which claims making by social movement actors becomes repetitive, routinized, and self-sustaining in response to the internal dynamics of social movements and the imperatives of the external environment (Meyer 1993; Meyer and Tarrow 1998). While these papers describe multiple stable clusters of mobilizing structures and movement cultures within second-wave feminism, they also reveal a variable level of resilience in responding to state reconfiguration that is not predetermined by these relatively stable institutional patterns. The clusters we have identified in European and North American feminism show varying degrees of flexibility in terms of the degree to which they are able to modify a position of inclusion versus marginalization, cooptation, or routinization – the dimensions of institutionalization identified by Meyer and Tarrow (1998). Flexibility or inertia seems largely a function of how successfully key constituencies are able to meet their primary goals through their current form of institutionalization.

Our original expectation, that the structuring of element clusters would largely prefigure the response of women's movements to both the long-term and short-term changes in state reconfiguration, has given way to a more nuanced analysis. Rather, we have found that, drawing upon the evidence mustered in the preceding chapters each cluster type – radical, liberal, and socialist – responded to the opportunities and threats of reconfiguration in a way that was only to some extent predictable from their mobilizing structure and movement culture. Their degree of resilience in breaking with original patterns of routinization, cooptation, and inclusion/marginalization, however, is accounted for among these cases at least by the degree to which their preexisting overall structural patterns have served them successfully. We consider the failure to break out of routinized mobilizing structures and predisposing movement cultures as evidence of a high level of institutionalization, regardless of whether this pattern involved inclusion and/or cooperation. To illustrate these patterns we describe examples of both more- and less-institutionalized responses for each of the three clusters.

Liberal Feminism

The most dramatic example of variability in level of institutionalization within a cluster type is that between liberal feminists in the United States and in Canada. For the United States, Katzenstein and Beckwith describe a high level of increasing institutionalization. Beckwith notes, for instance, an uneven but sustained increase in the proportion of women winning legislative office (22.4% in state legislatures by 1999; 12.4% in Congress by 1996), which shows no responsiveness to reconfiguration. Similarly, Katzenstein finds a high level of associationalism among middle-class women both inside and outside of government and other major institutions, which has served to protect the interests of middle-class women. She notes, "The right to equal pay, to merit-based employment and promotion, to reproductive choice, to credit, to insurance (free of provisions that discriminate based on sex), are all still fundamentally in place assuming the 'means' are there to make women competitive applicants and economically viable clients." Both authors also show that associationalism spread among middle-class women identified by differences in race, ethnicity, and occupation. A movement culture centered on providing opportunities for individual women is consistent with neoliberalism. It was only low-income women who were not similarly organized when state downsizing led to loss of welfare support and of national standards guaranteeing minimum levels of assistance and legal advocacy. We conclude from this work that liberal feminism in the United States made the least change of any of the national clusters described here because it has been successful in responding to the interests of its largely middle-class constituency of employed women and its culture was not challenged by neoliberalism. Reconfiguration has made little difference in meeting their concerns.

Dobrowolsky describes a very different response by liberal feminists to state reconfiguration and the associated constitutional crises in Canada. The women's movement came to life under Pierre Trudeau's Liberal administration which, like its counterpart in the United States, was highly supportive of an undifferentiated equal rights agenda for women. However, when Quebec created a constitutional crisis that threatened women's equality rights; when state downsizing (as well as increasingly oppositional political activities) led Mulroney's Conservative government to withdraw government financial support from the National Action Committee on the Status of Women (NAC); when NAFTA threatened the jobs of working-class women; and when a series of constitutional challenges presented new threats and opportunities, the largely liberal Canadian women's movement diversified its mobilizing structure by employing a flexible and varied repertoire of collective actions and by forging new ties across identities of race, class, ethnicity, and ability. Despite a neoliberal attack on "special interests," similar to that in the United States, the Canadian women's movement became more inclusive and more oppositional throughout the Mulroney period. Although ultimately their success was limited to opening up the constitutional debate and blocking specific governmental proposals, they had abandoned a low-risk political position based on a strategy of meeting the expectations of polity members and embraced a more confrontational approach defying the expectations of institutionalized political insiders. Thus, in contrast to their counterparts in the United States liberal feminists in Canada diversified their mobilizing structures and broadened their framing as they lost their primary source of material support from the state. Middle-class as well as working-class women were vulnerable to state reconfiguration.

Socialist Feminism

In contrast to liberal feminists whose considerable successes in North America during the 1970s were seriously compromised, particularly in Canada, by state reconfiguration in the 1980s, the responsiveness of feminists aligned with the left in Europe was strongly influenced by whether left-wing parties were in power during reconfiguration and what degree and type of reconfiguration was salient in a given country. Spain and Britain provide two of the most dramatic examples of variability on the positions of the left and reconfiguration, but feminists in each country have shown remarkable resilience.

Like the response to repression in Italy during the 1970s (della Porta this volume), Franco's authoritarian regime had led to a loose alliance of progressive forces in Spain by the time of his death in 1975. Valiente describes the strong ties of Spanish feminists to the leftist PSOE from the pre-Franco period throughout its fourteen-year ascendancy (1982–96) as a strategy for avoiding political marginalization. To overcome the long years of authoritarian rule, the left emphasized democratization, and socialist feminists emphasized equal rights for women. Through this propitious alliance, feminists won organizational status with the party machinery, party support for eliminating the most draconian laws against women, and the full development of an office for women (the Women's Institute). The latter has developed gender equality policies and provided funding for women's social services offered by feminists that have never been considered a state responsibility. With little welfare state apparatus to defund, reconfiguration has offered new opportunities for feminists to gain support through the European Women's Lobby that has exerted additional pressure on the parties to set quotas for women on the electoral lists, an exceptionally successful strategy that has placed Spain in the mid-level ranks of European countries in terms of the proportion of women in elected office.

The story of socialist feminists in Britain is, of course, somewhat different. Margaret Thatcher's Conservative government came to power in 1979 and remained until ousted by Tony Blair's Labour Party in 1997. The consequences for women, particularly those who depended on the state for support, were formidable. Beckwith describes the systematic downloading and offloading of state responsibilities for healthcare, unemployment protection, public education, child welfare, and housing coupled with widespread unemployment in the working class and among state-service employees. One of the most important responses by the British women's movement, which was formerly antistatist among both liberal and socialist feminists, was to move into the Labour Party. As Beckwith notes in this volume, they "... walked the long road within the Labour Party to bring that party to power...." Their infiltration of labor unions and the Labour Party began with establishing the Women's Action Committee in the 1980s. By 1988, feminists had successfully argued for an Equal Rights Department in the Trades Union Congress and, by 1989, a Shadow Ministry for Women in the Labour Party. Like their counterparts in Spain, they had also persuaded the Labour Party to support quotas for increasing the number of women elected to Parliament, resulting in significantly more women elected on Labour's tickets in 1992 and 1997.

Among socialist feminists in both Spain and Britain, we see a capacity to resist institutionalization. That resilience may appear somewhat less dramatic in Spain, where the left's long tenure in power with only a modest welfare state to defend mitigated against the severe losses felt by women in Britain. Instead socialist feminists in Spain were able to take advantage of new resources from the EU to increase the number of women in decision-making positions. The turnaround for British feminists, however, is quite dramatic as antistatist liberal and socialist feminists joined in bringing the Labour Party to power while increasing the influence of feminists within the party, unions, and the House of Commons. In both countries, women moved effectively to take advantage of openings on the left in Spain and to create those openings in Great Britain.

Radical Feminism

In asking how women's movements with radical tendencies have responded to state reconfiguration, it is well to keep in mind what was at stake in terms of women's issues that most concerned them. Throughout most of the chapters discussed here, downsizing of state responsibilities meant a reduction in commitment to social policies that required outlays for low-income women such as welfare, childcare, public housing, unemployment compensation, and job training. Closer to the focus of radical feminists' agendas, the trend toward state funding for battered women's shelters, rape crisis centers, crisis hotlines, and women's centers was threatened. These multiple threats posed major choices for radical feminists. The issues they had identified as key to women's oppression, centering on violence against women, required social services that no state provided and a major transformation in the law enforcement practices of every state. They could offer the services themselves (as they did for many years), but to the extent that they were successful, the need would outrun the supply of resources and personnel. Ultimately, they had to compromise.

In Italy, where a common response to state repression in the 1970s had brought women's small groups into alliance with the left, their problem had been to combine the framing of women's liberation on issues of reproduction, sexuality, and interpersonal relations with the traditional discourse of the left. Whereas in the 1970s, emancipation and liberation were in opposition, by the 1990s, reconfiguration ushered in a new pragmatism in which parity and diversity combined in a discourse on a "new citizenship." Despite a continued reliance on the parties of the Old Left, with reconfiguration the Third Sector offered a means of mediating relationships with the state by providing social services; money available through state downloading now offered a new meaning to "autonomy" as the movement could deliver or coordinate delivery of health, educational, and welfare services to women, children, and families. Such an opportunity was not widely available.

In Elman's description of shelter movements over the last thirty years in Britain, the United States, and Sweden, she describes a pattern in which radical feminists grudgingly sought support from and influence over the state and, in the United States, corporations as well. To some extent this compromise can be attributed to state reconfiguration in the United States and Britain. Yet the compromises go far beyond seeking partial state funding of shelters and personnel. In the United States there have been major campaigns by radical feminists to address violence against women through litigation and legislation bearing on the practice of law enforcement. When the U.S. Congress repeatedly refused to consider such legislation, radical feminists conducted state-by-state campaigns to change police practices (Tierney 1982). When the U.S. Congress finally passed the Violence Against Women Act in 1994, it represented years of state-level lobbying by radical feminists who abhor the state (see Tierney 1982, as well as Elman this volume). More recently, the issue of violence against women has been transferred to an even more contested site, the corporate workplace, through lawsuits against employers who fail to protect women and through administrative initiatives.

In Europe, radical feminists' compromises with the state have also been substantial. Although most shelter activists worked locally at piecemeal reform, by the mid-1970s, when Labour controlled the British Parliament, passage of the Domestic Violence Act (1976) and the Housing (Homeless) Persons Act (1977) first allowed for temporary eviction of the batterer, and second, established battered women as a priority for public housing. Lax enforcement rendered this legislation ineffective, however, until the Home

Office needed to improve its public image in the late 1980s. Although strategies of state-by-state lobbying or litigation were not alternatives in either Britain or Sweden, the pursuit of housing for battered women and other welfare initiatives required close cooperation with a variety of social agencies with often overlapping jurisdictions and contradictory regulations which led to multiagency initiatives. Shelter activists in Sweden have similarly pursued a relentless campaign through conservative, moderate, and social democratic governments seeking shelter and safety for battered women through state support for shelters, for legislation authorizing the prosecution of batterers, and for strong orders of protection.

With a mobilizing structure based in small collectives and nonhierarchical organizations and with a movement culture based on an analysis of patriarchy, radical feminists had the most to lose in seeking a *rapprochement* with the state. Yet the tenacity of radical feminists in coming back to the state over and over in the face of repeated disappointments and false promises indicates an unwillingness to be coopted, marginalized politically, or routinized as an ineffective, separatist enclave.

CONCLUSION

The logic of our general argument has challenged some of the traditional claims about the typical trajectories of individual life courses and the evolution of institutions. These include John Lofland (1978) and Howard Becker (1963) on deviant careers, organizational ecologists on organizations of all kinds (Scott 1992), and historians of path dependencies in political and social systems. Such accounts draw on concepts like "lines of action," "sunk costs" in identities and strategies and organizational forms, "resource dependencies," and images of the difficulties of changing a social course once it is set. All of these lines of analysis suggest lethargy and a lack of capacity of social movements to respond to altered environments. Yet we find considerable evidence of an ability by many well-established feminist movements to respond with surprising flexibility to radically altered political circumstances. The components of their "clusters" show differential continuity over time and great flexibility in their response to threats and opportunities to the interests of their key constituencies. Other feminist movements have survived state reconfiguration with cluster elements relatively intact because previous successes had left them in a comparatively secure position.

In terms of continuity, we have found that the framing of a movement's defining agenda, identity, and rationale largely prefigures the range of responses to threat/opportunity if not the level of innovation in exploiting the possibilities available. Thus, the most stable elements under state reconfiguration appear to be those associated with a movement's culture. Radical feminists continue to work from an agenda that prioritizes violence against women despite compromises in their relations to the state, their discourse with the state, and their mobilizing structures. Liberal feminists in Canada, Great Britain, and France continue to seek equal rights for women even though they may add other claims to their agenda, broaden their coalitions and alliances, and adopt a more confrontational stance vis-à-vis the state. Socialist feminists in Italy, Spain, and Great Britain continue to address the needs of poor, working-class, and immigrant women even if this means also addressing basic rights of women's participation in state decision making and electoral work within male-dominated unions and parties of the left.

Thus, change and innovation in mobilizing structures, alliance configurations, tactics, and strategies show greater flexibility in these women's movements than the broadly defined goals and identities of each movement cluster. This generalization is consistent with theorists of collective identities who see in cultural elements the primary source of movement continuity over time (della Porta and Diani 1999). These goals, identities, and agendas are also constrained to some extent by the political culture of a given polity.[12] That is, socialist clusters tend to be more viable in Europe than North America while the opposite is true for liberal feminists. Radical tendencies reflect a more fundamental challenge to political culture in both Europe and North America. We find that when radical women's movements are under siege from threats posed by state reconfiguration – particularly state downsizing – they have proved highly adaptive. When threatened, they have embraced new allies and tactics, engaged in actions that would earlier have been unthinkable, and sought out opportunities in new challenges of state building, of peace making, and of reconstituting the electorate. New transnational structures associated with state reconfiguration provided new allies and resources (the EU) and new threats (NAFTA) that created common cause for women (in Canada) with unions and indigenous peoples.

We have assumed that these processes are general. That is, they will also be applicable to other feminist movements and to movements in other substantive domains. It remains to be seen how generally applicable our conclusions may be for other movements by women in western industrial nations let alone feminist movements in other national contexts (but see Ray 1999 for similar divisions in the Indian women's movement). There is one major exception to these generalizations among the cases in this volume that suggests an explanation for the dramatically variable responses described here. Liberal feminists in the United States, described in this volume by Beckwith and Katzenstein, appear to have created such a vast network of associations that they have established themselves safely inside the outer boundaries of the polity. According to the arguments presented here, most of their core interests have not been undermined by state reconfiguration – despite serious

---

[12] This continuity of movement culture may form the context within which waves of feminism emerge. See, for instance, Whittier (1995) on generations of radical feminists. See also Castells (1997).

challenges to abortion rights. Employed, middle-class women have continued to rely on an associational superstructure to protect economic positions
that were won during the 1970s. If this is the case, then it appears that in-
flexibility is due largely to the successful institutionalization of employed,
middle-class women who are currently enjoying the fruits of their organizational efforts.[13] Thus, it may be that the resilience found elsewhere is due
largely to greater threats to the core values, identities, and agendas of other
strands of women's movements in North America and western Europe.

We remain cautious about whether the patterns described here will be
seen as other social movements confront state reconfiguration. How general
is the tactical and organizational adaptability we find across these several
women's movements in the face of changing political circumstances? Dieter
Rucht's comparative analysis of the changing character of five movements
associated with reconfiguration (this volume) provides us some tentative
answers. Although his analyses do not explicitly focus upon resiliency, they
do suggest that women's and environmental movements have shown far more
ability to adapt to changing political opportunities than have the labor, peace,
and antinuclear ones. So, it would seem, women's movements may be more
resilient in these respects than are other movements.

Why might this be the case? Is the resiliency we have identified the result
of factors external to the movement, or to internal factors? It may be the
case that, as Rucht argues, states respond to some classes of issues, ones
they view as inherently legitimate, in distinctive ways. If states are more
likely to respond to women's and environmental demands with regulatory
and institutionalizing approaches that encourage bargaining and adaptation,
then these movements may face very different political opportunity structures
than do other movements, even in the face of reconfiguration. Their apparent
adaptability may then simply reflect greater opportunities to adapt. Other
work (Smith 1997) suggests that the opportunities made available to different
movements by the transnationalization of authority and of responses through
the emerging network of international nongovernmental organizations (Keck
and Sikkink 1998) may vary considerably. To the extent that rewarding
opportunities to adapt are differentially available to different movements,
we will need to broaden our theoretical vision so that we do not mistake
movement/issue-specific responses and outcomes with more general adaptive
processes.

Women's and environmental movements are typically more decentralized
than other movements, based upon Rucht's analysis (this volume), and decentralized movements, he argues, tend to be more adaptable. And while
national women's movements vary among themselves in their level of decentralization, the continuing international vitality of the three cultural clusters

---

[13] As Myra Marx Ferree points out, this raises the question of whether there is not a natural
affinity between neoliberalism and liberal feminism (private communication).

we have discussed appears to exert an ongoing influence toward decentralization on national women's movements by nurturing a diversity of approaches. The same seems to be the case for environmental movements, where several coherent cultural frames continue to shape several organizationally distinct national branches of them (Brulle 2000; Rucht 1989). Following this logic it seems reasonable to suggest that women's movements tend to be more decentralized than other national movements, all things being equal, importantly as a result of their continuous cultural diversity. And that cultural diversity, therefore, serves indirectly to enhance women's movements' structural flexibility.

Interactions between Social Movements and States in Comparative Perspective*

Dieter Rucht

Interactions between social movements and states in the western hemisphere varied dramatically across the second half of the twentieth century, ranging from cooperation to tough bargaining to the use of violence. This variation is not, however, random across conflict issues and countries. Some movements may, by their very nature, be more aggressive than others. Certain states, by their historically rooted respect for the rule of law and their understanding of democratic rights, may be more tolerant and responsive to movement demands than are others. Even contemplating the same movement or a host of movements in the same country, we may find that their interactions vary considerably over time. Hence the question arises of whether or not one can identify specific patterns of movement-state interactions. If so, what factors account for such patterns?

This chapter seeks to provide answers to these two questions. Although the scope and complexity of the subject under study will not allow for a comprehensive and systematic description, let alone an exhaustive explanation, some empirical evidence and tentative explanations can be offered which put the interactions between women's movements and states into context by comparing them with other movements' interactions with states. The emphasis is more on comparison across movements than across time and space, although the latter two dimensions will also be considered.

This chapter is divided into three main sections. First, movement-state interactions for five movements in West Germany[1] will be described, focusing on issues of women, labor, peace, the environment, and nuclear power.

* I am grateful to the authors of this volume, in particular Lee Ann Banaszak and Karen Beckwith, for comments on earlier versions of this chapter. I also wish to thank all those who were involved, within the framework of the Prodat project in Germany, in the collection of protest event data, and Lee Ann Banaszak and Karen Beckwith for helping me with the English language version of this chapter.
[1] Germany here refers to West Germany since 1949 and, from 1990 onward, the unified Germany.

Second, this perspective will be broadened by references to other western countries in order to determine whether or not the findings for Germany are part of a more general pattern. Third, the factors that may underlie movement-state interactions will be discussed with special attention to the environmental and the women's movements. A brief overview of the general societal and political context in West Germany is provided before turning to the discussion of interactions between movements and the state.

POLITICAL CULTURE, POWER RELATIONS, AND THE STATE IN GERMANY

Few observers would doubt that Germany, at least in the postwar period, was still strongly shaped by an authoritarian heritage that goes back at least to the nineteenth century. In earlier writings, Germany's political culture was far from being characterized as truly democratic and liberal (Almond and Verba 1965; Dahrendorf 1968; Greiffenhagen and Greiffenhagen 1981), although, by 1949, all formal democratic institutions were in place and the state was decentralized to a large degree. From the very beginning, the newly created market economy was conceived as a *social* market economy (*Soziale Marktwirtschaft*), which gave great weight to state interventions. Moreover, some economic sectors were mostly or entirely controlled by the state so that several observers classified the economy as "mixed," being composed of a competitive market sector, an oligopolist market sector, and a monopolist state sector (Habermas 1973).

Together with the great significance of the state for many aspects of economic and social life, political parties also acquired such an important role in both constitutional and practical terms that the German system was dubbed a "party state." Major interest groups had, and still have, close links with political parties: trade unions with the Social Democratic Party; farmer organizations, business organizations, and the Catholic church with the conservative Christian Democratic Party; and some small enterprises and craft associations with the Liberal Party. The left-right cleavage, highly salient in the Weimar Republic, has lost much of its significance in the Bonn Republic, particularly since the Social Democrats officially abandoned their anticapitalist stance with the *Godesberger Programm* in 1959. Nevertheless, the left-right divide still remains the major cleavage, although it has been gradually offset by other cleavages, most notably that between materialism and post-materialism (Fuchs 1991). Given the existence of a major conservative and a social-democratic bloc with only a minor liberal party in between, political analysts, with good reason, referred to it as a "two-and-a-half-party system." Both from a domestic and an external viewpoint, this system was perceived as politically stable and economically viable. Due to its economic success, the average living standard constantly improved (Glatzer 1999). The widely accepted welfare state provided a substantial transfer of incomes and other forms of support for those who were economically deprived. Germany was a typical example of a corporatist version of a Keynesian state.

This apparently successful model experienced its first significant turbulence when the so-called extraparliamentary opposition gained momentum during the Grand Coalition of the conservative and social democratic parties from 1966–9. Headed by New Left groups and mainly supported by student activists, significant elements of a new generation began to question the status quo. They challenged the corporatist, elitist, and bureaucratized power structure, capitalist and imperialist exploitation (including the military engagement of western states in third-world countries), the rigidity, hypocrisy, and shallowness of bourgeois values and lifestyles, and silence in the face of the remnants of the Nazi regime.[2] After a relatively short but impressive revolt, this anticapitalist and antiauthoritarian movement rapidly decayed. It split apart into various pieces, chief among them a radical and eventually terrorist strand, a cluster of communist sects that engaged in bitter ideological struggles, many reform-minded activists who joined the Social Democratic Party and, most importantly, a considerable number of activists who inspired and fueled the so-called new social movements (Brand, Büsser, and Rucht 1986; Koopmans 1995; Roth 1994), including the second wave of the women's movement.

The new coalition of the Social Democratic Party and the Liberal Party that came into power in 1969 initiated a series of reforms. The Liberals were geared to modernize the state apparatus, strengthen citizen participation, and "normalize" the relationship with the East European communist bloc in general and East Germany in particular. With the exception of the latter aim, the reforms that had raised so many hopes largely failed in these years. Dissatisfaction and criticism rose. Moreover, the German economy, like those of most other western countries, exhibited shrinking growth rates and increasing unemployment. The "Model Germany" (Markovits 1982), as it was promoted by Social Democratic Chancellor Helmut Schmidt, came under dual pressure from the new social movements on one side and the ascendant neoconservatives and neoliberals on the other. Although the Social Democrats remained in federal government until the end of 1982, the overall power constellation had already begun to change. Yet even after the conservatives came to power, there was never a sharp political and ideological turn as with the neoconservatives in the United States and Great Britain (Pierson 1996). Nevertheless, from the mid-1970s on, the corporatist structure represented by the elites of the state, labor, and capital began to lose its stability

---

[2] It is important to mention two facts in this context. First, some representatives of the Nazi regime had managed to obtain public offices in the Bonn Republic. Second, during the period of the Grand Coalition, the rightist nationalist party NPD (*Nationaldemokratische Partei Deutschlands*) achieved considerable electoral success in several states, and, with 4.3% of the vote, was close to surpassing the 5% threshold for entering the German *Bundestag*.

and centrality. Gradually the state was restructured very much along the lines discussed in the first chapter of this volume. To a much lesser degree than, for example, in the United Kingdom, West Germany experienced processes of up- and downloading as well as offloading. The rhetoric of neoliberalism gained ground, though mitigated by a continuous commitment of even the conservative parties, in principle, to support of the welfare state.

The state, along with the system of parties and interest groups, became more open, more fragmented and diversified, and in some respects more participatory and responsive to the new social movements' demands. Two new parties, the Greens and later the socialist PDS (Party of Democratic Socialism, the successor of the former East German Communist Party), entered the lower house of Parliament (*Bundestag*) in 1983 and 1990, respectively. To some extent, this changing power constellation can also be attributed to the aggregate effect of many interactions between social movements and the state.

COMPARING PATTERNS OF STATE-MOVEMENT INTERACTIONS IN WEST GERMANY

Interactions between Selected Movements and the State in Germany

The Women's Movement

The "first" German women's movement, which was quite active until the Nazis seized power in 1933, never fully recovered after World War II. The few organizations that were revitalized or newly created remained small and insignificant. The political establishment promoted a conservative family policy based on the ideal of male breadwinners and caring wives and mothers at home.[3] In legal terms, with few exceptions, women were treated as equal to men. In practice, the degree of inequality was enormous.

This gap was the main reason for the rise of a "second wave" of women's and feminist groups that came into existence with the student revolt in the late 1960s. No bridge existed between those radical groups and the traditional women's groups, including some Old Left women's organizations (Schenk 1981). Initially, the first radical women's groups considered themselves as an integral part of the New Left. Very soon they moved from theoretical debates to practical concerns such as organizing antiauthoritarian collective childcare (*Kinderläden*) and, starting in the early 1970s, seeking to liberalize abortion. Abortion was the key issue that broadened the basis of the emerging second women's movement, bringing the radical autonomous women's groups into limited contact with women in established parties, trade unions, and civil rights organizations and leading to direct conflicts between women's groups and the state (Rucht 1994: ch. 8). However, with the exception of the

---

[3] Note that until 1957 a married woman needed the consent of her husband for employment.

abortion issue, the autonomous women's groups kept themselves apart from the established women's organizations inside and outside parties, unions, and churches. The autonomous women's groups developed a fundamental critique of patriarchy, including the role of the state as a tool for maintaining male domination. Their ultimate goal was women's liberation. They never accepted the idea of formal national organizations that could represent the diversity of groups and, therefore, fiercely maintained their autonomy (Ferree 1987). They also overwhelmingly rejected the occasional attempts to form a women's party. The more established liberal women's organizations, hardly perceiving themselves as part of a women's movement and keeping a very low profile, mildly criticized some forms of discrimination and inequality, which, they believed, could be overcome by working within the established institutions, including the state. Striving for more equality, these women saw men more as potential partners than as oppressive opponents.

In surveying the 1970s it becomes clear that there was not much interaction between women's groups and the state. The only significant exception is the abortion issue, which was formally settled in 1976 with a somewhat more liberal law (Ferree et al. 2002). The established women's groups, maintaining their low profile, worked within the institutions without much clamor or success. If there was interaction on behalf of women's issues, it was mainly the male-dominated umbrella organizations, and not their women's sections, that dealt with state authorities. The strategy of these organizations was clearly assimilative. The autonomous feminist movement, in spite (and probably also because) of its radical critique of the patriarchal state, did not enter the terrain of established policies to challenge the state. Instead, feminists sought to establish their own infrastructure and to offer services for needy women. The feminist strategy in this period was confrontational in theory and principle, but it was more a confrontation in daily life and on cultural grounds than in the policy arena. Even the streets were not widely used as an arena of contestation. Only occasionally did feminist groups stage provocative protest actions. The majority, however, preferred to exchange their experiences in consciousness-raising groups and to offer practical help, for example, for battered women. No wonder then that no significant new institutions on behalf of women were introduced into the public administration, few parliamentary debates on women's policies were held, and no coherent women's policy took shape.

Given this situation, the state and the established parties could remain relatively passive. Because there was no direct and strong challenge no strategy had to be developed. The more liberal forces, simply ignoring the feminist critique, rhetorically embraced moderate and reformist claims to give women a better standing without, however, making much effort to put them into practice. The conservative forces defended the status quo, hoping that the wave of women's groups would be a temporary fashion that would soon fade away.

During the 1980s and 1990s, this situation gradually changed. First, with a conservative government in power by 1982–3, increasing economic problems, and a growing emphasis on traditional values promoted by right-wing forces, it became obvious that there was to be no automatic progress in terms of women's issues. The major issues regarding equal rights remained unresolved and new problems, such as high female unemployment, were added. Women's groups both outside and inside the institutions felt that they needed a higher profile and a broadening of their strategic repertoire.

Second, these two strands began to talk to each other and, occasionally, to form alliances. This was possible because, on the one hand, the women within the institutions, perceiving their limited impact, gradually radicalized their demands, whereas, on the other hand, the autonomous feminist groups moderated their antiinstitutional stance and valued the importance of engaging in conventional politics. Last but not least, many young women who, mainly as students, had been politically socialized within radical women's groups were now in professions and, in part, occupied positions within (public) administration,[4] parties, universities, welfare organizations, and professional groups in which they could exert some influence. These women had a better understanding of the mechanisms of established politics, including a sense of the limits to a strategy of bringing about social change "from within," but they also developed a better understanding of how to use formal institutional positions to advance the cause of women.

Most activities and interchanges of this sort took place at the local level. Local administrations became ready to finance women's projects and, after a short but heated debate about the potential danger of accepting state money in the early 1980s (*Staatsknetedebatte*), most autonomous women's groups welcomed this financial support. Women's offices for equality (*Frauengleichstellungsbüros*) were established in virtually all major cities (Wiechmann and Kißler 1997).

From the local to the national and EU levels, the Green Party, with its strong emphasis on women's issues and the internal representation of women, helped to accelerate the building of bridges between women outside and inside the institutions. In general, women activists became more self-conscious and visible in established politics. Women's issues were treated more seriously and gains were made in many respects and on all political levels, as evidenced by the passing of laws and regulations supportive to women, the (slowly!) rising number of women in higher positions, and growing awareness of the continuing problems of discrimination and violence against women.

Overall, interactions between the women's movement and the state increased, intensified, and became nearly ubiquitous. Today, the dominant

---

[4] Nevertheless, it would be an exaggeration to talk in the case of Germany of a sizable number of "state feminists" or "femocrats."

pattern of interaction is conflictual, but the conflicts are mostly confined to institutional settings; a close observer of the German women's movement referred to this as the "NGOization of Feminism" and its "adaptation to the existing pillars of society and politics" (Lang 1997: 116). Negotiation and bargaining have become a matter of routine. The few but highly symbolic confrontational encounters and clashes that characterized the 1970s have become even rarer. And where these occur, for example, when women who have had illegal abortions publicize their acts, they no longer provoke the same strong reaction as they did in the past.

It is not easy to assess whether, in an overall perspective, the stakes of the conflict have changed to the same degree as the patterns of interaction. On the one hand, many of the once radical feminists have also softened their critique of patriarchy and the role of the state. Some of them, inspired by the relative success of "femocrats" in other countries (Stetson and Mazur 1995), no longer perceive state power as inherently repressive but rather as a tool that, in some instances and to some extent, can be used to promote the women's cause (Hernes 1987; Kolberg 1991). From a truly radical perspective, this in itself could be interpreted as a result of cooptation and thus as a sign of defeat. On the other hand, parts of the liberal strand of the women's movement have broadened and deepened their view of women's discrimination and accepted many of the insights of the autonomous movement. This, together with indications of progress in women's policies, could be interpreted as a partial success that could well lay the groundwork for further advances.

The Labor Movement

Since the end of the nineteenth century, the German labor movement, perceived as extraordinarily strong and well organized, has served as a model for movement organizers in many other countries. The historical movement consisted of three pillars: 1) the trade unions; 2) cooperatives for food or housing and leisure organizations (for example, sports, hiking, cycling, or singing groups); and 3) the Social Democratic and, at a later point, the Communist Party. With the seizure of power by the Nazi movement, this whole infrastructure was crushed or taken over to serve other purposes. Unlike the women's movement, however, the labor movement was quickly reorganized after World War II. In organizational terms, the movement soon reached or even surpassed its previous strength, though it was mainly reduced to the single pillar of trade unions. This reduction was partly a result of the decay of a vital and distinct workers' culture in the postwar period (Mooser 1984), but was also a consequence of the estrangement between the Social Democratic Party (SPD) and the very minor communist parties (Kommunistische Partei Deutschlands and its successor Deutsche Kommunistische Partei). The distance from the communists became apparent when, in the climate of the Cold War, the vast majority of the trade unions flatly rejected the communist ideology. The much less distinct dissociation of the trade unions from the Social Democratic Party was a result of a pragmatic division of labor, but also of the transformation of this party toward being a broad "people's party" (*Volkspartei*), seeking to represent social groups more than just workers. Similarly, the party also compromised with capitalism earlier and to a greater extent than did the trade unions in subsequent decades.

Given this situation, Germany's labor movement has become largely identical with the trade unions. The backbone of the unions consists of a single umbrella organization, the *Deutscher Gewerkschaftsbund* (DGB) (Markovits 1986). It is internally differentiated by industrial branches, which enjoy partial autonomy and constitute the real organizational strongholds. Overall, the DGB has had a relatively stable membership over the last decades with the exception of an increase during German unification. More recently, however, there has been a significant decline of membership, to approximately eight million in 2000. The whole organization is hierarchical, well structured and well staffed. The DGB is the major representative of the German workforce and the key actor representing workers in most labor conflicts, whether they be strikes, negotiations with the employers, or interactions with the state. Few conflicts with employers, aside from wildcat strikes and rare conflicts with the state, are beyond the control of the unions.

In spite of the fact that leftist critics of the labor unions describe them as pacified and supportive of the status quo, it would be an overstatement to classify the strategy of the labor movement as entirely assimilative. It is certainly true that the movement has nearly fully accepted the existing political order and, to a large but significantly lesser extent, the economic order as well. The movement has occasionally engaged in substantial political issues. For instance, it was initially very critical of the rearmament of Germany around the mid-1950s, of the passing of the Emergency Laws (*Notstandsgesetze*) in the second half of the 1960s, and of the NATO double-track decision in the early 1980s. In each of these cases, particularly when conflict threatened to escalate, and the broadening of issues led toward a more fundamental critique of the existing order, the unions shied away from open confrontation (Cooper 1995). Nevertheless, there were other, more labor-centered conflicts in which the unions took a strong stance against the political mainstream, including state authorities, or engaged in direct confrontation with employer associations (for example, the campaign for the thirty-five-hour work week or conflicts about wages, plant closures, and security standards). In many of these instances, the unions were backed by the SPD, which made it part of a powerful alliance.

The force of the unions as a potential reservoir of voters, protesters, and strikers becomes apparent not only in distinct conflicts and campaigns but also in structural arrangements with both employers and the state. This is true for laws that regulate participation at the workplace and the rights and limits to strike, but also for the representation of trade unions in state and semistate bodies, which, for example, advise governmental agencies (for example, the Federal Office for Labor) and control public television and radio. This is likewise the case for many semiformal or informal circles of negotiation and bargaining in which state, capital, and labor elites coordinate their activities. With good reason, Germany has been described as a clear-cut (neo-)corporatist system (Lehmbruch and Schmitter 1979) in which the leadership of the labor movement engages in crucial decisions and is integrated into the overall system but, as a consequence, is restrained in its activities or challenges to existing institutions. This corporatist configuration had already lost some of its significance by the second half of the 1970s, but tends to be reactivated when it comes to key economic decisions. Given the power of the trade unions, it is not surprising that the state and, more specifically, the government (even if conservative) shies away from harsh confrontation with the unions.

Overall, the quality of the interactions between the labor movement and state cannot be captured by one term. In some cases, the interactions are unabashedly cooperative. For instance, in the 1970s, the unions and the state acted side by side in promoting and implementing a governmental program on the "humanization of labor" which, among other things, tried to make the working place safer, healthier, and less stressful. In a few other cases, particularly when the unions went beyond their immediate economic concerns, the state and the unions engaged in open confrontation, although these confrontations hardly ever resulted in the use of violence. In most remaining cases, however, the interactions were conflictual, although confined to fairly regulated institutional settings such as litigation. Incidents of conflictual interaction have been more frequent when a conservative government is in power, as was the case from late 1982 to fall 1998. Yet, in spite of the relatively large number of conflicts in which it has engaged, the labor movement has relinquished its historical vision of a new social order. Typically the movement's protest does not go beyond routinized and even ritualized action (Rucht 2001). Although the movement may occasionally surprise and even impress its opponents, it no longer represents a fundamental challenge.

The Peace Movement

The peace movement in Germany in the twentieth century has a discontinuous history. Its waves of mobilization were largely bound to contingent decisions such as entering World War I, rearming Germany by the mid-1950s, attempting to equip the army with atomic weapons in 1957–8, escalating the war in Vietnam in the second half of the 1960s, deploying new nuclear missiles in western Europe in the early 1980s, initiating the Gulf War in 1991, and engaging in the wars in the former Yugoslavia in the 1990s.

Few and relatively weak organizations have worked continuously over the last decades, and only three of these preceded the Nazi regime. In Germany, the movement's mobilization was impressive in terms of numbers, but also erratic and short lived. Whenever a crucial decision was taken (whether positive or negative), mobilization rapidly declined. The only exceptions to this rule were the Vietnam War, which, while not involving Germany directly, gradually attracted growing resistance,[5] and the war in the former Yugoslavia. In the latter case, from the viewpoint of the peace movement, it was difficult to distinguish between the good guys and the bad guys. Moreover, the German state was only marginally and indirectly involved up until the recent war in Kosovo, an involvement that was not based on any single decision that might have focused the energies of the protesters.

The very nature and conditions of the peace movement have strong implications for its persistence, structure, and strategies. Given its reactive and erratic patterns of mobilization, together with the fact that, unlike the women's and labor movements, the peace movement has no "natural" constituency, the movement has lacked continuous and strong organizations that are rooted in a particular social environment. Moreover, matters of war and peace are usually at the discretion of national governments and/or parliaments. This makes it particularly hard for local groups to find leverage and to survive in periods when the peace issue is no longer on the national agenda. As a consequence, we find a distinctive pattern of high but short visibility and longer phases of latency or even complete inactivity.

In the periods of high mobilization, the few, relatively weak peace organizations are just one component of a much broader network of organizations and informal groups that, in other times, may have different primary concerns (for example parties, trade unions, churches, women's groups, Third World groups). The bloc recruitment of such broad alliances together with the appeal to unaffiliated but concerned individuals quickly produces a mass movement but only for a short time. When the issue is settled or no policy impact has been achieved, mobilization fades away and most of the groups return to their original concerns, leaving behind the minute core of committed peace activists who act as moral entrepreneurs rather than professional organizers.

This pattern also has implications for interactions between the movement and the state. The typical arenas during the high tide of the movement are the streets and the mass media. Because of their formal responsibility for matters of armament, war, and peace, it is the state and, more particularly, the national governments that are the main targets of the movement. Objectively, it is a confrontational situation because the movement usually wants exactly the opposite of what the state does. In practice, however, there were very few direct interactions between the movement and the state, apart from the state's role in policing the protests.

Peace movements' potential strengths rest on two strategies: first, to impress the wider public and politicians by the "power in numbers"

---

[5] Participation in the Easter marches increased from several hundred in 1960 to 350,000 in 1968 (Leif 1985).

(DeNardo 1985), that is the sheer mass of adherents that can be mobilized; and, second, to use "self-limited" confrontational tactics, such as blockades or other forms of civil disobedience. It is crucial that a movement that praises the virtue of peace and civility remain below the threshold of violence. Otherwise, it would not only lose its credibility among the mass public but would also legitimize state repression, which, given the sensitive nature of military issues for the state as a whole, may be more severe than in most other issues. Beyond these strategies, the peace movement has few opportunities to interact with the state. Defense policy is a special area where a few national political leaders take decisions behind closed doors. There is no way of downloading, let alone offloading, power and executive tasks, as in other policy areas. With the possible exception of some institutes of conflict and peace research, the movement has no bridgehead within the established institutions. Influencing political decisions requires working indirectly and without the existence of permanent channels of communication, of the types that exist for the labor movement and, to a lesser extent, for the women's and environmental movements. These indirect attempts to influence policy making usually bear fruit only over longer periods, whereas decisions on international conflicts tend to be taken quickly. The other challenge for peace movements is that their reliance on established actors – in Germany, mostly leftist parties and trade unions – can make them vulnerable to shifts of opinions within these established organizations. For instance, it was a bitter lesson for the German peace movement to see the withdrawal of the Social Democrats and trade unions from the struggle against rearmament in the 1950s (which they had originally backed), leaving the movement with almost no infrastructure and no resources (Rupp 1970).

The German peace movement, in general and despite its massive mobilization in some periods, has been in a weak position and has had little policy impact. This was true even after 1983, when the Greens were in the national parliament. The only exception to this general experience was the campaign against nuclear rearmament in 1958.[6]

To summarize, the interactions between the peace movement and the German state have been restricted to relatively short periods in which much mobilization but no negotiation took place. Physical encounters between representatives of the movement and the political decisionmakers were rare. Unlike movements in other policy fields, the peace movement, despite its mass support (albeit only temporarily), remained an outsider with no institutional leverage, no strong organizational base, and no accumulated experience. Given the fundamental dissent between the movement and the government,

---

[6] In 1958, a number of distinguished natural scientists publicly criticized the government for its attempts to obtain nuclear weapons. Instead, they suggested using nuclear energy for civil purposes only. It was the initiative of this small but highly regarded group, and not the masses in the streets, that eventually persuaded the government to pull back.

there was no way to cooperate. Movement mobilization concentrated on street action, mostly with no direct opponent. Confrontational direct interaction was limited to encounters between protesters and the police.

The Environmental and Antinuclear Movements

The "new" environmental movement started about the same time as the second wave of the women's movement (Brand 1999). Like the feminists, the environmentalists only later discovered and appreciated their historical forerunners. Unlike the new women's movement, however, the environmental movement received wider and quicker support from state authorities.[7] In some respects, state initiatives even preceded or preempted the emerging movement, with initial environmental programs dating from the early 1970s. Similar to its counterparts in many other countries, the German environmental movement was also inspired by international initiatives, such as the UN conference on the environment that took place in Stockholm in 1972. In addition, reports and warnings of concerned scientists spurred environmental action both within and outside the state.

Soon after local environmental groups began to flourish, they formed regional and national alliances. Over the years, the movement has developed a complex organizational structure (Rucht 1991; Rucht and Roose 2001). Its major components are a) autonomous local and regional environmental groups, b) nationwide membership organizations with state, district, and local sections, c) professional action groups, such as Greenpeace, that work mainly through the mass media and rely on the support of financial donors, d) foundations, e) scientific groups and institutes supported by the movement, and f) the Green Party, which, in electoral terms, is probably the most successful in the world.[8]

The environmental movement's issues, strategies, and ways of interacting with the state vary as much as its organizational forms. Some of the first local groups to organize were primarily concerned with the global dimension of environmental problems (for example, the pollution of the oceans); others dealt mainly with local environmental problems. As these groups became increasingly aware of each other, they began to understand their particular issue to be part of a wider and interconnected problem.

In general, the state was sympathetic to the idea of environmentalism. One major national environmental organization, the *Bundesverband Bürgerinitiativen Umweltschutz*, was founded with the help of state officials in 1972. Moreover, environmental advisory groups and governmental agencies

---

[7] An exception is probably the United States where governmental initatives in the first half of the 1960s preceded rather than followed the rise of the new women's movement.

[8] An exception to this overall pattern is the antinuclear movement, which consists mainly of local and regional groups that form a loose nationwide network without any formal structure at the national level.

were created in the 1970s, most notably the *Umweltbundesamt* (a kind of environmental protection agency) and environmental departments in several (and eventually all) state governments.[9] The movement was instrumental to the launch of the first series of environmental laws in the second half of the 1970s (see Weidner 1995), although these laws cannot be attributed primarily to the environmental movement, which, with the exception of the issue of nuclear energy, was not yet powerful at the national level.

Despite the state's engagement in environmental matters, environmental groups faced tough opposition in concrete struggles, particularly when large-scale infrastructure projects such as highways, airports, and nuclear plants were at stake. In many of these cases, state authorities, private enterprises, and major sections of the trade unions stood against the environmentalists, blaming them for blocking economic and technical progress and for threatening jobs (Jahn 1993). Between the mid-1970s and the mid-1980s, the environmental debate was overshadowed by significant and tenacious struggles which tended to include a broad range of movement tactics, such as mass demonstrations, petitions, litigation, local and statewide referenda,[10] boycotts, blockades, arson, and violent clashes with police forces. The conflict over nuclear power was, and still is, by far the most confrontational issue. In some instances of antinuclear protests, observers even feared their escalation to the level of civil war.

Behind these notable conflicts, however, many environmental groups engaged in less spectacular activities and promoted nonconflictual proposals (for example, on how to save energy, to reduce waste, and to live in healthier ways). Particularly at the local level, environmental groups began to cooperate with state authorities on issues that, by their very nature, are not conducive to polarization. The growing trend of cooperation and negotiation with the state has been extended, in recent years, to include parts of industry. Confrontation nonetheless continues. Even after thirty years of struggle, the antinuclear issue remains unresolved. Although plans were announced (and eventually agreed upon in 2001) to phase out nuclear power gradually across the next thirty years, the antinuclear movement has turned against nuclear waste facilities and the transport of nuclear waste. Given the most recent clashes with police forces in the years of 1995–7 and 2000, there are no signs of an institutionalization of the conflict that has occurred in other policy fields. Moreover, animal rights activists and opponents of outdoor genetic experiments have occasionally used violent tactics and have apparently developed underground structures. These radical groups are fairly marginal, but their existence and activities make it difficult to characterize the environmental movement as entirely pacifist.

---

[9] A federal ministry for environmental protection, however, was only established in 1986 in the aftermath of the nuclear accident in Chernobyl.
[10] National referenda are not an option in Germany.

Comparing and Interpreting Patterns of Interaction

A summary of the general pattern of prevailing movement strategies over time shows that the labor movement in Germany was marked by assimilative strategies in both the 1970s and the 1990s, while the antinuclear and the peace movement tended toward confrontational strategies in both periods. In contrast, the environmental movement and the women's movement shifted from predominantly confrontational strategies in the 1970s to more assimilative strategies in the 1990s.

It is striking that, in the same state and overall context, the patterns of state-movement interaction exhibit a remarkable degree of variation across movements and time. This is especially remarkable because these five movements are situated in the progressive spectrum of left and left-libertarian movements (della Porta and Rucht 1995) and therefore should exhibit common traits. Furthermore, these movements overlap (for example, women's groups in labor, peace, and environmental movements) and organizations from different movements occasionally ally for common campaigns.

The fact that, in spite of these conditions, we do not find greater similarities across movements and/or time can be attributed to the following factors. First and foremost, it is important to note that only in a very formal sense was the same state involved. On closer inspection we see that any given state is not a uniform machinery with similar parts following the same principles. Instead, it is a complex network with different branches, interests, actors, levels, strategies, and power resources. Second, different movements representing different degrees and kinds of challenges frequently address themselves to different parts of the state evoking heterogeneous patterns of interaction. Third, the various movements differ widely in terms of their organizational strength, characteristics, and strategic preferences. Let us first take a closer look at these features and how they may affect movement/state interactions.

When a movement's *organizational strength* is measured in terms of regular members, money, staff, and infrastructure, the labor movement is by far the leader, followed by the environmental movement; the women's and peace movements, in contrast, are relatively weak. However, if we measure organizational strength in terms of the number of existing and active groups at the local level, the picture is quite different. The labor movement relies mainly on its paid staff and elected representatives in the shops but tends to have few volunteers. The women's movement has few paid staff, but, at least at the local level, routinely has more active groups than the environmental movement and the peace movement.[11]

---

[11] This is the case apart from the latters' phases of high tide, at least when looking at the social movement sector in Berlin (Rucht, Blattert, and Rink 1997).

TABLE 11.1. *Proportion of Protest Events of Five Movements, West Germany, 1970–1996 (Percentages)*

Kind of Movement	1970–9	1980–9	1990–6	1970–96
Women	2.6	1.7	1.1	1.8
Labor	17.9	17.0	18.0	17.6
Peace	6.6	18.2	9.4	12.0
Environment	2.0	8.8	5.1	5.5
Antinuclear	5.2	9.8	6.2	7.2
All other domains	65.7	44.5	60.2	56.0
TOTAL	100	100	100	100
N	3,008	3,599	2,551	9,158

In terms of a movement's *organizational structure*, again the labor movement is an outstanding case. Its adherents are paying members of one comprehensive organizational body with a hierarchical structure, elected representatives, formal statutes, offices, and educational centers. Moreover, the movement has close links to the Social Democratic Party. The women's movement and the antinuclear movement are just the opposite, both based on a loose network of mainly local groups and initiatives. They rely on no major national organization, and have no formal center of power or authorized speakers. Contrary to common assumptions, they lack strong links to any of the existing parties, including the Greens. In these respects, the peace movement approximates the pattern of the women's movement. The major difference, however, is that the peace movement is essentially a temporary coalition of progressive organizations and ad hoc groups that, after phases of high mobilization, turns to other concerns. By contrast, the environmental movement includes extremely different components that are woven loosely together, ranging from informal groups to nationwide to international membership organizations.

Since protest is the most visible and most crucial tool of social movements, it may be interesting to compare *protest activities* of the movements under consideration.[12] The relative weight of the *protest activities* of the five movements in different time periods can be seen from 1) the number of protest events and 2) the number of participants of each movement (Tables 11.1 and 11.2). For reasons of comparability over time, only data on West Germany (including West Berlin) are displayed.

[12] Here we can draw on a large data set from the so-called Prodat project (Documentation and Analysis of Protest Events in Germany) that is run under the auspices of the author. For detailed information about the design and data collection, see Rucht and Ohlemacher (1992) and Rucht and Neidhardt (1999). The following data are derived from a systematic sample (all weekend protests plus five workday protests in each fourth week) of two nationwide "quality newspapers," the *Süddeutsche Zeitung* and the *Frankfurter Rundschau*.

TABLE 11.2. *Proportion of Participants in Five Movements, West Germany,* *1970–1996 (Percentages)*

Kind of Movement	1970–9	1980–9	1990–6	1970–96
Women	0.8	0.7	0.4	0.6
Labor	13.7	11.6	8.8	11.0
Peace	6.4	51.9	6.3	28.0
Environment	11.3	9.2	10.7	10.1
Anti-nuclear	9.1	6.6	2.8	5.7
All other domains	58.7	20.0	70.1	44.7
TOTAL	100	100	100	100
N	6,735,966	18,331,825	10,864,996	35,932,787

Among the five movements considered here, labor[13] and peace involve the highest number of protest events in the period from 1970–96. In terms of numbers of protesters, however, the peace movement, with a 28% proportion of the total mobilization, has more presence than the labor movement. In terms of mobilizing protest, women's issues range extremely low with a proportion of 1.9% out of all protests and only 0.6% out of all protesters. Another interesting finding is that the antinuclear issue attracts more protest (but fewer protesters) than all other environmental issues.

Compared across time, only the proportion of labor protests out of all protest events remains nearly constant, while peace, environmental, and antinuclear movement protests peaked in the 1980s. In terms of the number of people mobilized, the peace movement stands out in the 1980s with 51.9% of the total mobilization. Women, labor, environmental, and antinuclear movements attract lower proportions of participants over time.

What is the relative weight of confrontational and violent protests within these movement domains? As Table 11.3 shows, the labor movement is extraordinarily peaceful, with a tiny proportion of violent protests in the whole period under investigation. Surprisingly, with 5.7% violent protests and 14.7% confrontational protests, the peace movement is not as peaceful as its name suggests. Clearly, antinuclear protests are by far the most unruly when confrontational and violent activities are taken together. Compared to the 1970s, protests on issues of women and labor have become less disruptive, for the first half of the 1990s, while the opposite holds for the antinuclear issue.

---

[13] Consider, however, that labor protests are underrepresented. Strike activity is often lumped together in summary reports that do not allow identification of the time and place of concrete incidents of protests. In these cases, protests are not coded. According to well-grounded estimates, the number of labor protests should be roughly doubled.

TABLE 11.3. *Proportion of Confrontational and Violent Protests by Movement, West Germany, 1970–1996 (Percentages*)*

Protest Domain	Confrontational				Violent			
	1970–9	1980–9	1990–6	1970–96	1970–9	1980–9	1990–6	1970–96
Women	6.3	3.3	3.6	4.8	1.3	13.1	0.0	5.4
Labor	6.3	3.8	3.0	4.4	0.0	0.8	0.2	0.4
Peace	6.5	17.2	14.6	14.7	7.5	6.4	2.1	5.7
Environment	6.8	15.9	17.0	15.1	1.7	16.5	4.6	11.7
Antinuclear	15.3	26.2	27.7	23.9	2.6	11.2	20.8	11.4
All other domains	12.7	19.1	15.7	15.8	3.6	13.2	26.5	10.6
TOTAL	13.8	19.3	16.4	14.6	5.3	11.6	22.0	7.6
N	331	585	327	1,243	128	352	441	921

* Out of all protests per period.

TABLE 11.4. *Level and Target of Protests by Movements, West Germany,*
1970–1996 (Percentages)

Level of Mobilization	Women	Labor	Peace	Environment	Antinuclear
Local/regional	38.7	66.3	44.5	40.4	45.0
State	19.0	19.5	17.8	22.1	22.1
National	39.3	13.5	28.1	33.4	26.2
International	3.0	0.7	9.6	4.2	6.7
TOTAL	100	100	100	100	100
N	168	1,610	1,096	503	656
Target of Mobilization					
State	62.1	37.6	94.3	60.6	70.4
Parties	0.9	1.4	0.8	0.4	1.6
Employers/firms	12.1	59.6	1.0	30.2	25.6
Other interest groups	8.6	0.7	0.9	0.7	0.9
Other targets/unclear	16.4	0.8	2.9	8.1	1.4
TOTAL	100	100	100	100	100
N	116	1,424	971	454	554

Finally, we can compare the movement protests with respect to their levels of mobilization and their main targets (see Table 11.4).[14] Besides the environmental movement, the women's movement has a surprisingly strong emphasis on national mobilization when compared to the other movements. Labor protests, in contrast, involve mostly local and regional mobilization. In four out of the five protest domains, the state is by far the most important target. As one might expect, it is the overriding target for the peace movement, whereas nearly 60% of labor protests concentrate on employers/firms, followed by 37.6% focusing on the state.

Most protests, particularly those that are confrontational or violent, occur in the streets. Therefore, the numbers presented above do not adequately reflect the preferred arenas of interaction. Drawing on qualitative descriptive material, it is clear that the peace movement is a special case insofar as it is mainly geared to street action and influencing the mass media. The physical presence of masses of protesters is the key tool of the peace movement, as shown by its extraordinary mobilization (although only for brief periods). Given the high number of women's groups, on the one hand, and their low profile in terms of protest as registered in protest event analysis, on the other, it becomes clear that the women's movement focuses primarily on settings of

[14] Only the national sections of newspapers have been scanned to assess level of mobilization. As a consequence, small and local protests are underrepresented across all protest domains.

interaction other than the streets and the media, such as direct negotiations with public administration, parliamentary hearings, and committees. In contrast, both the labor movement and the environmental movement are present in every arena: that is, streets, courts, parliaments, committees, and advisory boards.

Summarizing movement-state interaction in Germany, several points should be stressed. First, comparing various movements, significantly different patterns of interactions with the state are evident. Second, even though the state may have shown little change in its overall structural and institutional setting, there are considerable changes in the relationship and exchanges with some movements over time. This underlines Tarrow's (1996) observation of "dynamic opportunities" which are not simply given, but, at least in some cases, can be shaped by social movements. Overall, it seems that the German state has become more permeable to those movements whose demands are not so much a matter of either/or (for example, war or peace; nuclear power yes/no) but rather of more or less, as is the case with the labor, environmental, and women's movements. Salaries, emission standards, and quotas for women are negotiable and suited to compromise. Hence these latter movements are, in contrast to the peace and antinuclear movements, engaged in more-or-less continuous interactions with the state – interactions that are marked by cooperation and conflict but little confrontation.

BROADENING THE PICTURE: MOVEMENT-STATE INTERACTIONS
IN OTHER COUNTRIES

Are the patterns found in Germany unique or similar to those in other western countries? Unfortunately we do not have the same detailed data on movement activities over several decades for other countries that we have for Germany. However, we can organize limited data that will provide an outline of the broader picture.

Women's Movements and States

The quality of interaction between women's movements and states has changed since the emergence of the second wave of women's movements in most western countries. By and large, the pattern described for Germany also holds for most other western countries.

The late sixties and early seventies were a period in which new feminist groups in most western countries engaged in marked conflicts, including an array of provocative activities (Kaplan 1992; Katzenstein and Mueller 1987; Rucht 1994). The radical branches of the women's movements overshadowed the more traditional and liberal groupings, mounting challenges to both the state and parts of civil society by attacking persistent inequalities in the workplace, restricted access of women to various professions and institutions, restrictive abortion laws, and hypocrisy and double standards in matters of sexuality (for example, contraception). Feminists publicly threw their bras and high-heeled shoes into a "freedom trash can," invaded meetings reserved for men only, disrupted beauty contests by presenting sheep as possible contestants, and organized counseling and trips for obtaining (illegal) abortions. Some groups such as the Danish Redstockings and the Dutch Dolle Minna gained a particular reputation for such provocative activities. In countries such as Italy and France, socialist and communist women's organizations also staged confrontational actions similar to those of the autonomous radical feminists. Many of these actions did not specifically target the state but rather were intended to create a more general awareness of the pervasiveness of patriarchy in all spheres of public and private life. Overall, interactions of the feminist groups with the state were confrontational and hostile. "Autonomy...and disruptive protest...are women's movements' strategic responses to closedness" (Beckwith this volume). Since the state was perceived as an integral part of the suppressive patriarchic system, radical feminists saw themselves as outsiders whose task was not to seek compromise but to mount challenges. Similarly, state institutions had little if any incentive to engage in talks with their radical critics, let alone to provide support to them.

It is difficult to conclude that women's movements were significantly more confrontational in some countries than in others in North America and western Europe during this period. It is clear, however, that the less radical and predominantly reform-minded branches of the women's movements had different weight in various countries, being relatively strong in North America and Scandinavia, but less so in Britain, France, Belgium, Germany, Austria, Switzerland, and Italy, let alone the authoritarian regimes of the 1970s in Greece, Spain, and Portugal (Kaplan 1992).

By the 1990s, this picture had changed considerably. The radical feminists were still there, but they were no longer concentrating on provocative tactics.[15] Interactions between women's movements and states shifted from confrontation to conflict and even cooperation which, for the most part, has now become almost routine. Radical feminists are taken more seriously than before by the political elites and sometimes have managed to obtain positions within the state apparatus. In addition, in many countries women's groups and projects, such as help lines and houses for battered women, are partially or fully state funded, though not necessarily always state controlled. This is particularly true for the Scandinavian countries (for Sweden, see Elman 1996b; Elman this volume), several central European countries, Spain, and, to a limited extent, North America. Britain and France seem to be exceptions to this rule, but for different reasons. In France, the autonomous women's movement has become extremely weak since the late 1970s, while at the same time much of the activity around women's issues – among these the campaign for parity – has shifted to the leftist parties (see Jenson and Valiente this

---

[15] Canada appears to be an exception to the general picture. Since the 1980s, the women's movement in Canada has radicalized (see Dobrowolsky in this volume).

volume). In Great Britain, the state is traditionally reluctant to support autonomous groups of whatever kind so that they tend to remain largely outside the political institutions and policy networks (Lovenduski and Randall 1993).

Overall, it appears that the changes in interactions between women's movements and states over time are more salient than the cross-national differences in given periods. Hence the German case does reflect a more general pattern. Nevertheless, some differences between countries cannot be denied. For example, while it is hard to identify in the Scandinavian countries a segment of the women's movement that is truly independent from the state, the same cannot be said for Britain, Germany, Italy, and the United States.

Labor Movements and States

Unlike the case of the women's movements, interactions between labor movements and states seem to show greater variety across western countries. In some countries, like Italy, France, and Great Britain, the movements tended to be prone to conflicts not only with private employers but also with the state – and not only regarding the state's role as an employer, as the events of France in May 1968 illustrate. In other places, such as the Nordic countries, the Netherlands, Germany, Austria, Switzerland, the United States, and Canada, the labor movements were more pragmatic and moderate, considering themselves as a negotiation partner of, rather than a challenger to, the state. For the most part, these are also countries where the movements are not organized along different ideological lines but rather represented by relatively unified and hierarchical bodies that are able to control their adherents. Especially in the countries with pronounced neocorporatist arrangements (for example, Sweden, Norway, Denmark, the Netherlands, Austria, and Germany), the unions are integrated in various statist and semistatist institutions where they actively and more-or-less regularly participate in processes of policy making.

Comparisons across time show that differences in movement-state interactions between countries have been mitigated since the 1970s. The labor movements in countries marked by relatively salient class conflicts have become more moderate. This becomes obvious when considering the working days lost in labor disputes, which, of course, predominantly occur in the private sector. Overall, with the exception of a few countries, labor disputes have decreased in the last decades.[16] Considering the more recent period, it

---

[16] According to calculations based on the figures provided by Crouch (1993: 155, 279), the average was 352.9 lost working days per 1,000 dependent labor force in 12 European countries in the period from 1971–5. The respective figure decreased to 311.0 working days in the period from 1986–90. Excluding Italy, which had an extraordinary wave of strikes in the second period, the respective figures are 257.1 days in the first and 112.1 days in the second period.

TABLE 11.5.   *Working Days Lost in Labor Disputes**

Area/Country	1987–1991	1992–1996
United States	68	42
Canada	344	172
EU average	246	93
OECD average	148	65

* Per 1,000 employees in all industries and services.
Source: OECD Economic Surveys 1998–9:73.

is clear that the decline in strike activity has continued in western countries, as Table 11.5 shows. Other indicators, such as number of people involved in strikes and lockouts per 10,000 employees, confirm this picture.

Overall, the labor movements have been compromised and are mainly confined to purely economic questions so that states are no longer fundamentally challenged by them. With a few remarkable exceptions (for example, Sweden), union density has been decreasing in the western world in the last decades (Ebbinghaus and Visser 1996; Golden, Wallerstein, and Lange 1999: 200). Corporatist arrangements seem to have lost some of their importance, except possibly in the Scandinavian countries. Interactions between labor movements and states seem to have stabilized and moderated in European countries such as France, Britain, and Germany, where left-wing governments returned to power in the second half of the 1990s.

Peace Movements and States

Peace movements stand in stark contrast to most other movements insofar as they never became involved in concrete processes of negotiation and routine interaction with the state. As stated above, this stems from the fact that these movements refer to issues that, from the viewpoint of the powerholders, are nonnegotiable and should be reserved for a small circle of experts. State authorities simply do not want any citizen participation in issues of military strategy, defense, and armament. No wonder that the peace movements were relegated to public campaigning and street action (Rochon 1988).

This negative attitude of the political decisionmakers toward the peace movement has not changed from the 1970s to the 1990s. However, because the stakes have been lowered since the end of the Cold War, state authorities can be more relaxed about extraparliamentary opposition in matters of war and armament. In the period of intense ideological rivalry and military bloc confrontation, peace movements were regarded with much suspicion because they appeared to undermine the state's own strength, if not – willingly or unwillingly – to serve the cause of the "enemy." This was particularly evident during the Vietnam War when many state officials in the United States felt that the war was eventually lost "at the home front." Not surprisingly, peace movements from the 1950s to the 1980s were often discredited as being "steered by Moscow." Because of this accusation, most noncommunist peace groups felt the need to distance themselves from the communist strand, making it harder for the movement to speak and act with one voice.

In the late 1980s and 1990s, the peace movements were perceived less as an internal threat for several reasons. First, the sharp ideological confrontation between the east and west had largely waned. Second, military conflicts (Falklands, Gulf War) tended to be immediate and short so that protest, if it occurred at all, was spontaneous and reactive and not accompanied by the creation of a more consistent and solid mobilization structure. Third, peace protesters had difficulties in identifying with the other side since figures such as Saddam Hussein and Slobodan Milosevic could hardly be praised as fighters for liberation and tolerance. With the exception of a relatively strong peace mobilization during the Gulf War in some countries, especially Germany, only scattered protests took place, leaving western governments free of serious challenge in the 1990s.

In summary, it seems that the nature of interactions between peace movements and states neither changed significantly over time nor across countries, in spite of the fact that the movements varied considerably in their organizational strength and levels of activity. If we consider only the 1990s, relatively strong movements existed in southern Europe, Germany, and the Netherlands, whereas they remained weak in Great Britain, France, and North America. As stressed above, with the exception of the policing of demonstrations and other protest activities, little if any interaction between movements and states took place. Unlike other movements, the peace movements never made an inroad into state institutions.

Environmental/Antinuclear Movements and States

Nonnuclear environmental issues[17] were embraced, both in theory and in practice, by many state authorities in western countries, although the embrace came more slowly for some states (for example, France, Great Britain, Spain, Greece) than for others (the Nordic countries, the United States, Canada). There was also disagreement between various agencies responsible for environmental issues, for example, the newly emerging environmental departments, on the one hand, and departments of industry, commerce, and agriculture, on the other. For the environmental movements, this meant that they had at least limited support from some of the political elites in various countries. This did not prevent the movements from facing intolerance and hostility, however, when confronting the state in concrete conflicts over the

---

[17] Antinuclear struggles are often seen as part of the wider environmental movement. However, as the analysis for Germany shows, antinuclear activities are quite distinct in their patterns and dynamics and therefore can be analyzed separately.

implementation of new highways, airports, waste deposits, and the like. But even such conflicts, not to mention less heated issues such as the protection of wildlife and natural "monuments," were often accompanied by talks, negotiation, and participation of movement organizations in public hearings. Environmental protection was accepted as a given so that the conflict was about the extent and pace of environmental protection rather than its basic legitimacy. Conflicts were particularly salient when environmental demands seemed to endanger economic competitiveness and jobs. Overall, however, environmental groups became more moderate during the last decades in most western countries. Among the few exceptions is Great Britain where conflicts around road construction and animal rights intensified around the mid-1990s (Rootes 2001). Also in the United States, a number of radical groups (for example, Earth First! and various animal rights groups) began to flourish during the 1980s and 1990s, though they remained a marginal phenomenon compared to the moderate activities of the large and more established environmental organizations such as the Sierra Club, Audubon Society, and Environmental Defense Fund (Brulle 2000).

For the antinuclear power movements of the 1970s the situation was markedly different. In many countries, nuclear power epitomized scientific and technological progress. Its development was nourished in almost all places with considerable public funding (Jasper 1990; Rüdig 1990). Moreover, in some countries, most notably in France, Great Britain, and the United States, nuclear power programs were closely linked to military purposes and sometimes even administered by the same bodies and institutions. No wonder that states tended to fight back when nuclear power came under attack, for they themselves could be seen to be, or were indeed, the ultimate target. The latter was true when antinuclear groups focused not so much on the potential dangers of radioactivity but rather on the centralized, elitist power structures and the link between big capital and the state – a critique which culminated in the notion of the "atomic state" (*Atomstaat, l'état nucléaire*). Such a state, for various reasons, was perceived as inherently tending toward exclusion of citizens, distrust, surveillance, and secrecy. France, the country with the strongest engagement in nuclear power and the closest link between its civil and military use, was also the country where the state remained most intransigent to the antinuclear movement (Rucht 1994a). In contrast, in the United States, where nuclear power was mostly perceived as a matter of private business, the state gradually took the role of a third party in the conflict (Jasper 1990).

By the 1990s, the picture had changed for both environmental and nuclear power issues. Across the board, western states became receptive to environmental demands. They created a new policy domain with extensive legislation and the establishment of a full-fledged polity. Today, state bodies embrace environmental protection in nearly all respects, if to a different degree in individual countries. Consequently, the environmental movements have gained much recognition from both the broader populace and the state

(Dunlap 1991). Environmental organizations are usually tax exempt, accepted as serious lobbyists, and integrated into committees and advisory boards due to their expertise and/or political significance. In some countries they are specifically entitled to engage in litigation. Occasionally, they act as allies to state authorities and even receive public funding (in, for example, the Netherlands, Germany,[18] Switzerland, France, and Sweden). Interactions between movements and states have broadened and intensified, covering the full spectrum from hostile clashes on building sites to partnership in joint campaigns. Overall, however, there is a trend toward assimilative strategies, with the remarkable exception of Great Britain. Differences over time appear more significant than differences between countries at given points of time. It is clear that some countries, particularly those in southern Europe, lag behind this process of mutual rapprochement, but these latecomers are also moving in the same direction.

Antinuclear movements developed more highly differentiated relationships with individual states in the 1990s than did environmental movements generally. In some states, political decisionmakers have become extremely critical of nuclear power or at least have bowed to the tenacious antinuclear campaigning that has gradually won the support of the broader populace. For example, in Austria, Italy, the Netherlands, and more recently Sweden, nuclear power is no longer an issue and therefore the antinuclear movement has disbanded.[19] In other countries, existing nuclear facilities and issues such as transport and storage of waste have resulted in ongoing, though not necessarily high-profile, antinuclear activities.[20] Strikingly, in France, where nuclear power plays an important role and has never been seriously questioned by the political elites, the antinuclear activities are scattered and weak, whereas in Germany, as we have seen, they represent a greater proportion of protest activities than all other environmental issues taken together.

Whatever the level of activity in these cases, interaction between states and antinuclear movements is mainly restricted to confrontation. With very few exceptions, the antinuclear groups have never had access to state institutions, let alone recognition or support from the state. There are now only a few countries (for example, Belgium, Finland), where nuclear power still plays an important role but is not challenged by a significant nuclear opposition, mooting the question of movement-state interaction.

---

[18] According to a 1998 survey of 56 national environmental organizations in Germany and 106 local environmental groups in Berlin, state funding was on average 23 and 31%, respectively, out of the groups' annual budget (Rucht and Roose 2001: 69).

[19] Only a very few antinuclear power groups remain (for example, those campaigning against power stations in neighbor countries – Sweden in the case of Denmark, the Czech Republic in the case of Austria).

[20] This is most notable in Germany but is evident as well in France, Switzerland, Spain, and Sweden.

TABLE 11.6. *Proportion of Moderate and Violent Protests of Selected Movements in Four Countries, 1975–1989 (Percentages*)*

Movement	Netherlands		Germany		France		Switzerland	
	Confr.	Viol.	Confr.	Viol.	Confr.	Viol.	Confr.	Viol.
Women	0.5	0.5	0.5	0.8	1.4	0.7	0.6	0.0
Labor	15.5	2.1	2.8	0.3	18.6	2,5	5.5	0.0
Peace	12.3	12.4	18.2	6.2	6.6	1.3	4.2	2.8
Environment	8.0	7.3	9.5	8.3	3.4	1.6	2.4	2.8
Anti-nuclear	5.3	3.6	14.2	8.5	8.8	9.0	3.6	4.0

* Out of the total of protest events per movement and per country.
Source: Data from Kriesi et al. 1995.

A Look at Comparative Protest Event Data

Beyond this impressionistic picture of movement-state interactions, no systematic and truly comparative data across movements and countries are available. We have, however, protest event data collected in a four-nation[21] study (Germany, the Netherlands, France, Switzerland) from 1975 to 1989 (Kriesi et al. 1995).[22] Protest does not necessarily involve interaction with the state and, even when it does, it is only one of many types of state-movement interactions. However, the proportion of more radical forms of protests in these four countries gives us some indication of the cases in which the movement-state relationship tends to be tense and even confrontational, especially when we know that the state is an important if not the main target of protests.

Table 11.6 shows that the women's movements are moderate in their forms of action across all four countries. The other four movements differ across the categories of confrontational and violent protests and across countries without representing a clear-cut pattern. Both the peace and environmental movements in the Netherlands and Germany stand out as relatively disruptive when compared to France and Switzerland. The labor movements in France and the Netherlands have a relatively high proportion of confrontational events. The antinuclear movements are more disruptive in Germany, France, and Switzerland when compared to the environmental movements in the same countries.[23] Unfortunately, no cross-national data for later periods are available. As for the new social movements, it is likely that their protests became more moderate after the 1990s.

---

[21] Koopmans (1996) later extended this work to Spain and the United Kingdom. However, the data base for these two countries is relatively small and covers only the period from 1980–9.
[22] I am grateful to the authors for providing me with the data set on which Table 11.6 is based.
[23] Comparing the proportion of confrontational and violent protests for the aggregate of all five movements in the earlier period (1975–81) and the later period (1982–9), no significant differences are evident in the four countries (figures are not displayed here).

Systematizing Comparison across Three Dimensions

The fairly complex patterns of interaction between movements and states presented previously can be summarized in three observations. First, the peace and the antinuclear movements share their status as outsiders with no access to the political system. In these cases, movement-state relations tend to be highly confrontational with little if any room for a mutual rapprochement (see Table 11.7).

Second, the interactions between labor movements and states showed marked national differences in the first period but became increasingly similar across time. Less conflictual relations even emerged in countries that previously were marked by a relatively strong left-right cleavage (Italy, France, Great Britain, Spain). By and large, class cleavages, and therefore movement-state conflict, have declined (Franklin, Mackie, Valen, et al. 1992).

Third and probably most significant, the interactions between states, on the one hand, and the women's and environmental movements, on the other, exhibit some striking parallels. In both cases, differences over time were more significant than differences across countries. In the 1970s, political elites tended to be divided over the issues raised by these two movements, so that these were met partly with suspicion and partly with sympathy. Interaction was still unstructured because a full-fledged policy domain was not yet in place. By the 1990s, both movements were treated by state actors as serious players. They became involved in the policy process and in some cases were even directly supported by the state. Within a short period of time, both movements have reached a level of recognition and policy involvement that the labor movement has sought for more than a century, although the extent to which both movements actually have access to the state and have become part of the established players in their respective policy fields clearly varies across countries and concrete issues. In all countries considered, we see a move toward more continuous and less tense interactions with the state.

EXPLAINING CHANGING PATTERNS OF INTERACTION

Which factors account for these three major patterns in movement-state interaction? Focusing on the changing interactions between states and the environmental and women's movements will highlight the reasons for their similar trends over time. The specific question here is why and how these two movements, having been political outsiders and very critical of the state authorities in the 1970s, managed to develop close, nonconfrontational interactions with state institutions and to become established players in their respective policy domains. I argue that this reflects a *learning process* on the part of both the movements and the states – a process that was greatly facilitated by the structural reconfiguration discussed in Chapter 1.

TABLE II.7. *A Synopsis of Interactions between Movements and States*

Kind of Movement	Description of Interaction 1970s	1990s
Women	Few differences between countries	Few differences between countries
	Confrontational; provocative symbolic action of the movement as an outsider challenger	Conflictual and cooperative; close and partly routinized interactions, some movement leaders in public offices
Labor	Marked differences between countries	Reduced differences between countries
	Conflictual and partly cooperative in some countries, particularly those with neocorporatist arrangements (Sweden, Germany, Austria); little interaction in United States and Canada	Conflictual and partly cooperative; decreased weight of general ideological conflict
	More confrontational in other countries (Italy, France, Great Britain) with marked general ideological conflict	
Peace	Few differences between countries	Few differences between countries
	Confrontational; movements act as outsiders with no institutional access to the state; movement is regarded with suspicion by state authorities; accusations of serving the cause of the "enemy"	Confrontational; movements act as outsiders with no institutional access to the state; more relaxed attitude of state authorities since mobilization tends to be less significant and the bloc confrontation is no longer in place
Environment	Some differences between countries	Few differences between countries
	Conflictual and confrontational in some countries (Germany, France, Austria, Switzerland); more cooperative in other countries (Great Britain, Scandinavia, The Netherlands)	Conflictual and co-operative; close and partly routinized interactions, some movement leaders in public offices; Green party established

(continued)

TABLE 11.7. *(continued)*

Kind of Movement	Description of Interaction 1970s	1990s
Antinuclear	Few differences between countries Confrontational; movements act as outsiders with no institutional access to the state; movement is accused of undermining technologic progress and economic performance	Significant differences according to different outcomes of the conflict Decline of movements and no more interactions due to abandonment of nuclear power (Italy, Austria, The Netherlands in the future – Sweden, United States, Canada?) Continuing confrontation in Germany, France, and Spain; movements remain outsiders with no institutional access to the state; hardly any antinuclear mobilization in Belgium and Finland in spite of large nuclear power production

When the new environmentalism and the second wave of the women's movements took shape, they were radical in their diagnosis of the situation, their political demands, and, partly, their actions. They both perceived the existing situation as profoundly immoral. For the environmental movement, the main problem was the degradation and destruction of the natural environment of humankind; for the women's movement it was the flagrant violation of basic values of equality, dignity, and self-determination. Both movements urged radical changes that would affect the deeper structure of society as well as people's daily lives. This sense of crisis and injustice, however, was not felt to the same dramatic extent by the preexisting and more traditional branches of both movements and certainly still less by political elites and the wider populace. The radical claims appealed particularly to a relatively small and already politicized segment of society, although their values were widely acknowledged, if often only rhetorically. Radical actions reminded the public that something was wrong, but they failed to attract mass support. In order to survive and grow, the movements gradually learned to accept the unlikelihood of immediate and profound change. Without necessarily abandoning their long-term perspective, these movement groups moderated their tone and actions, learning the bitter lesson that political change not only is slower than expected but also has its price.

A second lesson the movements had to learn was that the world cannot be easily divided into black and white, with movement solutions being good and easy and the existing world simply bad and mad. Particularly when moving from fundamental critique to practical solutions, it became clear that compromise both within the movements and with external forces was unavoidable. Again, this contributed to the overall shift toward more pragmatic stances within both movements.

Third, the movements learned that they could not achieve societal and political changes by remaining strictly outsiders. The state, with all its power, financial resources, and experts cannot be forcefully besieged. Instead, one has to find inroads into the state, create bridgeheads within its apparatus, and exploit differences of interest and opinion within the state, both between different sections and at different levels. The movements had to accept that policy reform is not just a matter of good will and sound arguments but mainly a power game. Such a game requires knowledge of the institutional rules and technicalities of policy making, the readiness and skills to form tactical alliances, and considerable patience – probably at the expense of spectacular action. To some extent, this also meant that the movement would be in a better situation if it took a more indirect course, for example in putting forward its demands via other interest groups such as trade unions, civil rights organizations, churches, or a new party like the Greens, while at the same time keeping a lower profile. For example, even many radical groups of the women's movement no longer strictly adhered to their initial policy of "women only." They recognized that mixed organizations and settings could well serve their cause. This was also reflected by feminists in academia who argued against a "ghettoization" of women enclosed in their own circles, study programs, journals, and the like. Similarly, over time environmentalists were less concerned about maintaining their ideological and organizational purity and became more openminded about cooperating with other actors, including the state and industry.

This shift toward more pragmatic, continuous, and less confrontational forms of interaction was not a one-sided affair. It was greatly facilitated by changes of the state. Here we have to consider both general and policy-specific changes. It seems that during the last decades most western states, to different degrees, have become more responsive to citizens' demands by changing some of their structures and adopting less authoritarian policy styles. In a number of states citizen participation has been facilitated, electoral systems made less restrictive to small and/or new parties, access to state-controlled information has been improved, hearings and advisory boards have become more accessible to dissenting groups, semistatist institutions and public-private partnerships have been set up, and voluntary associations have been invited to perform functions that traditionally were reserved for the state administration. Based on historical traditions and the respective parties in power, this overall trend occurred to a different extent and at a different pace in individual countries. The United States and Canada are traditionally more open political systems (Kitschelt 1985), so their changes were less pronounced than those of some European countries such as Germany, Great Britain, and Italy. The French state, in spite of its historic move toward decentralization since the 1980s, was more reluctant to follow this general trend (see Banaszak this volume).

Looking more specifically at environmental and women's policies, the western European states of the 1970s were not in a position to reject the movements' demands outright. While these claims may have been perceived as exaggerated or totally unrealistic, their underlying values were fully compatible with the underpinnings of modern liberal democracies. In the case of the women's movement, most of the claims were derived from constitutionally guaranteed rights. So, unlike in the case of peace and antinuclear power, the environmental and women's movements were met with some sympathy among parts of the (progressive) state elites. Moreover, both movements pointed to problems that were simply undeniable, making it hard for state authorities to remain totally passive. When it became clear that both movements were not simply short-lived phenomena, expressed well-founded critiques and demands, and were ready to engage in constructive solutions, state authorities, also influenced by other progressive groups outside the movements themselves, became more receptive. They even began to invite movement representatives to participate actively in processes of policy making, thus facilitating the movements' march into and through the institutions (Katzenstein 1998a).

It would be naive to assume that state authorities became more responsive to environmental and women's issues only by intrinsic conviction. Indifference and nonreaction to the movements' demands were simply not viable options. It would have put state elites under enormous pressure not only by the movements but by the wider populace. It was wiser to embrace the movements' cause rhetorically and to make some limited concessions instead of facing rising criticism and possible eventual delegitimation.

Each side had to pay its price in this process of coming closer together. For the state, this meant granting limited influence and support to critical and sometimes annoying societal forces; for the movements, it meant lowering their demands and shifting from sweeping criticism to the cumbersome details of formulating and implementing policies by piecemeal processes.[24]

This explanatory and interpretative account has highlighted a distinct trend while remaining largely silent about the differences within the two movements and, more importantly, differences across countries. Informed and close observers of one or the other movement may well argue that there

---

[24] Obviously, what has been interpreted here as a learning process can be read from a different angle. While elitist defenders of state autonomy may argue that the state has become a prey of pressure groups, deep ecologists and hard-core feminists may point to the fact that "institutional participation is...a double-edged sword" (Tarrow 1998: 208) and deplore that the movements have "sold out" while reaching none of their ambitious goals.

exists more variation across these lines. Taking a broad perspective and looking for the major trends, however, it is evident that these variations are less pronounced than the structural similarities of both movements. In terms of their interactions with the state, they have followed a surprisingly similar path. Taken together, it becomes clear that different kinds of factors determine the interactions between states and social movements. These factors can be grouped into three categories: 1) the properties of the actors, most importantly their degree of unity/centralization and their basic worldviews and values, 2) the stake of the conflict (limited or fundamental), and 3) the context of interaction which, in turn, can be specified by the overall political culture (more or less liberal), configuration of power (degree of establishment and regulation), and the forums of interaction (for example, streets, parliament, courts).

What can be hypothesized when considering these factors in the light of the previous comparisons? First, comparing the labor movement with the other movements, it appears that centralized actors exhibit less varied forms of interaction than decentralized actors. Second, dramatic perceptions of crisis and injustice and social cleavages, combined with a quest for radical change, tend to lead to more conflictual and confrontational forms of interaction. Third, when the stakes of the conflict are fundamental, more conflictual and confrontational forms of interaction result. Fourth, liberal political contexts (for example, the United States) and established, regulated power configurations (for example, Sweden) encourage cooperative and more-or-less permanent forms of interaction. Finally, forums of interaction that are highly institutionalized are associated with moderate forms of conflict.

CONCLUSION

This chapter has sought to put interactions of women's movements and states into a broader context by comparing them to other movements' interactions with states. From these comparisons, some observations and tentative explanations can be offered. A major finding of this chapter is that (changing) interactions between the women's movement and states cannot be said to be typical or representative for interactions between social movements and states in general. Though it was argued that the environmental movement exhibits a pattern very similar to that of the women's movement, this does not apply to other kinds of movements which display different patterns of interaction and/or little change over time.

Second, as far as the women's and the environmental movements are concerned, differences in interaction patterns across countries seem to be less pronounced than expected. In almost all western countries, these two movements have shifted from more confrontational to more assimilative strategies. Nonetheless, this pattern applies to no other movements. In some cases, the very logic and themes of the movement (for example, peace, antinuclear power) appear to be factors that override the structural differences of national contexts. In other cases, particular properties of given states seem to have a greater weight, leading to similar patterns of interaction for different movements.[25] Moreover, some movements (for example, labor, women) are more affected by the restructuring of states than others (for example, peace). If these observations are correct, we should regard with caution general decontextualized theories about the nature, logic, and determinants of interactions between movements and state (Birnbaum 1988). We might better start from more restricted but systematic and empirically grounded comparisons across movements, countries and time. Relating them to each other may guide us toward more encompassing theories about interactions between social movements and states.

[25] For example, Koopmans (1991) observes that the state in the Netherlands has reacted in a more relaxed manner to challenges from various kinds of movements than has the German state.

12

Restating the Woman Question

Women's Movements and State Restructuring*

David S. Meyer

In challenging the state on matters of policy or political process, social movements must confront a moving target, with some of the state's motion a response to their efforts. The experience of women's movements over the past thirty years demonstrates this problem, one of analysis and of politics, quite clearly. As the state responds to activists' claims, the bases of social movement politics can be fundamentally changed. The chapters in this volume confront the women's movements changing in response to state restructuring, some portions of which the movements themselves had affected. Although a template pattern of mobilization and apparent retreat and retrenchment holds to some degree across all of the cases represented here, the differences are illuminating. Most significantly, the differences inform about the character of claims making in the different states, a function of rules, institutions, and culture, as well as the strategic decisions activists made. They point up the differential starting points that women had in various states, the nature of political development in these advanced industrial nations, the contingencies associated with the timing of a particular claim, and the choices among available alliances that women made. They also reflect the impact of public policy in structuring subsequent opportunities for mobilization.

In this chapter, I will review and summarize some of the findings in the preceding chapters, taking the occasion to raise more general issues about the politics of social protest movements in advanced industrialized societies. The case of women's movements informs about the permeability of advanced industrialized states, which are restructuring, as described by the editors, in response to a number of exogenous pressures and altering possibilities for a wide range of social movement claimants. The comparisons of women's

* I am grateful to the editors of this volume for helpful comments on earlier drafts of this chapter.

movements in restructuring states presented here emphasize the interactions between movements and the state.

The history of women's mobilization is one of broad coalitions of women and various allies that coalesce and reformulate in response to external political circumstances, picking new claims and redefining issues that seem most urgent or most promising. Carol Mueller and John McCarthy look at the component parts of movement coalitions and find that individual organizations adapt fairly successfully to changing political circumstances, but the development and influence of the broader coalition is of greater importance if we are to understand the impact of social movements. How these coalitions change over time, and how the issues that comprise the agenda of a women's movement change over time, reflect both activist strategy and state capacity and openings. The free-market liberal reconfiguration that swept advanced industrial societies fractured the old political coalitions that defined the women's movements twenty and thirty years earlier. That reconfiguration, including a renegotiation of political coalitions, has limited the sorts of claims the new women's movements can effectively make. Neoliberal restructuring of advanced industrial states has made access to some institutions more available to some women, but other institutions have been foreclosed for new participation – or, alternatively, opened for participation but insulated from meaningful influence on the policy process. Contemporary women's movements have effectively reaffirmed the exclusion of some of their old concerns, acting opportunistically in picking allies, issues, and core constituencies. As we look at the contemporary women's movements, we must ask who or what they now represent, and what they are likely to be able to accomplish – and how, by working within and against these restructuring states.

I will begin by discussing the politics of social protest more generally, then turn to look at the changing political opportunities new women's movements face. I then look at how structure and political culture affected the tactics, coalitions, and issues women's movements embraced. I conclude, following the explicit suggestions of Jane Jenson, Celia Valiente, and Mary Katzenstein, with a discussion of the sorts of citizenship that is now most readily available to women in restructured states. My core argument here is that the story of developing women's movements is one of political institutionalization that brings differential costs and benefits to different groups in the coalition of groups that comprise women's movements. The trajectory of movement development is shaped by the interaction of women's movement groups with conventional politics, with influence on public policy both the prize and a prime determinant of subsequent social movement claims, constituencies, and tactics. Assessing the development of women's movements and the changing status of different women in advanced industrialized states tells us not only about these constituencies, I believe, but also about the nature of emergent social movement politics as they affect other constituencies.

POLITICS AND SOCIAL PROTEST

We can see both the origins and the outcomes of social protest in institutional conventional politics and policy. The groups of people who protest and engage in social movements are those whose relationship with institutional politics is dynamic and somewhat in between. Those who can get what they want by standard political means such as voting, making financial contributions, writing editorial pieces, or routine interest group politics, will use those means to press their claims; they don't need to take to the streets. Those who are so alienated from conventional politics that they can't make inroads in the polity will lack the safety or capacity to organize and make claims altogether, appearing quiescent or apathetic instead; they can't envision, risk, or stage protest.

Social movements emerge when a potential constituency can claim sufficient political legitimacy to express its claims, but is alienated enough to be unable to win much without making a tremendous fuss. Social movements are comprised of people engaged in a broad range of political actions, including conventional political participation such as voting and campaigning, but also less conventional, sometimes riskier, political actions like street protest, and a broad range of activities in between. It is not necessarily that the same people are engaged in the full range of activity – although sometimes some are – but that those on the margins and in the mainstreams see themselves united and engaged in a common struggle. Such a phenomenon is limited in time and the responses of the state to the movement alter the nature of dissident politics and identities. As the state moves to respond to the claims and actions of dissidents of any sort, participants in the loose coalition that defines most social movements recalculate what their best prospects and who their truest allies are.

The template story of the women's movements in western Europe, the United States, and Canada (for example, Costain 1992; Dahlerup 1986; Gelb 1989; Githens, Norris and Lovenduski 1994; Katzenstein and Mueller 1987; Lovenduski 1986; Taylor 1993; Teske and Tetreault 2000) beginning in the late 1960s, is one in which women in advanced industrial societies had gained sufficient education, employment, recognition, and resources to launch substantial social movements. This process begins with forging a collective political identity of women as potentially efficacious political actors with common interests, then organizing and mobilizing a latent constituency, staging public protests – in conjunction with filling the available opportunities for institutional participation, and making real gains. In the late 1960s, the exclusion of women from the arenas of decision making, both formal (for example, parliaments) and less formal (party leadership), created a viable political identity that, while actually mobilizing relatively few women, seemed to represent the interests of virtually all women by highlighting easily justifiable claims of equal access and inclusion. Middle-class, aspiring professional, and working-class women, with a range of substantive policy needs, all would seem to benefit from an increased presence of women, and from government action against gender discrimination by both government and private-sector actors. Even women who needed much more from the government would seem to benefit from these first steps. Focusing on eliminating discrimination and ensuring inclusion was also a way to avoid, or more accurately, to manage, difficult political debates about what women's interests were. Additionally, these first steps promised to improve the chances of women to make subsequent substantive claims more effectively.

This first break of the second "wave" of the women's movement achieved some successes. Although the range of representation in government and political parties varied across the wealthy countries, women generally won increased representation and enhanced access to the arenas of political decision making, as well as to the economy. That these gains were dramatic and real, of course, doesn't mean that they were enough to improve the lives of most women, or to satisfy the claims of leading activists. Nonetheless, as Lee Ann Banaszak points out, enhanced legitimacy for women in "nontraditional" roles, increased presence of women in the workforce, and sometimes modest increases in the number of women in political office changed the landscape for making claims on behalf of women. Women's movement efforts also often changed the rules of access, the availability of allies, and the capacity of the state to redress grievances. They also changed the nature of the grievances women shared – or didn't share. Thus, the nature of the constituencies, and the scope of the concerns, that could be represented by a women's movement changed, partly as a result of movement actions.

At the same time, for reasons quite apart from women's concerns and women's mobilization, the politics and the policies of the advanced industrialized nations shifted in other ways, with states backing away, again to varying degrees, from the welfare states established over the previous decades. It is not only the stakes of mobilization that changed since the emergence of the second wave of women's movement activism, but also the rules of the contest, and the nature of who would be willing to participate. This is a story of *political institutionalization* (Meyer and Tarrow 1998; also see Costain 1992), where movement actors negotiate some kind of more stable and routinized arrangement with the state and mainstream politics, even as the use of social movement forms and tactics becomes more widely employed and accepted. In the case of the women's movements, however, renegotiation is perpetual, with the constant reformulation of claims and coalitions.

POLITICAL OPPORTUNITIES AND POLITICAL MOBILIZATION

If we want to understand the nature of social movement challenges to the state, it makes sense to look at the state being challenged (Tarrow 1996; Tilly 1984). If indeed the nation-state itself was the political creation that made the social movement possible, surely changes within it are critical to understanding what constituencies launch extrainstitutional campaigns about which issues when. Social movements are opportunistic, even if activists are not conscious of their opportunism. Movements emerge representing somehow disadvantaged constituencies and carrying issues that are otherwise neglected, appear in open spaces at open moments (Gourevitch 1986), and reorganize and remobilize themselves in response to the effects they have on state structures, policies, and political opportunities, allowing for constraints of organization, resources, and ideology (see particularly Staggenborg 1995). The movements that emerged in the mid-1970s gravitated to political spaces in which mobilization was most possible, and used the tactics that were essentially mandated by the rules of entry to those political spaces. In other words, working through parties often required brokerage politics, litigating required legal briefs, and so forth. When political spaces were less permeable to women, activists made other, more accessible spaces, such as day-care centers and consciousness-raising groups, into political spaces. Rules of entrance were far less restrictive, but access to policy making was also more limited.

These chapters give us two ways to look at comparisons across states. The cross-national variations reflect the varied opportunities different states present to insurgents. Although the new women's movements of the late 1960s and early 1970s emerged across virtually all of the advanced industrialized nations, they did so in different ways. In general, women's movements were most active in states that were structurally more open, that is, those with numerous means of routine participation and low barriers to political participation, and less active in states that were more closed to citizen participation generally. At the same time, they were less identifiable as a critical force in states that were the most open to the participation of women.

At one end of the spectrum were liberal democracies, which, over time, opened already established routine means of participation to women pressing a variety of claims. As an example, the Nordic countries with extensive political participation and open political parties welcomed the participation of women in conventional politics. By the mid-1980s, for example, Norway's government was led by a woman, Gro Harlem Bruntland, who announced her intent to represent women's concerns as a route to promoting social justice (Skjeie 1991). This represented a stark contrast with her contemporary, Margaret Thatcher, the first woman to serve as prime minister of the United Kingdom, who claimed no allegiance to or identification with feminists or the women's movement (Lovenduski and Norris 1993).

Paradoxically, in settings such as Norway where the state and parties were relatively welcoming to women as feminists because there were so many openings for women to make claims, the women's movement did not develop a distinct and critical politics, as efforts for legal inclusion and protections were embraced by mainstream political parties. When mainstream political and economic institutions were most open to women's aspirations, the development of a social movement making broad claims was also slow in coming. The reformist wing of women's movements, Dieter Rucht notes, was strongest in states where such wings could find some institutional support; reformers were more established and visible in the United States, Canada, and Scandinavia, less strong in the United Kingdom, France, Belgium, Austria, Switzerland, and Italy, and still less strong in Greece, Spain, and Portugal. In other words, reformists flourished where reform efforts stood a reasonable prospect of success. At the same time, in the middle of the spectrum, where reformers were visible but less successful, particularly in the larger democracies, radical groups with broader political analyses also developed, and sometimes flourished.

At the far end of the spectrum was the fascist government of Franco-era Spain, as considered by Celia Valiente. With all politics stifled, there was insufficient political space for any kind of social movement to emerge, even one for democracy, and the development of a women's movement was stilted until Franco's death. When the possibilities for political participation opened, potential women's movement activists were taken up in pursuit of broader political reforms and tied their claims to the Socialist Party. So-called "women's issues" emerged slowly.

Where political openings were extensive, and the state more responsive, women's issues often developed in pieces. As Amy Elman notes in her comparison of shelter movements, the Swedish variant was largely service oriented, and not explicitly tied to other feminist issues or political empowerment. Indeed, one of her informants commented that the development of shelters was peculiar in that it was not tied to a women's movement. Because the state was more open to women in general, women in general shared fewer common grievances, and while the state was very responsive to the service-oriented claims of the shelter movement in Sweden (in contrast to other states responding to sister movements elsewhere), the issues of shelter developed in isolation from other issues commonly on a broad feminist agenda (see also Gornick and Meyer 1998; Matthews 1994). Shelter movements in the United Kingdom and the United States, as Elman notes, developed to establish something of a Swedish pattern, albeit with even less generous state support. Initially tied to political movements – and a political analysis of the problem of spousal abuse – they became client oriented, turning a political cause into a series of cases.

In the rest of the industrialized countries, the women's movements that developed in the 1970s were characterized by broad yet sometimes tense and tenuous coalitions between women oriented primarily to the state and institutional politics (often labeled "liberal") and others oriented to using women's mobilization to make broader claims against capitalism and/or patriarchy and working in local communities, or simply working on ideas and identities independently of any conventional political claims ("socialist" and "radical" feminists) (for example, Ferree and Hess 1994). There is a general pattern of women trying to work through all of the major political parties, though finding most inspiration and access from those on the left. In the 1970s there was often a tension in the larger democracies among these groups, as activists disagreed on what was possible within conventional political institutions, and how costly and worthwhile pursuing those possibilities would be.

In certain respects, the styles of mobilization that characterized this phase of the women's movements reflected the interaction of political culture and political structures. In the United Kingdom and in France, unitary states with strong party governance, feminist thought flourished and activists demanded some kind of proportional representation within the parties. They made few inroads, however, in matters of policy, as Jenson and Valiente point out, particularly as both states were cutting back on the social welfare policies that were part of women's political concerns (also see, Lovenduski 1986). Where women were shut out of the parties, they organized in venues that were more distant from conventional politics and policy making. In Italy, according to Donatella della Porta, where patronage-oriented parties dominated, brokerage went on through the parties, and issues took a backseat to inclusion, particularly after a brief period of mobilization on divorce and abortion laws. The movements themselves became agents of brokerage. In Spain, women focused on gaining representation through formal quotas on the party lists, and although refusing to enforce a formal quota, the Socialist Party increased the representation of women significantly. In these cases, the character and practices of the open parties affected the development of the women's movements. In both cases, women adopted a "dual presence" strategy, which essentially separated women's movement politics from the brokerage politics of working within established political parties.

Although the nature of the electoral system and rules of representation were important, as more rigid notions of political opportunity theory would suggest (see Kitschelt 1986; Kriesi et al. 1995), also critically important were norms and styles of conducting politics, both inside and outside institutions, what Dieter Rucht here describes as "political culture" in his treatment of social movement strategies in Germany. Formal structure is an appropriate starting place for analysis, but the chapters in this collection profitably push us beyond a narrow structuralist approach.

Federal states, by design, offer more arenas in which to make political claims, and function to disperse any social movement's efforts, but here again there is variation within the countries studied. In Canada and Germany, federal states with traditions of brokerage politics organized women's groups and gained support from the state (for example, Vickers, Rankin, and Appelle 1993), linked their efforts to specific policy demands, and made some concrete gains. In states where party organizations bore responsibility for choosing and supporting candidates for office, activists focused on increasing the number of women candidates. Where parties had to respond (or not respond) to specific demands for proportionate representation for women, this goal was particularly prominent. Because parties were responsible for nominating candidates, they could be challenged and, at least potentially, held accountable for their representation of women (for example, Lovenduski and Norris 1993).

In the United States, with a federal system and weak open parties, the range of organized interest groups and social movement activity was somewhat broader, split among numerous organizations. Indeed, the National Organization for Women became a site of struggle for different tendencies within the women's movement (Reger 2001). Nonetheless, gains in policy were more difficult to assess. The self-nomination system for candidates in the United States removed a critical, yet very elusive, target for activists seeking to include women in office. In contrast, in the United States, the call for more women in office led to mobilization outside the parties for independent fundraisers to contribute to women candidates, essentially allowing the parties to get off the hook. Activists formed and funded Political Action Committees, most notably Emily's List, to fund feminist candidates (Burrell 1994; McCarthy 1997). The self-nomination system also meant that women who gained office owed less to their party than to the personal coalitions they had assembled, perhaps including elements of the women's movement; in such cases, individual officeholders became brokers, well-positioned to deliver redress to individuals, but less capable of effecting structural reforms (Freeman 1987; Spalter-Roth and Schreiber 1995). This is a difficult balancing act for coalitions to manage.

Political Positioning and Available Opportunities

Formal structures and rules do not explain all of the variance even when coupled with the traditions and political culture of claims making in the advanced industrialized states. Of critical importance is the positioning of actors within the state, most significantly, the politics of who is in power. The fact that the Italian Communist Party (PCI) was most open to the women's movement was not wholly divorced from the fact that the PCI did not sit in a governing coalition during that long period. Having allies in government encourages a movement to frame its claims more pragmatically, that is to say, in terms of policy, but more narrowly.

When we look at the restructuring of advanced states over the past three decades, we see that the dominant parties at critical times influenced not only the character of restructuring, but also the open spaces and viable issues available for social movements. Importantly, as Dieter Rucht notes, not only were the women's movements of the 1980s and beyond different from those of the 1960s and 1970s, but the states they challenged had also changed. Although none of the other states considered in this volume witnessed the wholesale reconfiguration of Spain, before and after Franco, numerous smaller changes, chronicled in the introduction to this volume, affected the prospects for women's mobilization and influence. Drawing from the chapters presented here, we might array a range of reconfigurations, with Spain at one end, democratizing and joining the emerging European Union. At the other end of the spectrum was France, but even here the state ceded some authority and responsibility to the European Community, "uploading" in the editors' terms.

More commonly, in general terms, nation-states reduced the scope of what they did (offloading), and correspondingly, what political leaders considered to be legitimate claims on the national state. Decision making in many venues was redistributed to other levels of government, above and below the national state, and ceded to the market in many other areas. This general pattern holds true, even when there was no formal reconfiguration of governmental institutions, for the politics of those holding power also mattered.

Germany and the United Kingdom provide an instructive comparison here. Although both nations spent most of the 1980s under conservative governments led by very long-tenured leaders, Chancellor Helmut Kohl and Prime Minister Margaret Thatcher, the stories were very different. Kohl's center-right coalition government represented a much less dramatic departure from the center-left coalition government it replaced, particularly in matters of political economy, as Dieter Rucht observes. Similarly, the left-center coalition now governing Germany, although now leaning left, offers relatively modest changes in policy. Further, Kohl was firmly committed to European integration, and used his tenure to support, enhance, and speed European integration.

In stark contrast, Margaret Thatcher's government aggressively set about undoing not only the work of the previous Labour government, but much of the infrastructure of the welfare state. Hostile to Britain's integration into Europe, her government limited uploading of responsibility to the European Union, and, as Karen Beckwith notes here, committed to restructuring only to the degree that it took power out of the venues she did not control. With Thatcher actively hostile to the claims the women's movement ·

made, and the Labour Party completely insulated from the policy-making process, women's movement activists in the 1980s and beyond turned to direct action, and to mobilization within other movements, including labor (see Beckwith 1996) and peace (for example, Cook and Kirk 1983; Harford and Hopkins 1984; Junor 1995). Unsurprisingly, political alignments in the two states led the women's movements to adopt different strategies and forms, such that the German movement became more adept at and interested in bargaining, and the British movement more comfortable with a broader analysis of what comprised women's issues and direct action.

Opening Institutions

Although activists might like to open existing institutions and create new ones in which they might exercise greater influence, they are constrained by other actors and a range of exogenous factors. Celia Valiente's analysis of the rapid opening of political institutions in Spain describes a context that women's movement actors had little or no discernible influence in making. The few organizations that survived during Franco's time had little visible impact on the transition following his death. In contrast, Alexandra Dobrowolsky's analysis of constitutional reform and women's organizing in the British Commonwealth puts the process of negotiating restructuring in high relief. In the Canadian case, we see an explicitly open moment in politics, where not only political alignments are subject to renegotiation and reformation, but also the rules of claims making, as political leaders sought to reform the Constitution and renegotiate the federal arrangement. Driven primarily by dissatisfaction from geographically concentrated ethnic groups, French-speaking Québécois and indigenous people, the process of negotiation created a temporal opportunity for women to make claims as well, trying to establish constitutionally protected rights in the new Charter of Rights and Freedoms. As in the comparison cases elsewhere in the Commonwealth, advocates for women's interests by their actions blurred more conventional distinctions among party politics, interest group representation, and social movement activism, as the appellation "women's movement" came to unite, albeit tenuously.

The demands, however, increasingly turned to procedural openness, rather than to specific policy outputs. Most notably, Canadian women pressed, unsuccessfully, for a constitutional provision that would ensure 50% representation for women in the federal parliament, affecting not only participation, but representation as a right. The presumption beneath such a demand, frequently challenged within women's movement groups, is that women, by nature of experience or something even more undefined, will behave *differently* than men when in positions of power, and that the differences would create benefits for all women. The failure of the women's groups in Canada to secure formal quotas for representation meant that the renegotiation of federalism passed with neither new substantive guarantees for all sorts of women nor reserved access for particular women. Despite the best efforts of women's groups, this represented a missed opportunity (Sawyers and Meyer 1999). Similarly, when the open moment of a new parliament in Scotland or constitutional reorganization appeared, the demands that emerged from what seemed to be a women's movement again focused on formal quotas for representation rather than substantive policy outputs.

DEFINING WOMEN'S ISSUES

As in all social movements, debates within the women's movement were most heated on the interrelated issues of identity and political claims; specifically, which women would be represented by the women's movement and what they would ask from the state. In making claims, activists must assess needs, resources, and possibilities. Jane Jenson and Celia Valiente apply T.H. Marshall's (1950) classic notions of citizenship to assessing the possible. For Marshall, citizenship was evolutionary, beginning with civil rights, or protections of basic liberties and property, followed by political rights, specifically, suffrage and the right to hold office. Finally, Marshall suggested, advanced industrialized nations would move to ensure social rights, that is, protections from the uncertainties of the market.

Women have lagged well behind men in pacing through Marshall's stages of citizenship, with suffrage struggles in advanced industrialized nations continuing deep into the twentieth century. The reconfiguration of states in the last few decades, Jenson and Valiente contend, suggests a retreat from even the ambition of ensuring social rights, meaning that claims for political rights, essentially liberal inclusion, are more likely to be met with success than claims for social guarantees. The fact that proportionate representation of women, often by explicit quota, came to be the most visible claim of women's movements in open moments, presents a clear indication of how the women's movements of the preceding decades had adapted to the primacy of political claims.

During the 1960s and 1970s, women were excluded from so many aspects of government and commerce, and experienced such a wide range of discrimination, that the emergence of a women's movement was an attractive vehicle for a range of women with all kinds of grievances. From women who had experienced difficulties in reaching high levels of management in business to single mothers dependent upon the state for support, from young women who had experienced sexual violence to women who dealt with unwanted pregnancies or felt trapped in sex-segregated occupations, the women's movements that emerged were a means of articulating their own claims. Advocates sought to attach their concerns to this growing movement, fighting with would-be allies about the definitions of women's movement, feminism, or "women's liberation."

In this context, the debates about ideology, tactics, and definition of women's interests in the 1970s were understandably intense and divisive. Activists against sexual violence, for example, argued among themselves about whether it emerged from poor enforcement of criminal laws or was a result of some larger, and less tractable, system of oppression (Brownmiller 1975; Marsh, Geist, and Caplan 1982). Debates about the nature of patriarchy or capitalism animated, and frequently divided, the women's movements. At the same time, particularly in states where women won relatively quick entry into political institutions, other women's movement activists argued that working within those institutions was the most effective way to better the lives of women. Such debates were most heated in states in which there was some mix of openings, as in Germany and the United Kingdom.

In France, in contrast as Jenson and Valiente note, political activity was more limited. The Socialists and Communists in France rejected not only numerical quotas for representation in the 1980s, but even more modest sorts of accommodation. When the French Socialist Party did finally respond by increasing the number of women on its electoral list in the 1993 elections for European Parliament, the women were placed, the authors note, toward the bottom of the electoral list, essentially guaranteeing that the Socialist delegation would be overwhelmingly male. The number of women from left parties in government did increase over time, but this was not reflected in terms of increased openness from the state toward women in general, Karen Beckwith points out, nor in terms of policy outputs. The French state's general cession of power upward to the European Union meant that women's activists in France had limited prospects for achieving direct policy gains from their efforts. Although civil society was more welcoming, there was little room for grounding in policy within the state, and feminist theory was consequently divorced from political import. In contrast, theoretical analyses found little traction in the Scandinavian countries, where the state was sufficiently open to allow all political questions to turn into practical, often technical, issues of policy.

In states which presented a range of political options, activists argued about what to do when, which institutions to target, which issues to prioritize, and whom to trust as an ally. In the period of the 1970s, when essentially all issues seemed particularly urgent, the arguments were heated, and every compromise seemed to promise great gains or threaten the loss of essential identities (see, for example, Arnold 1995; Matthews 1994; Whittier 1995). Advocates of particular claims or positions on issues worked to attach them to a larger identity for the women's movement.

In the 1990s and beyond, however, when it appeared that what the state could do was far more limited, there was, as observed by most of the authors here, much more cooperation among women's groups. Perhaps this is a function of political learning, as in all of the nations considered here, a new group of experienced organizers and activists had developed having witnessed and participated in campaigns that they believed met with more-or-less success and rivalries that had caused more-or-less damage. Further, in many cases, women who had begun working outside the state had found more permanent and sustainable positions (see Whittier 1995) inside policy making or administrative bodies. Tensions between the margins and the mainstream ameliorated as the margins declined in significance and capacity, and the mainstream grew more connected with what had formerly been the margins. As an example, the issue of lesbianism, which had been divisive among women's movement activists in the 1970s, had become mainstreamed and sanitized (Bernstein 1997). Sexual orientation was divorced from a critique of the politics of patriarchy and became instead an alternative way of constructing conventional nuclear families. Although such a reframing of the issue made it easier for activists to gain acceptance and some advantages from the private sector and from the state, it also entailed a curtailing of demands. Rather than calling for a reconceptualization and reconstruction of the way in which sexuality and family were treated by mainstream society and the state, they asked instead for inclusion. The degree to which women in positions of power have opened the door for others remains a critical, and largely unexplored, question.

Paradoxically, as debate about what comprised feminist issues diminished so did passion for feminism defined as such. Issue activists within the women's movement found it easier to build support and to mobilize resources in support of more focused campaigns such as efforts against domestic violence (for example, Schechter 1982) based on much narrower claims. At the same time, appeals to other women to mobilize as feminists, rather than as women, became less frequent and less effective, as fewer women self-identified with feminism (Chancer 1998; Sawyers and Meyer 1999). There are several reasons for this pattern. First, as the national state reduced the issues it managed, activists looked elsewhere for redress of their grievances. In virtually all cases, the most recent wave of the women's movements had reemerged at the local levels, as women tried to make sense of their lives in changing times. The failures and limited successes of national mobilization and national politics effectively encouraged women to turn their attention back to the more accessible local venues and to issues immediately central to their lives. Some bypassed the state altogether, directing their efforts to direct service or to the market.

Women interested in domestic violence, for example, mobilized primarily at state and local levels – particularly in federal states – for that is where hospitals, police, and prosecutors could most easily be reached and influenced. As Amy Elman points out, the process of making claims that one expected concrete responses on, entering the political process led to a focus on defining practical ways of implementing policies. Working with people

and institutions who were not immediately sympathetic to anything beyond an immediate programmatic goal, if that, transformed the activists as
well as the state (see also Matthews 1994), making activists more pragmatic,
narrower in their claims, more modest in their analyses, and – at least over
the shorter term – much more effective – at least in pursuit of relatively
modest reforms. Instead of movement politics based on collective goods for
broad categories of people, domestic violence policy, as Elman notes, became
a matter of client service, in which causes are flattened into cases.

   Political culture and political institutions interacted to set the options
for activists, producing some predictable outcomes. Advocates for battered
women in the United States (Arnold 1995; Schechter 1982), for example,
where there is judicial review and a history of judicial activism and administration, were much more likely to use litigation to achieve their aims than
sister movements in Sweden or the United Kingdom. Although the judiciary
could provide some relief, essentially it played into the larger pattern Elman
describes of turning causes into cases.

   The same process, albeit at a national level, is replicated with issue activists
concerned with a range of issues that could conceivably be, and sometimes
were, treated as women's issues, including, as Lee Ann Banaszak notes in
her comparisons here, abortion rights and wages. The right to choose an
abortion, for example, over twenty-five years was insulated from the broader
analyses and claims of its initial champions in the women's movements,
particularly where the right was reasonably secure. Similarly, claims about
social justice or about children's welfare were also winnowed away from
any kind of broader feminist analysis. In the neoliberal state, such claims
were just baggage for women concerned with issues not connected to class,
ranging from electoral representation to sexual harassment.

   Cooperation among women's groups in the face of global restructuring
and the reconfiguration of advanced industrialized states in the West is then
a more ambiguous phenomenon than it might initially seem. Cooperation
comes with greater access to the state, but also with a sense that the stakes
of that access are somehow smaller than they formerly were. Cooperation
reflects a willingness of a range of women's movement groups to divide labor,
to leave identity and claims largely uncontested, and to let different tendencies within the movement compete not within a larger women's movement,
but with the much broader range of political actors active within the nation
state.

   The gains of political inclusion and access to certain rights effectively
divided rather than united women. Ensuring equal pay for equal position,
to turn to one of the issues Banaszak considers, which could be affected by
antidiscrimination regulations, is far less complicated and far reaching than
trying to guarantee equal pay for equal value. This less ambitious claim, however, substantially improves the workings of the marketplace for educated
women; it does less for poor and uneducated women, and deprives them of

powerful allies at the same time. In short, legal and political openings for all women, really only available to some women, fracture potentially broad coalitions of women with different needs and interests.

OTHER MOVEMENTS, ISSUES, AND ALLIES

The women's movements of the 1960s and 1970s grew out of other social movements of the time, and were affected by those movements, particularly in terms of discourse, which was generally framed in terms of rights and inclusion. The movements emerged to create an environment in which all kinds of things, including even the survival of the national governments in much of the West, could no longer be taken for granted. Protest was an increasingly common tactic, spawning a demonstration effect for other potential constituencies. As Dieter Rucht shows with comparative data on protest events, the first period examined was a time in which direct action and demonstrations seemed more attractive strategies for all kinds of social movement actors. In this case, the existence of other volatile social movements heightened the prospects for mobilization and for policy efficacy for the women's movement. The movements had a synergistic effect on each other and on a larger climate of intense participation and possibility.

This is not always the case. In the later 1970s and beyond, it was not only the women's movements that adapted less disruptive, more institutionally oriented strategies, but virtually all social movement claimants. Donatella della Porta's history of the Italian women's movement is instructive. Growing out of the New Left in Italy, the women's movement initially made claims based on class, worked closely with the institutionalized left, and staged several large demonstrations for reformed abortion and divorce laws in the late 1970s. Political violence in this period, however, legitimated a crackdown on street politics, and women turned to decentralized, service-oriented activism, working within the broad confines of politics as usual.

It was not only the tactics of the women's movement that changed; who these movements represented also changed. Even as antiwar and student movements disappeared, and ethnic minority rights movements transformed, other social movements emerged, changing the nature of potential alliances and opponents available to the women's movements. In the 1970s and 1980s, the strongest mobilizers focused on what can best be called "synthetic constituencies," that is, persons united by belief rather than some ascriptive personal characteristic. As a result, they could appeal to women's movement activists with new opportunities for activism. Peace and environmental movements flourished throughout the West, although sporadically in the past twenty years. The peace movements grew mostly in the early 1980s, in response to heightened tension in the Cold War, and grew most strongly in countries slated to host new nuclear missiles. Environmental movements waxed and waned in response to events that dramatized particular environmental threats, such as nuclear reactor accidents (for example, Libby 1998).

As the women's movements reconfigured in the 1970s and 1980s, these other movements offered vehicles for potentially efficacious mobilization, for the social connections and personal efficacy of protest movement participation, and the chance to define an individual identity as an activist. A woman interested in social justice broadly, seeing limited mobilization and limited prospects for influence on so-called women's issues, could mobilize for peace or environmental justice (Meyer and Whittier 1994). At the same time that movements on other issues offered alternatives, they also effectively offered competition to the women's movements, which struggled to find activists, resources, and public attention. In contemporary western societies, where the existence of social protest movements has become, to a large extent, accepted and accommodated (Meyer and Tarrow 1998), challenging movements, rather than enjoying a synergistic effect, come to be contenders not only against the state, but against each other in a limited-sum game for public attention.

The ways in which this competition and coordination played out in different countries varied, depending upon all of the political, structural, and cultural factors noted previously, and also depending upon the time at which each movement emerged in relation to other movements and the larger social movement sector (see Banaszak 1996). In Spain, for example, the autonomous political institutions needed to sustain a social movement had yet to develop in the 1970s, so that after Franco's death the newly opened political institutions managed virtually all manifestations of political discontent, and this was expressed primarily as partisan competition along a relatively conventional left-right spectrum. This crowded out the expression of an autonomous women's movement. Instead, women's movement activists were largely contained, at least politically, in the Socialist Party. In the United Kingdom, where a strong state crowded out all kinds of dissident politics, women's movement activists often expressed their concerns from within marginal social movements on the left, including labor and peace. Karen Beckwith's observation about radical mobilization of working-class women on behalf of miners' actions in Britain reflects some activist picking up a cause that the Labour Party was no longer pursuing aggressively or effectively.

In the United States, where the federal state and political culture allowed social movements to grow into the state more quickly, women's movement activists continued to work on some issues previously associated with feminism, particularly abortion rights, but also filled and altered movements for peace and the environment (Meyer and Whittier 1994), transforming the organization and style of social movement politics. Conservative movements, particularly on abortion, flourished in the 1980s, and forced women's movement activists into a defensive posture; although they were mostly successful at defending formal access to abortion (and less successful in ensuring the availability of abortion throughout the United States), the opportunity costs of playing defense meant an underdeveloped political agenda (Meyer and Staggenborg 1996; Staggenborg 1991).

In addition, the dependence on nonstate supported resources provided by middle-class members and foundation funders clearly advantaged some kinds of movements and claimants and hurt others. Women's policy claims became white, middle-class women's policy claims. As Mary Katzenstein notes, movements for poor women withered on the vine. As Jenson and Valiente suggest, political citizenship was more accessible than social rights. Formal legal rights – to fly combat aircraft in the military, for example, helped some individual women, but left many others behind. Although framed neutrally, legal reform affected different women dramatically differently, generally advantaging those who could make, and have the resources to pursue, such specific and narrow claims. In a different version of clientism, the legal system processed broad political grievances into narrower legal cases.

In Canada, the women's movement institutionalized, along with all sorts of other claimants, into a state-supported interest group, playing brokerage politics that often played out as zero-sum conflicts (Vickers, Rankin, and Appelle 1993). Perhaps most interestingly, in Germany, feminism linked with strong environmental and peace movements, and activists used the German electoral system of proportional representation and the electoral subsidies that come with party politics to form a unified front in the Greens. Although the Greens gave voice to the variety of claims expressed by women's movement activists, and gave a far greater share of its few parliamentary seats to women than any of the other parties, the success of the Green movement largely ghettoized feminist politics on the left, and activists made few inroads into government or marks on public policy. This is not to say that all women's movement activists were taken up in the Greens, but instead that the other parties were slow to respond to the claims of advocates representing so-called "women's issues" (Kolinsky 1989).

Contrasting these cases, we are left with more questions than answers. Every social movement organization struggles with defining itself in the context of other issues and other movements and potential movements. The most vigorous debates within movements take place about which issues ought to be linked, and which ought to be eschewed, or minimally, ignored. Debates occur along two basic dimensions, ideological and pragmatic politics. Women's movement activists argue about whether abortion rights, say, are integrally related to the status of women in society; and whether making claims about abortion rights helps or hurts the movement in terms of public support and political efficacy. Activists have no magic formula for resolving these questions of *realpolitik* or ideology. Even when there is generally agreement on the consequence of linking with a particular issue, activists disagree on the relative importance of speaking truth or seeking power. To date, social scientists have not yet figured out a means for determining the calculus of issue linkages. The chapters offered in the volume taken together raise these questions critically. The problem of linking issues becomes only more difficult and more acute as the venues for claims making are internationalized.

UPLOADING AUTHORITY AND ACTIVISM: STATES AND SHELL GAMES

It is clear that activists gravitate to the places where they can mobilize safely, or toward open spaces, places where they can articulate at least some portion of their concerns. It is not clear, however, that the venues that are most attractive for mobilization are those that are most closely linked to actual policy making. In other words, the venues that suck up political participation from women, and presumably others, are frequently not those that are connected to policy reform or service delivery. The concerns that come from the lived experience of women in advanced industrial nations are incentives to participate, to do something, but concerns themselves do not generate mobilization or strategy. The choice of venues and tactics reflects the most available means of participation, not necessarily, and frequently not at all, the places most likely to redress grievances. The reconfiguration of advanced industrialized states reallocated both open spaces and policy making, often in different directions.

The creation and integration of the European Community, to cite the most notable example, provided a wholly new setting for making claims, but thus far the capacity of the European Community institutions, including the European Parliament, to change policy within states has been circumscribed (Imig and Tarrow 2001). It is reasonable to inquire into the degree to which this venue has encouraged activists for women's rights, without much explicit acknowledgment, to swap relatively easy access for limited policy efficacy. In general, activists have been extremely interested in creating any additional venues for making claims, regardless of efficacy.

Increasingly, as the authors to this volume point out in their introduction, decisions about people's lives formerly made at the national level are made at levels above the state, in surpranational bodies, or alongside the state, by markets. The reality of increased economic and political integration presents a critical challenge for social movements, one which is posed in this volume, but which requires a great deal more research. Without doubt, uploading of national authority radically changes the nature of the structure of political opportunity that all kinds of challengers face. Immediately, national states are encumbered in ways that they have not been previously by economic agreements about trade and international regimes about issues like human rights (Brysk 1993) although, as Karen Beckwith observes, such constraints are not felt equally by all member states. The constraints of Europe, for example, are felt more heavily on that continent than the North American Free Trade Agreement is felt in the United States or Canada.

For women's movements, there are two important questions that uploading and offloading raise. The first question involves the coordination of insurgent groups transnationally. The hypothesis is that changing means of communication and politics will provide an infrastructure that makes it easier for activists to make claims across borders (Keck and Sikkink 1998; Tarrow 2000). Although the women's movements have always made allusions to the internationalism of its organization and claims, there is little evidence presented in these chapters that coordination beyond borders is increasing.[1] Of course, this merits more attention, both from scholars and activists, but it seems likely that in terms of transnational coordination and activism, women's movements have lagged behind states and multinational businesses, to the detriment of their constituents.

Second, and perhaps more significantly, increased integration and supranational coordination of states would suggest that women in advanced industrialized states will be facing conditions that are increasingly similar, and, correspondingly, will devise ways of making claims that are also similar. To the extent that the essays here confront this second issue, early evidence suggests a trend toward homogenization, with women moving increasingly to institutionally oriented means of making claims, to direct service, and to associationalism within organizations, while recognizing that women's movements in different countries are at different stages of development along this path. On the one hand, this means that individual women are better positioned to win positions within mainstream institutions than ever before. On the other hand, as Mary Katzenstein points out, it also means that women without means and access to political institutions are, minimally, without allies in making their lives better, and perhaps, even worse off than when considered a key constituency of a volatile and diverse social movement. In this way, access and institutionalization are means of, in Suzanne Mettler's (1998) terms, "dividing citizens." If indeed the homogenization of women's movements continues, and does so in this way, it occurs at quite a substantial cost. The discussion of abortion politics in Lee Ann Banaszak's chapter suggests a more complicated and disturbing picture. Increased European integration offers travel unimpeded within the Community save by individual financial constraints. In this reality, legal restrictions on abortion in Germany and Ireland create inconveniences for wealthier women, while imposing far harsher strictures on working-class and poor women.

Increased international integration presents would-be activists on all sorts of issues, including women, with additional venues in which to make claims. States remain, but operate in a political universe in which other institutions also make some of the decisions that nation-states formerly monopolized. The state as a political institution has not withered away or been outmoded,

---

[1] Importantly, the women's movement has demonstrated a transnational component for more than a century. See, for example, Anderson (2000).

but the areas in which advanced industrialized states enjoy autonomy have been circumscribed. Access to particular institutions does not mean influence on policy, an important limitation for actors who frame their claims in terms of political inclusion. Indeed, it may be that women have gained access to institutions even as that access itself is less valuable. Activists effectively play a political shell game in which access is only part of the question. Restrictions on state autonomy have not affected all areas equally, as several of the authors point out, and some women are better positioned in the new restructuring than others.

CONCLUSION

The chapters presented in this book do us a service in empirically examining the interaction of a movement with the state, in which both the challenger and the challenged are changing, at least partly in response to each other. Particularly useful here are the cross-national comparisons that are conducted explicitly in many of the chapters, and raised explicitly among all of the chapters by the volume itself. Thus, we are treated to the scholars responding to the challenge of understanding the process of social protest and claims making over time and across geographic space.

In all of the cases presented here, there are certain commonalities. Most significantly, the states adopted and adapted some portion of the initial women's movement's concerns and the coalitions that staged those movements altered in response to their changing political circumstances; some issues became more promising or urgent to some claimants, while others seemed easier to ignore. Mary Katzenstein's chapter argues that in the United States this has been good news for middle-class women and very bad news for poor women. It seems quite likely, based on the other cases presented, that a similar accounting can be found in the other wealthy countries.

Of course, the women's movement has not been the only force in pushing liberal states to restructure, nor has it been the most powerful one. Particularly since the end of the Cold War, wealthy countries have thrown themselves at the mercy of free trade and free markets, as nation-states have ceded power to make important decisions effectively. The new neoliberal order has been more helpful to actors who need less from the state. At the same time, the eroding of institutionalized prejudices and pressures that discriminate against women has meant, unsurprisingly, that more women have found visible and important positions within the state and civil society. From these chapters, however, it appears that women have been most successful in gaining access to institutions with little power over important policy matters. The question that remains is whether the ascension of women to positions in which they can manipulate the levers of government has come at a time when those levers are connected to much less that actually affects the nature of women's lives.

References

Albrecht, Lisa and Rose M. Brewer. 1990. *Bridges of Power: Women's Multicultural Alliances*. Philadelphia: New Society Publishers.

Almond, Gabriel and Sidney Verba. 1965. *The Civic Culture: Political Attitudes and Democracy in Five Nations*. Boston: Little, Brown and Company.

Alvarez, Sonia. 1990. *Engendering Democracy in Brazil: Women's Movements in Transition Politics*. Princeton, NJ: Princeton University Press.

Anderson, Bonnie S. 2000. *Joyous Greetings: The First International Women's Movement, 1830–1860*. New York: Oxford University Press.

Anderson, Perry. 1974a. *Lineages of the Absolutist State*. London: Verso.

Anderson, Perry. 1974b. *Passages from Antiquity to Feudalism*. London: Verso.

Appleton, Andrew and Amy G. Mazur. 1993. "Transformation or Modernization: the Rhetoric and Reality of Gender and Party Politics in France." In *Gender and Party Politics*, ed. Joni Lovenduski and Pippa Norris. London: Sage, pp. 86–112.

Arbetsmarknadsdepartementet. 1998. *Kvinnofrid*. http://www.kvinnofrid.gov.se. Accessed November 11, 1998.

Ardagh, John. 1994. *Ireland and the Irish: Portrait of a Changing Society*. London: Hamish Hamilton.

Aretxaga, Begoña. 1997. *Shattering Silence: Women, Nationalism and Political Subjectivity in Northern Ireland*. Princeton, NJ: Princeton University Press.

Arnold, Gretchen. 1995. "Dilemmas of Feminist Coalitions: Collective Identity and Strategic Effectiveness in the Battered Women's Movement." In *Feminist Organizations: Harvest of the New Women's Movement*, ed. Myra Marx Ferree and Patricia Yancey Martin. Philadelphia: Temple University Press, pp. 276–290.

Ashford, Douglas E. 1990. "Decentralizing France; How the Socialists Discovered Pluralism." *West European Politics* 13(4), October: 46–65.

Assises nationales des droits des femmes. 1998. Paris: Assises nationales.

Badie, Bertrand and Pierre Birnbaum. 1979. *Sociologie de l'Etat*. Paris: Grasset.

Banaszak, Lee Ann. 1996. *Why Movements Succeed or Fail: Opportunities, Culture and the Struggle for Woman Suffrage*. Princeton, NJ: Princeton University Press.

Barreiro, Belén. 1998. *Democracia y Conflicto Moral: la Política del Aborto en Italia y España*. Madrid: Instituto Juan March de Estudios e Investigaciones.

Barron, Jackie. 1990. *Not Worth the Paper: The Effectiveness of Legal Protection for Women and Children Experiencing Domestic Violence*. London: WAFE.

Bashevkin, Sylvia. 1998. *Women on the Defensive: Living through Conservative Times*. Chicago: University of Chicago Press.

Bashevkin, Sylvia. 1989. "Free Trade and Canadian Feminism: The Case of the National Action Committee on the Status of Women." *Canadian Public Policy* 15: 4.

Bataille, Phillipe and Françoise Gaspard. 1999. *Comment les femmes changent la politique et pourquoi les hommes resistent*. Paris: La Découverte.

Baumgartner, Frank and Bryan D. Jones. 1993. *Agendas and Instability in American Politics*. Chicago: University of Chicago Press.

Beccalli, Bianca. 1984. "From Equality to Difference: Women and Trade Unions in Italy." *Feminist Review* 16: 43–73.

Becker, Howard S. 1963. *The Outsiders*. Glencoe, IL: The Free Press.

Beckwith, Karen. 2000. "Beyond Compare? Women's Movements in Comparative Perspective." *European Journal of Political Research* 37: 431–468.

Beckwith, Karen. 1997. "Movement in Context: Women and Miners' Campaigns in Britain." In *The Political Context of Collective Action*, ed. Ricca Edmondson. London and New York: Routledge, pp. 15–32.

Beckwith, Karen. 1996. "Lancashire Women against Pit Closures: Women's Standing in a Men's Movement." *Signs* 21(4): 1034–1068.

Beckwith, Karen. 1987. "Response to Feminism in the Italian Parliament: Divorce, Abortion and Sexual Violence Legislation." In *The Women's Movements of the United States and Western Europe*, ed. Mary Fainsod Katzenstein and Carol McClurg Mueller. Philadelphia: Temple University Press, pp. 153–171.

Beckwith, Karen. 1985. "Feminism and Leftist Politics in Italy: The case of UDI-PCI relationships." In *Women and Politics in Western Europe*, ed. Sylvia Bashevkin. London: Frank Cass, pp. 19–37.

Beetham, David and Stuart Weir. 1999. "Auditing British Democracy." *The Political Quarterly* 70: 2.

Bella, Amparo 1999. "La ADMA, la AAM y las Radicales del Color Morado: Organizaciones de Mujeres en Zaragoza en los Primeros Años de la Transición." In *Mujeres, Regulación de Conflictos Sociales y Cultura de la Paz*, ed. Anna Aguado. Valencia: Universidad de Valencia, pp. 157–176.

Benz, Arthur. 1989. "Intergovernmental Relations in the 1980s." *Publius: The Journal of Federalism* 19 (Fall): 203–220.

Berelson, Bernard R., Paul F. Lazarsfeld, and William N. McPhee. 1954. *Voting*. Chicago: University of Chicago Press.

Berkovitch, Nitza. 1999. *From Motherhood to Citizenship: Women's Rights and International Organizations*. Baltimore, MD and London: Johns Hopkins University Press.

Bernstein, Mary. 1997. "Celebration and Suppression: The Strategic Uses of Identity by the Lesbian and Gay Movement." *American Journal of Sociology* 103:3.

Berrington, Hugh. 1998. "Britain in the Nineties: The Politics of Paradox." *Western European Politics* 21:1.

Berrington, Hugh. 1987. "The Changing Party System." In *Political Institutions in Britain: Development and Change*, ed. Lynton Robins. New York: Longman, pp. 132–150.

Berry, Mary Frances. 1986. *Why ERA Failed: Women's Rights and the Unending Process of the Constitution.* Bloomington: Indiana University Press.

Bianchi, Marina and Maria Mormino. 1984. "Militanti di se stesse." In *Altri Codici*, ed. Alberto Melucci. Bologna: Il Mulino, pp. 127–173.

Birch, Anthony. 1998. *The British System of Government*, 10th ed. London and New York: Routledge.

Birkinshaw, Patrick, Ian Harden, and Norman Lewis. 1990. *Government by Moonlight: The Hybrid Parts of the State.* London: Unwin Hyman.

Birnbaum, Pierre. 1988. *States and Collective Action.* Cambridge: Cambridge University Press.

Black, Naomi. 1980. "Feminism and Integration." *Journal of European Integration* 4(1): 83–103.

Blackburn, Robert and Raymond Plant. 1999. *Constitutional Reform: The Labour Government's Constitutional Reform Agenda.* London: Longman.

Blattert, Barbara. 1998. *Aus(sen)wirkungen staatlicher Frauenpolitik*, vol. 356 of *European University Studies Series XXXI: Political Science.* Frankfurt am Main: Peter Lang.

Boccia, Maria Luisa. 1980. "Percorsi del femminismo." *Critica Marxista* 3: 63–80.

Bogdanor, Vernon. 1999. "Devolution: Decentralisation or Disintegration?" *Political Quarterly* 70 (2), April–June: 185–194.

Bogdanor, Vernon. 1997. "Devolving for a Stronger Union." In *Comparative Politics, 1998–99*, ed. Christian Soe. Guilford, CT: Dushkin/McGraw, pp. 38–41.

Boles, Janet K. 1979. *The Politics of the Equal Rights Amendment: Conflict and the Decision Process.* New York: Longman.

Boli, John and George M. Thomas. 1999. *Constructing World Culture: International Nongovernmental Organizations Since 1875.* Stanford, CA: Stanford University Press.

Bondi, Liz. 1993. "Locating Identity Politics." In *Place and the Politics of Identity*, ed. Michael Keith and Steve Pile. London: Routledge, pp. 84–101.

Bonefeld, Werner, Alice Brown, and Peter Burnham. 1995. *A Major Crisis? The Politics of Economic Policy in the 1990s.* Aldershot: Dartmouth.

Bookman, Ann and Sandra Morgen, eds. 1988. *Women and the Politics of Empowerment.* Philadelphia: Temple University Press.

Borreguero, Concha, Elena Catena, Consuelo de la Gándara, and María Salas, eds. 1986. *La Mujer Española: de la Tradición a la Modernidad (1960–1980).* Madrid: Tecnos.

Bowman, Gary W., Simon Hakim, and Paul Seidenstat, eds. 1993. *Privatizing Correctional Institutions.* New Brunswick, NJ and London: Transaction Publishers.

Boyle, Kevin and Tom Hadden. 1999. "Northern Ireland." In *Constitutional Reform: The Labour Government's Constitutional Reform Agenda*, ed. Robert Blackburn and Raymond Plant. London: Longman.

BRÅ, PM. 1989. *Lagen om besöksförbud: En uppföljning* [The law concerning orders of protection: An investigation of their implementation]. Government Memorandum. Stockholm: The National Council for Crime Prevention.

Bradley, Karen and Francisco O. Ramirez. 1996. "World Polity Promotion of Gender Parity: Women's Share of Higher Education, 1965–1985." *Research in Sociology of Education and Socialization* 11: 63–91.

Brand, Karl-Werner. 1999. "Dialectics of Institutionalisation: The Transformation of the Environmental Movement in Germany." *Environmental Politics* 8 (1): 35–58.

Brand, Karl-Werner, Detlef Büsser, and Dieter Rucht. 1986. *Aufbruch in eine andere Gesellschaft. Neue soziale Bewegungen in der Bundesrepublik* (aktualisierte Neuausgabe, zuerst 1983). Frankfurt/M.: Campus.

Brandenburg. Ministerium der Finanzen. 2000. *Haushaltsplan 2000 und 2001: Ministerium für Arbeit, Soziales, Gesundheit, und Frauen.* http://www.brandenburg.de/land/mdf/lh/hhpl/hhpl2000/Haushalt/ep07.htm. Accessed July 18, 2001.

Brennan Center for Justice, NYU School of Law, Access to Justice Series. 2000. "How Congress Left the Poor with Only Half a Lawyer." New York.

Brennan Center for Justice, NYU School of Law, Access to Justice Series. 1999. "Making the Case: Legal Services for the Poor." New York.

Brenner, Johanna. 1996. "The Best of Times, The Worst of Times: Feminism in the United States." In *Mapping the Women's Movement: Feminist Politics and Social Transformation in the North*, ed. Monica Threlfall. London and New York: Verso, pp. 17–72.

Bretherton, Charlotte and Liz Sperling. 1996. "Women's Networks and the European Union: Towards an Inclusive Approach?" *Journal of Common Market Studies* 34(4), December: 487–508.

Briët, Martien, Bert Klandermans, and Frederike Kroon. 1987. "How Women Become Involved in the Women's Movement in the Netherlands." In *The Women's Movements of the United States and Western Europe*, ed. Mary Fainsod Katzenstein and Carol M. Mueller. Philadelphia: Temple University Press, pp. 44–63.

Bright, Charles and Harding, Susan, eds. 1984. *Statemaking and Social Movements.* Ann Arbor: University of Michigan Press.

Brown, Alice. 1998. "Building a Representative House in Scotland and the Role of Women in the Developmental Process." *PS: Political Science and Politics* XXX (1), March: 17–20.

Brown, Alice, David McCrone, and Lindsay Paterson. 1996. *Politics and Society in Scotland.* London: Macmillan.

Brown, Wendy. 1995. *States of Injury: Power and Freedom in Late Modernity.* Princeton, NJ: Princeton University Press.

Brownmiller, Susan. 1975. *Against Our Will: Men, Women, and Rape.* New York: Simon and Schuster.

Brulle, Robert J. 2000. *Agency, Democracy and Nature: The U.S. Environmental Movement from a Critical Perspective.* Cambridge, MA and London: The MIT Press.

Brysk, Alison. 1993. "From Above and Below: Social Movements, the International System, and Human Rights in Argentina." *Comparative Political Studies* 26 (3): 259–285.

Bryson, Valerie and Jo Campling. 1999. *Feminist Debates: Issues of Theory and Political Practice.* New York: New York University Press.

Buechler, Steven. 2000. *Social Movements in Advanced Capitalism: The Political Economy and Cultural Construction of Social Activism.* New York: Oxford University Press.

Buechler, Steven M. 1990. *Women's Movements in the United States.* New Brunswick, NJ: Rutgers University Press.

Bunch, Charlotte. 1990. "Women's Rights as Human Rights: Toward a Re-Vision of Human Rights." *Human Rights Quarterly* 12, November: 486–500.

Burns, Nancy, Kay Lehman Schlozman, and Sidney Verba. 1998. "Active Intersection: Gender, Race or Ethnicity, and Participation." Presented at the Annual Meeting of the Midwest Political Science Association, Chicago, April 23–25.

Burrell, Barbara C. 1994. *A Woman's Place is in the House: Campaigning for Congress in the Feminist Era.* Ann Arbor: University of Michigan.

Burstein, Paul, Rachel L. Einwohner, and Jocelyn A. Hollander. 1995. "The Success of Political Movements: A Bargaining Perspective." In *The Politics of Social Protest: Comparative Perspectives on States and Social Movements,* ed. J. Craig Jenkins and Bert Klandermans. London: UCL Press.

Burt, Martha R, Nancy Pindus, and Jeffrey Capizzano. 2000. "The Social Safety Net at the Beginning of Federal Welfare Reform: Organization of Access to Social Services for Low-Income Families." In *Assessing the New Federalism.* Washington, DC: Urban Institute.

Burt, Sandra. 1990. "Organized Women's Groups and the State." In *Policy Communities and Public Policy in Canada: A Structural Approach,* ed. William D. Coleman and Grace Skogstad. Mississauga: Copp Clark and Pitman, pp. 191–211.

Burt, Sandra. 1988. "The Charter of Rights and the Ad Hoc Lobby: The Limits of Success." *Atlantis* 14:4.

Bustelo, Carlota. 1992. "La democracia paritaria." *El País* 20, October.

Bustelo, María 1999. "Políticas Públicas de Igualdad de Género en España: Evolución y Evaluación." In *Género y Ciudadanía: Revisiones desde el Ámbito Privado,* ed. Margarita Ortega, Cristina Sánchez, and Celia Valiente. Madrid: Universidad Autónoma de Madrid, pp. 367–389.

Butler, David and Martin Westlake. 1995. *British Politics and European Elections, 1994.* New York: St. Martin's Press.

Butler, Judith. 1990. *Gender Trouble: Feminism and the Subversion of Identity.* New York: Routledge.

Byrne, Paul. 1997. *Social Movements in Britain.* London and New York: Routledge.

Byrne, Paul. 1996. "The Politics of the Women's Movement." *Parliamentary Affairs* 49(1): 55–70.

Bystydzienski, Jill. 1995. *Women in Electoral Politics: Lessons from Norway.* Westport, CT: Praeger.

Carlucci, Paola. 1999. *Associazioni di donne a Firenze negli anni '80 e '90.* Firenze: Centro Editoriale Toscano.

Carter, April. 1988. *The Politics of Women's Rights.* London and New York: Longman.

Castells, Manuel. 1997. *The Information Age: Volume II, The Power of Identity.* Malden, MA: Blackwell.

Castles, Francis G. 1995. "Welfare State Development in Southern Europe." *West European Politics* 18: 291–313.

Castles, Francis and Deborah Mitchell. 1993. "Worlds of Welfare and Families of Nations." In *Families of Nations: Patterns of Policy in Western Democracies,* ed. Francis G. Castles. Aldershot: Dartmouth, pp. 93–128.

Chamberlayne, Prue. 1993. "Women and the State: Changes in Roles and Rights in France, West Germany, Italy and Britain, 1970–1990." In *Women and Social Policies in Europe: Work, Family and the State*, ed. Jane Lewis. Brookfield, VT: Edward Elgar, pp. 170–193.

Chancer, Lynn S. 1998. *Reconcilable Differences*. Berkeley: University of California Press.

Charlot, Monica. 1980. "Women in Politics in France." In *The French National Assembly Elections of 1978*, ed. Howard R. Penniman. Washington, DC: American Enterprise Institute, pp. 171–191.

Childs, Sarah. 2001. "Hitting the Target: Are Labour Women MPs 'Acting For' Women?" Presented at the Annual Meeting of the American Political Science Association, San Francisco, August 30–September 2.

Clarke, Steve. 2001. "Earnings of men and women in the EU: the gap narrowing but only slowly." *Statistics in Focus: Population and Social Conditions*. Theme 3-5/2001. Catalogue Number KS-NK-01-005-EN-1. Published by Eurostat. http://europa. eu.int/comm/eurostat/Public/datashop/print-catalogue/EN?catalogue=Eurostat& product =KS-NK-01-005-I-EN. Accessed August 1, 2001.

Cockburn, Cynthia. 1998. *The Space between Us: Negotiating Gender and National Identities in Conflict*. London: Zed Books.

Cockburn, Cynthia, Bianca Beccalli, Paola Piva, and Chiara Ingrao. 1984. "Trade Unions and the Radicalizing of Socialist Feminism." *Feminist Review* 16, Summer: 43–74.

Cole, M. 1999. "Adversary Politics and Proportional Representation." *The Political Quarterly* 70:2.

Collins, Neil and Frank McCann. 1991. *Irish Politics Today*. Manchester: Manchester University Press.

Connelly, Alpha. 1999. "Women and the Constitution of Ireland." In *Contesting Politics: Women in Ireland, North and South*, ed. Yvonne Galligan, Eilis Ward, and Rick Wilford. Boulder, CO: Westview Press, pp. 18–37.

Cook, Alice and Gwyn Kirk. 1983. *Greenham Women Everywhere: Dreams, Ideas, and Actions from the Women's Peace Movement*. London: Pluto Press.

Cooper, Alice Holmes. 1995. *Paradoxes of Peace: German Peace Movements Since 1945*. Ann Arbor: University of Michigan Press.

Coote, Anna and Polly Pattullo. 1990. *Power and Prejudice: Women and Politics*. London: Weidenfeld and Nicholson.

Corbett, Richard, Francis Jacobs, and Michael Shackleton. 1995. *The European Parliament*, 3rd ed. New York: Stockton.

Corcoran, Jennifer. 1988. "Enforcement Procedures for Individual Complaints: Equal Pay and Equal Treatment." In *Women, Equality and Europe*, ed. Mary Buckley and Malcolm Anderson. London: Macmillan Press.

Costain, Anne N. 1992. *Inviting Women's Rebellion: A Political Process Interpretation of the Women's Movement*. Baltimore, MD: Johns Hopkins University.

Costain, Anne N. 1988. "Women's Claims as a Special Interest." In *The Politics of the Gender Gap*, ed. Carol McClurg Mueller. Newbury Park, CA: Sage, pp. 150–172.

Cowley, Philip and Sarah Childs. 2001. "Critical but not Rebellious? New Labour Women in the House of Commons." Presented at the Annual Meeting of the American Political Science Association, San Francisco, August 30–September 2.

Cress, Daniel M. and David A. Snow. 1996. "Mobilization at the Margins: Resources, Benefactors and the Viability of Homeless Social Movement Organizations." *American Sociological Review* 61:1089–1109.

Crouch, Colin. 1993. *Industrial Relations and European State Traditions.* Oxford: Claredon Press.

Dahlerup, Drude. 1986. *The New Women's Movements: Feminism and Political Power in Europe and the USA.* Belmont, CA: Sage.

Dahrendorf, Ralf. 1968. *Gesellschaft und Demokratie in Deutschland.* München: Piper.

Daley, Anthony. 1999. "The Hollowing Out of French Unions: Politics and Industrial Relations after 1981." In *The Brave New World of European Labor,* ed. Andrew Martin and George Ross. New York: Berghahn Books, pp. 167–216.

Daley, Suzanne. 2001 "France's Most Courted: Women to Join the Ticket." *New York Times,* February 6, p. 1.

D'Amelia, Marina. 1985. "Dalla differenza alle differenziazioni. Le difficili innovazioni dei gruppi." *Memoria. Rivista di storia delle donne* 13: 122–131.

Darcy, R. and Karen Beckwith. 1991. "Political Disaster, Political Triumph: The Election of Women to National Parliaments." Presented at the Annual Meeting of the American Political Science Association, Washington, DC, August 29–September 1.

Darcy, Robert, Susan Welch, and Janet Clark. 1994. *Women, Elections and Representation,* 2nd ed. Lincoln: University of Nebraska Press.

Deckard, Barbara. 1975. *The Women's Movement.* New York: Harper and Row.

della Porta, Donatella. 1999. *La politica locale.* Bologna: Il Mulino.

della Porta, Donatella. 1996. "Movimenti collettivi e sistema politico." *Italia, 1960–1995.* Bari: Laterza.

della Porta, Donatella. 1995. *Social Movements, Political Violence, and the State.* Cambridge: Cambridge University Press.

della Porta, Donatella and Mario Diani. 1999. *Social Movements: An Introduction.* Oxford: Blackwell.

della Porta, Donatella and Hanspeter Kriesi. 1999. "Social Movements in a Globalizing World." In *Social Movements in a Globalizing World,* ed. Donatella della Porta, Hanspeter Kriesi, and Dieter Rucht. London: Macmillan. pp. 3–22.

della Porta, Donatella and Herbert Reiter, eds. 1998. *Policing Protest.* Minneapolis: University of Minnesota Press.

della Porta, Donatella and Dieter Rucht. 1995. "Left-Libertarian Movements in Context: A Comparison of Italy and West Germany." In *The Politics of Social Protest: Comparative Perspectives on States and Social Movements,* ed. J. Craig Jenkins and Bert Klandermans. Minneapolis: University of Minnesota Press, pp. 229–272.

della Porta, Donatella, Celia Valiente, and Maria Kousis. Forthcoming. "Women's Movements and Women's Rights in Southern Europe." In *Democratic Consolidation in Southern Europe,* ed. Nikiforos Diamandouros and Hans-Juergen Puhle. Washington, DC: Johns Hopkins University Press.

della Porta, Donatella, Celia Valiente, and Maria Kousis. 1997. "Women's Movement and Democratization: Paths to Women's Rights in Southern Europe." Typescript.

della Sala, Vincent. 1997. "Hollowing Out and Hardening the State: European Integration and the Italian Economy." *West European Politics* 20(1), January: 14–33.

DeNardo, James. 1985. *Power in Numbers: The Political Strategy of Protest and Rebellion*. Princeton, NJ: Princeton University Press.

Di Febo, Giuliana 1979. *Resistencia y Movimiento de Mujeres en España 1936–1976*. Barcelona: Icaria.

Dobash, R. Emerson and Russell P. Dobash. 1992. *Women, Violence and Social Change*. New York: Routledge.

Dobrowolsky, Alexandra. 2000. *The Politics of Pragmatism: Women, Representation and Constitutionalism in Canada*. Toronto: Oxford University Press.

Dobrowolsky, Alexandra. 1998. "Of 'Special Interest': Interest Identity and Feminist Constitutional Activism." *Canadian Journal of Political Science* 31: 4.

Dodson, Debra. Forthcoming. *The Impact of Women in Congress*. Oxford: Oxford University Press.

Dodson, Debra. 1995. *Voices, Views, Votes; The Impact of Women in the 103rd Congress*. New Brunswick, NJ: Center for the American Woman and Politics, Eagleton Institute.

Dolan, Julie. 1997. "Support for Women's Interests in the 103rd Congress: The Distinct Impact of Congressional Women." *Women & Politics* 18(4): 81–94.

Duchen, Claire. 1986. *Feminism in France: From May '68 to Mitterrand*. London and Boston: Routledge and Kegan Paul.

Dunlap, Riley E. 1991. "Trends in Public Opinion Toward Environmental Issues: 1965–1990." *Society and Natural Resources* 4 (3): 285–312.

Dunleavy, Patrick, Andrew Gamble, Ian Holliday, and Gillian Peele. 1993. *Developments in British Politics 4*. London: Macmillan.

Durán, María A. and María T Gallego. 1986. "The Women's Movement in Spain and the New Spanish Democracy." In *The New Women's Movement: Feminism and Political Power in Europe and the USA*, ed. Drude Dahlerup. London: Sage, pp. 200–216.

Dyson, Kenneth. 1996. "The Economic Order – Still Modell Deutschland?" In *Developments in German Politics 2*, ed. Gordon Smith, William Paterson, and Stephen Padgett. Durham, NC: Duke University Press, pp. 194–210.

Ebbinghaus, Bernhard and Jelle Visser. 1996. "When Institutions Matter: Union Growth and Decline in Western Europe, 1950–1995." *European Sociological Review* 15 (2): 135–158.

Echols, Alice. 1989. *Daring to be Bad: Radical Feminism in America 1967–1975*. Minneapolis: University of Minnesota Press.

Edmondson, Ricca, ed. 1997. *The Political Context of Collective Action: Power, Argumentation, and Democracy*. London and New York: Routledge.

Edsall, Thomas Byrne. 1988. *Power and Money: Writing about Politics, 1971–1987*. New York: W. W. Norton.

Edsall, Thomas Byrne. 1984. *The New Politics of Inequality*. New York: W. W. Norton.

Eduards, Maud. 1997. "The Women's Shelter Movement." In *Towards a New Democratic Order? Women's Organizing in Sweden in the 1990s*, ed. Gunnel Gustafsson, Maud Eduards, and Malin Rönnblom. Stockholm: Publica, pp. 120–168.

Egidi, Piera. 1985. "Cronaca di una città. Torino." *Memoria. Rivista di storia delle donne* 13: 103–116.

Eisenstein, Hester. 1995. "The Australian Femocratic Experiment: A Feminist Case for Bureaucracy." In *Feminist Organizations: Harvest of the New Women's Movement*, ed. Myra Marx Ferree and Patricia Yancey Martin. Philadelphia: Temple University Press, pp. 69–83.

Eisinger, Peter K. 1973. "The Conditions of Protest Behavior in American Cities." *American Political Science Review* 67:11–28.

El País. April 29, 2000: 26; December 7, 2000: 34; January 31, 1999; February 19, 1999; September 28, 1999: 70; August 31, 1998; November 2, 1998; December 27, 1998; May 18, 1997; August 8, 1997; October 27, 1997.

Elizondo, Arantxa and Eva Martínez 1995. "Presencia de Mujeres y Política para la Igualdad entre los Sexos: el Caso de las Instituciones Políticas Vascas (1980–1994)." *Revista de Estudios Políticos* 89: 345–368.

Ellwood, Marilyn R. and Kimball Lewis. 1999. "On and Off Medicaid: Enrollment Patterns for California and Florida in 1995." In *Assessing the New Federalism.* Washington, DC: The Urban Institute.

Elman, R. Amy. 2001. "Testing the Limits of European Citizenship: Ethnic Hatred and Male Violence." *National Women's Studies Association Journal* 13(3): 49–69.

Elman, R. Amy. 2001a. "Unprotected by the Swedish Welfare State Revisited: Assessing a Decade of Reforms for Battered Women." *Women's Studies International Forum* 24(1): 39–52.

Elman, R. Amy, ed. 1996a. *Sexual Politics and the European Union.* Providence, RI: Berghahn Books.

Elman, R. Amy. 1996b. *Sexual Subordination and State Intervention: Comparing Sweden and the United States.* Oxford: Berghahn Books.

Elman, R. Amy. 1993. "Debunking the Social Democrats and the Myth of Equality." *Women's Studies International Forum* 16(5): 513–522.

Elman, R. Amy and Maud L. Eduards. 1991. "Unprotected by the Swedish Welfare State: A Survey of Battered Women and the Assistance They Received." *Women's Studies International Forum* 14(5): 413–421.

Engender. 1996. "The Importance of the Civic Assembly in the Democratic Process in Scotland." *Engender Newsletter* 12: 2.

Engender. 1995. *Gender Audit.* Edinburgh: Engender.

Engstrom, Richard L. 1987. "District Magnitude and the Election of Women to the Irish Dail." *Electoral Studies* 6: 2.

Epp, Charles R. 1998. *The Rights Revolution: Lawyers, Activists, and Supreme Courts in Comparative Perspective.* Chicago: University of Chicago Press.

"Equal Pay for Women." *The Financial Times* (London), August 25, 1993, p. 13. Accessed via LEXIS-NEXIS Academic Universe, July 25, 2001.

Ergas, Yasmine. 1992. "La costruzione del soggetto femminile: il femminismo negli anni '60/'70." In *Storia delle donne in Occidente,* ed. G. Duby and M. Perrot. Il Novecento: Bari: Laterza, pp. 564–593.

Ergas, Yasmine. 1986. *Nelle maglie della politica.* Milano: Angeli.

Escario, Pilar, Inés Alberdi, and Ana I. López-Accotto. 1996. *Lo Personal es Político: el Movimiento Feminista en la Transición.* Madrid: Instituto de la Mujer.

Esping-Andersen, Gosta. 1990. *The Three Worlds of Welfare Capitalism.* Cambridge: Polity Press.

European Court of Justice. 2000. *Katarina Abrahamsson and Leif Anderson v. Elisabet Fogelqvist.* Case C-407/98. Available on Celex. Commission of the European Union, Brussels. Referenced July 30, 2001.

European Court of Justice. 2000. *Bärbel Kachelmann v. Bankhaus Hermann Lampe KG.* Case C-322/98. Available on Celex. Commission of the European Union, Brussels. Referenced August 1, 2001.

European Court of Justice. 2000. *Deutsche Post AG v. Elisabeth Sievers.* Case C-270/97. Available on Celex. Commission of the European Union, Brussels. Referenced August 1, 2001.

European Court of Justice. 2000. *Deutsche Telekom AG v. Agnes Vick.* Case C-234/96. Available on Celex. Commission of the European Union, Brussels. Referenced August 1, 2001.

European Court of Justice. 2000. *Shirley Preston and Others v. Wolverhampton Health-care NHS Trust and Others and Dorothy Fletcher and Others v. Midland Bank plc.* Case C-78/98. Available on Celex. Commission of the European Union, Brussels. Referenced August 1, 2001.

European Court of Justice. 1998. *Kathleen Hill and Ann Stapleton v. The Revenue Commissioners and Department of Finance.* C-243/95. Available on Celex. Commission of the European Union, Brussels. Referenced July 30, 2001.

European Court of Justice. 1997. *Hellmut Marschall v. Land Nordrhein-Westfalen.* C-409/95. Available on Celex. Commission of the European Union, Brussels. Referenced July 26, 2001.

European Court of Justice. 1993. *Eckhard Kalanke v. Freie Hansestadt Bremen.* Case C-450/93. Available on Celex. Commission of the European Union, Brussels. Referenced July 30, 2001.

European Court of Justice. 1991. *Society for the Protection of Unborn Children Ireland Ltd. v. Stephen Grogan and others.* Case C-159/90. Available on Celex. Commission of the European Union, Brussels. Referenced July 20, 2001.

European Court of Justice. 1976. *Gabrielle Defrenne v. Société Anonyme Belge de Navigation Aérienne Sabena.* Case vC-43/75. Text taken from *Equality in Law Between Men and Women in the European Community,* ed. Michel Verwilghen. 1987. Louvain-la-Neuve: Presses Universitaires de Louvain, pp. 135–162.

European Parliament. 1994. *Europe Elections, 1994.* Luxembourg Central Press Division.

European Union. 1997. "Council Directive 97/81/EC of 15 December 1997 Concerning the Framework Agreement on Part-Time Work Concluded by UNICE, CEEP and the ETUC – Annex : Framework Agreement on Part-Time Work." *Official Journal* L 014, 20/01/1998 p. 0009–0014. Accessed on Eur-Lex (Document 397L0081), August 15, 2001.

European Union. European Parliament. Committee on Women's Rights. 1999. *Second Report on the Report from the Commission to the Council, the European Parliament, the Economic and Social Committee and the Committee of the Regions on the State of Women's Health in the European Community.* January 22, 1999. (A4-0029/99). Accessed July 18, 2001.

Eurostat. The Statistical Office of the European Communities. 2000. *Earnings in Industry and Services: Hours of Work in Industry, 1996–1998.* Luxembourg-Kirchberg: Statistical Office of the European Communities.

Eurostat. The Statistical Office of the European Communities. 1996. *Earnings: Industry and Services 1995.* Luxembourg-Kirchberg: Statistical Office of the European Communities.

Eurostat. The Statistical Office of the European Communities. 1987. *Eurostat Review 1976–1985*. Luxembourg-Kirchberg: Statistical Office of the European Communities.

Evans, Rob and David Hencke. 1999. "Straw to climb down on freedom of information." *Guardian Weekly* October 14–20.

Evans, Sara. 1979. *Personal Politics: The Roots of Women's Liberation in the Civil Rights Movement and the New Left*. New York: Knopf.

Fawcett Society. 1997. *The Best Man for the Job? The Selection of Women Parliamentary Candidates*. London: Fawcett.

Fawcett Society. 1995/96. *Working Towards Equality. Annual Report*. London: Fawcett.

Fearon, Kate. 1999. *Women's Work: The Story of the Northern Ireland Women's Coalition*. Belfast: Blackstaff Press.

Featherstone, Joseph. 1970. "Kentucky Fried Children," *The New Republic* 163, September 5: 12–16.

Fernández, José M. and Xavier Aierdi. 1997. "Entramado Organizativo del Movimiento Feminista en el País Vasco." *Revista Española de Investigaciones Sociológicas* 80: 183–201.

Ferraro, Kathleen J. 1993. "Cops, Courts, and Woman Battering." In *Violence Against Women: The Bloody Footprints*, ed. Pauline Bart and Eileen Moran. London: Sage, pp. 165–192.

Ferraro, Kathleen J. 1989. "The Legal Response to Woman Battering in the United States." In *Women, Policing, and Male Violence: International Perspectives*, ed. Jalna Hanmer and Elizabeth Stanko. New York: Routledge, pp. 155–184.

Ferree, Myra Marx. 1995. "Making Equality: The Women's Affairs Offices in the Federal Republic of Germany." In *Comparative State Feminism*, ed. Dorothy McBride Stetson and Amy Mazur. Thousand Oaks, CA: Sage, pp. 95–113.

Ferree, Myra Marx, 1987. "Equality and Autonomy: Feminist Politics in the United States and West Germany." In *The Women's Movements of the United States and Western Europe*, ed. Mary Fainsod Katzenstein and Carol McClurg Mueller. Philadelphia: Temple University Press, pp. 172–195.

Ferree, Myra Marx, William A. Gamson, Jürgen Gerhards, and Dieter Rucht. 2002. *Shaping Abortion Discourse: Democracy and the Public Sphere in Germany and the United States*. Cambridge: Cambridge University Press.

Ferree, Myra Marx and Beth Hess. 1994. *Controversy and Coalition: The New Feminist Movement Across Three Decades of Change*, rev. ed. New York: Twayne.

Ferree, Myra Marx and Patricia Yancey Martin. 1995. *Feminist Organizations: Harvest of the Women's Movement*. Philadelphia: Temple University Press.

Ferrera, Maurizio. 1996. "Il modello sud europeo di welfare state." *Rivista italiana di scienza politica* 26: 67–101.

Ferrera, Maurizio. 1993. *Modelli di solidarietà*. Bologna: Il Mulino.

Findlay, Sue. 1987. "Facing the State: The Politics of the Women's Movement Reconsidered." In *Feminism and Political Economy*, ed. Heather Jon Maroney and Meg Luxton. Toronto: Methuen.

Firestone, Shulamith. 1970. *The Dialectic of Sex*. New York: Bantham Books.

Fix, Michael E. and Karen Tumlin 1999. "Welfare Reform and the Devolution of Immigrant Policy." In *New Federalism: Issues and Options for States* Series. Washington DC: The Urban Institute. Number A-15.

Flam, Helena, ed. 1994. *States and Anti-Nuclear Oppositional Movements*. Edinburgh: Edinburgh University Press.

Flockton, Christopher. 1996. "Economic Management and the Challenge of Reunification." In *Developments in German Politics 2*, ed. Gordon Smith, William E. Paterson, and Stephen Padgett. Durham, NC: Duke University Press, pp. 211–232.

Folguera, Pilar. 1988a. "De la Transición Política a la Democracia: La Evolución del Feminismo en España durante el Periódo 1975–1988." In *El Feminismo en España: Dos Siglos de Historia*, ed. Pilar Folguera. Madrid: Fundación Pablo Iglesias.

Folguera, Pilar, ed. 1988b. *El Feminismo en España: Dos Siglos de Historia*. Madrid: Fundación Pablo Iglesias.

Forbes, Ian. 1997. "The Privatisation of Equality Policy in the British Employment Market for Women." In *Sex Equality Policy in Western Europe*, ed. Frances Gardiner. New York: Routledge, pp. 161–179.

Frabotta, Biancamaria and Giuseppina Ciuffreda, eds. 1976. *Le politiche del femminismo*. Roma: Savelli.

Franklin, M.N., Thomas T. Mackie, Henry Valen, et al. 1992. *Electoral Change: Responses to Evolving Social and Attitudinal Structures in Western Countries*. Cambridge: Cambridge University Press.

Fraser, Nancy. 1989. *Unruly Practices: Power, Discourse and Gender in Contemporary Social Theory*. Minneapolis: University of Minnesota Press.

Freeman, Jo. 1987. "Whom You Know vs. Whom You Represent: Feminist Influence in the Democratic and Republican Parties." In *The Women's Movements of the United States and Western Europe*, ed. Mary Fainsod Katzenstein and Carol McClurg Mueller. Philadelphia: Temple University Press, pp. 215–244.

Freeman, Jo. 1975. *The Politics of Women's Liberation*. New York: Longman.

Friedrichsen, Gisela. 1989. *Abtreibung: Der Kreuzzug von Memmingen*. Wiesbaden: Orell Füssli.

Fuchs, Dieter. 1991. "Zum Wandel politischer Konfliktlinien: Ideologische Gruppierungen und Wahlverhalten." In *Die Bundesrepublik in den achtziger Jahren*, ed. Werner Süß. Opladen: Westdeutscher Verlag, pp. 69–88.

Fuhrman, Susan. 1994. "Clinton's Education Policy and Intergovernmental Relations in the 1990s." *Publius: The Journal of Federalism* 24, Summer: 83–97.

Gaffney, John. 1996. "France." In *The 1994 Elections to the European Parliament*, ed. Juliet Lodge. London: Pinter, pp. 84–106.

Galligan, Yvonne. 1998. *Women and Politics in Contemporary Ireland: From the Margins to the Mainstream*. London: Pinter.

Gamson, William A. 1990 [1975]. *The Strategy of Social Protest*. Belmont, CA: Wadsworth.

Gamson, William A. and David S. Meyer. 1996. "Framing Political Opportunity." In *Comparative Perspectives on Social Movements: Political Opportunities, Mobilizing Structures and Cultural Framings*, ed. Doug McAdam, John D. McCarthy, and Mayer N. Zald. Cambridge: Cambridge University Press, pp. 275–290.

Gamson, William A. and Andre Modigliani. 1989. "Media Discourse and Public Opinion on Nuclear Power: A Constructionist Approach." *American Journal of Sociology* 95: 1–37.

Gaspard, Françoise. 1998a. "La parité, principe ou stratégie." *Le Monde Diplomatique*. November: 26–27.

Gaspard, Françoise. 1998b. "Parity: Why Not?" *Differences: A Journal of Feminist Cultural Studies* 9(2): 93–104.

Gaspard, Françoise, Claude Servan-Schreiber, and Anne Le Gall. 1992. *Au pouvoir citoyennes: Liberté, Egalité, Parité.* Paris: Le Seuil.

Gelb, Joyce. 1995. "Feminist Organization Success and the Politics of Engagement." In *Feminist Organizations: Harvest of the New Women's Movement,* ed. Myra Marx Ferree and Patricia Yancey Martin. Philadelphia: Temple University Press, pp. 128–134.

Gelb, Joyce. 1989. *Feminism and Politics: A Comparative Perspective.* Berkeley: University of California Press.

Gelb, Joyce and Vivien Hart. 1999. "Feminist Politics in a Hostile Environment: Obstacles and Opportunities." In *How Social Movements Matter,* ed. Marco Giugni, Doug McAdam, and Charles Tilly. Minneapolis: University of Minnesota, pp. 149–181.

Gelb, Joyce and Marian Lief Palley. 1987. *Women and Public Policies,* 2nd ed. Princeton, NJ: Princeton University Press.

Gélédan, Alain. 1993. *Le Bilan économique des années Mitterrand, 1981–1993.* Paris: Le Monde.

Geller-Schwartz, Linda. 1995. "An Array of Agencies." In *Comparative State Feminism,* ed. Dorothy McBride Stetson and Amy Mazur. Thousand Oaks. CA: Sage, pp. 40–58.

Georghiou, Mary. 1993. *Labour's Road to Electoral Reform: What's Wrong With First Past the Post?* London: LCER.

Gerhards, Jürgen, Friedhelm Neidhardt, and Dieter Rucht. 1998. *Zwischen Palaver und Diskurs: Strukturen öffentlicher Meinungsbildung am Beispiel der deutschen Diskussion zur Abtreibung.* Opladen: Westdeutscher Verlag.

Gerlach, Luther and Virgina Hine. 1970. *People, Power and Change.* Indianapolis: Bobbs-Merrill.

"Germany: Catholic Church to End Abortion Counseling Certificates." *Off Our Backs* March 28, 1998: 6.

Ginsburg, Norman. 1993. "Sweden: The Social Democratic Case." In *Comparing Welfare States: Britain in International Context,* ed. Alan Cochrane and John Clarke. London: Sage, pp. 173–203.

Githens, Marianne, Pippa Norris, and Joni Lovenduski, eds. 1994. *Different Roles, Different Voices: Women and Politics in the United States and Europe.* New York: HarperCollins.

Giugni, Marco G. 1998. "Was It Worth the Effort? The Outcomes and Consequences of Social Movements." *Annual Review of Sociology* 98: 371–393.

Glatzer, Wolfgang 1999. "Lebensstandard und Lebensqualität. "In *Handwörterbuch zur Gesellschaft Deutschlands,* ed. Bernhard Schäfers und Wolfgang Zapf. Opladen: Leske + Budrich, pp. 427–438.

Glendinning, Caroline and Jane Millar. 1992. *Women and Poverty in Britain: The 1990s.* New York: Harvester Wheatsheaf.

Goggin, Malcolm, ed. 1998. *Understanding the New Politics of Abortion.* Newbury Park: Sage Publications.

Golden, Miriam, Michael Wallerstein, and Peter Lange. 1999. "Postwar Trade-Union Organization and Industrial Relations in Twelve Countries." In *Continuity and Change in Contemporary Capitalism*, ed. Herbert Kitschelt, Peter Lange, Gary Marks, and John D. Stephens. Cambridge: Cambridge University Press, pp. 194–230.

Goodstein, Laurie. 2001. "Eager States Have Been Steering Religious Charities Toward Aid." *New York Times*, July 21, A1.

Gornick, Janet C. and David S. Meyer 1998. "Changing Political Opportunity: The Anti-Rape Movement and Public Policy." *Journal of Policy History* 10(4), December: 367–398.

Gotell, Lise. 1990. "The Canadian Women's Movement, Equality Rights and the Charter." A Report Prepared for The Canadian Research Institute for The Advancement of Women. Paper no. 16. Ottawa: CRIAW/ICREF.

Gourevitch, Peter. 1986. *Politics in Hard Times*. Ithaca, NY: Cornell University Press.

Grace, Sharon. 1995. *Policing Domestic Violence in the 1990s*. London: HMSO.

Granados, Elena. 1999. "El Instituto Andaluz de la Mujer: la Creación de un Órgano Autonómico para la Igualdad entre los Géneros." In *Género y Ciudadanía: Revisiones desde el Ámbito Privado*, ed. Margarita Ortega, Cristina Sánchez, and Celia Valiente. Madrid: Universidad Autónoma de Madrid, pp. 391–405.

Grazioli, Marco and Giovanni Lodi. 1984. "La mobilitazione collettiva degli anni ottanta: tra condizione e convinzione." In *Altri Codici*, ed. Alberto Melucci. Bologna: Il Mulino, pp. 267–313.

Greer, Germaine. 1971. *The Female Eunuch*. London: Paladin.

Greiffenhagen, Martin and Sylvia Greiffenhagen. 1981. *Ein schwieriges Vaterland: Zur Politischen Kultur Deutschlands*. Frankfurt/M.: List.

Griffin, Gabriele. 1994. "The Struggle Continues – An Interview with Hannana Siddiqui of Southhall Black Sisters." In *Feminist Activism in the 1990s*, ed. Gabriele Griffin. London: Taylor and Francis, pp. 79–89.

Guadagni Anna Maria. 1985. "Nuove facce dell'Udi." *Memoria. Rivista di storia delle donne* 13: 13–30.

Guadagnini, Marila. 1995. "The Late-Comers: Italy's Equal Status and Equal Opportunity Agencies." In *Comparative State Feminism*, ed. Dorothy McBride Stetson and Amy G. Mazur. Thousand Oaks, CA: Sage, pp. 150–167.

Haase-Dubosc, Danielle. 1999. "Sexual Difference and Politics in France Today." *Feminist Studies* 25 (1), Spring: 183–210.

Habermas, Jürgen. 1973. *Legitimationsprobleme im Spätkapitalismus*. Frankfurt/M.: Suhrkamp.

Handler, Joel F. 1997. "Welfare Reform in the United States." *Osgoode Hall Law Journal* 35, Summer: 289.

Hardiman, Niamh. 1998. "Inequality and the Representation of Interests." In *Ireland and the Politics of Change*, ed. William Crotty and David E. Schmitt. London: Longman, pp. 122–143.

Harford, Barbara and Sarah Hopkins. 1984. *Greenham Common: Women at the Wire*. London: Women's Press.

Harne, Lynne. 1996. "Valuing Women: Young Lesbians Talk." In *All the Rage: Reasserting Radical Lesbian Feminism*, ed. Lynne Harne and Elaine Miller. London: The Women's Press, pp. 231–246.

Hartmann, Heidi. 1981. "The Unhappy Marriage of Marxism and Feminism: Towards a More Progressive Union." In *Women and Revolution*, ed. Lydia Sargent. Boston: South End Press, pp. 1–41.

Hartmann, Susan M. 1998. *The Other Feminists: Activists in the Liberal Establishment.* New Haven, CT and London: Yale University Press.

Haughton, Jonathan. 1998. "The Dynamics of Economic Change." In *Ireland and the Politics of Change*, ed. William Crotty and David E. Schmitt. London: Longman, pp. 27–50.

Haussman, Melissa. 1992. "The Personal is Constitutional: Feminist Struggles for Equality Rights in the United States and Canada." In *Women Transforming Politics: Worldwide Strategies for Empowerment*, ed. Jill Bystydzienski. Bloomington: Indiana University Press, pp. 108–123.

Healey, Jon. 1996. "VA-HUD Spending Bill Clears with Bipartisan Support." *Congressional Quarterly Report* September 28: 2762.

Healy, Geraldine and Gill Kirton. 2000. "Women, Power and Trade Union Government in the UK." *British Journal of Industrial Relations* 38(3): 343–360.

Heenan, Dierdre and Anne Marie Gray. 1999. "Women and Nominated Boards in Ireland." In *Contesting Politics: Women in Ireland, North and South*, ed. Yvonne Galligan, Eilis Ward, and Rick Wilford. Boulder, CO: Westview, pp. 185–200.

Held, David and Joel Krieger. 1981. "Theories of the State: Some Competing Claims." In *The State in Capitalist Europe*, ed. Stephen Borstein, David Held, and Joel Krieger. London: George Allen & Unwin, pp. 1–20.

Helfferich, Barbara and Felix Kolb. 2001. "Multilevel Action Coordination in European Contentious Politics: The European Women's Lobby." In *Contentious Europeans: Protest and Politics in an Integrating Europe*, ed. Doug Imig and Sidney Tarrow. Boulder, CO: Rowman and Littlefield, pp. 143–162.

Hellman, Judith Adler. 1987a. "Women's Struggle in a Workers' City: Feminist Movements in Turin." In *The Women's Movements of the United States and Western Europe*, ed. Mary Fainsod Katzenstein and Carol McClurg Mueller. Philadelphia: Temple University Press, pp. 111–131.

Hellman, Judith. 1987b. *Journeys among Women: Feminism in Five Italian Cities.* Cambridge: Polity Press.

Hellman, Stephen. 1987. "Feminism and the Model of Militancy in an Italian Communist Federation: Challenges to the Old Style of Politics." In *The Women's Movements of the United States and Western Europe*, ed. Mary Fainsod Katzenstein and Carol McClurg Mueller. Philadelphia: Temple University Press, pp. 132–152.

Henderson, M. 2000. "Scottish Women's Consultative Forum." *Engender Newsletter* Spring, 23.

Hernes, Helga Maria. 1988. "The Welfare State Citizenship of Scandinavian Women." In *The Political Interests of Gender*, ed. Kathleen B. Jones and Anna G. Jónasdóttir. London: Sage, pp. 187–213.

Hernes, Helga. 1987. *Welfare State and Women Power: Essays on State Feminism.* Oslo: Norwegian University Press.

Hesse, Barnor, Dhanwant K. Rai, Christine Bennett, and Paul McGilchrist. 1992. *Beneath the Surface: Racial Harassment.* Aldershot: Avebury.

Hester, Marianne and Lorraine Radford. 1997. "Contradictions and compromises." In *Women, Violence and Male Power*, ed. Marianne Hester, Liz Kelly, and Jill Radford. Buckingham: Open University Press, pp. 80–98.

Hiebert, Janet L. 1999. "Parliament, Courts and Rights: Sharing the Responsibility for Interpreting the Charter." In *Canadian Politics*, ed. James Bickerton and Alain G. Gagnon. Peterborough: Broadview, pp. 185–205.

Hinds, Bronagh. 1999. "Women Working for Peace in Northern Ireland." In *Contesting Politics: Women in Ireland, North and South*, ed. Yvonne Galligan, Eilís Ward, and Rick Wilford. Boulder, CO: Westview Press, pp. 109–129.

Hipsher, Patricia. 1998. "Democratic Transitions and Social Movement Outcomes: The Chilean Shantytown Dweller's Movement in Comparative Perspective." In *From Contention to Democracy*, ed. Marco G. Giugni, Doug McAdam, and Charles Tilly. Lanham, MD: Rowman and Littlefield, pp. 149–168.

Hirsch, Joachim. 1991. "From the Fordist to the Post-Fordist State." In *The Politics of Flexibility: Restructuring State and Industry in Britain, Germany and Scandinavia*, ed. Bob Jessop, Hans Kastendiek, Klaus Nielsen, and Ove K. Pedersen. Brookfield, VT: Edward Elgar, pp. 67–81.

Hirsch, Joachim. 1985. "Fordismus und Post-Fordismus: die gegenwärtige gesellschaftliche Krise und ihre Folgen." *Politische Vierteljahreschrift* 26 (2): 160–182.

Hirsch, Joachim and Roland Roth. 1986. *Das neue Gesicht des Kapitalismus: Vom Fordismus zum Postfordismus*. Hamburg: VSA.

Hirschman, Alfred O. 1982. *Shifting Involvements: Private Interest and Public Action*. Princeton, NJ: Princeton University Press.

Hoff-Wilson, Joan, ed. 1986. *Rights of Passage: The Past and Future of the Equal Rights Amendment*. Bloomington: Indiana University Press.

Hole, Judith and Helen Levine. 1971. *The Rebirth of Feminism*. New York: Quadrangle.

Home Office and Welsh Office. 1995. *Interagency Circular: Interagency Co-Ordination to Tackle Domestic Violence*. London: Home Office of Public Relations Branch.

Hosek, Chaviva. 1983. "Women and The Constitutional Process." In *And No One Cheered*, ed. Keith Banting and Richard Simeon. Toronto: Methuen, pp. 280–300.

Hoskyns, Catherine. 1996. *Integrating Gender: Women, Law and Politics in the European Union*. London: Verso.

Houston, Muiris. 2001. "Council Rift over Abortion Could Mean Judicial Review." *The Irish Times*, June 7, city edition, p.7. Accessed via LEXIS-NEXIS Academic Universe, July 19, 2001.

Howe, Neil and Phillip Longman. 1992. "The Next New Deal." *Atlantic Monthly* April: 88–90.

Hutton, Will. 1995. *The State We're In*. London: Jonathan Cape.

Hyvarinen, Matti. 1997. "The Merging of Context into Collective Action." In *The Political Context of Collective Action: Power, Argumentation, and Democracy*, ed. Ricca Edmondson. London and New York: Routledge, pp. 33–46.

Imig, Doug and Sidney Tarrow, eds. 2001. *Contentious Europeans: Protest and Politics in an Integrating Europe*. Boulder, CO: Rowman and Littlefield.

Ingle, Stephen. 1989. *The British Party System*. Oxford: Basil Blackwell.

Instituto de la Mujer. 2000. *Las Mujeres en Cifras 2000*. Available on May 6, 2000 at http://www.mtas.es/mujer/mcifras.

Instituto de la Mujer. 1994. *La Mujer en Cifras: Una Década, 1982–1992.* Madrid: Instituto de la Mujer.

Jackson, Robert Max. 1998. *Destined for Equality: The Inevitable Rise of Women's Status.* Cambridge, MA: Harvard University Press.

Jahn, Detlef. 1993. *New Politics and Trade Unions: An Organization Theoretical Analysis of the Debate on Nuclear Energy in Swedish and German Trade Unions.* Aldershot: Dartmouth.

Jaquette, Jane S. and Sharon L. Wolchik, eds. 1998. *Women and Democracy: Latin America and Central and Eastern Europe.* Baltimore, MD: Johns Hopkins University Press.

Jasper, James M. 1990. *Nuclear Politics: Energy and the State in the United States, Sweden and France.* Princeton, NJ: Princeton University Press.

Jeffery, Charlie. 1996. "The Territorial Dimension." In *Developments in German Politics 2,* ed. Gordon Smith, William Paterson, and Stephen Padgett. Durham, NC: Duke University Press, pp. 76–95.

Jenkins, J. Craig and Bert Klandermans. 1995. "The Politics of Social Protest." In *The Politics of Social Protest: Comparative Perspectives on States and Social Movements,* ed. J. Craig Jenkins and Bert Klandermans. Minneapolis: University of Minnesota Press, pp. 3–13.

Jenkins, J. Craig and Charles Perrow. 1977. "Insurgency of the Powerless: Farm Workers' Movements, 1946–1972." *American Sociological Review* 42: 249–268.

Jenson, Jane. 1998. "Les réformes des services de garde pour jeunes enfants en France et au Québec: Une analyse historico-institutionaliste?" *Politique et Sociétés* 17: 1–2.

Jenson, Jane. 1996. "Representations of Difference: The Varieties of French Feminism." In *Mapping the Women's Movement: Feminist Politics and Social Transformation in the North,* ed. Monica Threlfall. London: Verso, pp. 73–114.

Jenson, Jane. 1990. "Representations in Crisis: The Roots of Canada's Permeable Fordism." *Canadian Journal of Political Science* 23: 653–83.

Jenson, Jane. 1988. "The Limits of 'and the' Discourse: French Women as Marginal Workers." In *Feminization of the Labor Force: Paradoxes and Promises,* ed. Jane Jenson, Elisabeth Hagen, and Ceallaigh Reddy. New York: Oxford University Press, pp. 155–172.

Jenson, Jane. 1987. "Changing Discourse, Changing Agendas: Political Rights and Reproductive Policies in France." In *The Women's Movements of the United States and Western Europe,* ed. Mary Fainsod Katzenstein and Carol McClurg Mueller. Philadelphia: Temple University Press, pp. 64–88.

Jenson, Jane. 1987a. "Both Friend and Foe: Women and State Welfare." In *Becoming Visible: Women in European History,* ed. Renate Bridenthal, Claudia Koonz, and Susan Stuard. Boston: Houghton Mifflin, pp. 535–556.

Jenson, Jane. 1982. "The Modern Women's Movement in Italy, France and Great Britain: Differences in Life Cycles." *Comparative Social Research* 5: 341–375.

Jenson, Jane and Mariette Sineau. 1995. *Mitterrand et les Françaises. Un rendez-vous manqué.* Paris: Presses de la fondation nationale des sciences politiques.

Jenson, Jane and Mariette Sineau. 1994. "France: The Same or Different? An Unending Dilemma for French Women." In *Women and Politics Worldwide,* ed. Barbara J. Nelson and Najma Chowdhury. New Haven, CT: Yale University Press, pp. 243–260.

Jessop, Bob. 1991a. "The Welfare State in the Transition from Fordism to Post-Fordism." In *The Politics of Flexibility: Restructuring State and Industry in Britain, Germany and Scandinavia*, ed. Bob Jessop, Hans Kastendiek, Klaus Nielsen, and Ove K. Pedersen. Brookfield, VT: Edward Elgar, pp. 82–105.

Jessop, Bob. 1991b. "Thatcherism and Flexibility: The White Heat of a Post-Fordist Revolution." In *The Politics of Flexibility: Restructuring State and Industry in Britain, Germany and Scandinavia*, ed. Bob Jessop, Hans Kastendiek, Klaus Nielsen, and Ove K. Pedersen. Brookfield, VT: Edward Elgar, pp. 135–161.

Jessop, Bob. 1990. *State Theory: Putting the Capitalist State in Its Place.* University Park: Pennsylvania State University Press.

Jiménez, Manuel 1999. "Consolidation Through Institutionalization? Dilemmas of the Spanish Environmental Movement in the 1990s." *Environmental Politics* 8 (1): 149–171.

Joël, Marie-Ève and Claude Martin. 1998. *Aider les personnes âgées dépendantes: Arbitrages économiques et familiaux.* Rennes: Éd. ENSP.

Johnston, Hank and Bert Klandermans, eds. 1995. *Social Movements and Culture.* Minneapolis: University of Minnesota Press.

Junor, Beth. 1995. *Greenham Common Women's Peace Camp: A History of Non-Violent Resistance, 1984–1995* (with illustrations by Katrina Howse). London: Working Press.

Kairys, David, ed. 1998. *The Politics of Law : A Progressive Critique.* New York: Basic Books.

Kamenitsa, Lynn. 1997. "East German Feminists in the New German Democracy: Opportunities, Obstacles, and Adaptation." *Women and Politics* 17(3): 41–68.

Kaplan, Gisela. 1992. *Contemporary Western European Feminism.* London: UCL Press and Allen & Unwin.

Kaplan, Temma. 1999. "Luchar por la Democracia: Formas de Organización de las Mujeres en los Años Cincuenta y los Años Setenta." In *Mujeres, Regulación de Conflictos Sociales y Cultura de la Paz*, ed. Anna Aguado. Valencia: Universidad de Valencia, pp. 89–107.

Katzenstein, Mary Fainsod. 1998a. *Faithful and Fearless: Moving Feminist Protest Inside the Church and Military.* Princeton, NJ: Princeton University Press.

Katzenstein, Mary Fainsod. 1998b. "Stepsisters: Feminist Movement Activism in Different Institutional Spaces." In *The Social Movement Society: Contentious Politics for a New Century*, ed. David S. Meyer and Sidney Tarrow. Boulder, CO: Rowman & Littlefield, pp. 195–216.

Katzenstein, Mary Fainsod and Carol McClurg Mueller, eds. 1987. *The Women's Movements of the United States and Western Europe.* Philadelphia: Temple University Press.

Katzenstein, Peter. 1987. *Policy and Politics in West Germany: The Growth of a Semisovereign State.* Philadelphia: Temple University Press.

Kavanagh, Dennis. 1998. "Power in the Parties: R.T. McKenzie and After." *West European Politics* 21: 1.

Keck, Margaret and Kathryn Sikkink. 1998. *Activists Beyond Borders: Advocacy Networks in International Politics.* Ithaca, NY: Cornell University Press.

Kelly, Ellen. 1998. "Reaching Women in Scotland: The Scottish Parliament-the Devil's in the Detail." In *Gender and Scottish Society: Polities, Policies and*

Participation. Report of Conference sponsored by the Unit for the Study of Government in Scotland. Edinburgh: University of Edinburgh.

Kenney, Sally. 1992. *For Whose Protection? Reproductive Hazards and Exclusionary Policies in the United States and Britain*. Ann Arbor: University of Michigan Press.

Keogh, Dermot. 1994. *Twentieth-Century Ireland: Nation and State*. Dublin: Gill and Macmillan.

Kessler-Harris, Alice. 1988. "The Just Price, the Free Market, and the Value of Women." *Feminist Studies* 14, Summer: 235–250.

Ketting, Evert and Philip van Praag. 1986. "The Marginal Relevance of Legislation Relating to Induced Abortion." In *The New Politics of Abortion*, ed. Joni Lovenduski and Joyce Outshoorn. Beverly Hills, CA: Sage Publications, pp. 154–169.

King, Mary. 1987. *Freedom Song: A Personal Story of the 1960s Civil Rights Movement*. New York: Morrow.

Kirkpatrick, Jeane J. 1976. *The New Presidential Elite: Men and Women in National Politics*. New York: Russell Sage.

Kirp, David. 1982. "Professionalization as a Policy Choice: British Special Education in Comparative Perspective." *World Politics* 34: 137–174.

Kitschelt, Herbert. 1986. "Political Opportunity Structures and Political Protest: Anti-Nuclear Movements in Four Democracies." *British Journal of Political Science* 16 (1): 57–85.

Kitschelt, Herbert. 1985. "New Social Movements in West Germany and the United States." *Political Power and Social Theory* 5: 273–324.

Kitzinger, Celia and Rachel Perkins. 1993. *Changing Our Minds: Lesbian Feminism and Psychology*. New York: New York University Press.

Klandermans, Bert. 1997. *The Social Psychology of Protest*. Oxford: Blackwell.

Klatch, Rebecca. 1992. "The Two Worlds of Women in the New Right." In *Women, Politics and Change*, ed. Louise Tilly and Pat Gurin. New York: Russell Sage, pp. 529–549.

Klein, Ethel. 1987. "The Diffusion of Consciousness in the United States and Western Europe." In *The Women's Movements of the United States and Western Europe*, ed. Mary Fainsod Katzenstein and Carol McClurg Mueller. Philadelphia: Temple University Press, pp. 23–43.

Kolberg, Jon Eivind. 1991. "The Gender Dimensions of the Welfare State." *International Journal of Sociology* 21 (2): 119–148.

Kolinsky, Eva, ed. 1989. *The Greens in West Germany: Organisation and Policy Making*. New York: St. Martin's Press.

Kome, Penney. 1983. *The Taking of 28: Women Challenge the Constitution*. Toronto: Women's Press.

Koopmans, Ruud. 1999. "Political. Opportunity. Structure. Some Splitting to Balance the Lumping." *Sociological Forum* 14: 93–106.

Koopmans, Ruud. 1996. "New Social Movements and Changes in Political Participation in Western Europe." *West European Politics* 19 (2): 28–50.

Koopmans, Ruud. 1995. *Democracy From Below: New Social Movements and the Political System in West Germany*. Boulder, CO: Westview Press.

Koopmans, Ruud. 1991. "Demokratie von unten. Neue soziale Bewegungen und politisches System in der Bundesrepublik Deutschland im internationalen Vergleich. "In *Neue soziale Bewegungen in der Bundesrepublik Deutschland*, 2nd and rev. ed., ed. Roland Roth and Dieter Rucht. Bonn: Bundeszentrale für politische Bildung, pp. 71–88.

Koopmans, Ruud and Paul Statham. 1999. "Ethnicity and Civic Conceptions of Nationhood and the Differential Success of the Extreme Right in Germany and Italy." In *How Social Movements Matter*, ed. Marco Giugni, Doug McAdam, and Charles Tilly. Minneapolis: University of Minnesota.

Krieger, Joel. 1996. "Britain." In *Comparative Politics at the Crossroads*, ed. Mark Kesselman, Joel Krieger, and William Joseph. Lexington, MA: D.C. Heath, pp. 29–99.

Krieger, Verena. 1987. *Entscheiden: Was Frauen (und Männer) über den Paragraph 218 wissen sollten*. Hamburg: Konkret Literatur Verlag.

Kriesi, Hanspeter. 1996. "The Organizational Structure of New Social Movements in a Political Context." In *Comparative Perspectives on Social Movements: Political Opportunities, Mobilizing Structures, and Cultural Framings*, ed. Doug McAdam, John D. McCarthy, and Mayer N. Zald. Cambridge: Cambridge University Press, pp. 152–184.

Kriesi, Hanspeter. 1995. "The Political Opportunity Structure of New Social Movements: Its Impact on Their Mobilization." In *The Politics of Social Protest: Comparative Perspectives on States and Social Movements*, ed. J. Craig Jenkins and Bert Klandermans. Minneapolis: University of Minnesota Press, pp. 167–198.

Kriesi, Hanspeter. 1989. "The Political Opportunity Structure of the Dutch Peace Movement." *West European Politics* 12: 295–312.

Kriesi, Hanspeter, Ruud Koopmans, Jan Willem Duyvendak, and Marco Giugni. 1995. *New Social Movements in Western Europe: A Comparative Analysis*. Minneapolis: University of Minnesota Press.

Ku, Leighton and Brian Bruen. 1999. "The Continuing Decline in Medicaid Coverage, Policy Brief A-37." In *Assessing the New Federalism*. Washington, DC: The Urban Institute.

Labour Campaign for Electoral Report. 1997. *Political Report*. April 1996–1997.

Laitin, David D. 1997. "The Cultural Identities of a European State." *Politics & Society* 25, September: 277–302.

Landau, Eve. 1985. *The Rights of Working Women in the European Community*. Luxembourg: Office for Official Publications of the European Communities.

Lang, Sabine. 1997. "The NGOization of Feminism." In *Transitions, Environments, Translations: Feminisms in International Politics*, ed. Joan W. Scott, Cora Kaplan, and Debra Keates. New York and London: Routledge, pp. 101–120.

Lanquetin, Marie-Thérèse. 2000. "Equality at Work: What Difference does Legislating Make?" In *The Gendering of Inequalities: Women, Men and Work*, ed. Jane Jenson, Jacqueline Laufer, and Margaret Maruani. Aldershot: Ashgate, pp. 239–250.

Laufer, Jacqueline. 2000. "Public Sphere, Private Sphere: The Issue of Women's Rights." In *The Gendering of Inequalities: Women, Men and Work*, ed. Jane Jenson, Jacqueline Laufer, and Margaret Maruani. Aldershot: Ashgate, pp. 231–238.

Laufer, Jacqueline. 1998. "Equal Opportunity between Men and Women: The Case of France." *Feminist Economics* 4(1): 53–69.

Laufer, Jacqueline. 1994. "Equal Opportunity of Men and Women and Organizational Change." In *Gender and Organizations – Changing Perspectives*, ed. Jeanne de Bruijn and Eva Cyba. Amsterdam: VU University Press, pp. 171–187.

Lavalette, Michael and Jane Kennedy. 1996. *Solidarity on the Waterfront: The Liverpool Lock Out of 1995/96*. Birkenhead: Liverpool Press.

Lawson, Roger. 1996. "Germany: Maintaining the Middle Way." In *European Welfare Policy: Squaring the Welfare Circle*, ed. Vic George and Peter Taylor-Gooby. New York: St. Martin's Press, pp. 31–50.

Le Monde. March 8, 2001; April 22–23, 2001: 6; September 21, 2001; December 19, 1998; March 11, 1997; May 23, 1997; November 5, 1997; January 16, 1993; February 19, 1993; March 7–8, 1993; November 10, 1993.

Lehmbruch, Gerhard and C. Philippe Schmitter, eds. 1979. *Patterns of Corporatist Policy-making*. London: Sage.

Leicester, Graham. 1999. "Scottish and Welsh Devolution." In *Constitutional Reform: The Labour Government's Constitutional Reform Agenda*, ed. Robert Blackburn and Raymond Plant. London: Longman, pp. 251–263.

Leif, Thomas. 1985. *Die professionelle Bewegung. Friedensbewegung von innen*. Bonn: Forum Europa Verlag.

Letablier, Marie-Thérèse. 1996. "L'activité professionnelle des femmes en France sur fond de pénurie d'emplois." *Lien social et politiques – RIAC* 36: 93–102.

Levine, Marsha and Roberta Trachtman. 1988. *American Business and the Public School*. New York: Teachers College Press.

Lewis, Jane. 1998. "'Work,' 'Welfare,' and Lone Mothers." *Political Quarterly* 69 (1): 4–13.

Lewis, Norman. 1991. "Changes in Socio-Legal Structures: The British Case." In *The Politics of Flexibility: Restructuring State and Industry in Britain, Germany and Scandinavia*, ed. Bob Jessop, Hans Kastendiek, Klaus Nielsen, and Ove K. Pedersen. Brookfield, VT: Edward Elgar, pp. 195–216.

Libby, Ronald T. 1998. *Eco-wars: Political Campaigns and Social Movements*. New York: Columbia University Press.

Liebfried, Stephan and Paul Pierson, eds. 1995. *European Social Policy*. Washington, DC: Brookings.

Lindsay, Isobel. 2001. "Constitutional Change and the Gender Deficit." In *Women and Contemporary Scottish Politics: An Anthology*, ed. Esther Breitenbach and Fiona MacKay. Edinburgh: Polygon, pp. 171–178.

Linton, Martin and Mary Southcott. 1998. *Making Votes Count: The Case for Electoral Reform*. London: Profile Books.

Lodge, Juliet. 1996. "The Future of the European Parliament." In *The 1994 Elections to the European Parliament*, ed. Juliet Lodge. London: Pinter, pp. 198–226.

Lofland, John. 1996. *Social Movement Organizations: Guide to Research on Insurgent Realities*. New York: Aldine de Gruyter.

Lofland, John. 1993. *Polite Protesters: The American Peace Movement of the 1980s*. Syracuse, NY: Syracuse University Press.

Lofland, John. 1978. *Deviance and Identity*. Englewood Cliffs, NJ: Prentice-Hall.

Long, Sharon K., Gretchen G. Kirby, Robin Kurka, and Shelley Waters. 1998. "Child Care Assistance under Welfare Reform: Early Responses by the States." Occasional Paper Number 15, *Assessing the New Federalism*. Washington, DC: The Urban Institute Press.

López-Accotto, Ana I. 1999. "Las Mujeres en la Transición Política Española." In *Mujeres: de lo Privado a lo Público*, ed. Laura Nuño. Madrid: Tecnos, pp. 108–131.

Lorber, Judith, ed. 1998. *Gender Inequality: Feminist Theories and Politics*. Los Angeles, CA.: Roxbury Publishing Co.

Lovenduski, Joni. 1995. "An Emerging Advocate: The Equal Opportunities Commission in Great Britain." In *Comparative State Feminism*, ed. Dorothy McBride Stetson and Amy Mazur. Thousand Oaks, CA: Sage, pp. 114–131.

Lovenduski, Joni. 1994. "Rules of the Political Game: Feminism and Politics in Great Britain." In *Women and Politics Worldwide*, ed. Barbara J. Nelson and Najma Chowdhury. New Haven, CT: Yale University Press, pp. 298–310.

Lovenduski, Joni. 1988. "The Women's Movement and Public Policy in Western Europe: Theory, Strategy, Practice and Politics." In *Women, Equality and Europe*, ed. Mary Buckley and Malcolm Anderson. London: Macmillan Press, pp. 107–125.

Lovenduski, Joni. 1986. *Women and European Politics: Contemporary Feminism and Public Policy*. Amherst: University of Massachusetts Press.

Lovenduski, Joni and Pippa Norris. 1996. *Women in Politics*. Oxford: Oxford University Press.

Lovenduski, Joni and Pippa Norris, eds. 1993. *Gender and Party Politics*. London: Sage Publications.

Lovenduski, Joni and Vicky Randall. 1993. *Contemporary Feminist Politics: Women and Power in Britain*. Oxford: Oxford University Press.

Luker, Kristin. 1984. *Abortion and the Politics of Motherhood*. Berkeley: University of California Press.

MacDonald, Martha. 1995. "Economic Restructuring and Gender in Canada: Feminist Policy Initiatives." *World Development* 23:11.

MacKay, Fiona. 1997. "Women and Representation: Discourses of Equality and Difference." In *New Waverley Papers, Politics Series 96–97*. Edinburgh: University of Edinburgh. pp. 1–34.

MacKinnon, Catharine A. 1989. *Toward a Feminist Theory of the State*. Cambridge, MA: Harvard University Press.

MacKinnon, Catharine A. 1982. "Feminism, Marxism, Method and the State: An Agenda for Theory." *Signs* 7 (3), Spring: 515–544.

Maclean, Mairi. 1995. "Privatisation in France 1993–94: New Departures, or a Case of plus ça change?" *West European Politics* 18 (2), April: 273–290.

MacLennan, Emma. 1992. "Politics, Progress, and Compromise: Women's Work and Lives in Great Britain." In *Women's Work and Women's Lives: The Continuing Struggle Worldwide*, ed. Hilda Kahne and Janet Giele. Boulder, CO: Westview, pp. 187–204.

Mainwaring, Scott. 1992. "Transitions to Democracy and Democratic Consolidation: Theoretical and Comparative Issues." In *Issues in Democratic Consolidation: The New South American Democracies in Comparative Perspective*, ed. Scott Mainwaring, Guillermo O'Donnell, and J. Samvela Valenzuela. Notre Dame, IN: University of Notre Dame Press, pp. 294–341.

Malos, Ellen and Gill Hague. 1997. "Women, Housing, Homelessness and Domestic Violence." *Women's Studies International Forum* 20(3): 397–409.

Mangen, Steen. 1996. "German Welfare and Social Citizenship." In *Developments in German Politics 2*, ed. Gordon Smith, William E. Paterson, and Stephen Padgett. Durham, NC: Duke University Press, pp. 250–266.

Mansbridge, Jane J. 1986. *Why We Lost the ERA*. Chicago: University of Chicago Press.

Margets, Helen. 1997. "The 1997 British General Election: New Labour, New Britain?" *West European Politics* 20(4), October: 180–191.

Markovits, Andrei S. 1986. *The Politics of the German Trade Unions: Strategies of Class and Interest Representation in Growth and Crisis*. Cambridge: Cambridge University Press.

Markovits, Andrei S., ed. 1982. *The Political Economy of West Germany: Modell Deutschland*. New York: Praeger.

Marlowe, Lara. 2001. "Treaty Has To Be Ratified by Each Member State Before Enlargement" *The Irish Times* June 12, city edition, p. 8. Accessed via LEXIS-NEXIS Academic Universe, July 12, 2001.

Marsh, Jeanne C., Alison Geist, and Nathan Caplan. 1982. *Rape and the Limits of Law Reform*. Boston: Auburn House.

Marshall, Thomas H. 1950. *Citizenship and Social Class and Other Essays*. Cambridge: Cambridge University Press.

Martin, Dell. 1976. *Battered Wives*. San Francisco, CA: Glide.

Martínez, Eva. 1997. "Políticas Públicas para la Igualdad entre los Sexos: Reflexiones sobre el Caso Español (1975–1997)" In *Mujeres en Política: Análisis y Práctica*, eds. Edurne Uriarte and Arantxa Elizondo. Barcelona: Ariel, pp. 211–232.

Mason, David. 1995. *Race and Ethnicity in Modern Britain*. Oxford: Oxford University Press.

Massé, Véronique. 1996. "Les grandes associations féminines convergent sur la parité?" *Parité-Infos* 16.

Mather, Janet. 2000. *The European Union and British Democracy: Towards Convergence*. London: Macmillan.

Matland, Richard. 1993. "Institutional Variables Affecting Female Representation in National Legislatures: The Case of Norway." *Journal of Politics* 55, August: 737–755.

Matland, Richard and Donley T. Studlar. 1996. "The Contagion of Women Candidates in Single-Member District and Proportional Representation Electoral Systems: Canada and Norway." *Journal of Politics* 58, August: 707–733.

Matthews, Nancy. 1994. *Confronting Rape: The Feminist Anti-Rape Movement and the State*. London: Routledge.

Mazey, Sonia. 1994. "Power Outside Paris." In *Developments in French Politics*, rev. ed., ed. Peter A. Hall, Jack Hayward, and Howard Machin. London: Macmillan, pp. 152–167.

Mazey, Sonia. 1988. "European Community Action on Behalf of Women: The Limits of Legislation." *Journal of Common Market Studies* 27(1), September: 63–84.

Mazur, Amy G. 1995. *Gender Bias and the State: Symbolic Reform at Work in Fifth Republic France*. Pittsburgh: University of Pittsburgh Press.

McAdam, Doug. 1996. "Conceptual Origins, Problems, Future Directions." In *Comparative Perspectives on Social Movements: Political Opportunities, Mobilizing*

Structures, and Cultural Framing, ed. Doug McAdam, John D. McCarthy, and Mayer N. Zald. Cambridge: Cambridge University Press, pp. 23–40.

McAdam, Doug. 1988. *Freedom Summer*. New York : Oxford University Press.

McAdam, Doug. 1982. *Political Process and the Development of Black Insurgency, 1930–1970*. Chicago: University of Chicago Press.

McAdam, Doug, Sidney Tarrow, and Charles Tilly. 2001. *Dynamics of Contention*. Cambridge: Cambridge University Press.

McCabe, Barbara. 1997. "Forum for whom?" *Fortnight* 358 (February), 19.

McCarthy, Abigail. 1997. "Women & Money & Politics: Can Susan & Emily Work Together?" *Commonweal* 124 (14), August: 8–9.

McCarthy, John D. 1997. "The Globalization of Social Movement Theory." In *Transnational Social Movements and Global Politics: Solidarity Beyond the State*, ed. Jackie Smith, Charles Chatfield, and Ron Pagnucco. Syracuse, NY: Syracuse University Press, pp. 243–259.

McCarthy, John D. 1996. "Mobilizing Structures: Constraints and Opportunities in Adopting, Adapting and Inventing." In *Comparative Perspectives on Social Movements: Political Opportunities, Mobilizing Structures, and Cultural Framing*, ed. Doug McAdam, John D. McCarthy, and Mayer N. Zald. Cambridge: Cambridge University Press, pp. 141–151.

McCarthy, John D. 1987. "Pro-Life and Pro-Choice Mobilization: Infrastructure Deficits and New Technologies." In *Social Movements in an Organizations Society*, ed. Mayer N. Zald and John D. McCarthy. New Brunswick, NJ: Transaction Books, pp. 49–66.

McCarthy, John D., David Britt, and Mark Wolfson. 1991. "The Institutional Channeling of Social Movements by the State in the United States." In *Research in Social Movements, Conflicts and Change 13*. Greenwich, CT: JAI Press, pp. 45–76.

McCarthy, John D., Jackie Smith, and Mayer N. Zald. 1996. "Accessing Public, Media and Electoral Agendas." In *Comparative Perspectives on Social Movements: Political Opportunities, Mobilizing Structures, and Cultural Framing*, ed. Doug McAdam, John D. McCarthy, and Mayer N. Zald. Cambridge: Cambridge University Press, pp. 312–337.

McWilliams, Monica. 1996. "Dinosaurs not extinct." *Fortnight* 354: 9–10.

Meehan, Elizabeth. 1985. *Women's Rights at Work: Campaigns and Policy in Britain and the United States*. London: Macmillan.

Meehan, Elizabeth and Evelyn Collins. 1996. "Women, the European Union and Britain." In *Women in Politics*, ed. Joni Lovenduski and Pippa Norris. Oxford: Oxford University Press, pp. 223–236.

Melucci, Alberto. 1996. *Challenging Codes: Collective Action in the Information Age*. Cambridge: Cambridge University Press.

Melucci, Alberto. 1996b. *The Playing Self: Person and Meaning in the Planetary Society*. Cambridge: Cambridge University Press.

Melucci, Alberto. 1995. "The Process of Collective Identity." In *Social Movements and Culture*, ed. Hank Johnston and Bert Klandermans. Minneapolis: University of Minnesota, pp. 41–63.

Melucci, Alberto. 1989. *Nomads of the Present: Social Movements and Individual Needs in Contemporary Society*. Philadelphia: Temple University Press.

Mény, Yves. 1998. *The French Political System*. Paris: La Documentation Française.

Messina, Anthony. 1989. *Race and Party Competition in Britain*. Oxford: Clarendon Press.

Mettler, Suzanne. 1998. *Dividing Citizens: Gender and Federalism in the New Deal*. Ithaca, NY: Cornell University Press.

Meulders, Danièle. 2000. "European Policies Promoting More Flexible Labour Forces." In *The Gendering of Inequalities: Women, Men and Work*, ed. Jane Jenson, Jacqueline Laufer, and Margaret Maruani. Aldershot: Ashgate, pp. 251–263.

Meulders, Danièle, Robert Plasman, and Valérie Vander Stricht. 1993. *Position of Women on the Labour Market in the European Community*. Aldershot: Dartmouth.

Meyer, David S. 1993. "Institutionalizing Dissent: The United States Political Opportunity Structure and the End of the Nuclear Freeze Movement." *Sociological Forum* 8 (2), June: 157–179.

Meyer, David S. and Suzanne Staggenborg. 1996. "Movements, Countermovements, and the Structure of Political Opportunity." *American Journal of Sociology* 101 (6), May: 1628–1660.

Meyer, David S. and Sidney Tarrow, eds. 1998. *The Social Movement Society: Contentious Politics for a New Century*. Lanham, MD: Rowman and Littlefield.

Meyer, David S. and Sidney Tarrow. 1998a. "A Movement Society: Contentious Politics for a New Century." In *The Social Movement Society*, ed. David S. Meyer and Sidney Tarrow. New York: Rowman and Littlefield, pp. 1–28.

Meyer, David S. and Nancy Whittier. 1994. "Social Movement Spillover." *Social Problems* 41(2), May: 277–298.

Meyer, John W., John Boli, George M. Thomas, and Francisco O. Ramirez. 1997. "World Society and the Nation-State." *American Journal of Sociology* 103: 144–181.

Michel, Sonya. 1999. *Children's Interests, Mothers' Rights: The Shaping of America's Child Care Policy*. New Haven, CT: Yale University Press.

Miller, Robert Lee, Rick Wilford, and Freda Donoghue. 1996. *Women and Political Participation in Northern Ireland*. Aldershot: Avebury.

Millett, Kate. 1970. *Sexual Politics*. Garden City, NY: Doubleday.

Milne, Seumas. 1998. "After the Brothers, Here's Sister; Derided as 'Male, Pale and Stale', Unions are Radically Re-thinking the Role of Women in Work." *The Guardian*, March 14, 1998. money page, p. 2. Accessed via LEXIS-NEXIS Academic Universe, July 12, 2001.

Mink, Gwendolyn. 1998. *Welfare's End*. Ithaca, NY: Cornell University Press.

Minkoff, Debra. 1999. "Bending with the Wind: Strategic Change and Adaptation by Women's and Racial Minority Organizations." *American Journal of Sociology*. 104 (6), May: 1666–1703.

Minkoff, Debra. 1995. *Organizing for Equality: The Evolution of Women's and Racial Ethnic Organizations in America, 1955–1985*. New Brunswick, NJ: Rutgers University Press.

Minow, Martha. 1995. "Not Only for Myself: Identity, Politics and Law." *Oregon Law Review* 75: 647–648.

Mirza, Heidi Safia. 1997. "Introduction: Mapping a Genealogy of Black British Feminism." In *Black British Feminism: A Reader*, ed. Heidi Safia Mirza. London: Routledge, pp. 1–30.

Mitchell, Alison. 2001. "Gramm Joins the Republicans Who Plan to Quit the Senate." *New York Times*, September 5, p. A1.

Monk, Janice and Maria Dolors García-Ramon. 1996. "Placing Women of the European Union." In *Women of the European Union: The Politics of Work and Daily Life*, ed. Maria Dolors García-Ramon and Janice Monk. London: Routledge, pp. 1–30.

Mooser, Josef. 1984. *Arbeiterleben in Deutschland 1900–1970: Klassenlagen, Kultur und Politik*. Frankfurt/M: Suhrkamp.

Morgan, Patricia. 1981. "From Battered Wife to Program Client: The State's Shaping of Social Problems." *Kapitalistate* 9: 17–39.

Morgan, Robin, ed. 1970. *Sisterhood Is Powerful*. New York: Vintage.

Morison, John and Stephen Livingstone. 1995. *Reshaping Public Power: Northern Ireland and the British Constitutional Crisis*. London: Sweet and Maxwell.

Mormino, Maria and Federico Guarnieri. 1988. "Milano: Il Collettivo di Via Cherubini." In *Le strategie delle minoranze attive*, ed. Franco Crespi and Angelica Mucchi Faina. Napoli: Liguori, pp. 31–44.

Morrison, John. 2001. *Reforming Britain: New Labour, New Constitution?* London: Reuters.

Mossuz-Lavau, Janine. 1998. *Femmes/Hommes pour la Parité*. Paris: Presses de Sciences Po.

Ms. 1994. "No More! Stopping Domestic Violence." September/October: 33–65.

Mueller, Carol McClurg. 1994. "Conflict Networks and the Origins of Women's Liberation." In *New Social Movements: From Ideology to Identity*, ed. Enrique Larana, Hank Johnston, and Joseph R. Gusfield. Philadelphia: Temple University Press, pp. 234–63.

Mueller, Carol McClurg. 1988. *The Politics of the Gender Gap*. Newbury Park, CA: Sage.

Mujeres. 1994. (13). Madrid: Women's Institute.

Mullender, Audrey. 1996. *Rethinking Domestic Violence: The Social Work and Probation Response*. London: Routledge.

Müller-Rommel, Ferdinand. 1989. *New Politics in Western Europe: The Rise and Success of Green Parties and Alternative Lists*. Boulder, CO: Westview Press.

Munro, Anne. 1999. *Women, Work and Trade Unions*. London: Mansell.

Mushaben, Joyce Marie. 1997. "Concession or Compromise?: The Politics of Abortion in United Germany." *German Politics* 6(3): 70–88.

Nandy, Dipak. 1980. "Administering Anti-discrimination Legislation in Great Britain." In *Equal Employment Policy for Women*, ed. Ronnie Steinberg Ratner. Philadelphia: Temple University Press, pp. 142–159.

Naples, Nancy A. 1998. *Community Activism and Feminist Politics: Organizing Across Race, Class, and Gender*. New York: Routledge.

New Statesman. 1998. "Women on the Verge of a Nervous Breakthrough." January 30, p. 27.

New Suffragettes. No date. *Votes for Women*. Unpublished campaign flyer.

Nielsen, Klaus. 1991. "Towards a Flexible Future: Theories and Politics." In *The Politics of Flexibility: Restructuring State and Industry in Britain, Germany, and Scandinavia*, ed. Bob Jessop, Klaus Nielsen, Hans Kastendiek, and Ove K. Pedersen. Brookfield, VT: Edward Elgar, pp. 3–30.

Nordenfors, Gunilla. 1996. *Fadersrätt: Kvinnofrid och Barns Säkerhet* [Father's Right: Women's Freedom and Children's Safety]. Umeå: Solfjädern Offset.

Norris, Pippa. 1985. "Women's Legislative Participation in Western Europe." *West European Politics* 8(4): 90–101.

Norris, Pippa and Joni Lovenduski. 1993. "Gender and Party Politics in Britain." In *Gender and Party Politics*, ed. Joni Lovenduski and Pippa Norris. London: Sage, pp. 35–59.

Northern Ireland Women's Coalition. 1996. *Newsletter* 1.

Norton, Laurence E. II. 1997. "Not Too Much Justice for the Poor." *Dickinson Law Review* 101, Spring: 601.

"Numbers of Women in Office: State Summaries." 2001. *Center for the American Woman and Politics*. www.rci.rutgers.edu/~cawp/Facts/html. June 1.

O'Brien, Tony. 1998. "Abortion Law in the Republic of Ireland." In *Abortion Law and Politics Today*, ed. Ellie Lee. London: Macmillan Press, pp. 110–115.

Odone, Christina. 2001. "Such a Turn-Off for Women." *The Observer*, May 27.

Odone, Christina. 2001a. "Work: Inequality Street: Women Are Still Being Paid Less for Doing the Same Job as Men, According to a New Survey." *The Guardian* February 27, sec. 2 p. 10. Accessed via LEXIS-NEXIS Academic Universe, July 25, 2001.

Oliver, Pamela. 1989. "Bringing the Crowd Back In." *Research in Social Movements, Conflict and Change* 11: 1–30.

Oliver, Pamela E. and Hank Johnston. 2000. "What a Good Idea! Ideology and Frames in Social Movement Research." *Mobilization* 5(1), Spring: 37–54.

O'Neill, Michael. 1999. "'Appointment with History': The Referendum on The Stormont Peace Agreement, May 1988." *West European Politics* 22 (1), June: 160–171.

Orloff, Ann Shola. 1996. "Gender in the Welfare State." *Annual Review of Sociology* 22: 51–78.

Ornstein, Norman J., Thomas E. Mann, and Michael J. Malbin. 1998. *Vital Statistics on Congress, 1997–1998*. Washington, DC: American Enterprise Institute.

Outshoorn, Joyce. 1988. "Abortion Law Reform: A Woman's Right to Choose?" In *Women, Equality and Europe*, ed. Mary Buckley and Malcolm Anderson. London: Macmillan Press, pp. 204–219.

Outshoorn, Joyce. 1986. "The Rules of the Game: Abortion Politics in the Netherlands." In *The New Politics of Abortion*, ed. Joni Lovenduski and Joyce Outshoorn. London: Sage Publications, pp. 5–26.

Pagnucco, Ron. 1995. "The Comparative Study of Social Movements and Democratization: Political Interaction and Political Process Approaches." *Research in Social Movements, Conflict and Change* 18: 145–183.

Pardo, Rosa 1988. "El Feminismo en España: Breve Resumen, 1953–1985." In *El Feminismo en España: Dos Siglos de Historia*. ed. Pilar Folguera. Madrid: Pablo Iglesias, pp. 133–140.

Pascal, Jean. 1990. *Les femmes députés [sic] de 1945 à 1988*. Paris: Edité par l'auteur Jean Pascal.

Peces-Barba, Gregorio. 1999. "La cuota femenina en las candidaturas electorales." *El País* July 1: 15–16.

Perkins, A. 1999. "Take Two." *The Guardian*, June 1, p. 6.

Perrigo, Sarah. 1996. "Women and Change in the Labour Party 1979–1995." In *Women in Politics*, ed. Joni Lovenduski and Pippa Norris. Oxford: Oxford University Press, pp. 118–131.

"The Personal Responsibility and Work Opportunity Reconciliation Act of 1996." 1996. United States Congress Public Law 104–193, 110 Stat. 2105.

Phillips, Anne. 1997. "From Inequality to Difference: A Severe Case of Displacement?" *New Left Review* 224 (July/August): 143–153.

Phillips, Anne. 1995. *The Politics of Presence*. Oxford: Clarendon Press.

Pierson, Paul. 1996. "The New Politics of the Welfare State." *World Politics* 48, January: 143–179.

Pierson, Paul. 1994. *Dismantling the Welfare State? Reagan, Thatcher, and the Politics of Retrenchment*. Cambridge: Cambridge University Press.

Pineda, Empar. 1995. "Algunas Reflexiones sobre el Estado Actual del Feminismo en España." *Género y Sociedad* 3: 95–116.

Piven, Frances Fox and Richard A. Cloward. 1979. *Poor People's Movements: Why They Succeed and How They Fail*. New York: Vintage.

Poggi, Gianfranco. 1990. *The State: Its Nature, Developments, and Perspectives*. Stanford: Stanford University Press.

Praud, Jocelyne. 1998. "La seconde vague féministe et la féminisation du Parti socialiste français et du Parti québécois?" *Politique et Sociétés* 17: 1–2.

"Presentation." 1999. *Association PARITE*. http://www.parité.asso.fr. July 6.

President's Commission on Privatization. 1988. *Privatization: Toward More Effective Government*. Washington, DC.

Pringle, Rosemary and Sophie Watson. 1990. "Fathers, Brothers, Mates: The Fraternal State in Australia." In *Playing the State: Australian Feminist Interventions*, ed. Sophie Watson. London and New York: Verso, pp. 229–243.

Przeworski, Adam. 1989. *Capitalism and Social Democracy*. New York: Cambridge University Press.

Puleo, Alicia. 1996. "Feminismo y Política en España." *Leviatán* 63: 49–62.

Pye, Sylvia. 1996. Telephone interview with K. Beckwith. March 28.

Radford, Jill, Liz Kelly, and Marianne Hester. 1997. "Introduction." In *Women, Violence and Male Power*, ed. Marianne Hester, Liz Kelly, and Jill Radford. Buckingham: Open University Press, pp. 1–16.

Radford, Jill, Liz Kelly, Marianne Hester, and Elizabeth Stanko. 1997. "Violence Against Women and Children: The Contradictions of Crime Control Under Patriarchy." In *Women, Violence and Male Power*, ed. Marianne Hester, Liz Kelly, and Jill Radford. Buckingham: Open University Press, pp. 65–80.

Rai, Shirin M. 1996. "Women and the State in the Third World: Some Issues for Debate." In *Women and the State: International Perspectives*, ed. Shirin M. Rai and Geraldine Lievesley. London: Taylor and Francis, pp. 5–22.

Ramirez, Francisco O., Yasemin Soysal, and Suzanne Shanahan. 1997. "The Changing Logic of Political Citizenship: Cross-National Acquisition of Women's Suffrage Rights, 1890–1990." *American Sociological Review* 62: 735–745.

Randall, Vicky. 1998. "Gender and Power: Women Engage the State." In *Gender, Politics, and the State*, ed. Georgina Waylen and Vicky Randall. London and New York: Routledge, pp. 185–205.

Randall, Vicky. 1995. "The Irresponsible State? The Politics of Child Daycare Provision in Britain." *British Journal of Political Science* 25 (3), July: 327–348.

Randall, Vicky. 1992. "Great Britain and Dilemmas for Feminist Strategy in the 1980s: The Case of Abortion and Reproductive Rights." In *Women Transforming Politics*, ed. Jill M. Bystydzienski. Bloomington: Indiana University Press, pp. 80–94.

Randall, Vicky. 1987. *Women and Politics: An International Perspective*. Chicago: University of Chicago Press.

Randall, Vicky. 1986. "The Politics of Abortion in Ireland." In *The New Politics of Abortion*, ed. Joni Lovenduski and Joyce Outshoorn. London: Sage Publications, pp. 67–85.

Ray, Raka. 1999. *Fields of Protest: Women's Movements in India*. Minneapolis: University of Minnesota Press.

Razack, Sherene. 1991. *Canadian Feminism and the Law: The Women's Legal Education and Action Fund*. Toronto: Second Story Press.

Rechnungshof Baden-Württemberg. 2000. *Besondere Prüfungsergebnisse (Denkschrift 2000): Förderung der Schwangerschaftskonfliktberatungsstellen*. Beitrag 18. http://www.baden-wuerttemberg.de/sixcms_upload/media/282/b0182000.pdf. Accessed July 19, 2001.

Reger, Jo. 2001. "More than One Feminism: Organizational Structure and the Construction of Collective Identity." In *Social Movements: Identity, Culture, and the State*, ed. David S. Meyer, Nancy Whittier, and Belinda Robnett. New York: Oxford University Press, pp. 171–184.

Regeringskansliet. 1998. *Violence Against Women: Government Bill 1997/98:55*. Stockholm: Regeringskansliets Offsetcentral.

Reimer, Jeremiah M. 1996. "Reproduction and Reunification: The Politics of Abortion in United Germany." In *From Bundesrepublik to Deutschland: German Politics after Unification*, ed. Michael Huelshoff, Andrei Markovits, and Simon Reich. Ann Arbor: University of Michigan Press, pp. 167–187.

Reinelt, Claire. 1995. "Moving on to the Terrain of the State: The Battered Women's Movement and the Politics of Engagement." In *Feminist Organizations: Harvest of the New Women's Movement*, ed. Myra Max Ferree and Patricia Yancey Martin. Philadelphia: Temple University Press, pp. 84–104.

Resources for Community Change, ed. 1974. *Demand for Day Care: An Introduction for Campus and Community*. Washington DC: Resources for Community Change.

Rhodes, Dusty and Sandra McNeill. 1985. *Women Against Violence Against Women*. London: Onlywomen Press.

Rieger, Elmar and Stephan Liebfried. 1995. *Globalization and the Western Welfare State*. New York: Social Science Research Council, Center for Social Policy Research.

Riewe, Julie M. 1997. "Note: The Least Among Us: Unconstitutional Changes in Prisoner Litigation under the Prison Litigation Reform Act of 1995." *Duke Law Journal* 117 (47), October: 117–159.

Roberts, Barbara. 1988. "Smooth Sailing or Storm Warning? Canadian and Quebec Women's Groups and the Meech Lake Accord." A Report Prepared for The Canadian Research Institute for The Advancement of Women. Ottawa: CRIAW/ICREF, pp.1–46.

Robertson, Sue. 1998. "Benefit Cuts for Lone Mothers." *Engender Newsletter*, March 17, p. 2.

Rochon, Thomas. 1988. *Between Society and State: Mobilizing for Peace in Western Europe*. Princeton, NJ: Princeton University Press.

Rochon, Thomas R. and Daniel A. Mazmanian. 1993. "Social Movements and the Policy Process." *The Annals of the American Academy* 528: 75–87.

Rootes, Christopher. 2001. "Environmental Movements in Western Europe Compared: Accounting for British Exceptionalism... Again!" Presented at the the Annual Meeting of the American Political Science Association, San Francisco, August 30–September 2.

Roseneil, Sasha. 1995. *Disarming Patriarchy: Feminism and Political Action at Greenham.* Buckingham: Open University Press.

Roth, Roland. 1994. *Demokratie von unten. Neue soziale Bewegungen auf dem Wege zur politischen Institution.* Bonn: Bund.

Roulston, Camel. 1997. "Gender, Nation, Class: The Politics of Difference in Northern Ireland." *Scottish Affairs* 18 (Winter): 54–67.

Rowbotham, Sheila. 1996. "Introduction: Mapping the Women's Movement." In *Mapping the Women's Movement: Feminist Politics and Social Transformation in the North*, ed. Monica Threlfall. London and New York: Verso, pp. 1–16.

Ruane, Joseph and Jennifer Todd. 1996. *The Dynamics of Conflict in Northern Ireland: Power, Conflict and Emancipation.* Cambridge: Cambridge University Press.

Rubery, Jill, Francesca Bettio, Colette Fagan, Friederike Maier, Sigrid Quack, and Paola Villa. 1998. "Payment Systems and Gender Pay Differentials: Some Societal Effects." In *Equal Pay in Europe? Closing the Gender Wage Gap*, ed. Jill Rubery. New York: St. Martin's, pp. 1–31.

Rubery, Jill and Colette Fagan. 1995. *Social Europe: Wage Determination and Sex Segregation in Employment in the European Community. Supplement 4/94.* Document #: V/408/94-EN. Luxembourg: Office for the Official Publications of the European Communities.

Rubery, Jill, Mark Smith, and Colette Fagan. 1999. *Women's Employment in Europe: Trends and Prospects.* London: Routledge.

Rucht, Dieter. 2001. "'Heraus zum 1. Mai!' – Ein Protestritual im Wandel." In *Protest in der Bundesrepublik*, ed. Dieter Rucht. Frankfurt/M: Campus, pp. 143–172.

Rucht, Dieter. 1994. *Modernisierung und neue soziale Bewegungen: Deutschland, Frankreich und USA im Vergleich.* Frankfurt/M: Campus.

Rucht, Dieter. 1994a. "The Anti-Nuclear Power Movement and the State in France." In *States and Anti-Nuclear Movements*, ed. Helena Flam. Edinburgh: Edinburgh University Press, pp. 129–162.

Rucht, Dieter. 1991. "Von der Bewegung zu Institution? Organisationsstrukturen der Ökologiebewegung." In *Neue soziale Bewegungen in der Bundesrepublik Deutschland*, ed. Roland Roth and Dieter Rucht. Bonn: Bundeszentrale für politische Bildung, pp. 334–358.

Rucht, Dieter. 1990. "The Strategies and Action Repertoire of New Movements." In *Challenging the Political Order: New Social and Political Movements in Western Democracies*, ed. Russell J. Dalton and Manfred Küchler. Cambridge: Polity Press, pp. 156–175.

Rucht, Dieter. 1989. "Environmental Movement Organizations in West Germany and France: Structure and Interorganizational Relations." *International Social Movement Research* 2: 61–94.

Rucht, Dieter, Barbara Blattert, and Dieter Rink. 1997. *Soziale Bewegungen auf dem Weg zur Institutionalisierung: Zum Strukturwandel "alternativer" Gruppen in beiden Teilen Deutschlands.* Frankfurt am Main: Campus.

Rucht, Dieter and Friedhelm Neidhardt. 1999. "Methodological Issues in Collecting Protest Event Data: Units of Analysis, Sources and Sampling, Coding Problems." In *Acts of Dissent: New Developments in the Study of Protest*, ed. Dieter Rucht, Ruud Koopmans, and Friedhelm Neidhardt. Lanham, MD: Rowman and Littlefield, pp. 65–89.

Rucht, Dieter and Thomas Ohlemacher. 1992. "Protest Event Data: Collection, Uses and Perspectives." In *Issues in Contemporary Social Movement Research*, ed. Ron Eyerman and Mario Diani. Beverly Hills, CA: Sage, pp. 76–106.

Rucht, Dieter and Jochen Roose. 2001. "Neither Decline nor Sclerosis: The Organisational Structure of the German Environmental Movement." *West European Politics*, Autumn: 55–81.

Rüdig, Wolfgang. 1990. *Anti-Nuclear Movements: A World Survey of Opposition to Nuclear Energy.* Essex: Longman.

Ruggie, Mary. 1987. "Workers' Movements and Women's Interests: The Impact of Labor-State Relations in Britain and Sweden." In *The Women's Movements of the United States and Western Europe*, ed. Mary Fainsod Katzenstein and Carol McClurg Mueller. Philadelphia: Temple University Press, pp. 247–266.

Ruggie, Mary. 1984. *The State and Working Women: A Comparative Study of Britain and Sweden.* Princeton, NJ: Princeton University Press.

Ruiz-Miguel, Alfonso. 1999. "Paridad electoral y cuotas femeninas." *Claves de razón práctica* 94, July–August: 48–53.

Rule, Wilma. 1987. "Electoral Systems, Contextual Factors, and Women's Opportunity for Election to Parliament in 23 Democracies." *Western Political Quarterly* 40, Spring: 477–498.

Rupp, Hans Karl. 1970. *Außerparlamentarische Opposition in der Ära Adenauer.* Köln: Pahl-Rugenstein.

Rupp, Leila J. and Verta Taylor. 1987. *Survival in the Doldrums: The American Women's Right Movement, 1945 to the 1960s.* New York: Oxford University Press.

Ryan, Barbara. 1992. *Feminism and the Women's Movement.* New York: Routledge.

Ryan, Barbara. 1989. "Ideological Purity and Feminism: The U.S. Women's Movement from 1966 to 1975." *Gender and Society* 3: 239–257.

Sainsbury, Diane. 1996. *Gender, Equality and Welfare States.* New York: Cambridge University Press.

Salas, María. 1996. "Una Mirada sobre los Sucesivos Feminismos." *Documentación Social* 105: 13–32.

Sales, Rosemary. 1997. *Women Divided: Gender, Religion and Politics in Northern Ireland.* London: Routledge.

Salper, Roberta, ed. 1972. *Female Liberation: History and Current Politics.* New York: Knopf.

Sampedro, María R. 1992. *Administración Local y Políticas de Igualdad de la Mujer.* Madrid: Federación Española de Municipios y Provincias.

Saraceno, Chiara and Nicola Negri. 1996. *Le politiche sulla povertà.* Bologna: Il Mulino.

Savoie, Donald. 1994. *Thatcher, Reagan and Mulroney.* Pittsburgh: University of Pittsburgh Press.

Sawyers, Traci M. and David S. Meyer. 1999. "Missed Opportunities: Social Movement Abeyance and Public Policy." *Social Problems* 46 (2), May: 187–206.

Scanlon, Geraldine M. 1990. "El Movimiento Feminista en España, 1900–1985: Logros y Dificultades." In *Participación Política de las Mujeres*, ed. Judith Astelarra. Madrid: Centro de Investigaciones Sociológicas and Siglo XXI, pp. 83–100.

Scanlon, Geraldine M. 1976. *La Polémica Feminista en la España Contemporánea (1868–1974).* Madrid: Siglo XXI.

Schattschneider, Elmer Eric. 1960. *The Semi-Sovereign People: A Realist's View of Democracy in America.* New York: Holt, Rinehart and Winston.

Schechter, Susan. 1988. "Building Bridges Between Activists, Professionals, and Researchers." In *Feminist Perspectives on Wife Abuse*, ed. Kersti Yllö and Michele Bograd. Newbury Park, CA: Sage, pp. 299–312.

Schechter, Susan. 1982. *Women and Male Violence: The Visions and Struggles of the Battered Women's Movement.* Boston: South End Press.

Schenk, Herrad. 1981. *Die feministische Herausforderung: 150 Jahre Frauenbewegung in Deutschland.* München: C.H. Beck.

Schmidt, Frederika E. and Patricia Yancey Martin. 1999. "Unobtrusive Mobilization by an Institutionalized Rape Crisis Center." *Gender and Society* 13 (3), June: 364–384.

Schmitt, David E. 1998. "Conclusion: Continuity, Change and Challenge." In *Ireland and the Politics of Change*, ed. William Crotty and David E. Schmitt. London: Longman, pp. 210–222.

Schmitter, Phillipp. 1989. "Corporatism is Dead! Long Live Corporatism!" *Government and Opposition* 24: 54–73.

Schneider, Elizabeth M. 1994. "The Violence of Privacy." In *The Public Nature of Private Violence: The Discovery of Domestic Abuse*, ed. Martha Albertson Fineman and Roxanne Mykitiuk. New York: Routledge, pp. 36–58.

Schneider, Saundra K. 1999. "The Impact of Welfare Reform on Medicaid." In *Welfare Reform: A Race to the Bottom?*, ed. Sanford F. Schram and Samuel H. Beer. Baltimore, MD: Johns Hopkins University Press.

Schram, Sanford F. and Carol S. Weissert. 1997. "The State of American Federalism, 1996–1997." *Publius* 27, Spring: 1–31.

Scott, W. Richard. 1992. *Organizations: Rational, Natural and Open Systems*, 3rd ed. Englewood Cliffs, NJ: Prentice-Hall.

Seminario de Estudios sobre la Mujer 1986a. "El Movimiento Feminista en España." In *La Mujer Española: de la Tradición a la Modernidad (1960–1980)*, ed. Concha Borreguero, Elena Catena, Consuelo de la Gándara, and María Salas. Madrid: Tecnos, pp. 29–40.

Seminario de Estudios sobre la Mujer 1986b. "Introducción." In *La Mujer Española: de la Tradición a la Modernidad (1960–1980)*, ed. Concha Borreguero, Elena Catena, Consuelo de la Gándara, and María Salas. Madrid: Tecnos, pp. 11–15.

Sensat, Núria and Reyes Varella. 1998. "Las Políticas Dirigidas a las Mujeres: La Acción Pública para la Igualdad de los Sexos." In *Políticas Públicas en España: Contenidos, Redes de Actores y Niveles de Gobierno*, ed. Joan Subirats and Ricard Gomà. Barcelona: Ariel.

Servan-Schreiber, Claude. 1997. "La fausse-vraie maire de Vitrolles : une insulte pour toutes les femmes?" *Parité-Infos* 17.

SFS 1988: 688 *Lag om besöksförbud.* [Swedish legal reference to restraining orders.]

Sharrock, David. 1997. "All Together Now." *The Guardian*, 17 February, p. 7.

Sheldrick, Byron. 2000. "The Contradictions of Welfare to Work: Social Security Reform in Britain." *Studies in Political Economy* 62 (Summer): 99–121.

Short, Clare. 1996. "Women and the Labour Party." *Parliamentary Affairs* 49(1): 16–25.

Sineau, Mariette. 1997a. "La parité à la française : Un contre-modèle de l'égalité républicaine ?" In *Les femmes et la politique*, ed. A. LeBras-Chopard and J. Mossuz-Lavau. Paris: L'Harmattan, pp. 117–142.

Sineau, Mariette. 1997b. "Quel pouvoir politique pour les femmes? État des lieux et comparaisons européennes." In *Les Femmes dans la Prise de Décision en France et en Europe*, ed. Françoise Gaspard. Paris: L'Harmattan, pp. 89–110.

Sineau, Mariette. 1988. *Des Femmes en Politique.* Paris: Economica.

Skjeie, Hege. 1991. "The Rhetoric of Difference: On Women's Inclusion into Political Elites." *Politics & Society* 19(2), June: 233–263.

Skocpol, Theda. 1992. *Protecting Soldiers and Mothers: The Political Origins of Social Policy in the United States.* Cambridge, MA: Harvard University Press.

Smith, Andrea. 2000–2001. "The Color of Violence." *Color Lines: Race Culture Action* Winter: 14–15.

Smith, Andrea and Beth Richie. 2000–2001. "On the Cutting Edges: Andrea Smith Talks to Beth Richie about Heterosexism and Racism in Anti-Violence Organizing." *Color Lines: Race Culture Action* Winter: 24–25.

Smith, Barbara Ellen, ed. 1999. *Neither Separate Nor Equal: Women, Race and Class in the South.* Philadelphia: Temple University Press.

Smith, Jackie. 1997. "Characteristics of the Modern Transnational Social Movement Sector." In *Transnational Social Movements and Global Politics: Solidarity Beyond the State*, ed. Jackie Smith, Charles Chatfield, and Ron Pagnucco. Syracuse, NY: Syracuse University Press, pp. 42–58.

Smyth, Ailbhe. 1996. "'And Nobody Was Any the Wiser': Irish Abortion Rights and the European Union." In *Sexual Politics and the European Union: The New Feminist Challenge*, ed. R. Amy Elman. Providence, RI: Berghahn Books, pp. 109–130.

Snow, David and Robert D. Benford. 1992. "Master Frames and Cycles of Protest." In *Frontiers in Social Movement Theory*, ed. Aldon Morris and Carol McClurg Mueller. New Haven, CT: Yale University Press, pp. 133–155.

Snow, David and Robert D. Benford. 1988. "Ideology, Frame Resonance, and Participant Mobilization." In *From Structure to Action: Social Movement Participation Across Cultures*, ed. Bert Klandermans, Hanspeter Kriesi, and Sidney Tarrow. Greenwich, CT: JAI Press, pp. 197–217.

Snow, David, E. Burke Rochford, Jr., Steven K. Worden, and Robert D. Benford. 1986. "Frame Alignment Processes, Micromobilization, and Movement Participation." *American Sociological Review* 51: 464–481.

SOU. 1995:60. *Kvinnofrid* [Women's Freedom from Male Violence]. Del A. Stockholm: Fritzes.

Southcott, Mary. 1996. "A Stake in our Democracy." *The Chartist*, May-June.

Southcott, Mary. 1993. "Labour's Road to Electoral Reform: What's Wrong with First-Past-the-post?" (July). London: LCER. 6.

Spalter-Roth, Roberta and Ronnee Schreiber. 1995. "Outsider Issues and Insider Tactics: Strategic Tensions in the Women's Policy Network during the 1980s." In *Feminist Organizations: Harvest of the New Women's Movement*, ed. Myra Marx Ferree and Patricia Yancey Martin. Philadelphia: Temple University Press, pp. 105– 127.

Staggenborg, Suzanne. 1995. "Can Feminist Organizations Be Effective?" In *Feminist Organizations: Harvest of the New Women's Movement*, ed. Myra Marx Ferree and Patricia Yancey Martin. Philadelphia: Temple University Press, pp. 339–355.

Staggenborg, Suzanne. 1991. *The Pro-Choice Movement: Organization and Activism in the Abortion Conflict*. New York: Oxford.

Stämpfli, Regula. 1994. "Direct Democracy and Women's Suffrage: Antagonism in Switzerland." In *Women and Politics Worldwide*, ed. Barbara Nelson and Najma Chowdhury. New Haven, CT: Yale University Press, pp. 690–704.

Steinmetz, George, ed. 1999. *State/Culture: State-Formation after the Cultural Turn*. Ithaca, NY: Cornell University Press.

Stetson, Dorothy McBride. 1987. *Women's Rights in France*. Westport, CT: Greenwood Press.

Stetson, Dorothy McBride and Amy Mazur, eds. 1995. *Comparative State Feminism*. Thousand Oaks, CA: Sage Publications.

Stiehm, Judith. 1989. *Arms and the Enlisted Woman*. Philadelphia: Temple University Press.

Streeck, Wolfgang. 1995. "From Market Making to State Building? Reflections on the Political Economy of European Social Policy." In *European Social Policy: Between Fragmentation and Integration*, ed. Stephan Liebfried and Paul Pierson. Washington, DC: Brookings Institution, pp. 389–431.

Streeck, Wolfgang and Phillip Schmitter. 1983. "Community, Market, State – and Associations? The Prospective Contribution of Interest Governance to Social Order." In *Private Interest Government*, ed. Wolfgang Streeck and Phillip Schmitter. Thousand Oaks, CA: Sage Publications, pp. 1–29.

Studlar, Donley T. 1996. *Great Britain: Decline or Renewal?* Boulder, CO: Westview.

Studlar, Donley T. and Richard E. Matland. 1996. "The Contagion of Women Candidates in Single-Member District and Proportional Representation Electoral Systems: Canada and Norway." *Journal of Politics* 58: 707–733.

Sundman, Kerstin. 1999. *Between the Home and the Institutions: The Feminist Movement in Madrid, Spain*. Gothenburg: Acta Universitatis Gothoburgensis.

Swann, Dennis. 1988. *The Retreat of the State: Deregulation and Privatization in the U.K. and U.S.* Ann Arbor: University of Michigan Press.

Swedish Institute. 1993. "Equality between Men and Women in Sweden." *Fact Sheets on Sweden*. Stockholm.

Swidler, Ann. 1986. "Culture in Action: Symbols and Strategies." *American Sociological Review* 51: 273–286.

Tanner, Leslie, ed. 1971. *Voices from Women's Liberation*. New York: New American Library.

Tarrow, Sidney. 2000. "Mad Cows and Social Activists: Contentious Politics in the Trilateral Democracies." In *Why Western Publics Don't Trust Their Governments*, ed. Susan Pharr and Robert Putnam. Princeton, NJ: Princeton University Press, pp. 270–290.

Tarrow, Sidney. 1998. *Power in Movement: Social Movements and Contentious Politics*, 2nd ed. Cambridge: Cambridge University Press.

Tarrow, Sidney. 1996. "States and Opportunities: The Political Structuring of Social Movements." In *Comparative Perspectives on Social Movements: Political Opportunities, Mobilizing Structures, and Cultural Framing*, ed. Doug McAdam, John D. McCarthy, and Mayer N. Zald. Cambridge: Cambridge University Press, pp. 41–61.

Tarrow, Sidney. 1996b. "The People's Two Rhythms: Charles Tilly and the Study of Contentious Politics. A Review Article." *Comparative Studies in Society and History* 38: 3.

Tarrow, Sidney. 1994. *Power in Movement: Social Movements, Collective Action and Politics*. Cambridge: Cambridge University Press.

Tarrow, Sidney. 1989. *Struggle, Politics and Reform: Collective Action, Social Movements and Cycles of Protest*. Cornell University, Western Societies Paper No. 21. Ithaca, NY: Center for International Studies, Cornell University.

Taylor, Judith. 1998. "Feminist Tactics and Friendly Fire in the Irish Women's Movement." *Gender and Society* 12(6): 674–691.

Taylor, Verta. 1999. "Gender and Social Movements: Gender Processes in Women's Self-Help Movements." *Gender and Society* 13 (1), February: 8–33.

Taylor, Verta. 1993. "The New Feminist Movement." In *Feminist Frontiers III*, ed. Laurel Richardson and Verta Taylor. New York: McGraw Hill, pp. 533–548.

Taylor, Verta. 1989. "Social Movement Continuity: The Women's Movement in Abeyance." *American Sociological Review* 54: 761–775.

Taylor, Verta and Nancy Whittier. 1997. "The New Feminist Movement." In *Feminist Frontiers IV*, ed. Laurel Richardson, Verta Taylor, and Nancy Whittier. New York: McGraw Hill, pp. 544–545.

Teske, Robin L. and Mary Ann Tétreault, eds. 2000. *Conscious Acts and the Politics of Social Change: Feminist Approaches to Social Movements, Community, and Power*. Columbia, SC: University of South Carolina Press.

Thomas, Sue. 1994. *How Women Legislate*. New York and Oxford: Oxford University Press.

Thomas, Sue. 1991. "The Impact of Women on State Legislative Policies." *Journal of Politics* 53: 958–976.

Threlfall, Monica. 1998. "State Feminism or Party Feminism?: Feminist Politics and the Spanish Institute of Women." *The European Journal of Women's Studies* 5: 69–93.

Threlfall, Monica. 1996. "Feminist Politics and Social Change in Spain." In *Feminist Politics and Social Transformation in the North*, ed. Monica Threlfall. London and New York: Verso, pp. 115–151.

Threlfall, Monica. 1985. "The Women's Movement in Spain." *New Left Review* 151: 44–73.

Tierney, Kathleen. 1982. "The Battered Women's Movement and the Creation of the Wife Beating Problem." *Social Problems* 29(3): 207–220.

Tilly, Charles. 1995. *Popular Contention in Great Britain 1758–1834*. Cambridge, MA: Harvard University Press.

Tilly, Charles. 1984. "Social Movements and National Politics." In *Statemaking and Social Movements*, ed. Charles Bright and Susan Harding. Ann Arbor: University of Michigan Press, pp. 297–317.

Tilly, Charles. 1978. *From Mobilization to Revolution*. Reading, MA: Addison-Wesley.

Times Guide to the European Parliament. 1979, 1984, 1989. London: Times Books.

Touraine, Alain. 1997. *What is Democracy?* Boulder, CO: Westview.

Touraine, Alain. 1981. *The Voice and the Eye: An Analysis of Social Movements*. Cambridge: Cambridge University Press.

Trujillo, Gracia. 1999. "El Movimiento Feminista como Actor Político en España: el Caso de la Aprobación de la Ley de Despenalización del Aborto de 1985." Presented at the Meeting of the Spanish Association of Political Science and Public Administration, Granada, Spain, September 30–October 2.

Turner, Atuki. 1996. *Building Blocks: A Women's Aid Guide to Running Refuges and Support Services*. London: WAFE.

U.S. Department of Justice. 1997. *Violence Against Women Act NEWS 2(3)*. Washington, DC: U.S. Department of Justice Violence Against Women Office.

Uriarte, Edurne and Arantxa Elizondo, eds. 1997. *Mujeres en Política: Análisis y Práctica*. Barcelona: Ariel.

Valenza, Sara. 1999. *Il movimento delle donne di Firenze: dalla mobilitazione degli anni settanta all'associazionismo degli anni novanta*. Facoltà di scienze politiche di Firenze: Tesi di Laurea.

Valiente, Celia. 2001. "Implementing Women's Rights in Spain." In *Globalization, Religion, and Gender: The Politics of Implementing Women's Rights in Catholic and Muslim Contexts*, ed. Jane Bayes and Nayereh Tohidi. New York: St. Martins Press, pp. 107–125.

Valiente, Celia. 2000. "Género y Ciudadanía: Los Organismos de Igualdad y el Estado de Bienestar en España." In *Ciudadanía y Democracia*, ed. Manuel Pérez. Madrid: Pablo Iglesias, pp. 199–229.

Valiente, Celia. 1998–1999. "Feminismo de Estado en los Ayuntamientos de la Comunidad Autónoma de Madrid." *Gestión y Análisis de Políticas Públicas* 13–14: 181–197.

Valiente, Celia. 1998. "Sexual Harassment in the Workplace: Equality Policies in Post-Authoritarian Spain." In *Politics of Sexuality: Identity, Gender, and Citizenship*, ed. Terrell Carver and Véronique Mottier. London and New York: Routledge, pp. 169–179.

Valiente, Celia. 1997a. *Políticas de Género en Perspectiva Comparada: la Mujer Trabajadora en Italia y España (1900–1996)*. Madrid: Universidad Autónoma de Madrid.

Valiente, Celia. 1997b. "State Feminism and Gender Equality Policies: The Case of Spain (1983–95)." In *Sex Equality Policy in Western Europe*, ed. Frances Gardiner. London and New York: Routledge, pp. 127–141.

Valiente, Celia. 1996. "Partial Achievements of Central-State Public Policies against Violence Against Women in Post-authoritarian Spain (1975–1995)." In *Women in a Violent World: Feminist Analyses and Resistance Across 'Europe'*, ed. Chris Corrin. Edinburgh: Edinburgh University Press, pp. 166–185.

Valiente, Celia. 1995a. "Children First: Central Government Child Care Policies in Post-Authoritarian Spain (1975–1994)." In *Childhood and Parenthood: Proceedings of ISA Committee for Family Research Conference on Children and Families, 1995*, ed. Julia Brannen and Margaret O'Brien. London: Institute of Education/University of London, pp. 249–266.

Valiente, Celia. 1995b. "The Power of Persuasion: *The Instituto de la Mujer* in Spain." In *Comparative State Feminism*, ed. Dorothy M. Stetson and Amy G. Mazur. Thousand Oaks, CA: Sage, pp. 221–236.

Vallance, Elisabeth and Elisabeth Davies. 1986. *Women of Europe: Women MEPs and Equality Policy*. Cambridge: Cambridge University Press.

Vickers, Jill. 1993. "The Canadian Women's Movement and a Changing Constitutional Order." *International Journal of Canadian Studies* 7–8 (Spring/Fall): 261–284.

Vickers, Jill, Pauline Rankin, and Christine Appelle. 1993. *Politics as if Women Mattered: A Political Analysis of the National Action Committee on the Status of Women*. Toronto and Buffalo: University of Toronto Press.

Volden, Craig. 1997. "Entrusting the States with Welfare Reform." In *The New Federalism: Can the States be Trusted?*, ed. John A. Ferejohn and Barry R. Weingast. Stanford, CA: Hoover Institution Press, pp. 65–96.

Wadham, John. 1999. "A British Bill of Rights." In *Constitutional Reform: The Labour Government's Constitutional Reform Agenda*, ed. Robert Blackburn and Raymond Plant. London and New York: Longman. pp. 348–368.

Walby, Sylvia. 1999. "The New Regulatory State: The Social Powers of the European Union." *British Journal of Sociology* 50 (1), March: 118–140.

Walby, Sylvia. 1997. *Gender Transformations*. New York: Routledge.

Walker, Graham. 1995. *Intimate Strangers: Political and Cultural Interaction Between Scotland and Ulster in Modern Times*. Edinburgh: John Donald.

Ward, Lucy. 1999. "Women: Equal Pay? No Way." *The Guardian*. July 15, P.T6. Accessed via LEXIS-NEXIS Academic Universe, July 25, 2001.

Warner, Harriet. 1984. "EC Social Policy in Practice: Community Action on Behalf of Women and Its Impact in the Member States." *Journal of Common Market Studies* 23(2), December: 141–167.

Warrior, Betsy. 1985. *Battered Women's Directory*, 9th edition. Richmond, IN: Terry Mehlman.

Warrior, Betsy. 1976. *Wife Beating*. Somerville, MA: New England Free Press.

Waschbüsch, Rita. 2000. "Pressemitteilung: Statement von Rita Waschbüsch: Pressekonferenz Donum Vitae – 1 Jahr Donum Vitae." October 13, 2000. http://www.donumvitae.org//public/presse-mitteilung.php3?id=14. Accessed July 18, 2001.

Waylen, Georgina. 1998. "Gender, Feminism and the State: An Overview." In *Gender, Politics, and the State*, ed. Vicky Randall and Georgina Waylen. London: Routledge, pp. 1–17.

Weidner, Helmut. 1995. *25 Years of Modern Environmental Policy in Germany: Treading a Well-Worn Path to the Top of the International Field*. Paper FS II 95-301. Berlin: Wissenschaftszentrum Berlin.

Welch, Susan. 1985. "Are Women More Liberal Than Men in the U.S. Congress?" *Legislative Studies Quarterly* 10: 125–134.

Whitaker, R. 1998. "Northern Ireland Women's Coalition (NIWC)." *Engender Newsletter* 18 (June): 8.

White, M. 2000. "Radicals Dismayed at Plans for Lords." *Guardian Weekly* January 27–February 2.

Whittier, Nancy. 1995. *Feminist Generations: The Persistence of the Radical Women's Movement*. Philadelphia: Temple University Press.

Wiechmann, Elke and Leo Kißler. 1997. *Frauenförderung zwischen Integration und Isolation. Gleichstellungspolitik im kommunalen Modernisierungsprozeß*. Modernisierung des öffentlichen Sektors, Bd. 11. Berlin: Edition Sigma.

Wilcox, Clyde. 1994. "Why Was 1992 the 'Year of the Woman?' Explaining Women's Gains in 1992." In *The Year of the Woman: Myths and Realities*, ed. Elizabeth Adell Cook, Sue Thomas, and Clyde Wilcox. Boulder, CO: Westview Press, pp. 1–24.

Wilford, Rick. 1999. "Women's Candidacy and Electability in A Divided Society: The Northern Ireland Women's Coalition and the 1996 Forum Election." *Women and Politics* 20: 1.

Wilson, Robin and Paul Nolan. 1996. "No Reconciliation, No Receipts." *Fortnight* 353 (September): 16–17.

Wistrand, Birgitta. 1981. *Swedish Women on the Move*. Stockholm: Swedish Institute.

Wolbrecht, Christina. 2000. *The Politics of Women's Rights*. Princeton, NJ: Princeton University Press.

Wolfe, Joel. 2001. "Citizenship and State Power in Britain and the European Union." Paper Presented at the Annual Meeting of the American Political Science Association, San Francisco, California, August 30–September 2.

"Women in Decision-Making: Results of the Election to the European Parliament." 1999. http:/www.db-decision.de/news/EUParl.htm.

"Women in National Parliaments." 1999. Interparliamentary Union. http:/www.ipu.org/wmn-e/classif.htm. June 10.

"Women in National Parliaments: Situation as of 20 March 2000." Interparliamentary Union. Available on April 12, 2000 at http:/www.ipu.org/wmn-e/classif.htm.

"Women in the U.S. Congress, 1917–2001." 2001. *Center for the American Woman and Politics*. www.rci.rutgers.edu/~cawp/Facts/html. June 1.

"Women On Waves." 2001. *The Irish Times* June 25, city edition p. 15. Accessed via LEXIS-NEXIS Academic Universe, July 12, 2001.

Women's Action Alliance. 1974. *How to Organize a Child Care Center*. Unpublished Brochure.

Women's Unit. 1999. www.open.gov.uk/womens-unit/index.htm.

Wuthnow, Robert. 2002. "The Changing Character of Social Capital in the US." In *Democracies in Flux*, ed. Robert Putnam. New York: Oxford University Press.

Yishai, Yael. 1993. "Public Ideas and Public Policy: Abortion Politics in Four Democracies." *Comparative Politics* 25, January: 207–228.

Young, Brigitte. 1996. "The German State and Feminist Politics: A Double Gender Marginalization." *Social Politics* 3(2–3): 159–184.

Young, Lisa. 2000. *Feminists and Party Politics*. Vancouver: University of British Columbia Press.

Zahariadis, Nikolaos. 1995. *Markets, States, and Public Policy: Privatization in Britain and France*. Ann Arbor: University of Michigan Press.

Index

aboriginal peoples, and constitutional politics in Canada, 119, 121, 123, 125, 284

abortion: and conservative movements in the 1980s, 290–1; and feminist movement in France, 184; and feminist movement in Spain, 40, 42, 43–4; and gender parity movements in France and Spain, 81, 82, 83, 85; neoliberalism and contemporary women's movement, 288; policy successes and constraints of state reconfiguration, 141–68; and women's movement in Germany, 5–6, 148–55, 166–8, 245–6; and women's movement in Ireland, 141–4, 148–55, 166–8; and women's movement in Italy, 48, 56, 59. *See also* reproductive rights

Abrahamsson and Anderson v. Fogelqvist (2000), 158

Action Canada Network (ACN), 124

Action for Children's Television, 212

Action Programmes for Women's Equality, 145

Advisory, Conciliation, and Arbitration Service (Britain), 162

affirmative action: and European Union, 158–9; Left and women's movement in Italy, 63; and local government policies in Great Britain, 160

Aid to Families with Dependent Children (AFDC), 205

Alberdi, Cristina, 91n22

Alberdi, Inés, 91

Alliance Party (Northern Ireland), 131n9

alliances. *See* political parties; trade unions

All Women's House (Sweden), 99–100

Almunia, Joaquin, 91

Alvarez, Sonia, 170–1

American News Women's Club, 212

American Women in Radio and Television, 212

Amos, Valerie, 160

animal rights, and environmental movement, 254, 265

antinuclear movement: crossnational comparisons of interactions between states and, 265, 266, 270; and social movements in Germany, 253n8, 254, 257, 264n17, 266. *See also* peace movement

Appleton, Andrew, 185n15

Ashford, Douglas E., 10n11

Asociación Democrática de la Mujer (Women's Democratic Association), 33

Assemblée des femmes, 75, 78, 80

associationalism, U.S. culture and feminist, 213–14, 216–17, 228, 234